# FREAK

## vol. 4

Yi DongEun · Yu Chung

Yen Press

# CONTENTS

CAR 10. THE TEARS OF THE MERMAID, PART 1............5

CAR 10. THE TEARS OF THE MERMAID, PART 2..........27

CAR 10. THE TEARS OF THE MERMAID, PART 3.........45

CAR 11. AN INDICATION.................................................63

CAR 12. THE BEGINNING OF THE END............................87

CAR 13. THE SECOND STAGE OF THE END....................111

CAR 14. THE CONTINUATION OF THE END...................137

CAR 15. THE END OF THE END.....................................163

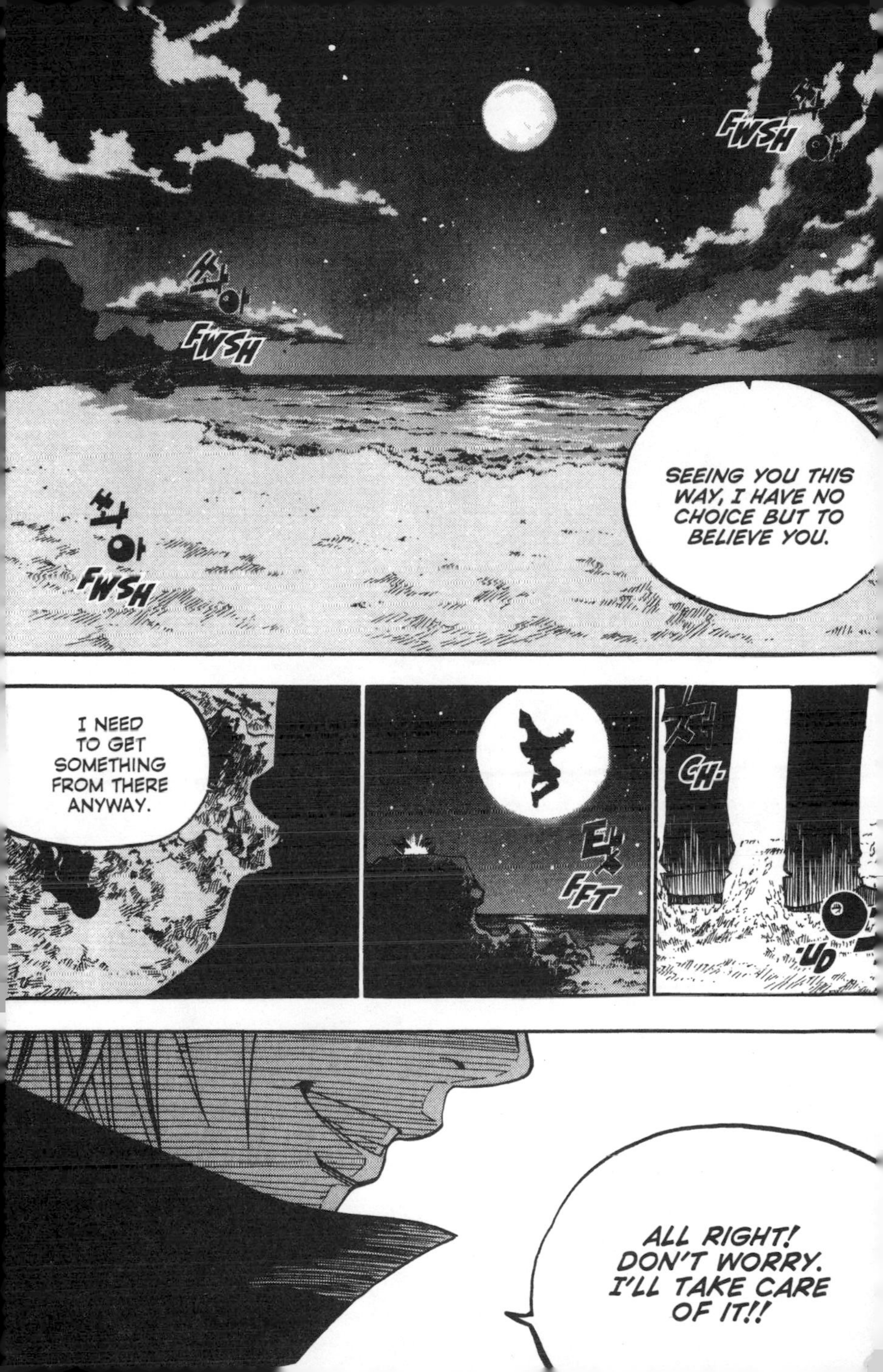
쏴아
FWSH
쏴아
FWSH
쏴아
FWSH
SEEING YOU THIS WAY, I HAVE NO CHOICE BUT TO BELIEVE YOU.
I NEED TO GET SOMETHING FROM THERE ANYWAY.
FFT
CH-
-UD
ALL RIGHT! DON'T WORRY. I'LL TAKE CARE OF IT!!

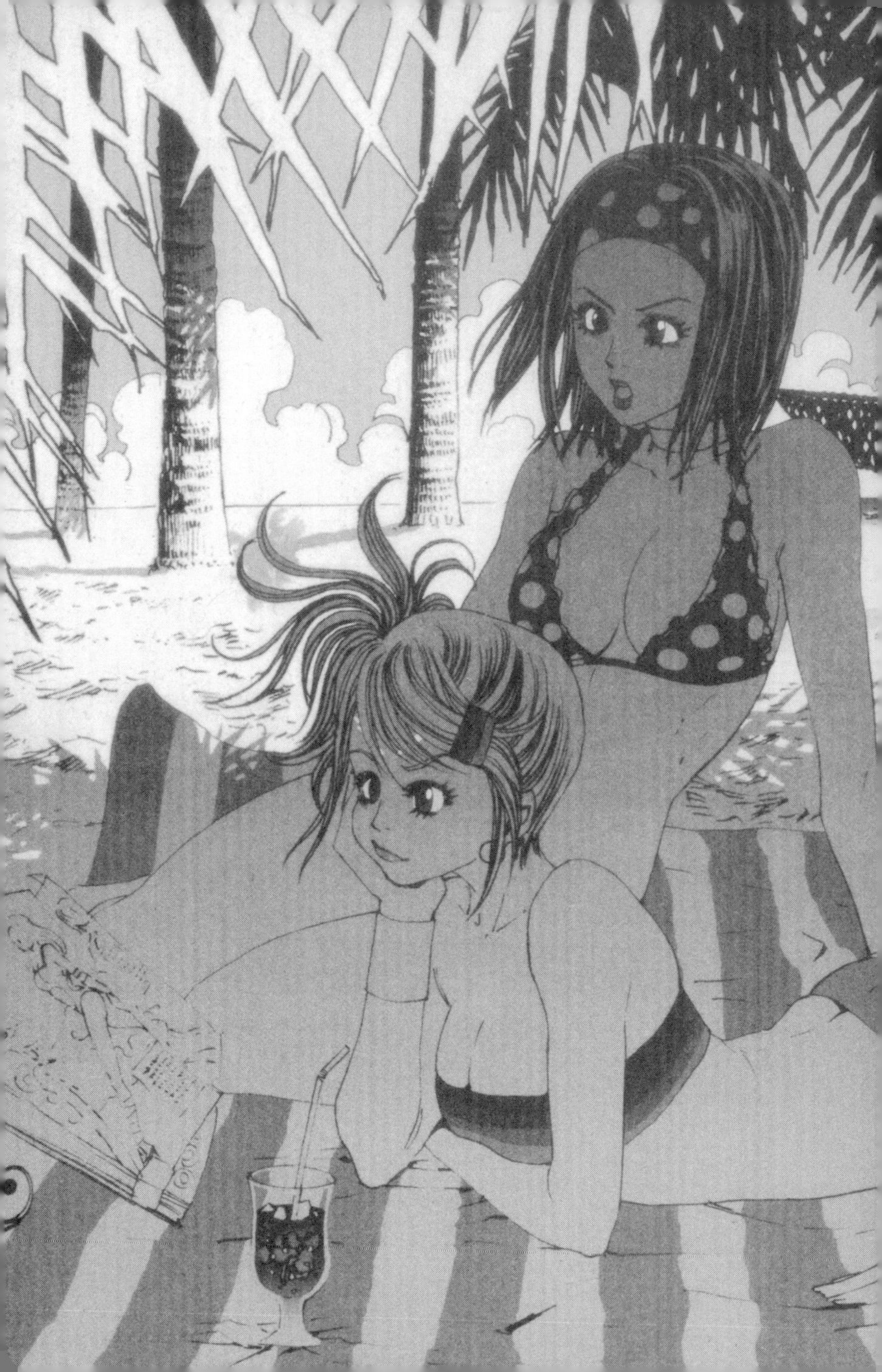

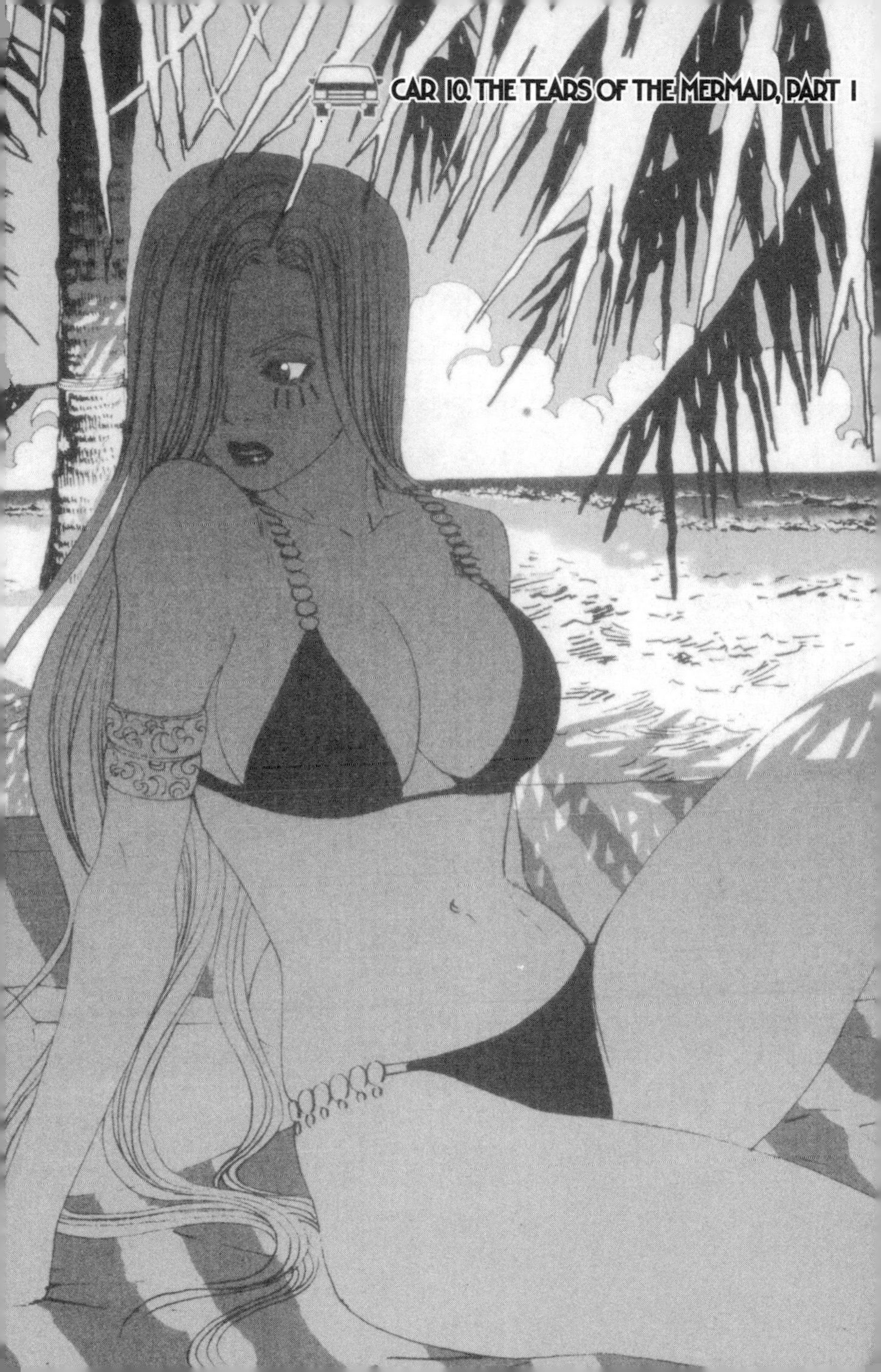
CAR 10. THE TEARS OF THE MERMAID, PART 1

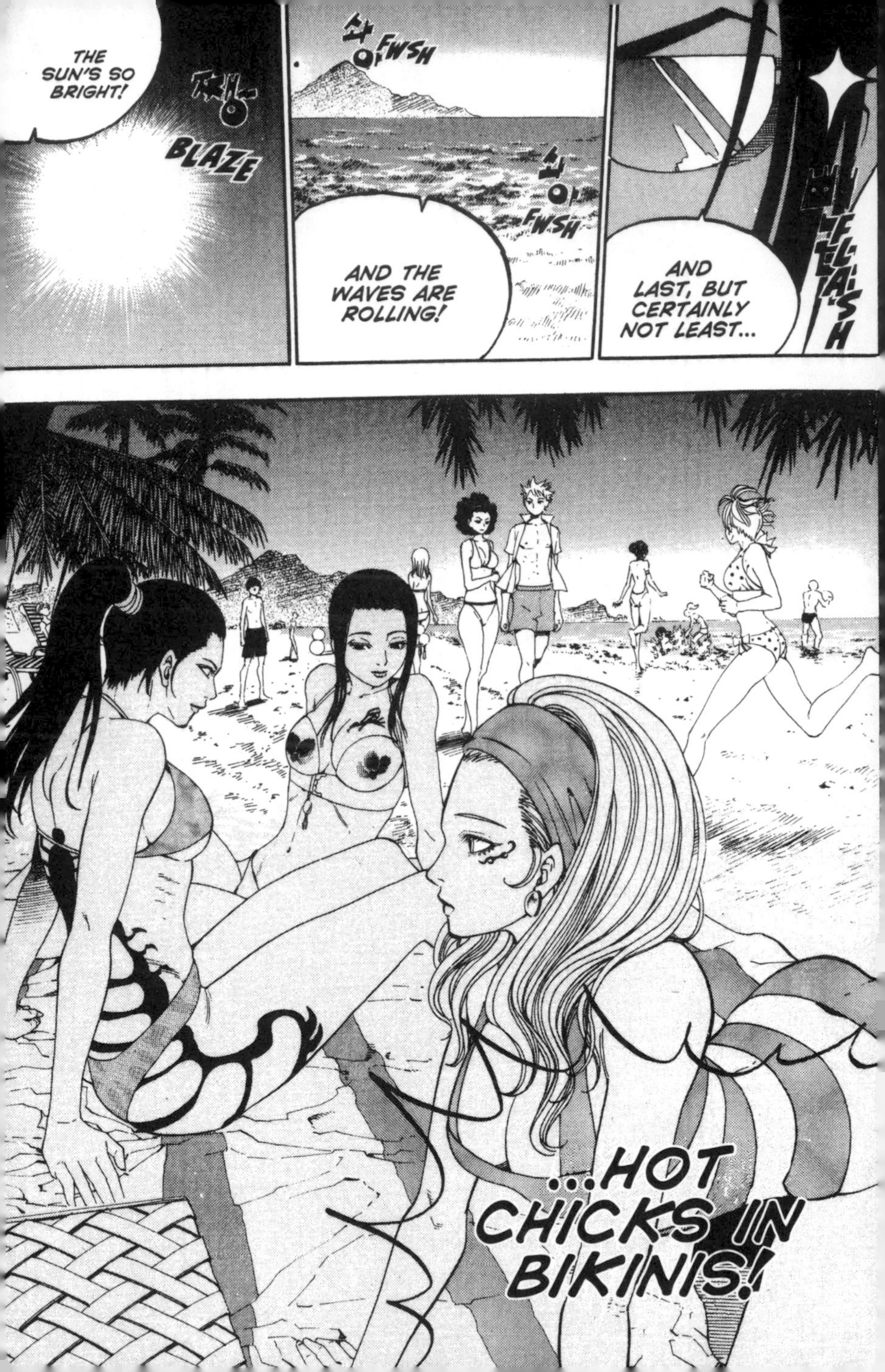
THE SUN'S SO BRIGHT!
BLAZE
FWSH
FWSH
AND THE WAVES ARE ROLLING!
AND LAST, BUT CERTAINLY NOT LEAST...
FLASH
...HOT CHICKS IN BIKINIS!

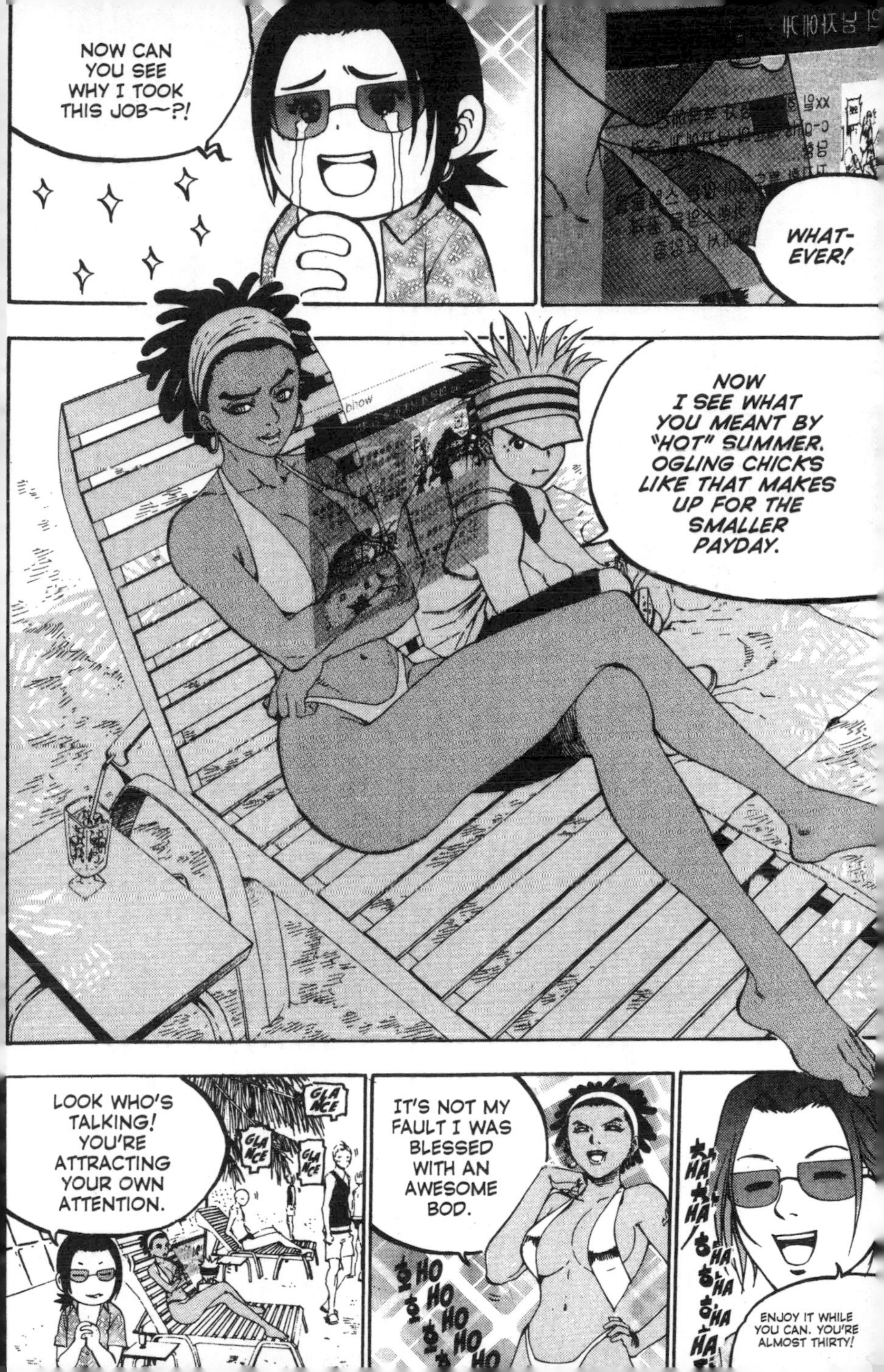
NOW CAN YOU SEE WHY I TOOK THIS JOB~?!
WHAT-EVER!
NOW I SEE WHAT YOU MEANT BY "HOT" SUMMER. OGLING CHICKS LIKE THAT MAKES UP FOR THE SMALLER PAYDAY.
LOOK WHO'S TALKING! YOU'RE ATTRACTING YOUR OWN ATTENTION.
GLANCE
GLANCE
GLANCE
IT'S NOT MY FAULT I WAS BLESSED WITH AN AWESOME BOD.
호 HO 호 HO 호 HO HO HO
하 HA 하 HA 하 HA 하 HA 하 HA HA
ENJOY IT WHILE YOU CAN. YOU'RE ALMOST THIRTY!

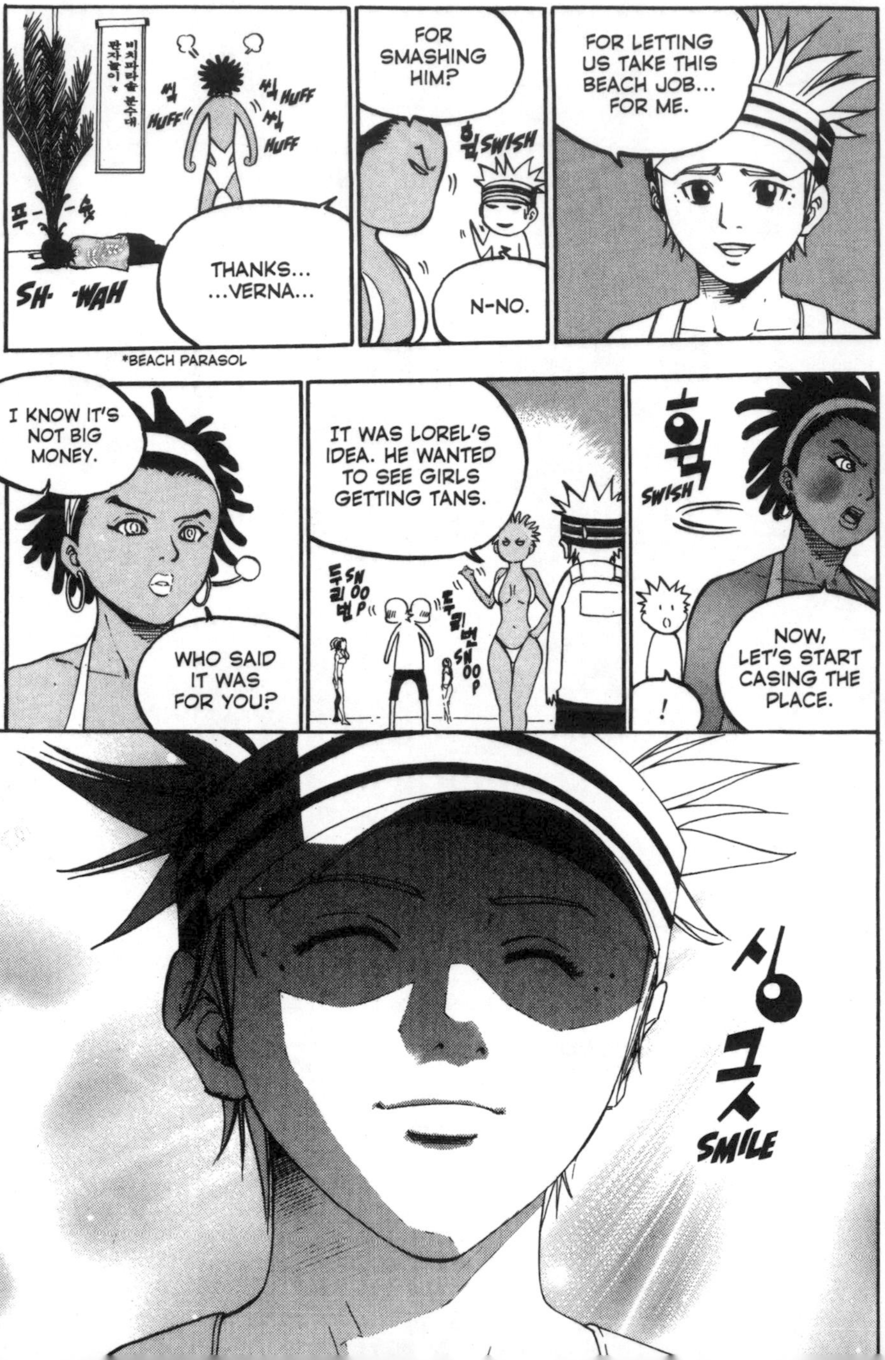

HUFF
HUFF
HUFF
HUFF
SH- -WAH
THANKS... ...VERNA...
*BEACH PARASOL
FOR SMASHING HIM?
SWISH
N-NO.
FOR LETTING US TAKE THIS BEACH JOB... FOR ME.
I KNOW IT'S NOT BIG MONEY.
WHO SAID IT WAS FOR YOU?
IT WAS LOREL'S IDEA. HE WANTED TO SEE GIRLS GETTING TANS.
SNOOP
SNOOP
SWISH
NOW, LET'S START CASING THE PLACE.
!
SMILE

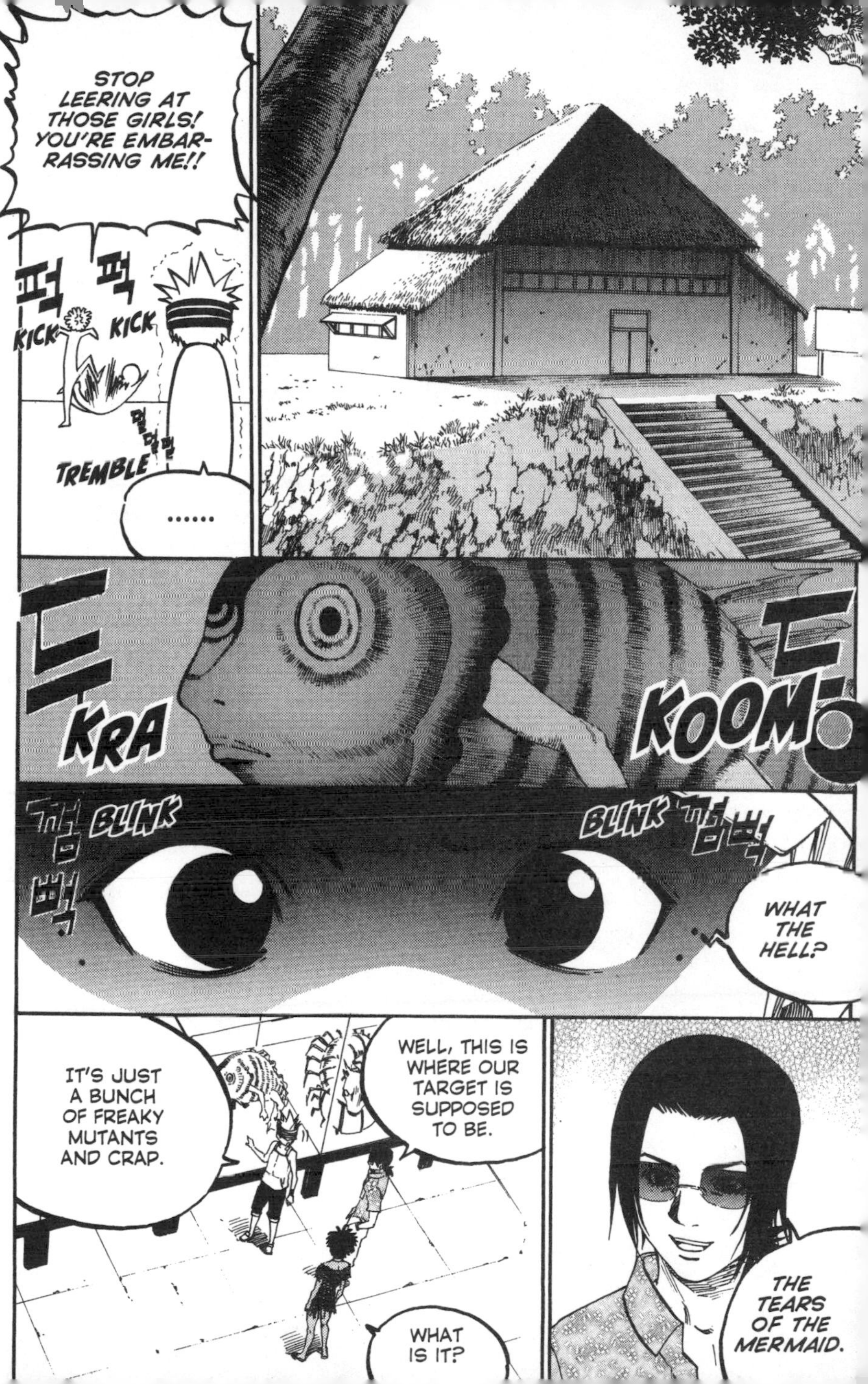
STOP LEERING AT THOSE GIRLS! YOU'RE EMBAR-RASSING ME!!
퍽 퍽
KICK KICK
덜덜덜
TREMBLE
......
드
KRA
드
KOOM
껌뻑
BLINK
BLINK
껌뻑
WHAT THE HELL?
IT'S JUST A BUNCH OF FREAKY MUTANTS AND CRAP.
WELL, THIS IS WHERE OUR TARGET IS SUPPOSED TO BE.
WHAT IS IT?
THE TEARS OF THE MERMAID.

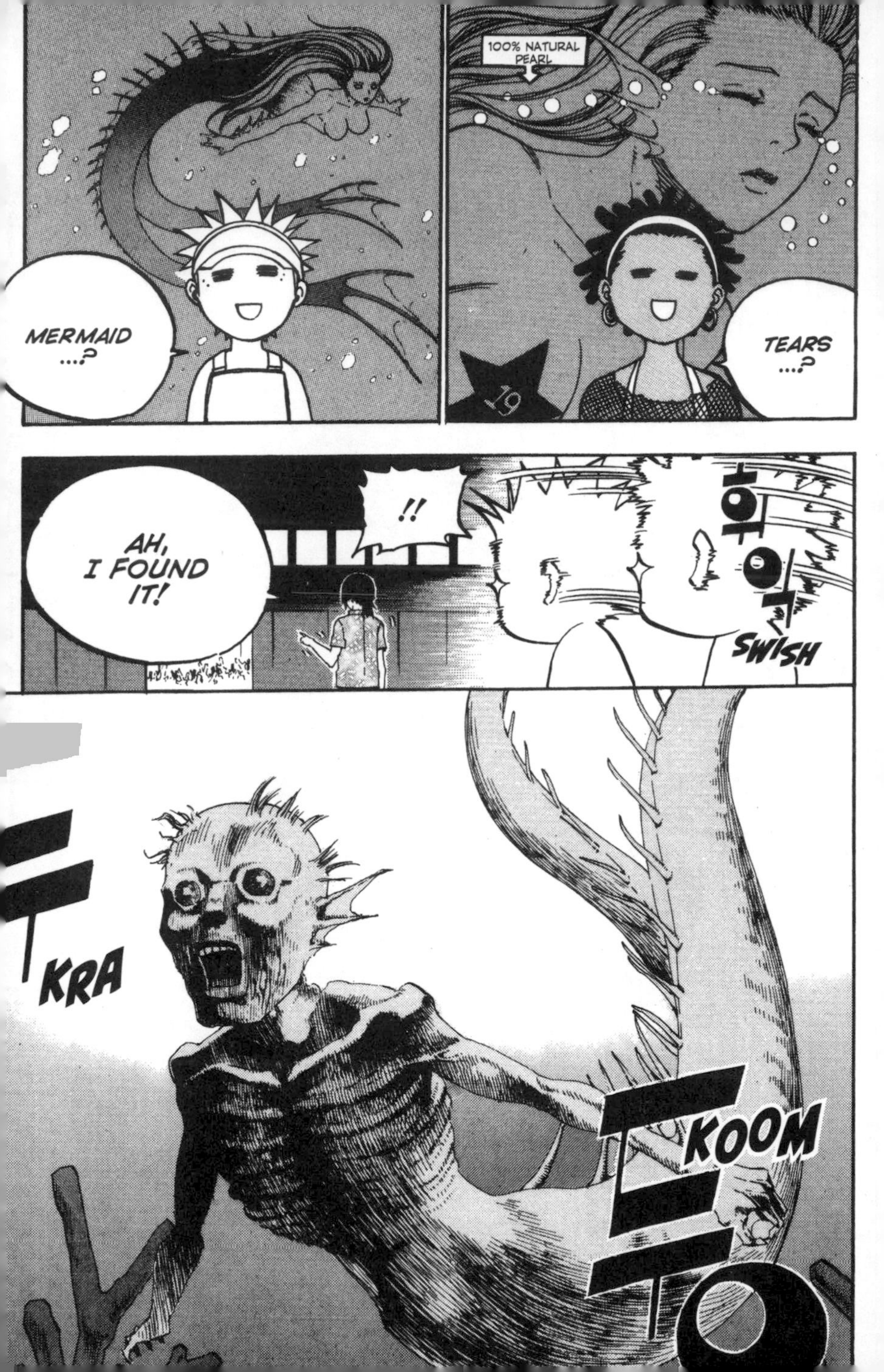
MERMAID ...?
100% NATURAL PEARL
TEARS ...?
AH, I FOUND IT!
!!
SWISH
KRA
KOOM

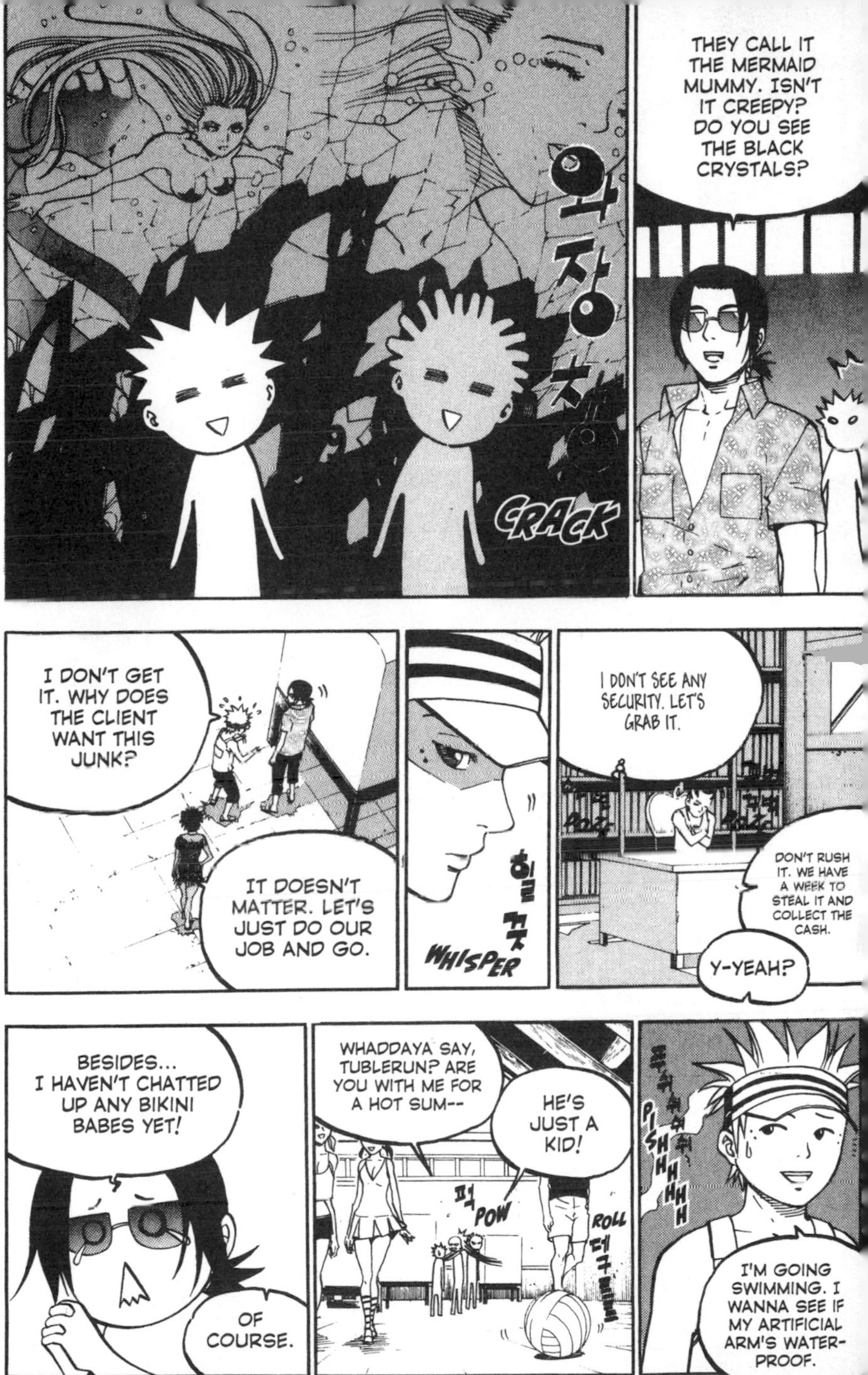
CRACK
THEY CALL IT THE MERMAID MUMMY. ISN'T IT CREEPY? DO YOU SEE THE BLACK CRYSTALS?
I DON'T GET IT. WHY DOES THE CLIENT WANT THIS JUNK?
IT DOESN'T MATTER. LET'S JUST DO OUR JOB AND GO.
WHISPER
I DON'T SEE ANY SECURITY. LET'S GRAB IT.
DON'T RUSH IT. WE HAVE A WEEK TO STEAL IT AND COLLECT THE CASH.
Y-YEAH?
BESIDES... I HAVEN'T CHATTED UP ANY BIKINI BABES YET!
OF COURSE.
WHADDAYA SAY, TUBLERUN? ARE YOU WITH ME FOR A HOT SUM--
HE'S JUST A KID!
POW
ROLL
PISHHHHHH
I'M GOING SWIMMING. I WANNA SEE IF MY ARTIFICIAL ARM'S WATER-PROOF.

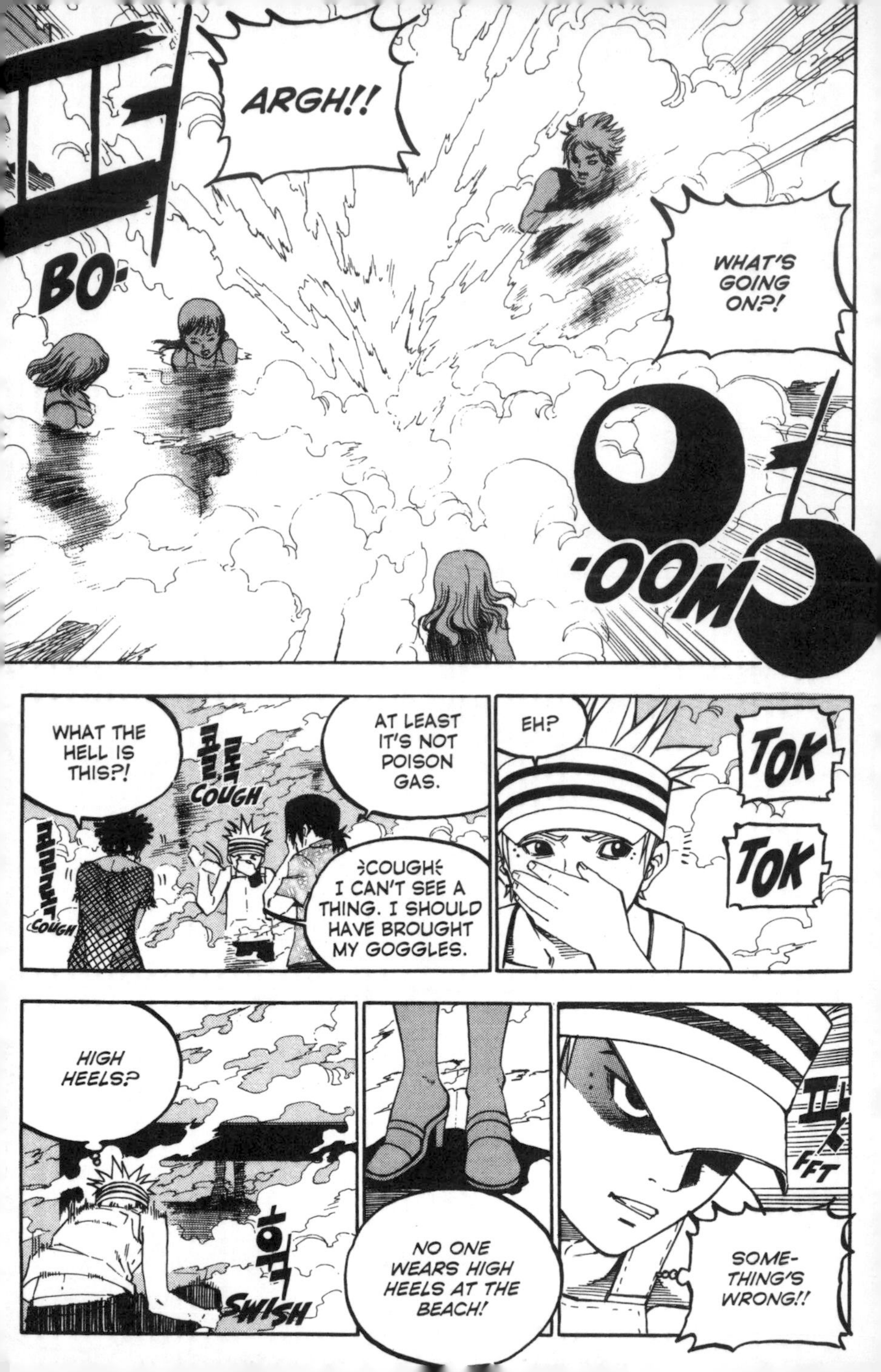
ARGH!!
BO-
WHAT'S GOING ON?!
-OOM
WHAT THE HELL IS THIS?!
COUGH
AT LEAST IT'S NOT POISON GAS.
COUGH
*COUGH* I CAN'T SEE A THING. I SHOULD HAVE BROUGHT MY GOGGLES.
EH?
TOK
TOK
HIGH HEELS?
SWISH
NO ONE WEARS HIGH HEELS AT THE BEACH!
FFT
SOME-THING'S WRONG!!

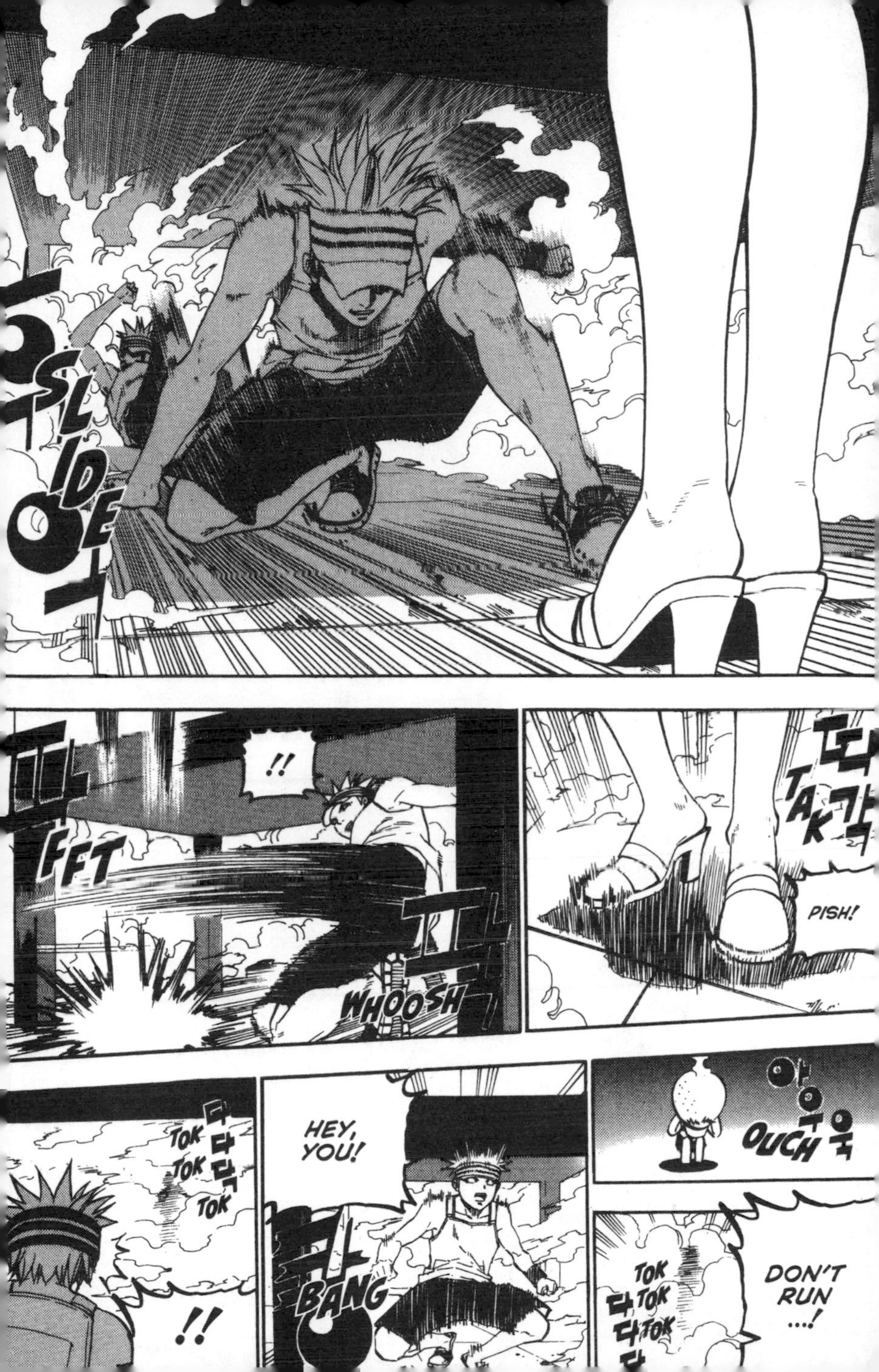
SLIDE
!!
FFT
WHOOSH
TAK
PISH!
TOK
TOK
TOK
!!
HEY, YOU!
BANG
OUCH
TOK
TOK
TOK
DON'T RUN ...!

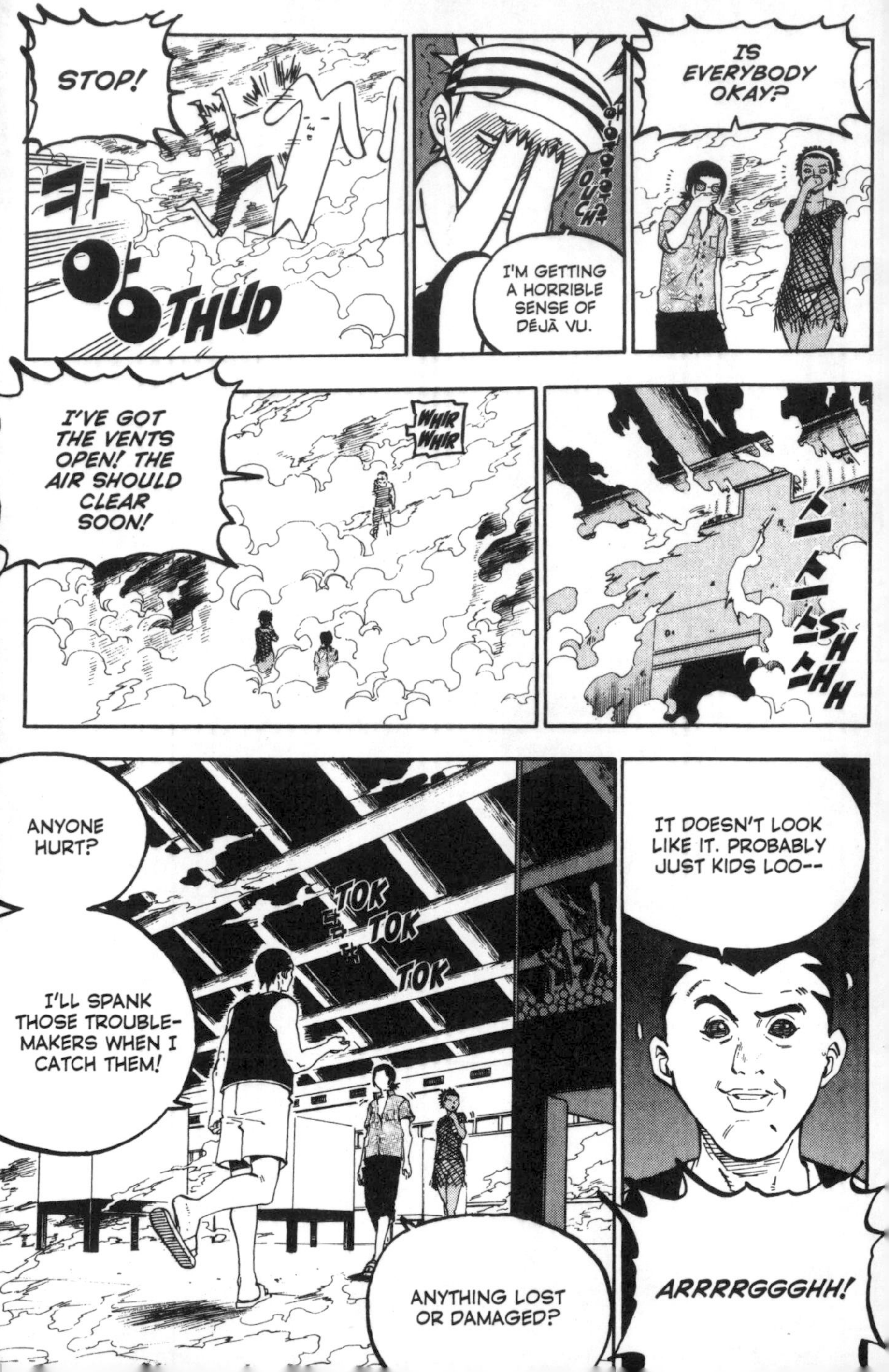
STOP!
카
앙
THUD
OUCH
I'M GETTING A HORRIBLE SENSE OF DÉJÃ VU.
IS EVERYBODY OKAY?
I'VE GOT THE VENTS OPEN! THE AIR SHOULD CLEAR SOON!
WHIR WHIR
SHHHH
ANYONE HURT?
TOK TOK TOK
I'LL SPANK THOSE TROUBLE-MAKERS WHEN I CATCH THEM!
ANYTHING LOST OR DAMAGED?
IT DOESN'T LOOK LIKE IT. PROBABLY JUST KIDS LOO--
ARRRRGGGHH!

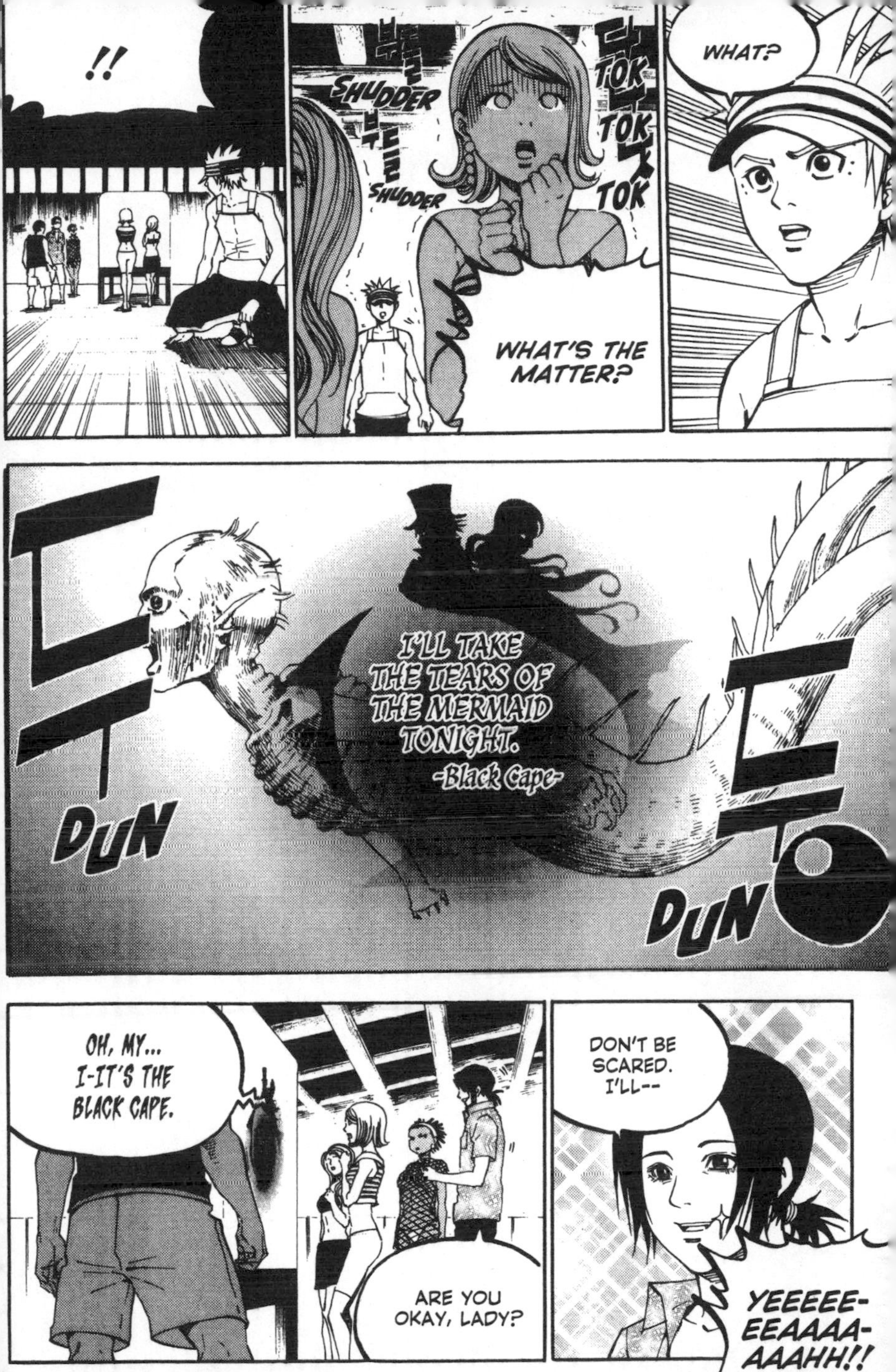

!!
SHUDDER
SHUDDER
TOK
TOK
TOK
TOK
WHAT'S THE MATTER?
WHAT?
DUN
I'LL TAKE THE TEARS OF THE MERMAID TONIGHT.
-Black Cape-
DUN
OH, MY... I-IT'S THE BLACK CAPE.
ARE YOU OKAY, LADY?
DON'T BE SCARED. I'LL--
YEEEEE-EEAAAA-AAAHH!!

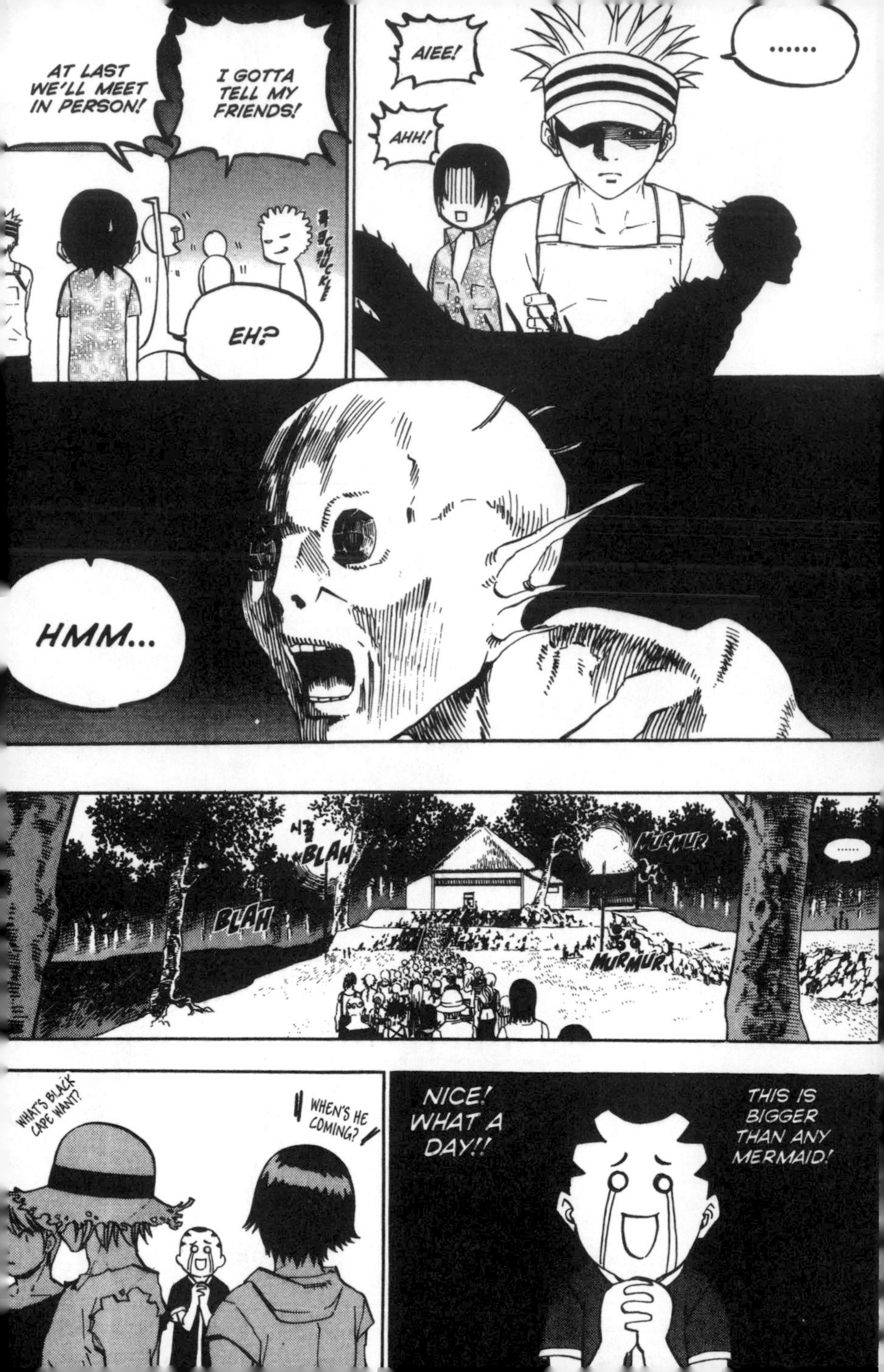

AT LAST WE'LL MEET IN PERSON!
I GOTTA TELL MY FRIENDS!
CHUCKLE
EH?
AIEE!
AHH!
.......
HMM...
BLAH
MURMUR
......
BLAH
MURMUR
WHAT'S BLACK CAPE WANT?
WHEN'S HE COMING?
NICE! WHAT A DAY!!
THIS IS BIGGER THAN ANY MERMAID!

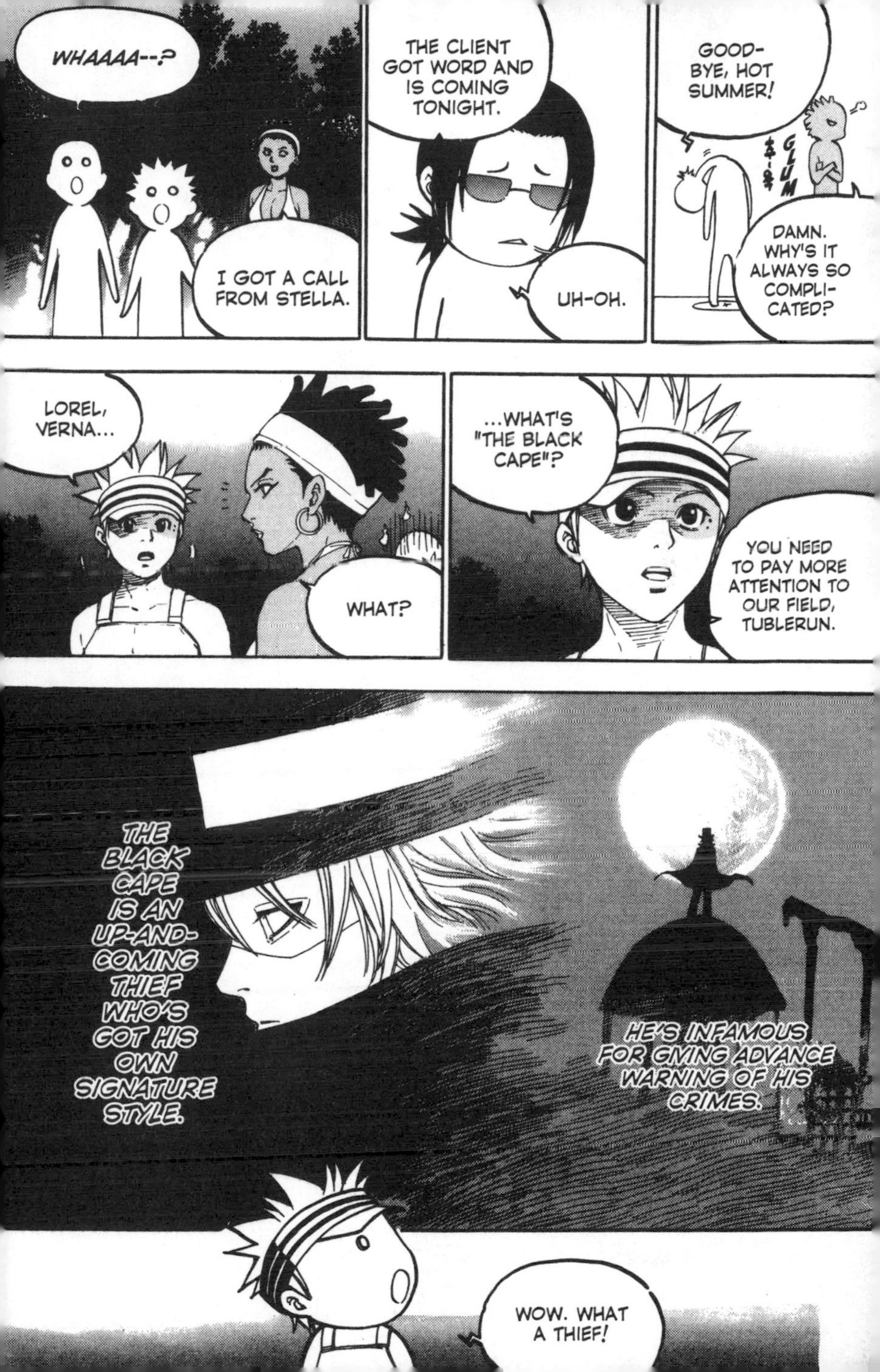
WHAAAA--?
I GOT A CALL FROM STELLA.
THE CLIENT GOT WORD AND IS COMING TONIGHT.
UH-OH.
GOOD-BYE, HOT SUMMER!
GLUM
DAMN. WHY'S IT ALWAYS SO COMPLI-CATED?
LOREL, VERNA...
WHAT?
...WHAT'S "THE BLACK CAPE"?
YOU NEED TO PAY MORE ATTENTION TO OUR FIELD, TUBLERUN.
THE BLACK CAPE IS AN UP-AND-COMING THIEF WHO'S GOT HIS OWN SIGNATURE STYLE.
HE'S INFAMOUS FOR GIVING ADVANCE WARNING OF HIS CRIMES.
WOW. WHAT A THIEF!

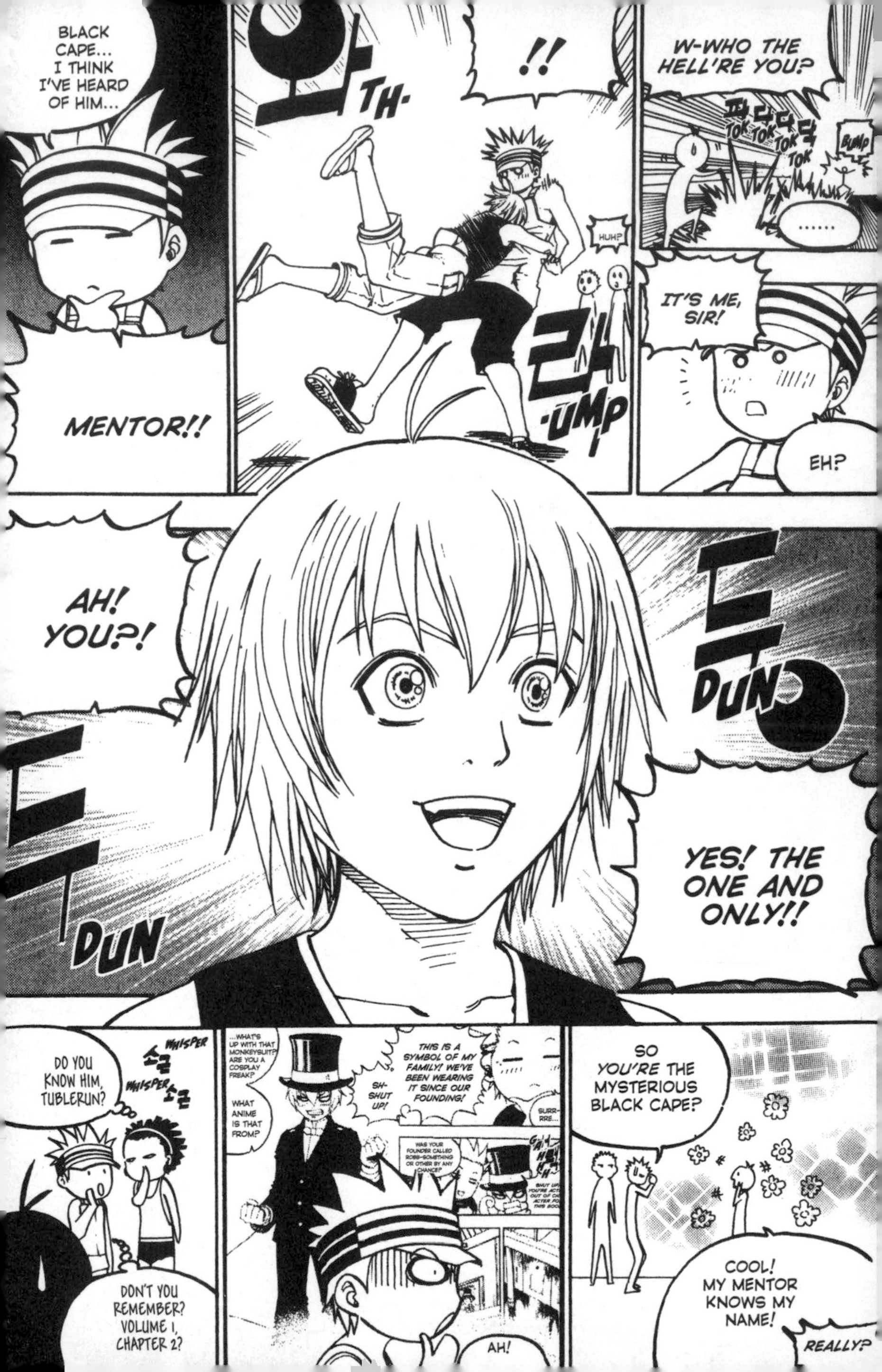
BLACK CAPE... I THINK I'VE HEARD OF HIM...
MENTOR!!
!!
TH-
HUH?
-UMP
W-WHO THE HELL'RE YOU?
TOK TOK TOK TOK
BUMP
......
IT'S ME, SIR!
EH?
AH! YOU?!
DUN
DUN
YES! THE ONE AND ONLY!!
DO YOU KNOW HIM, TUBLERUN?
WHISPER
WHISPER
DON'T YOU REMEMBER? VOLUME 1, CHAPTER 2?
...WHAT'S UP WITH THAT MONKEYSUIT? ARE YOU A COSPLAY FREAK?
WHAT ANIME IS THAT FROM?
SH-SHUT UP!
THIS IS A SYMBOL OF MY FAMILY! WE'VE BEEN WEARING IT SINCE OUR FOUNDING!
SURR-RRE...
WAS YOUR FOUNDER CALLED ROBB-SOMETHING OR OTHER BY ANY CHANCE?
AH!
SO YOU'RE THE MYSTERIOUS BLACK CAPE?
COOL! MY MENTOR KNOWS MY NAME!
REALLY?

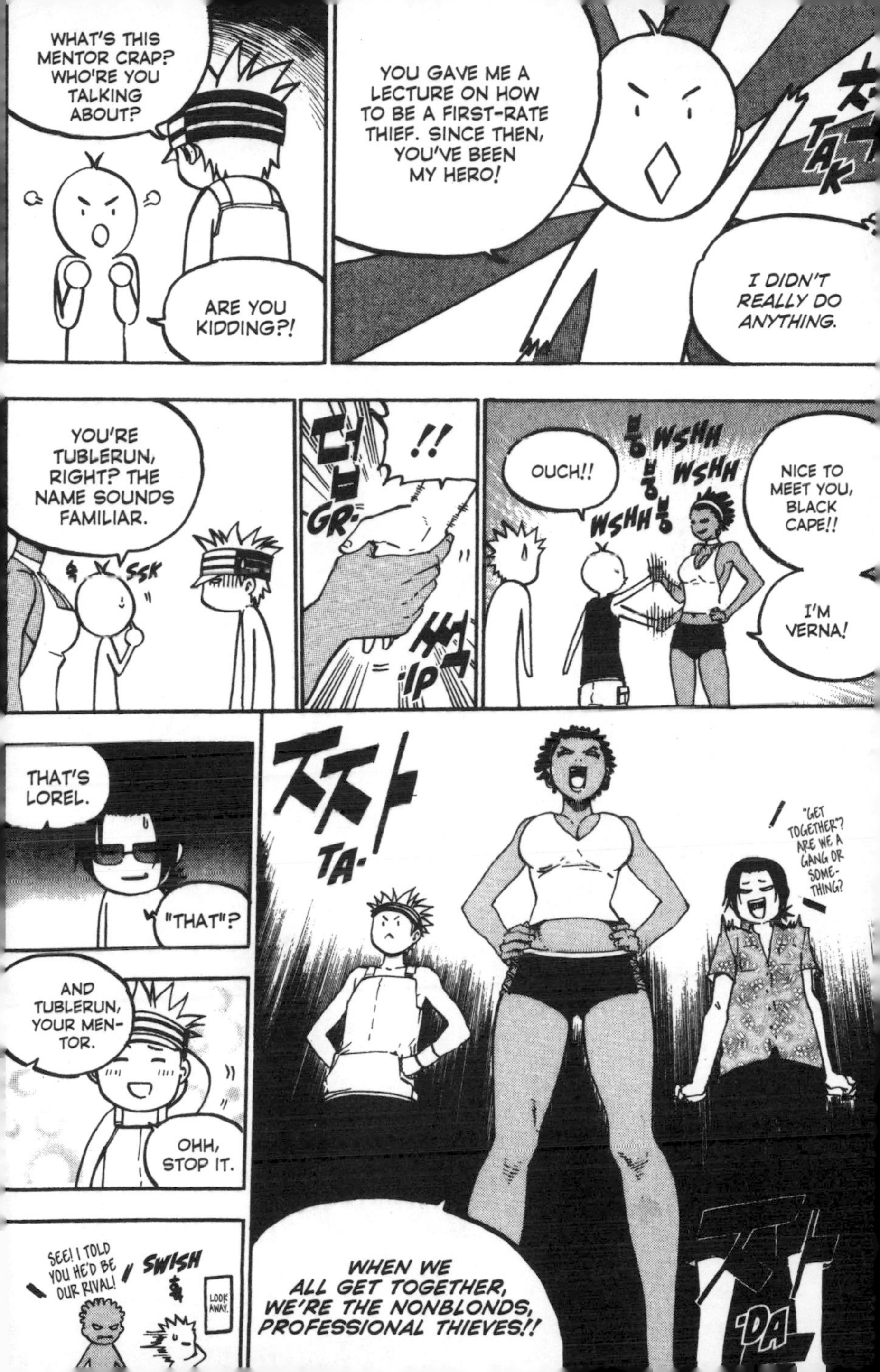
WHAT'S THIS MENTOR CRAP? WHO'RE YOU TALKING ABOUT?
ARE YOU KIDDING?!
YOU GAVE ME A LECTURE ON HOW TO BE A FIRST-RATE THIEF. SINCE THEN, YOU'VE BEEN MY HERO!
TAK
I DIDN'T REALLY DO ANYTHING.
YOU'RE TUBLERUN, RIGHT? THE NAME SOUNDS FAMILIAR.
SSK
!!
GR-
-IP
OUCH!!
WSHH
WSHH
WSHH
NICE TO MEET YOU, BLACK CAPE!!
I'M VERNA!
THAT'S LOREL.
"THAT"?
AND TUBLERUN, YOUR MEN-TOR.
OHH, STOP IT.
SEE! I TOLD YOU HE'D BE OUR RIVAL!
SWISH
LOOK AWAY.
TA-
"GET TOGETHER"? ARE WE A GANG OR SOME-THING?
WHEN WE ALL GET TOGETHER, WE'RE THE NONBLONDS, PROFESSIONAL THIEVES!!
-DAL

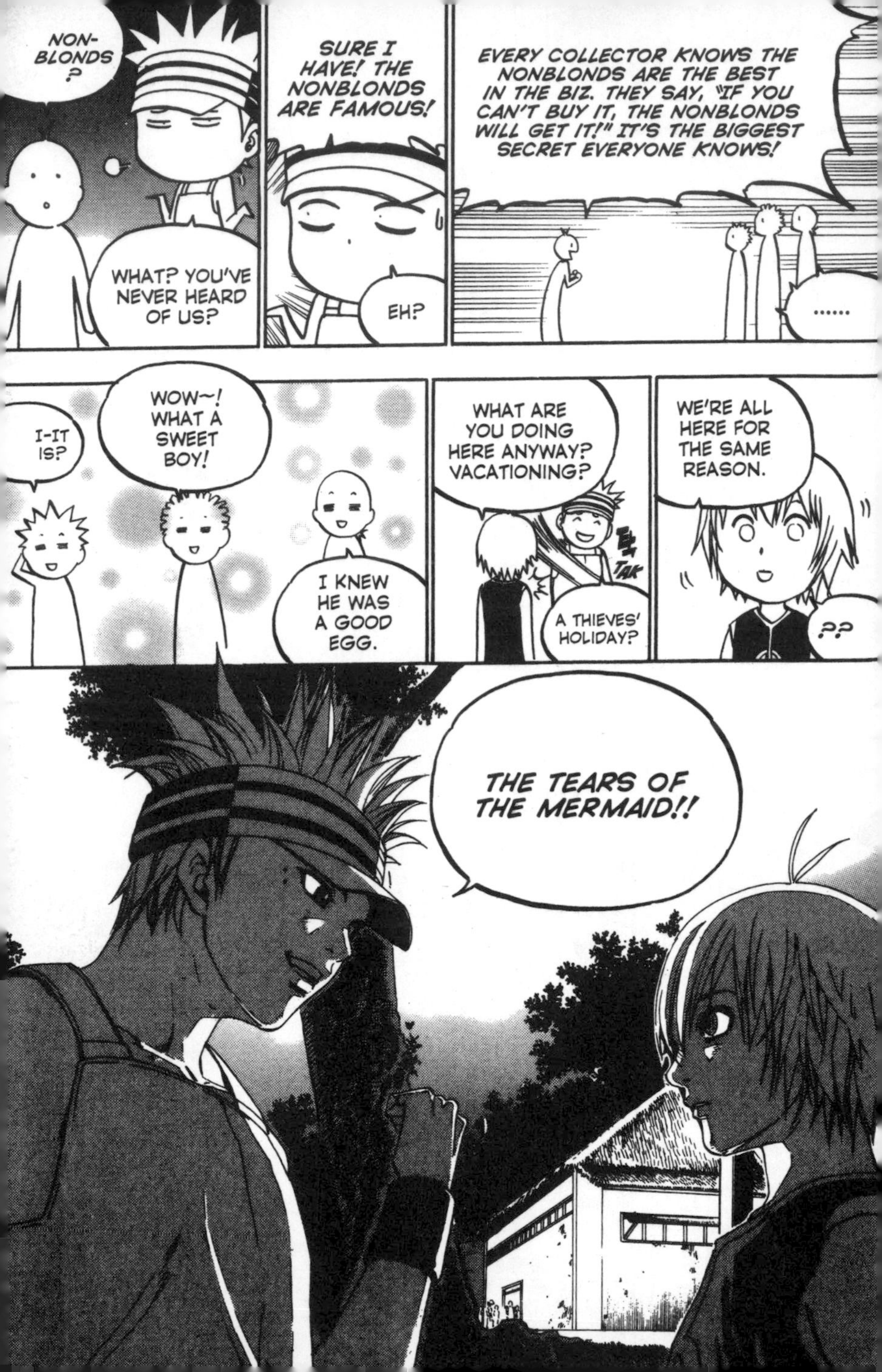
NON-BLONDS?
WHAT? YOU'VE NEVER HEARD OF US?
SURE I HAVE! THE NONBLONDS ARE FAMOUS!
EH?
EVERY COLLECTOR KNOWS THE NONBLONDS ARE THE BEST IN THE BIZ. THEY SAY, "IF YOU CAN'T BUY IT, THE NONBLONDS WILL GET IT!" IT'S THE BIGGEST SECRET EVERYONE KNOWS!
......
I-IT IS?
WOW~! WHAT A SWEET BOY!
I KNEW HE WAS A GOOD EGG.
WHAT ARE YOU DOING HERE ANYWAY? VACATIONING?
TAK
A THIEVES' HOLIDAY?
WE'RE ALL HERE FOR THE SAME REASON.
??
THE TEARS OF THE MERMAID!!

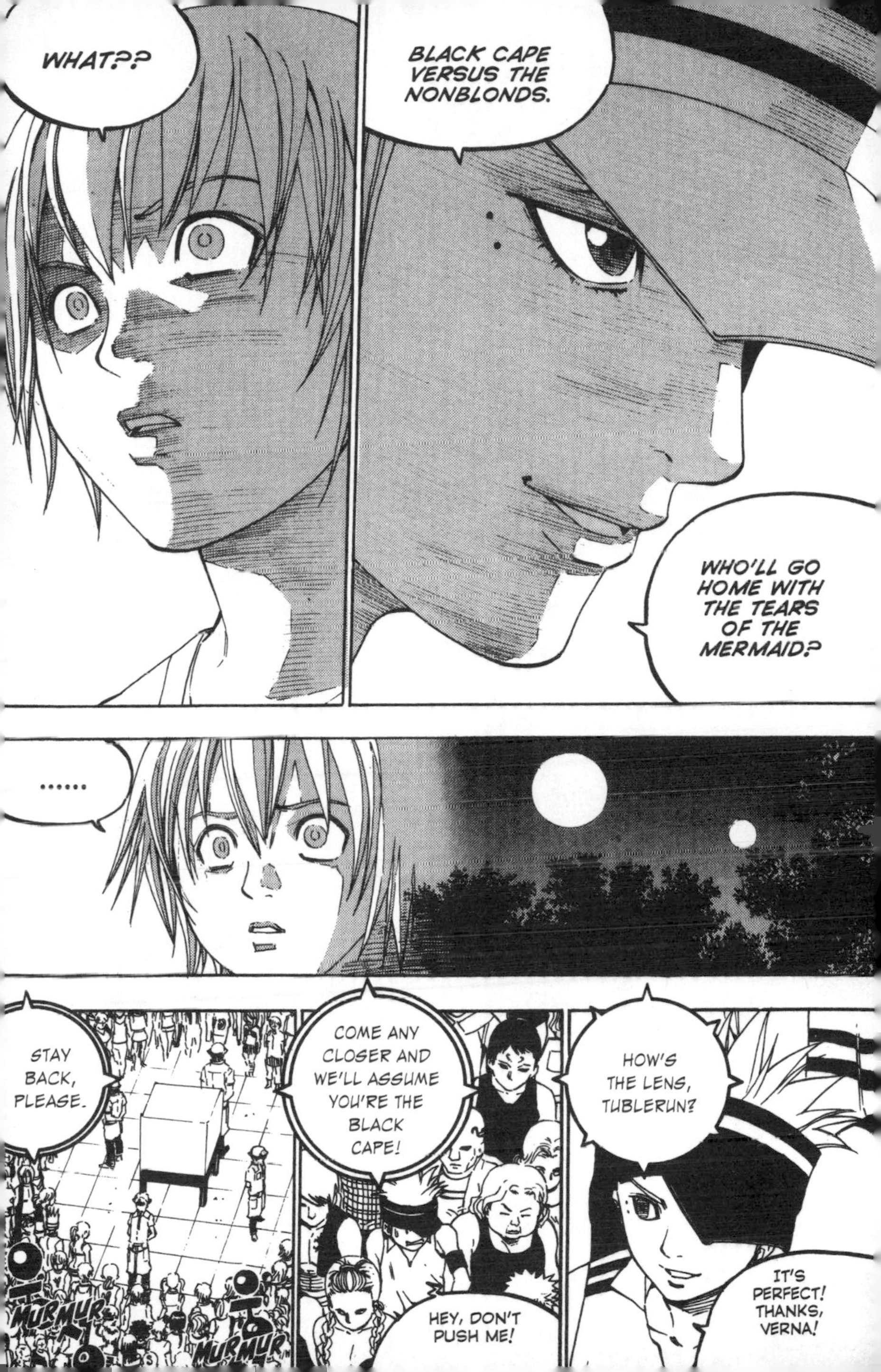
WHAT??
BLACK CAPE VERSUS THE NONBLONDS.
WHO'LL GO HOME WITH THE TEARS OF THE MERMAID?
......
STAY BACK, PLEASE.
MURMUR
MURMUR
COME ANY CLOSER AND WE'LL ASSUME YOU'RE THE BLACK CAPE!
HEY, DON'T PUSH ME!
HOW'S THE LENS, TUBLERUN?
IT'S PERFECT! THANKS, VERNA!

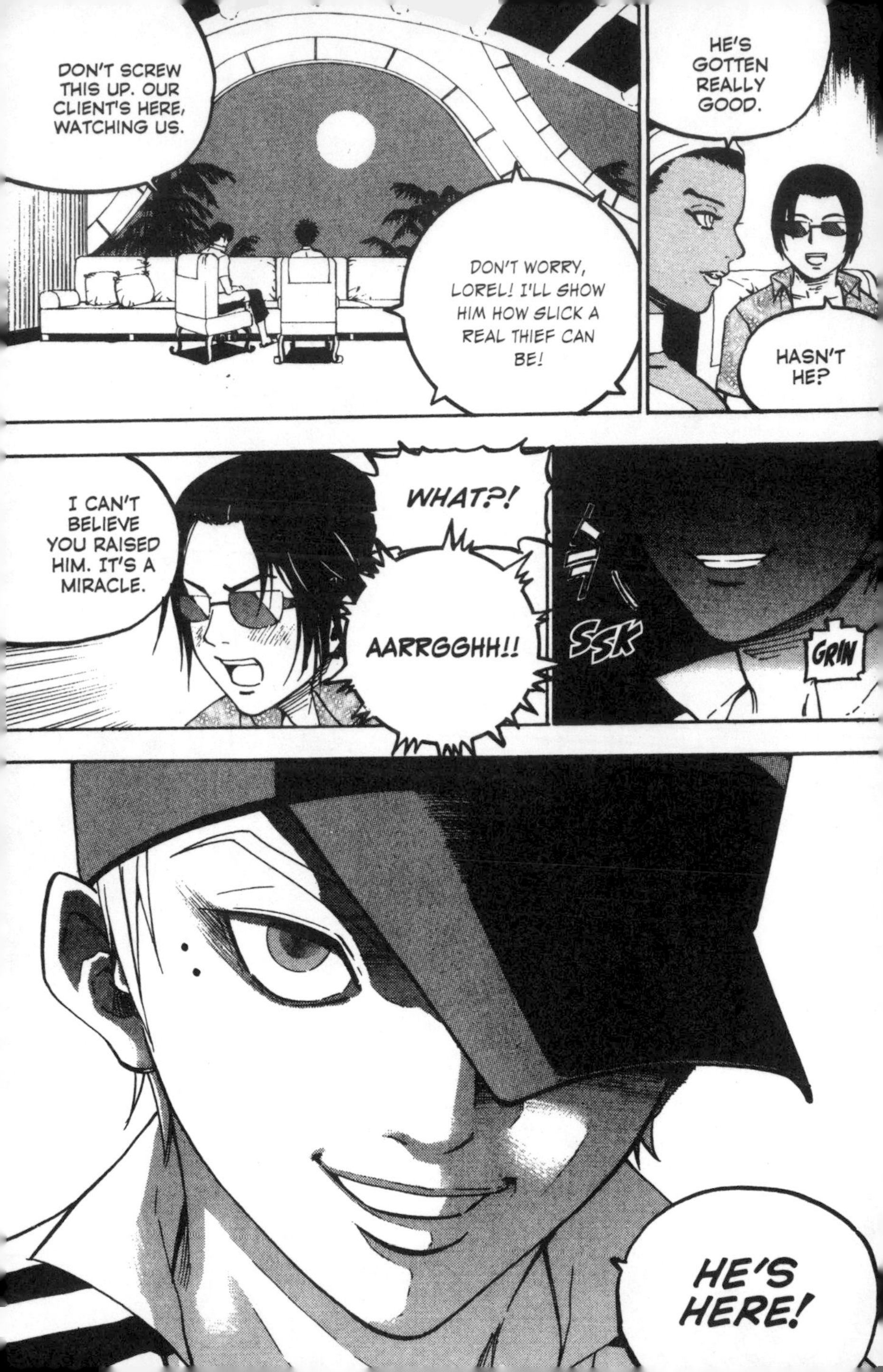
DON'T SCREW THIS UP. OUR CLIENT'S HERE, WATCHING US.
DON'T WORRY, LOREL! I'LL SHOW HIM HOW SLICK A REAL THIEF CAN BE!
HE'S GOTTEN REALLY GOOD.
HASN'T HE?
I CAN'T BELIEVE YOU RAISED HIM. IT'S A MIRACLE.
WHAT?!
AARRGGHH!!
SSK
GRIN
HE'S HERE!

SUMMER SPECIAL BONUS
하 HA-
하 HA-
하 HA-
HA-
하 HA-
하 HA

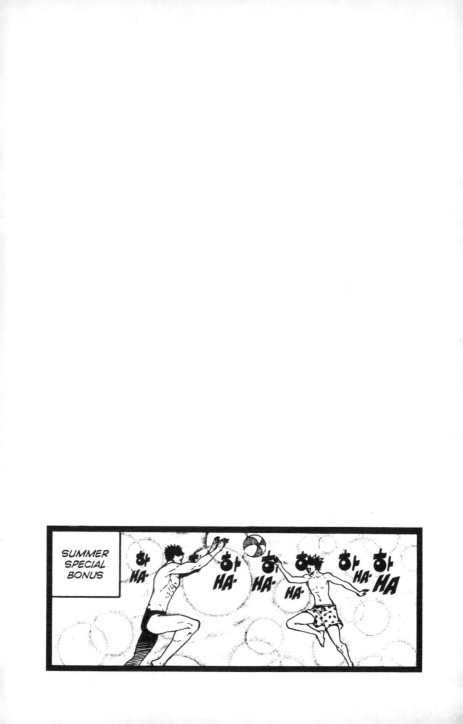

# FREAK

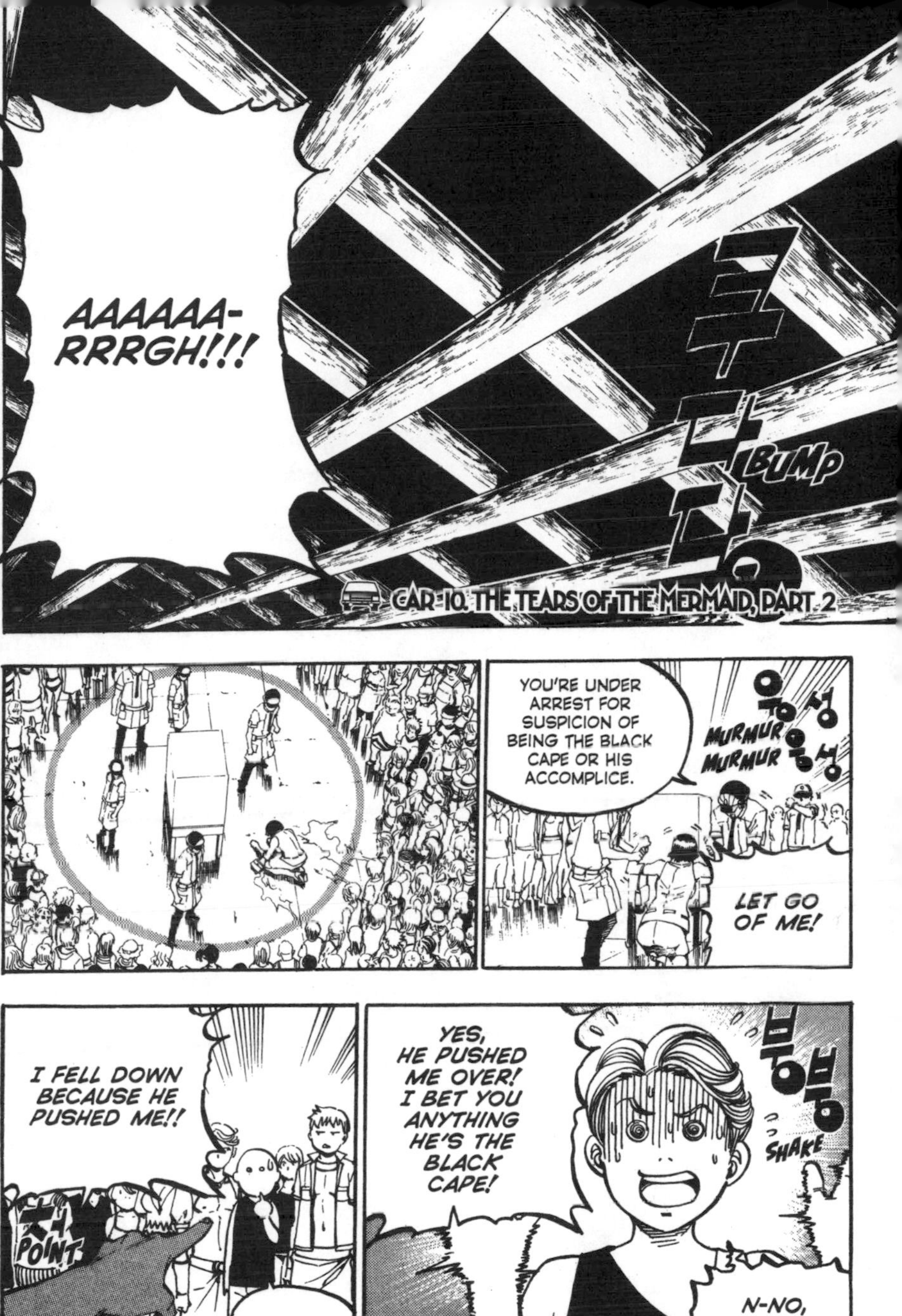

AAAAAA-RRRGH!!!
BUMP
CAR-10. THE TEARS OF THE MERMAID, PART 2
YOU'RE UNDER ARREST FOR SUSPICION OF BEING THE BLACK CAPE OR HIS ACCOMPLICE.
MURMUR MURMUR
LET GO OF ME!
I FELL DOWN BECAUSE HE PUSHED ME!!
POINT
ME?
YES, HE PUSHED ME OVER! I BET YOU ANYTHING HE'S THE BLACK CAPE!
SHAKE
N-NO, I'M NOT!

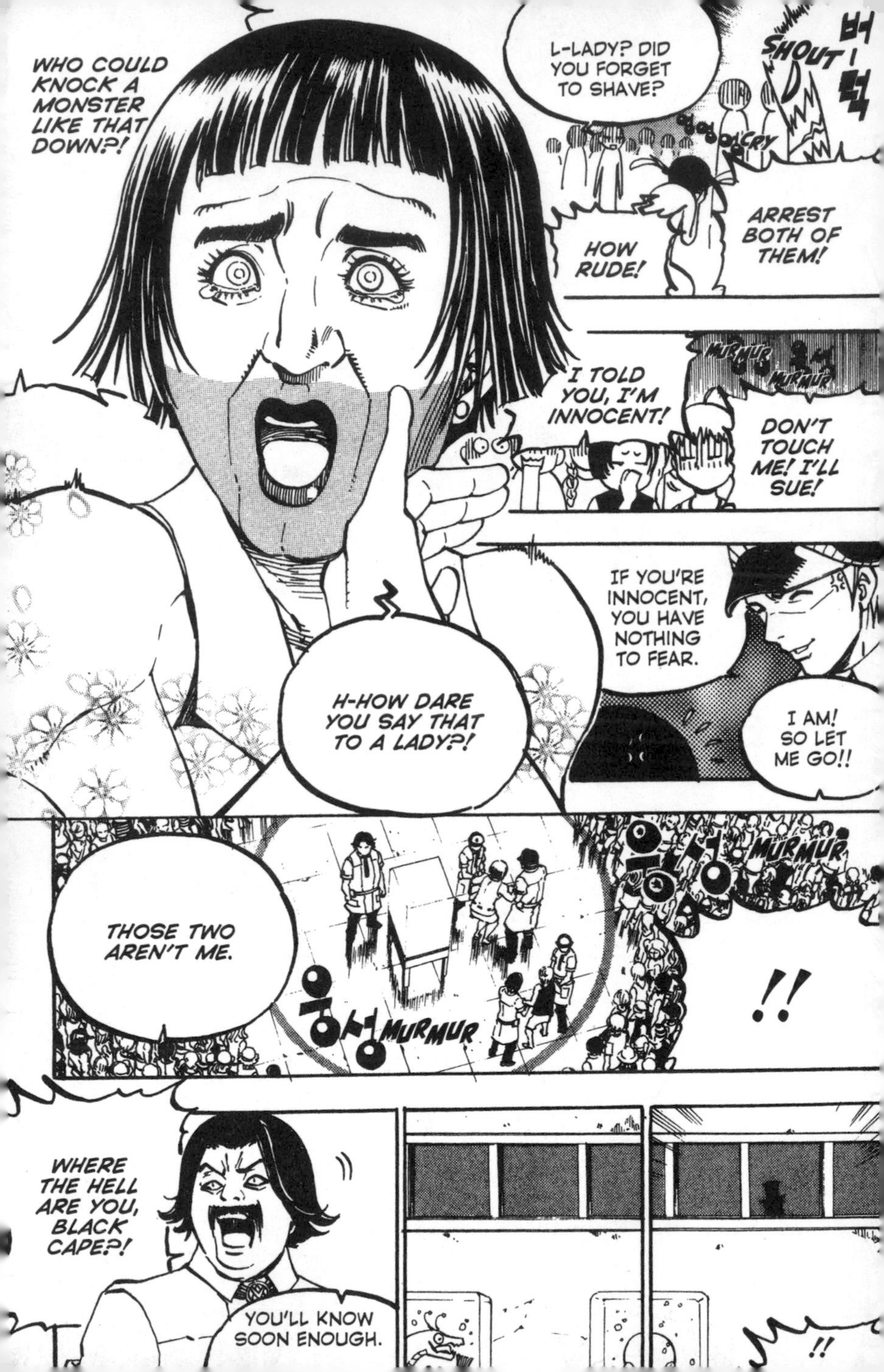
WHO COULD KNOCK A MONSTER LIKE THAT DOWN?!
H-HOW DARE YOU SAY THAT TO A LADY?!
L-LADY? DID YOU FORGET TO SHAVE?
SHOUT
CRY
HOW RUDE!
ARREST BOTH OF THEM!
MURMUR
MURMUR
I TOLD YOU, I'M INNOCENT!
DON'T TOUCH ME! I'LL SUE!
IF YOU'RE INNOCENT, YOU HAVE NOTHING TO FEAR.
I AM! SO LET ME GO!!
THOSE TWO AREN'T ME.
MURMUR
MURMUR
!!
WHERE THE HELL ARE YOU, BLACK CAPE?!
YOU'LL KNOW SOON ENOUGH.
!!

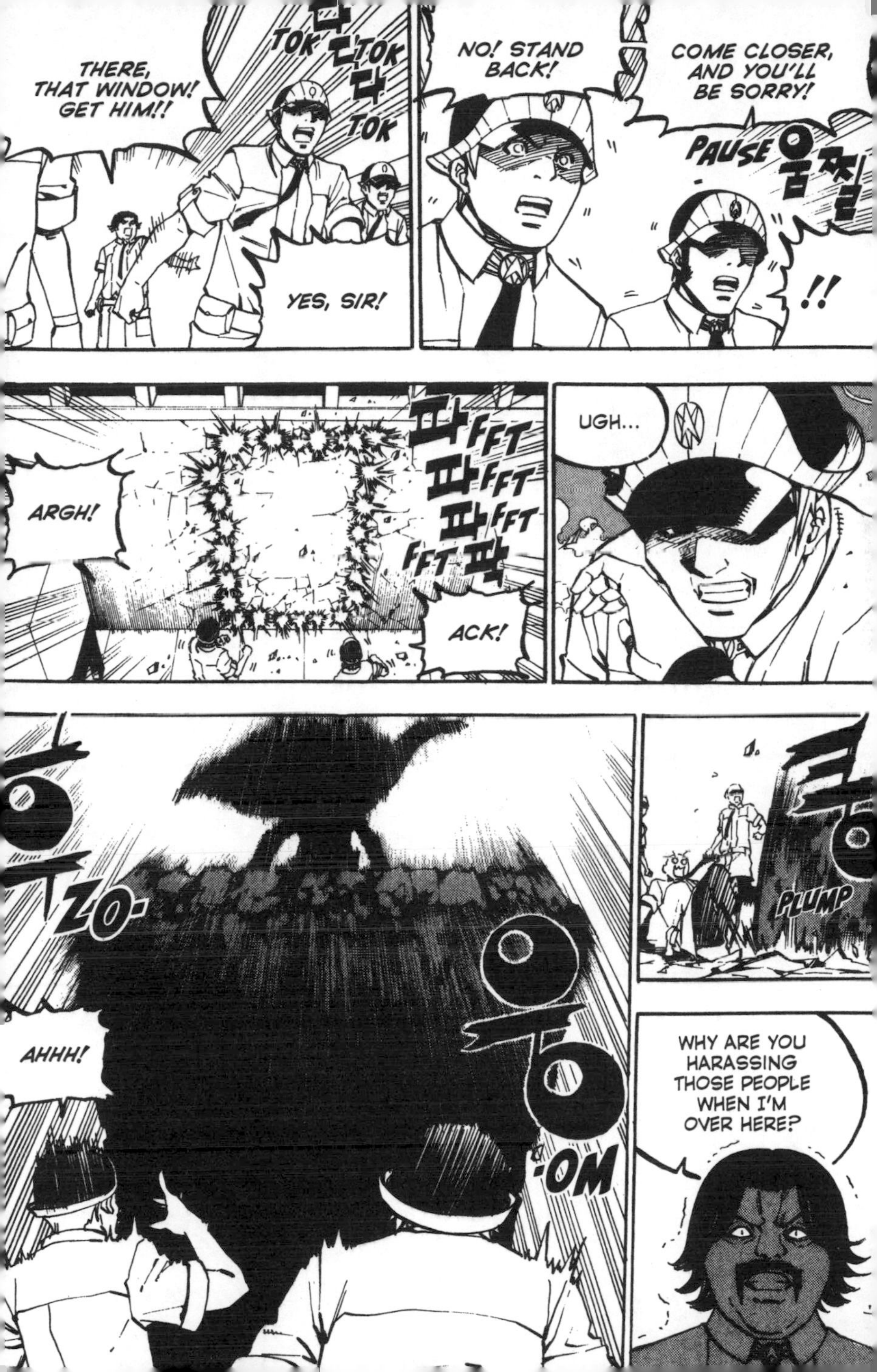
THERE, THAT WINDOW! GET HIM!!
TOK TOK TOK
YES, SIR!
NO! STAND BACK!
COME CLOSER, AND YOU'LL BE SORRY!
PAUSE 움찔
!!
ARGH!
파 FFT 파 FFT 파 FFT FFT 팍
ACK!
UGH...
ZO-
-OM
AHHH!
PLUMP
WHY ARE YOU HARASSING THOSE PEOPLE WHEN I'M OVER HERE?

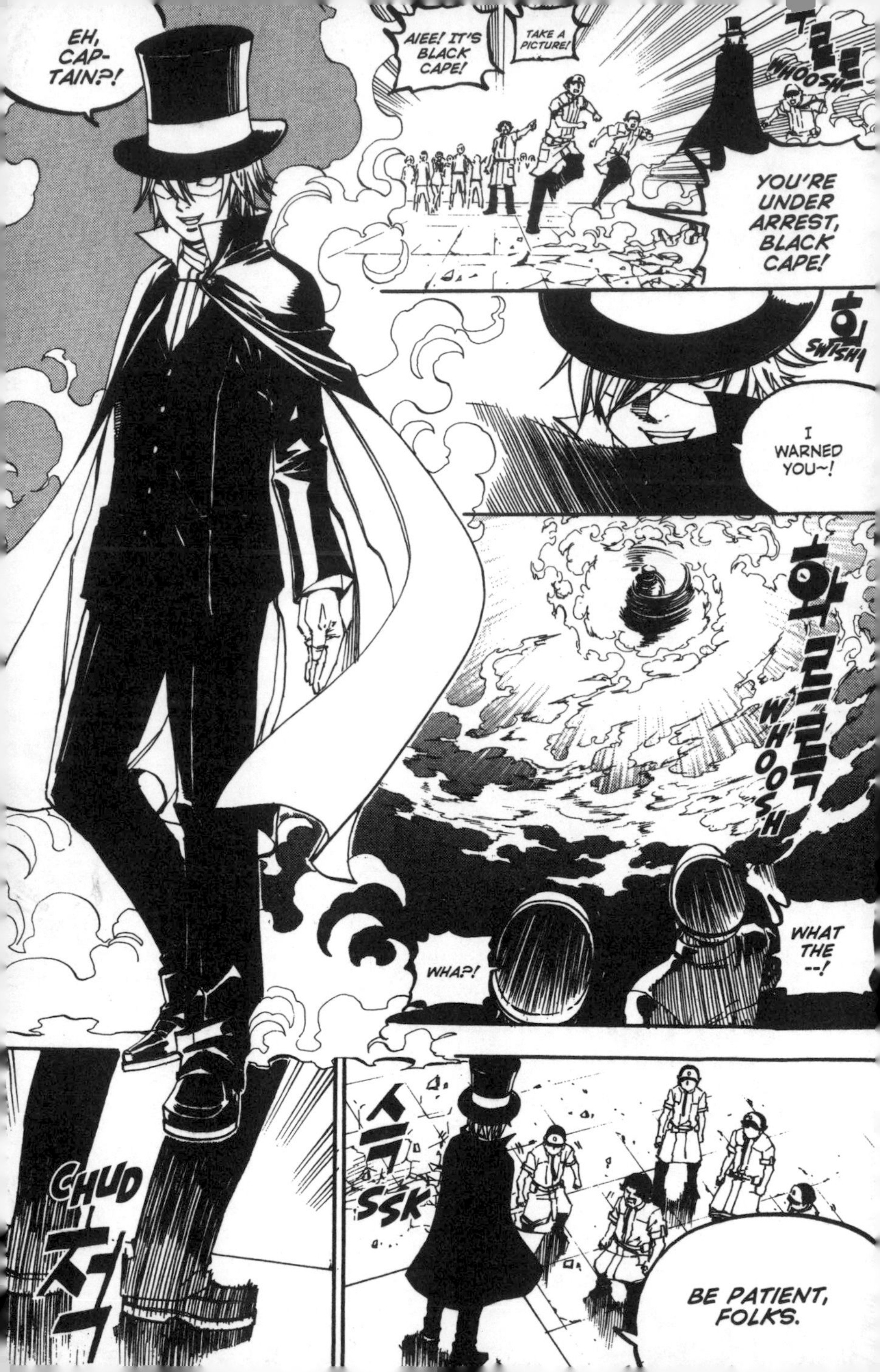
EH, CAP-TAIN?!
AIEE! IT'S BLACK CAPE!
TAKE A PICTURE!
WHOOSH
YOU'RE UNDER ARREST, BLACK CAPE!
SWISH
I WARNED YOU~!
WHOOSH
WHA?!
WHAT THE --!
CHUD
SSK
BE PATIENT, FOLKS.

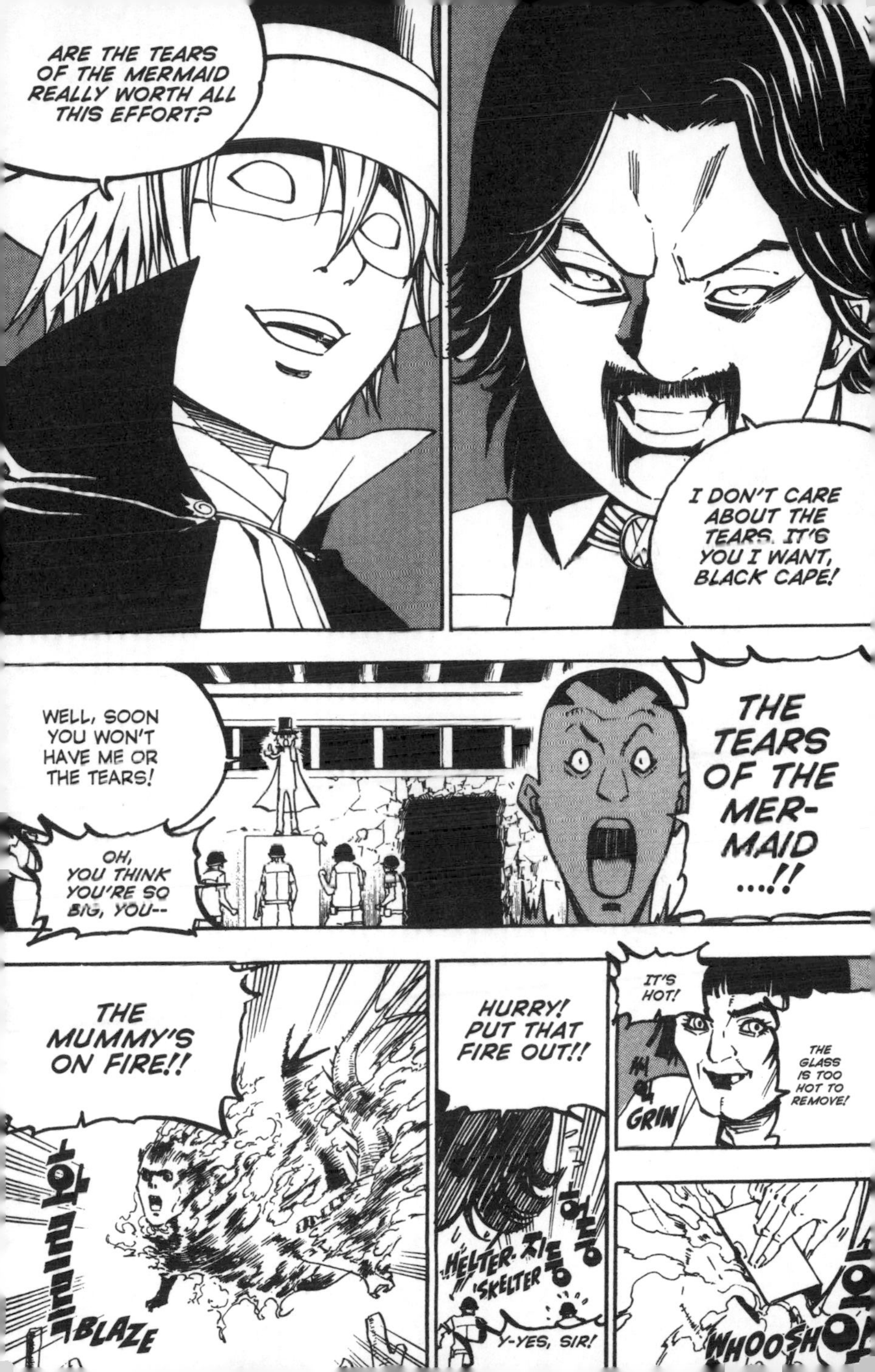
ARE THE TEARS OF THE MERMAID REALLY WORTH ALL THIS EFFORT?
I DON'T CARE ABOUT THE TEARS. IT'S YOU I WANT, BLACK CAPE!
WELL, SOON YOU WON'T HAVE ME OR THE TEARS!
OH, YOU THINK YOU'RE SO BIG, YOU--
THE TEARS OF THE MER-MAID ...!!
THE MUMMY'S ON FIRE!!
BLAZE
HURRY! PUT THAT FIRE OUT!!
HELTER-SKELTER
Y-YES, SIR!
IT'S HOT!
GRIN
THE GLASS IS TOO HOT TO REMOVE!
WHOOSH

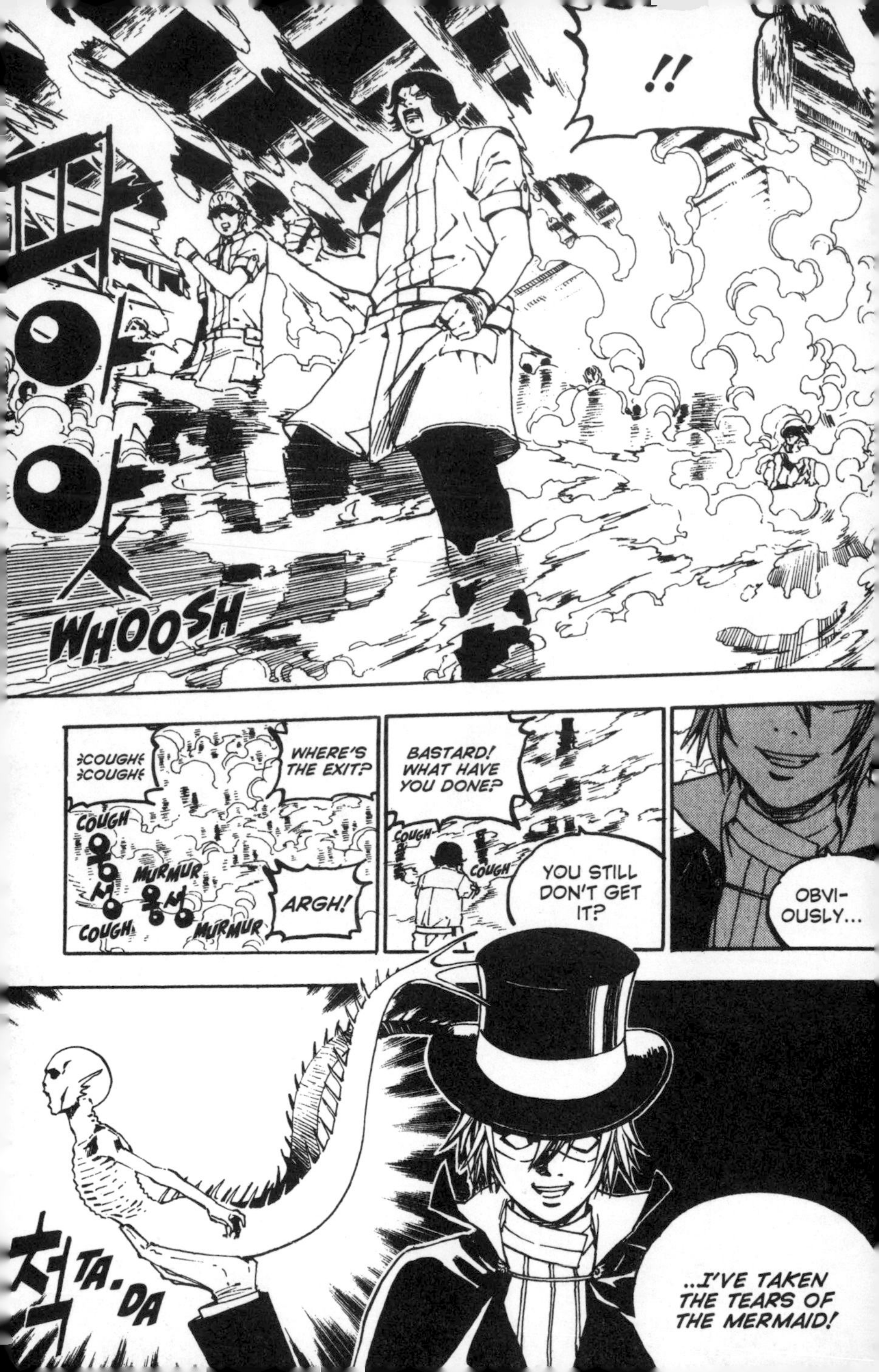
!!
WHOOSH
≈COUGH≈ ≈COUGH≈
WHERE'S THE EXIT?
COUGH
웅성
MURMUR
웅성
COUGH
MURMUR
ARGH!
BASTARD! WHAT HAVE YOU DONE?
COUGH
COUGH
YOU STILL DON'T GET IT?
OBVI-OUSLY...
착
TA-DA
...I'VE TAKEN THE TEARS OF THE MERMAID!

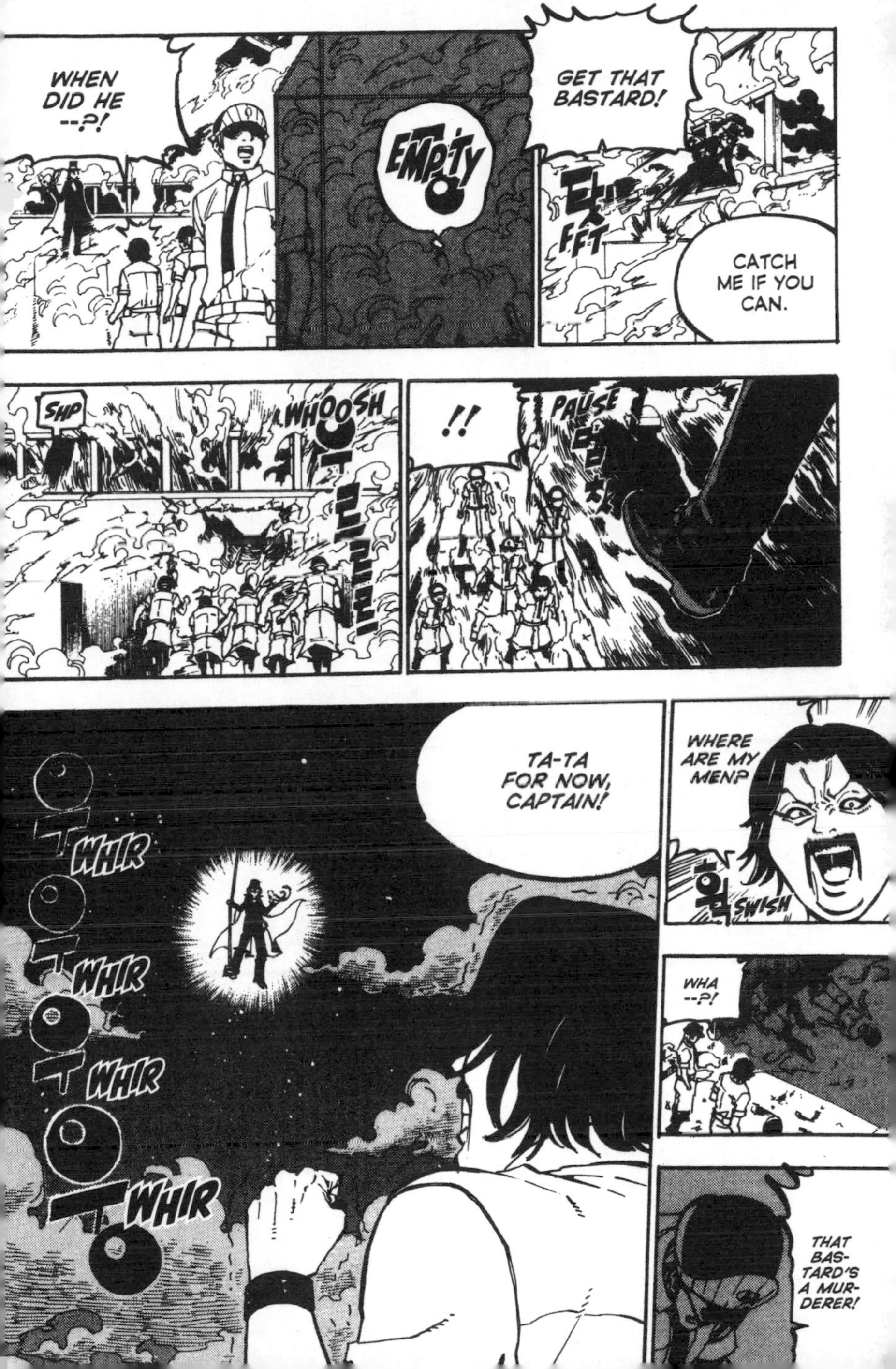

WHEN DID HE --?!
EMPTY
GET THAT BASTARD!
FFT
CATCH ME IF YOU CAN.
SHP
WHOOSH
!!
PAUSE
WHIR
WHIR
WHIR
WHIR
TA-TA FOR NOW, CAPTAIN!
WHERE ARE MY MEN?
SWISH
WHA --?!
THAT BAS-TARD'S A MUR-DERER!

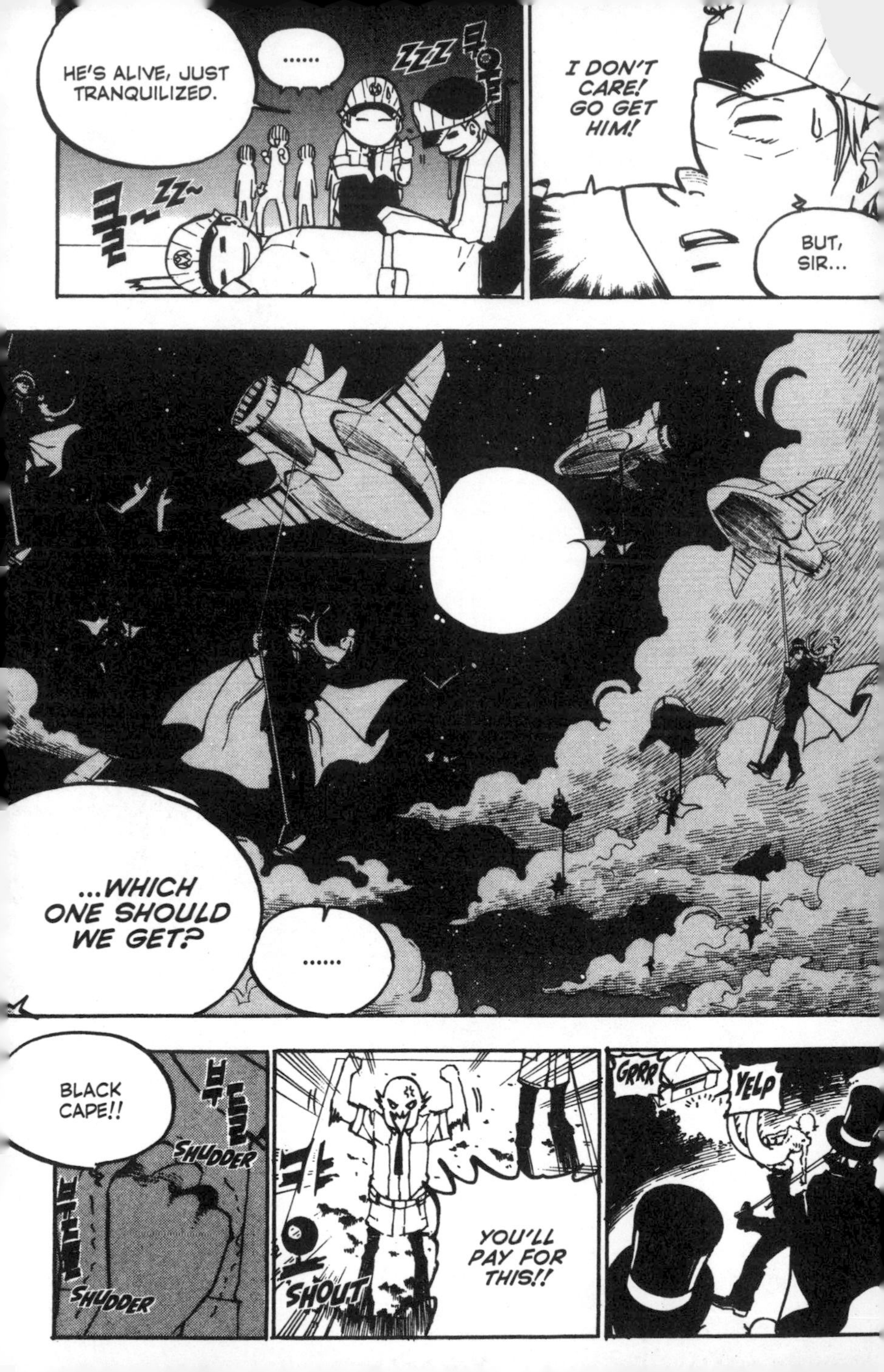
HE'S ALIVE, JUST TRANQUILIZED.
......
ZZZ
ZZ~
I DON'T CARE! GO GET HIM!
BUT, SIR...
...WHICH ONE SHOULD WE GET?
......
BLACK CAPE!!
SHUDDER
SHUDDER
SHOUT
YOU'LL PAY FOR THIS!!
GRRR
YELP

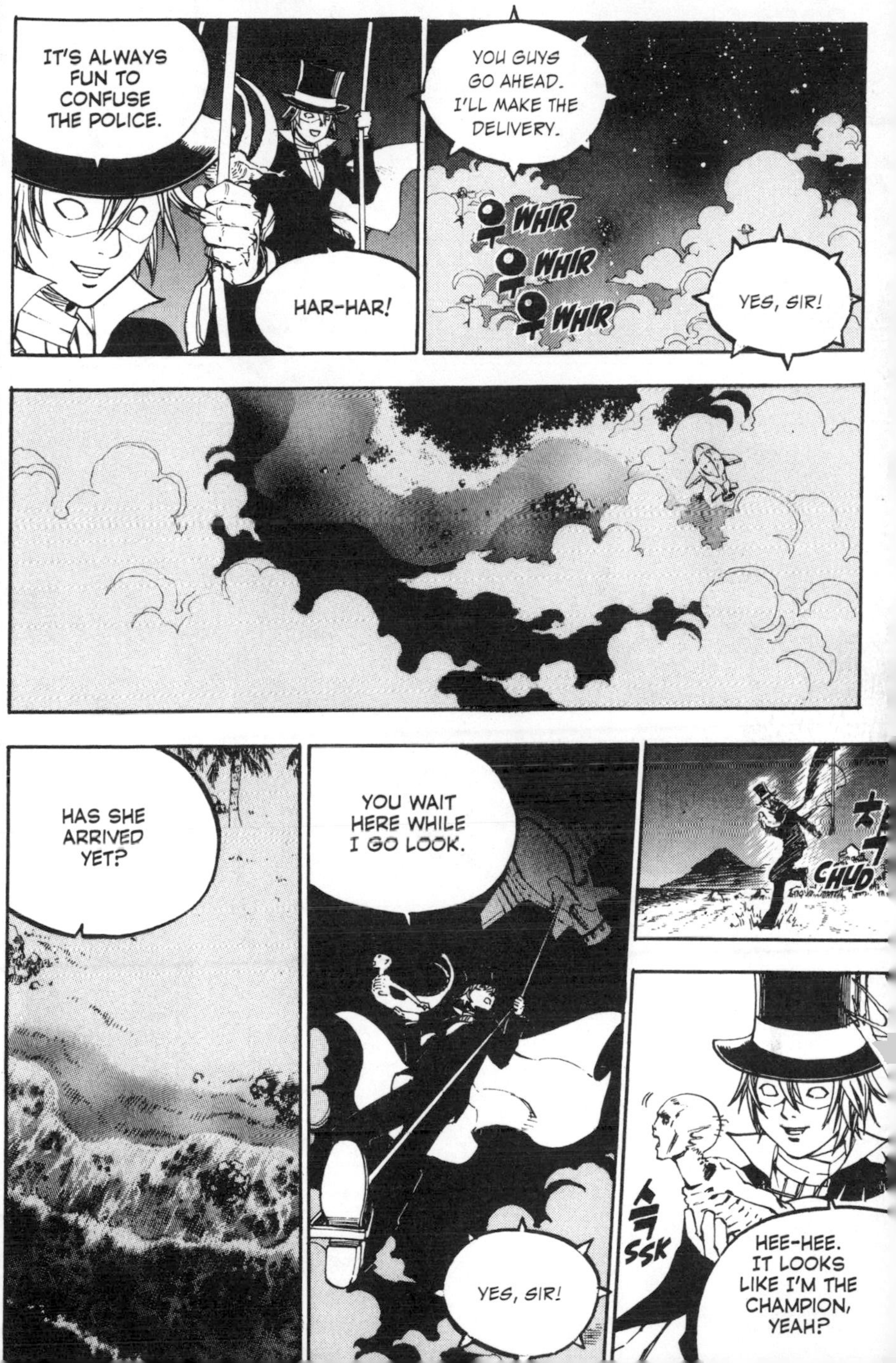
IT'S ALWAYS FUN TO CONFUSE THE POLICE.
HAR-HAR!
YOU GUYS GO AHEAD. I'LL MAKE THE DELIVERY.
WHIR
WHIR
WHIR
YES, SIR!
HAS SHE ARRIVED YET?
YOU WAIT HERE WHILE I GO LOOK.
YES, SIR!
CHUD
SSK
HEE-HEE. IT LOOKS LIKE I'M THE CHAMPION, YEAH?

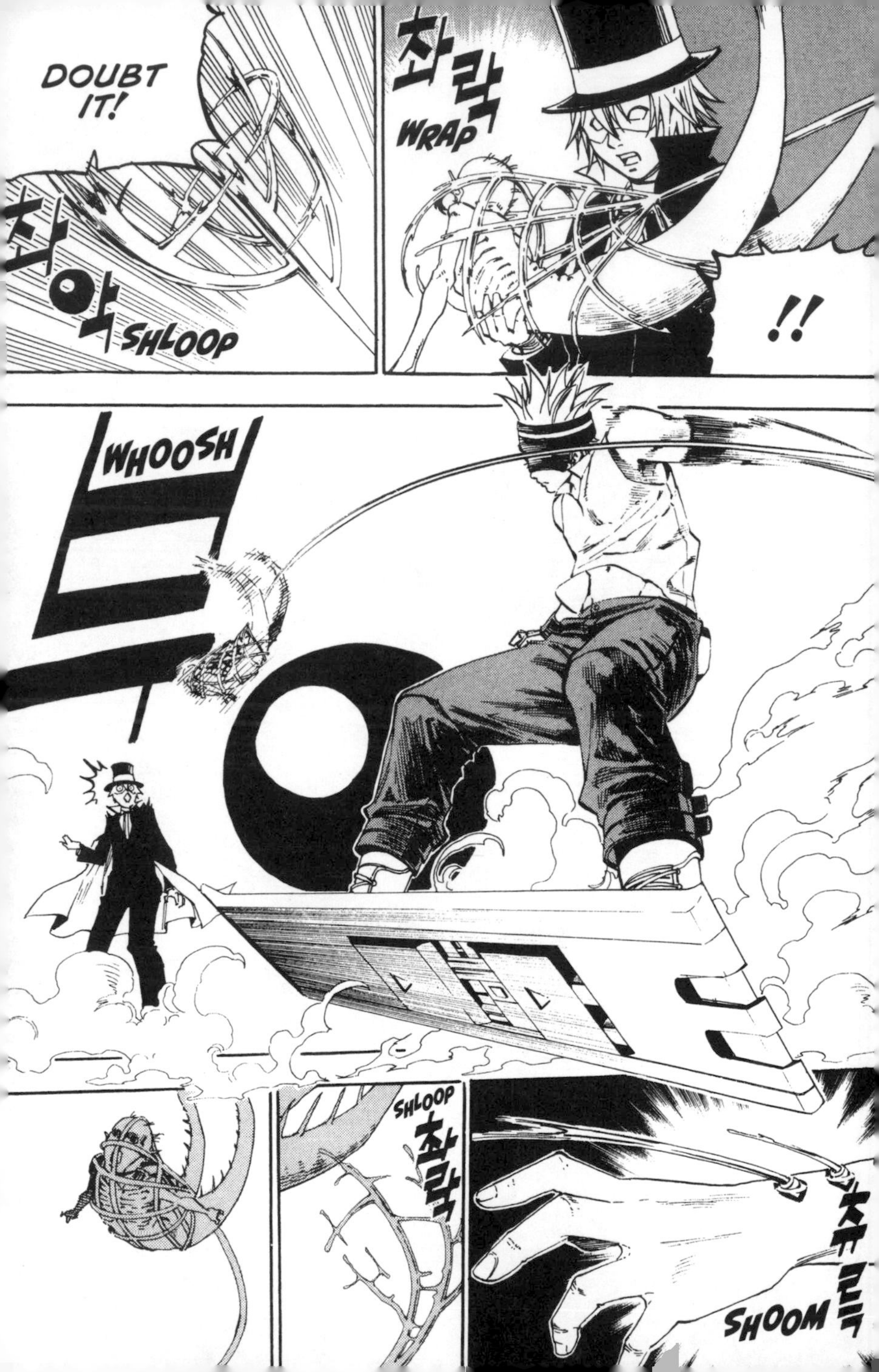
DOUBT IT!
촤악
SHLOOP
촤락
WRAP
!!
WHOOSH
SHLOOP
촤락
SHOOM

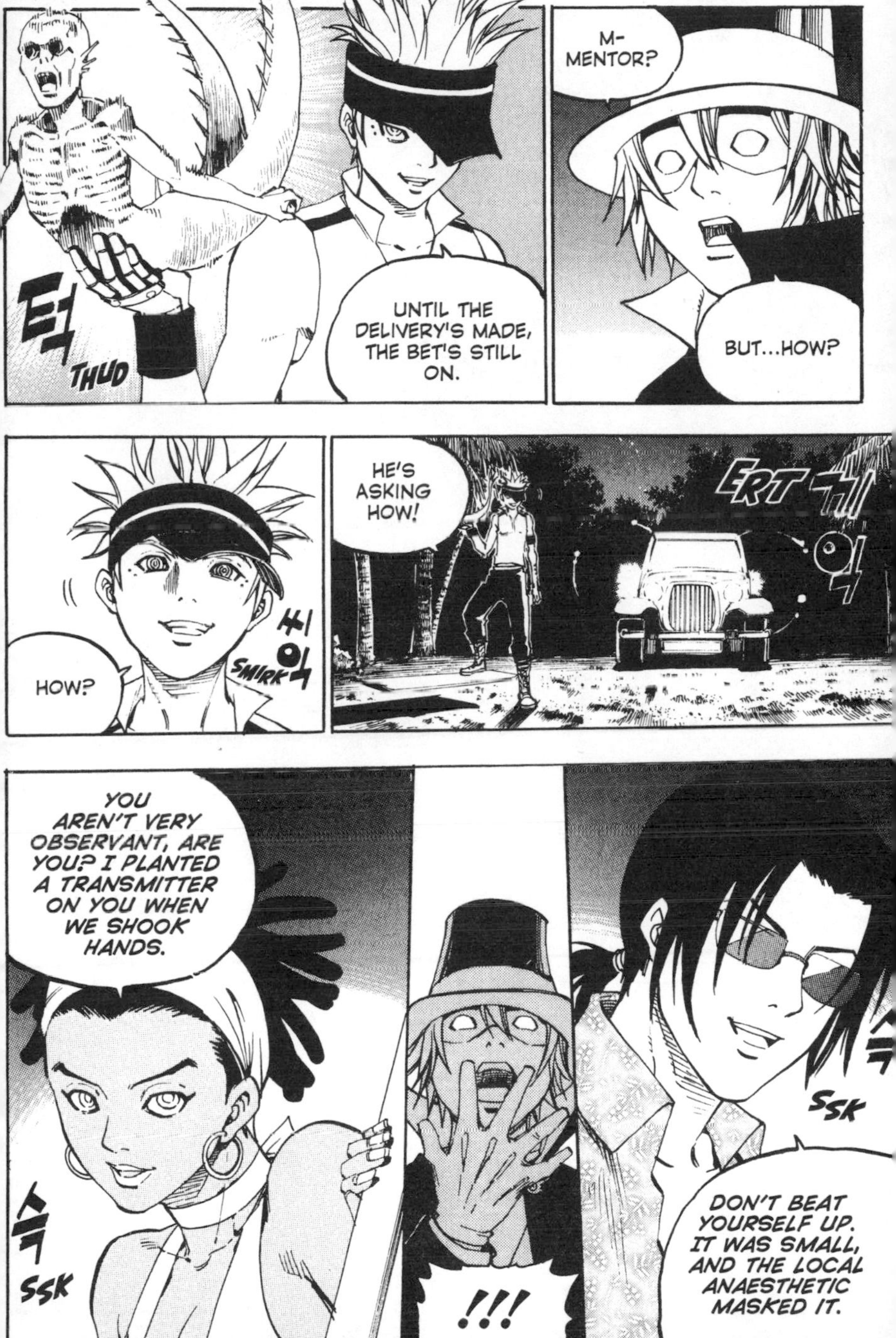
THUD
UNTIL THE DELIVERY'S MADE, THE BET'S STILL ON.
M- MENTOR?
BUT...HOW?
HOW?
SMIRK
HE'S ASKING HOW!
ERT
YOU AREN'T VERY OBSERVANT, ARE YOU? I PLANTED A TRANSMITTER ON YOU WHEN WE SHOOK HANDS.
SSK
!!!
SSK
DON'T BEAT YOURSELF UP. IT WAS SMALL, AND THE LOCAL ANAESTHETIC MASKED IT.

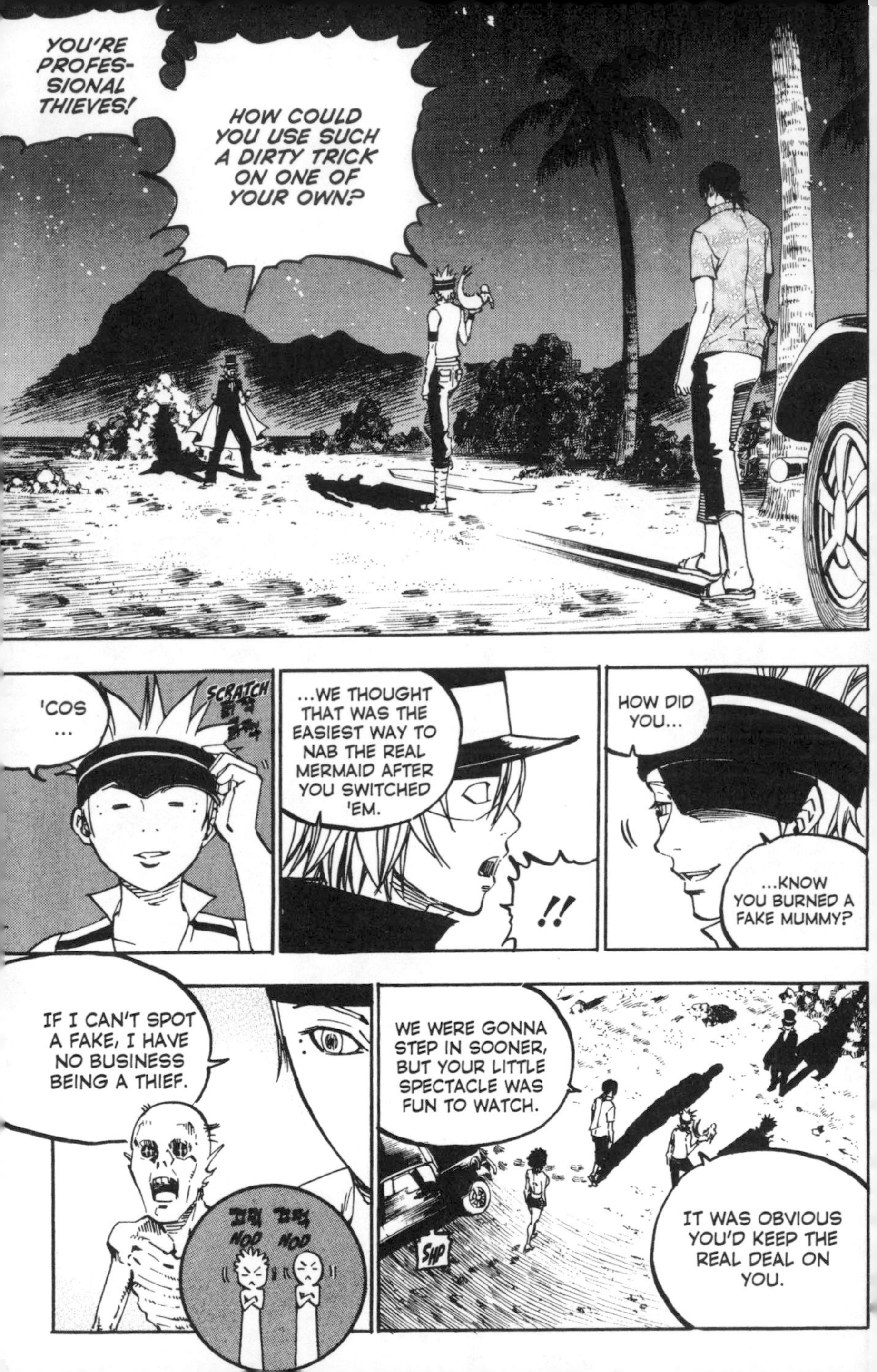
YOU'RE PROFES-SIONAL THIEVES!
HOW COULD YOU USE SUCH A DIRTY TRICK ON ONE OF YOUR OWN?
'COS ...
SCRATCH
...WE THOUGHT THAT WAS THE EASIEST WAY TO NAB THE REAL MERMAID AFTER YOU SWITCHED 'EM.
!!
HOW DID YOU...
...KNOW YOU BURNED A FAKE MUMMY?
IF I CAN'T SPOT A FAKE, I HAVE NO BUSINESS BEING A THIEF.
NOD NOD
WE WERE GONNA STEP IN SOONER, BUT YOUR LITTLE SPECTACLE WAS FUN TO WATCH.
SHP
IT WAS OBVIOUS YOU'D KEEP THE REAL DEAL ON YOU.

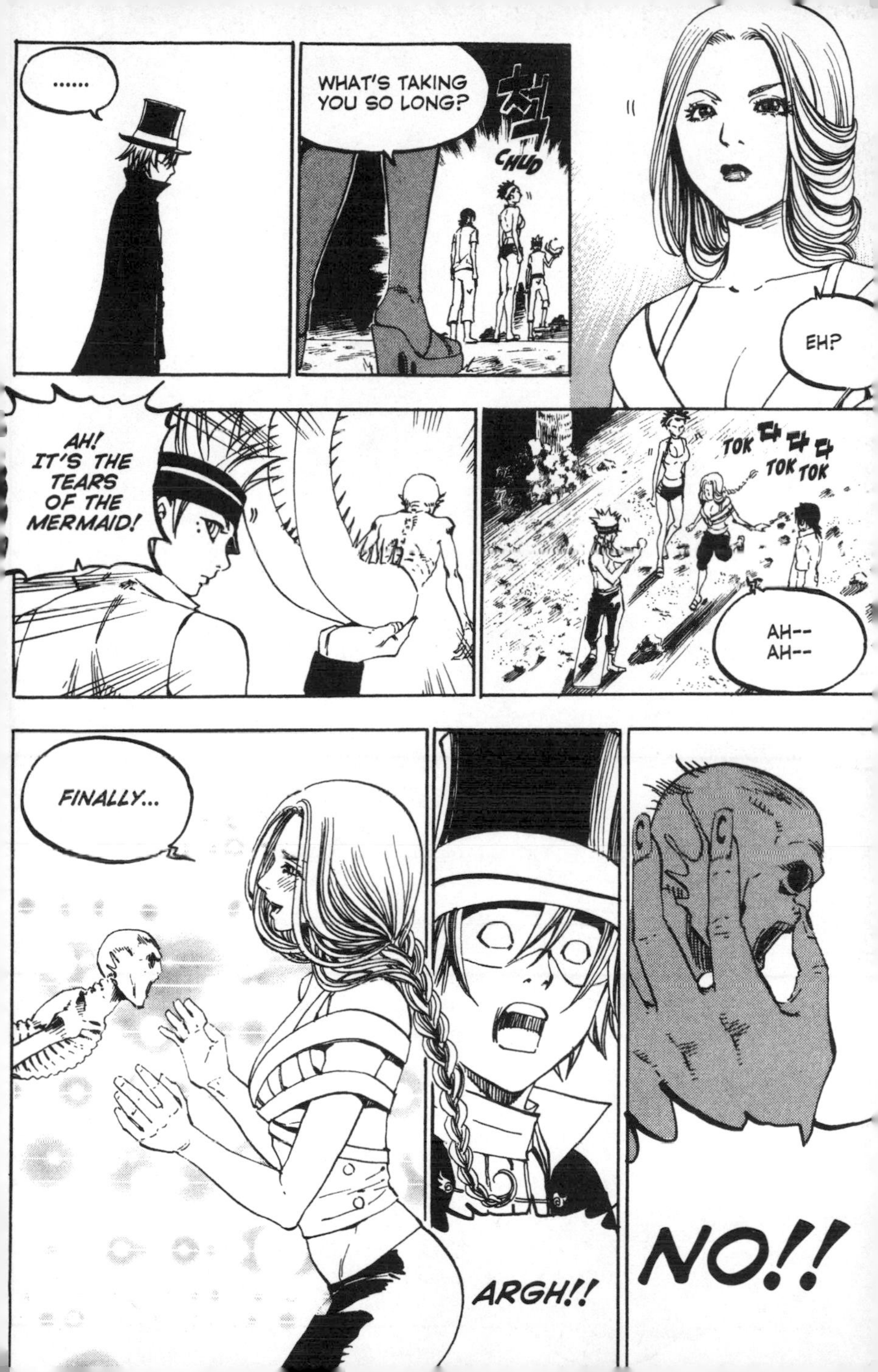
......
WHAT'S TAKING YOU SO LONG?
척
CHUD
EH?
AH! IT'S THE TEARS OF THE MERMAID!
TOK 다다다 TOK TOK
AH-- AH--
FINALLY...
ARGH!!
NO!!

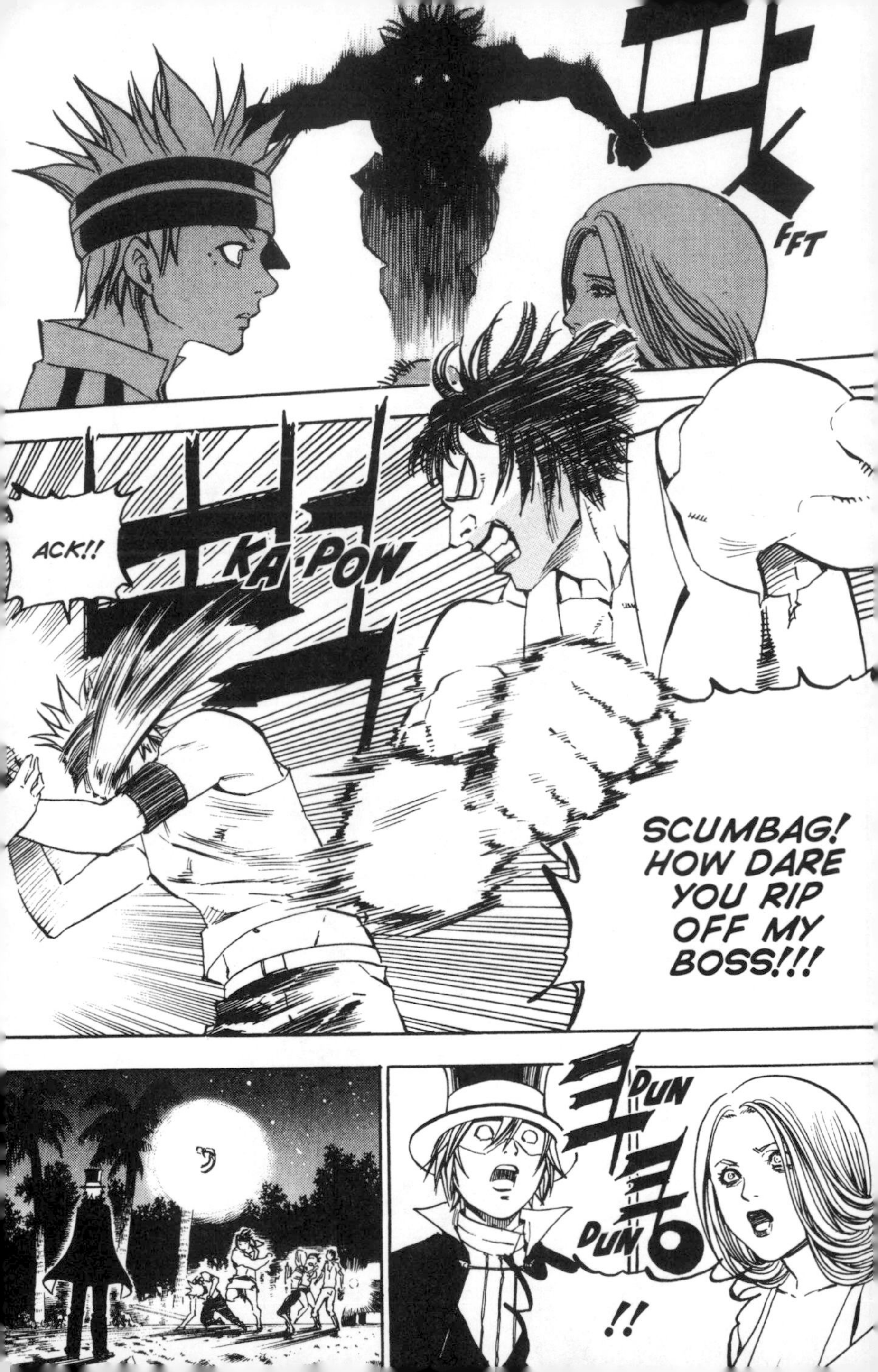
FFT
ACK!!
KA-POW
SCUMBAG! HOW DARE YOU RIP OFF MY BOSS!!!
DUN
DUN
!!

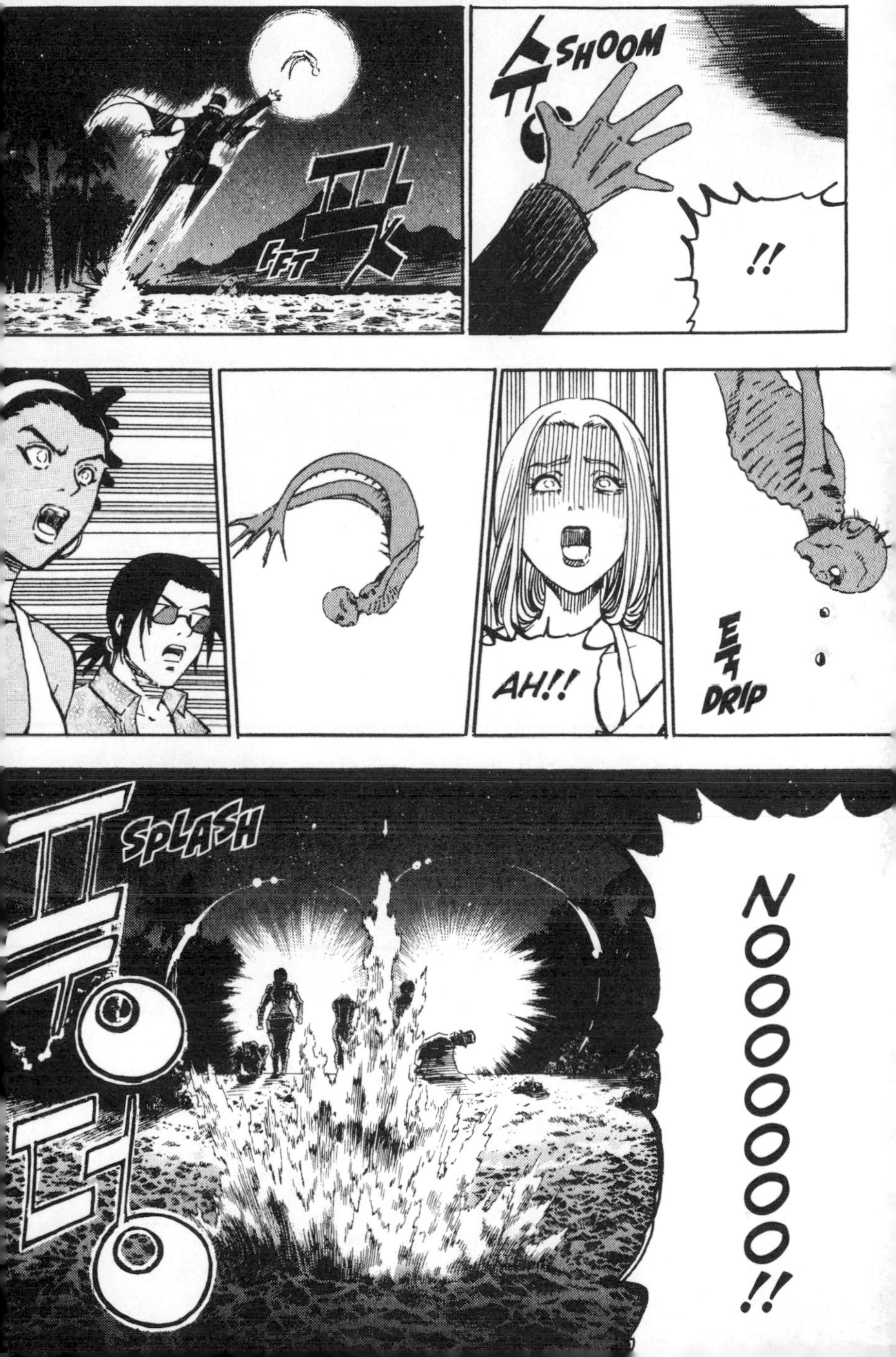
FFT
SHOOM
!!
AH!!
DRIP
SPLASH
NOOOOOOOOOO!!

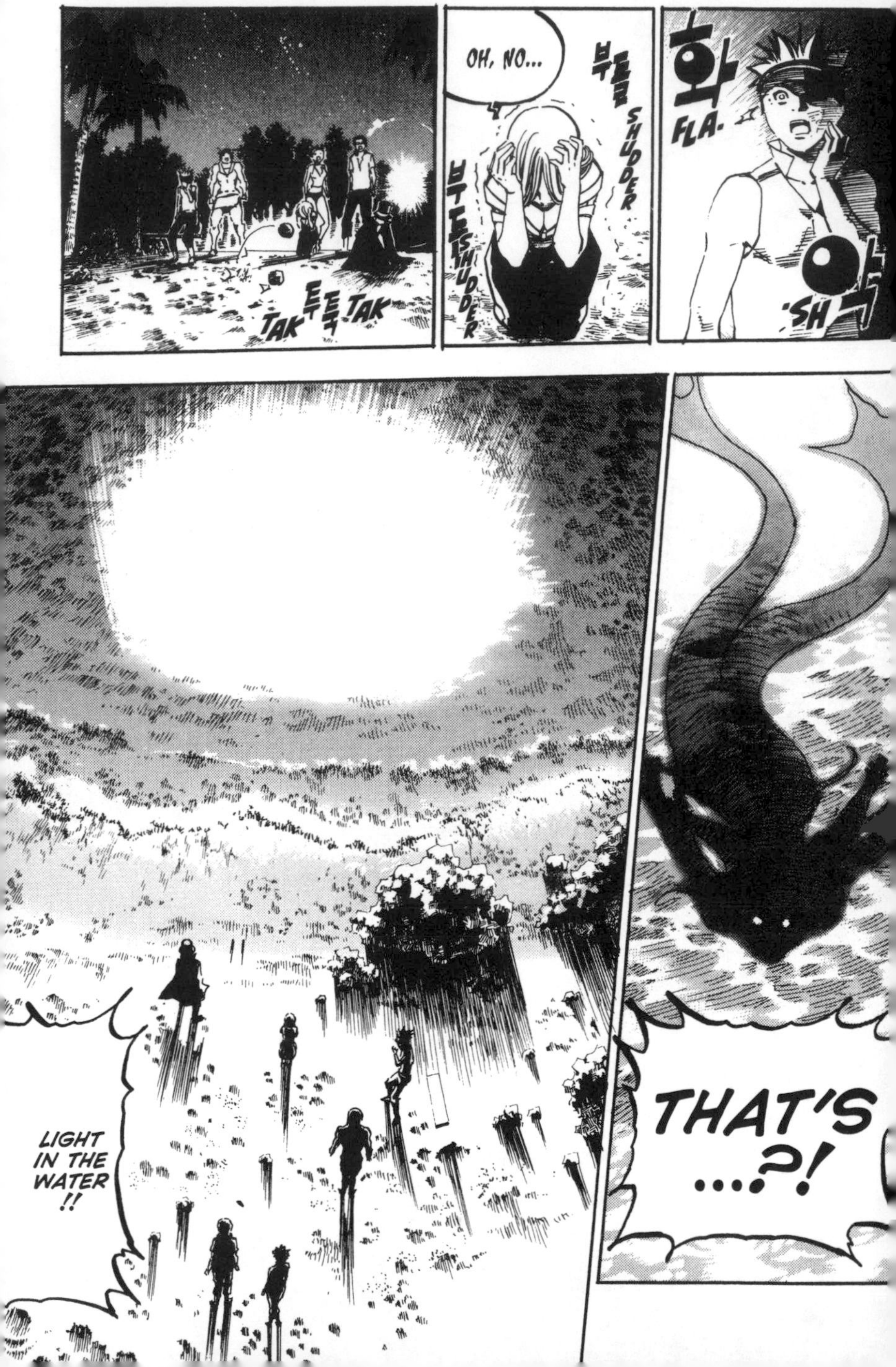

TAK TAK
OH, NO...
부들
SHUDDER
SHUDDER
화악
FLA.
SH
LIGHT IN THE WATER !!
THAT'S ...?!

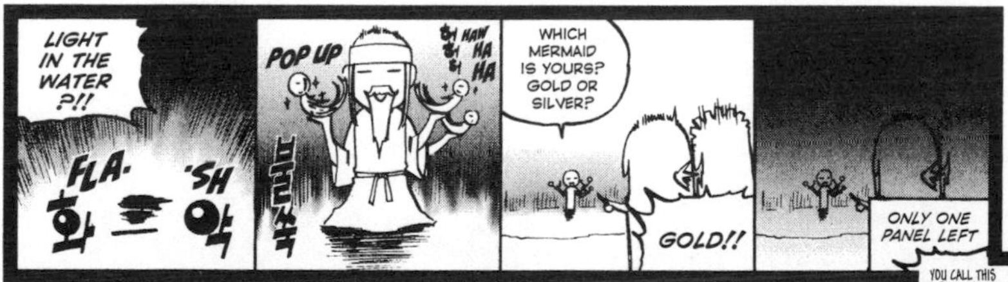
LIGHT IN THE WATER ?!!
FLA- 'SH
POP UP
불쑥
허허허
HAW HA HA
WHICH MERMAID IS YOURS? GOLD OR SILVER?
GOLD!!
ONLY ONE PANEL LEFT
YOU CALL THIS A FOUR-PANEL COMIC?

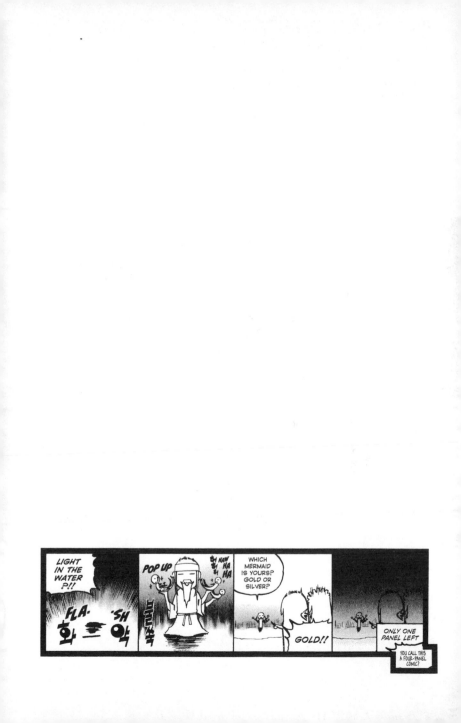

FREAK

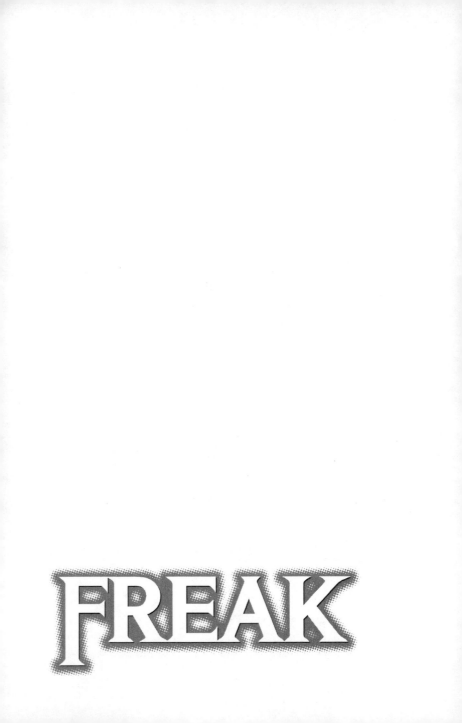

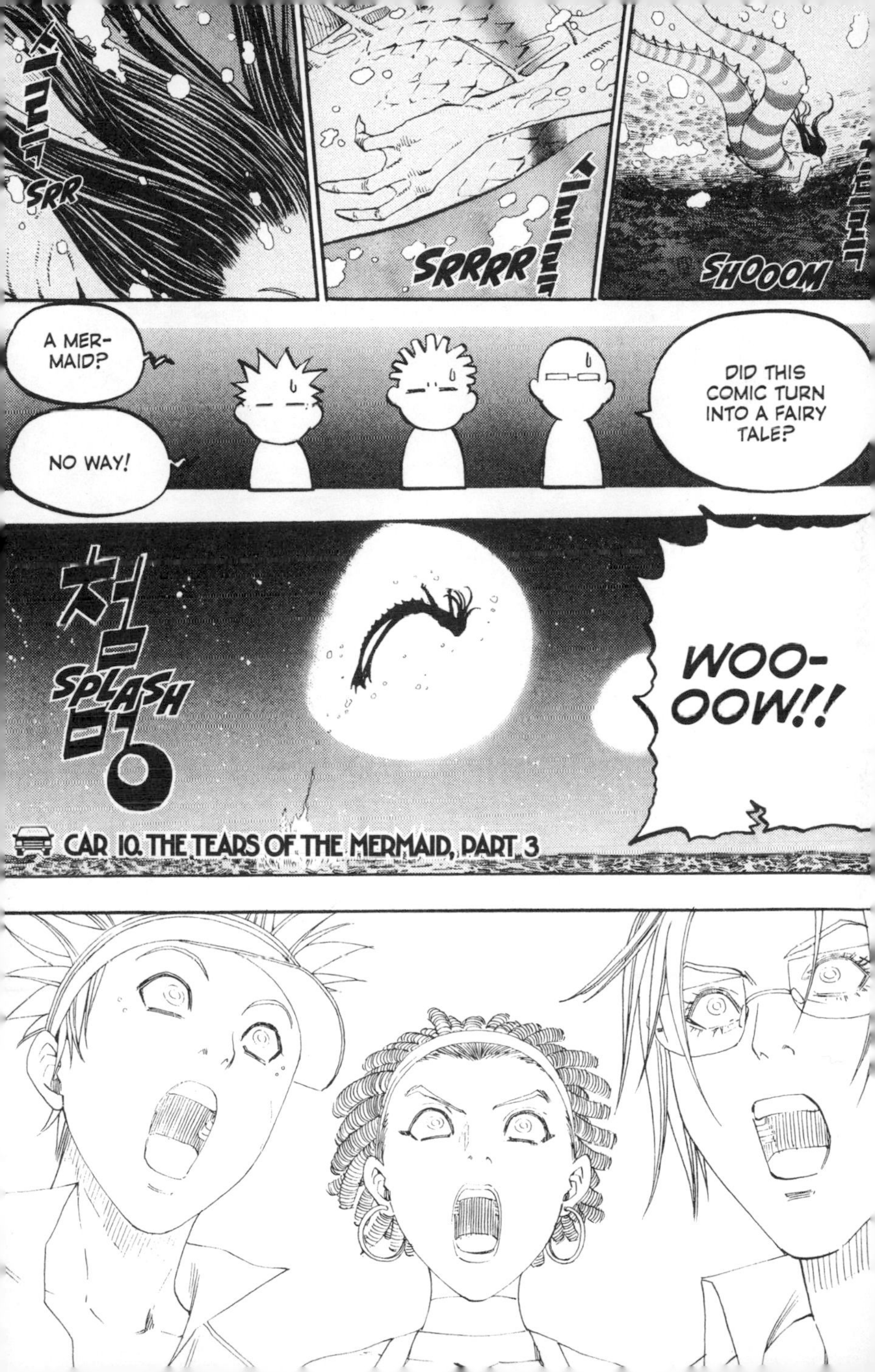
SRR
SRRRR
SHOOOM
A MER-MAID?
NO WAY!
DID THIS COMIC TURN INTO A FAIRY TALE?
SPLASH
WOO-OOW!!
CAR 10. THE TEARS OF THE MERMAID, PART 3

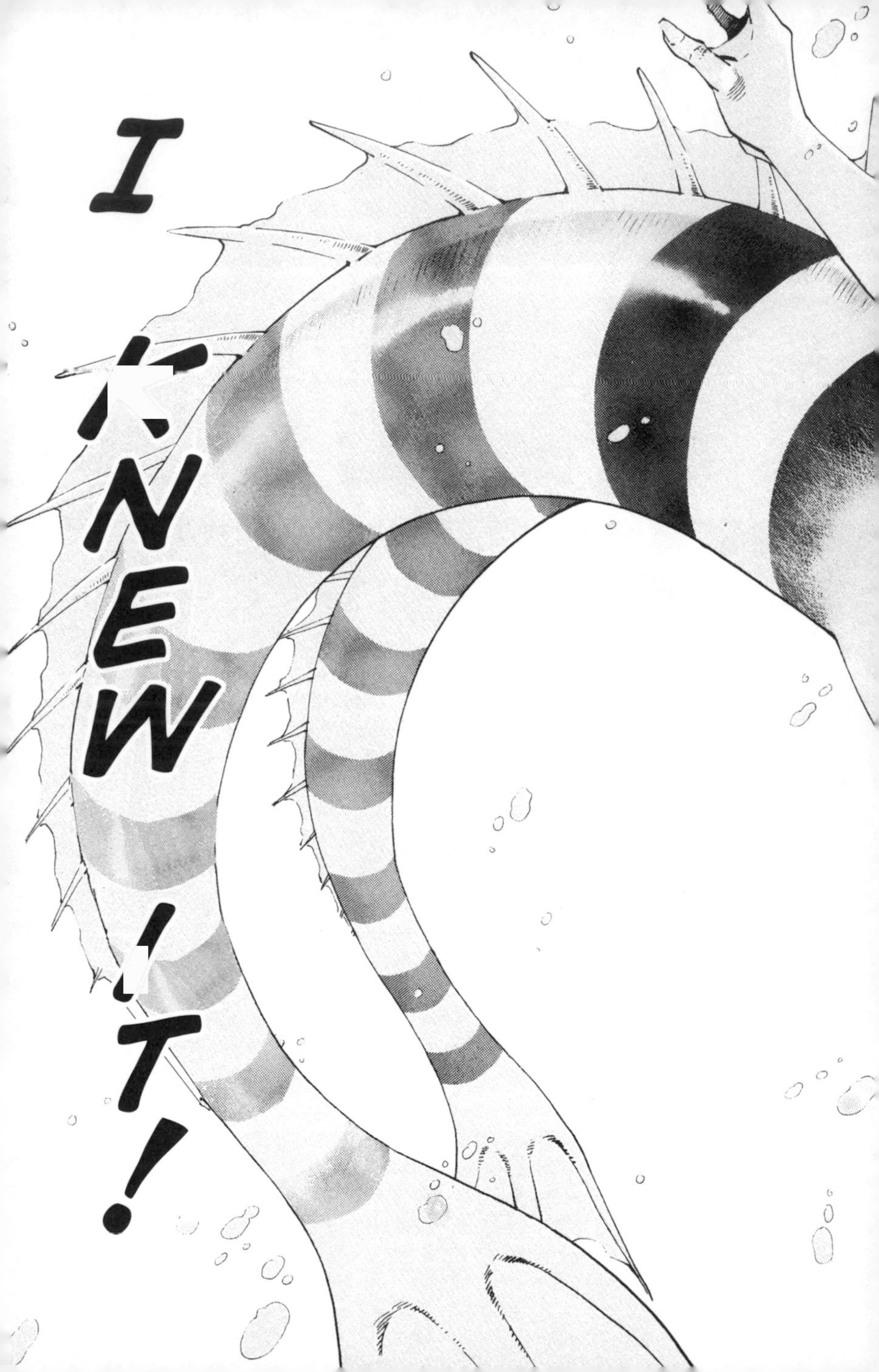
I KNEW IT!

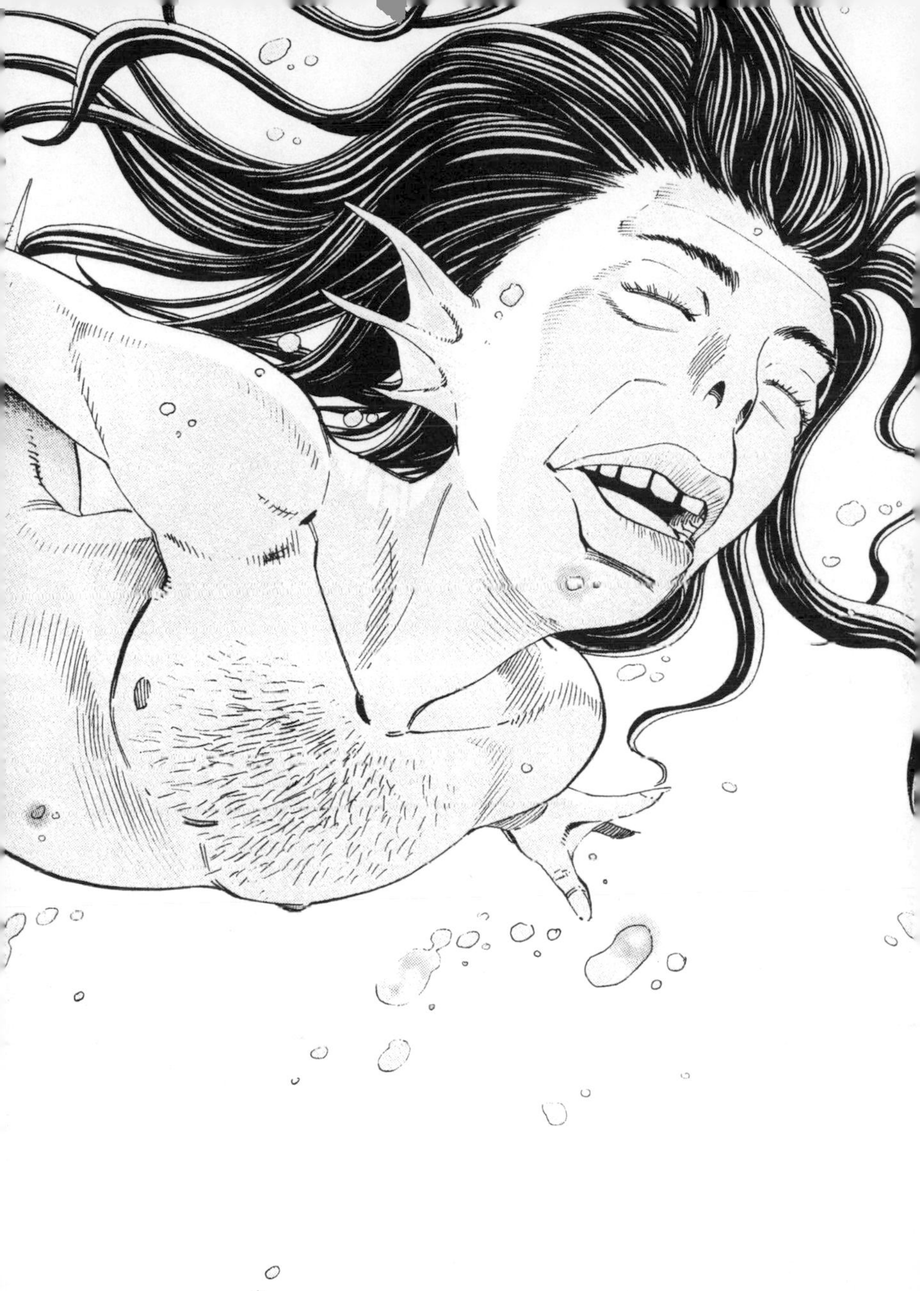

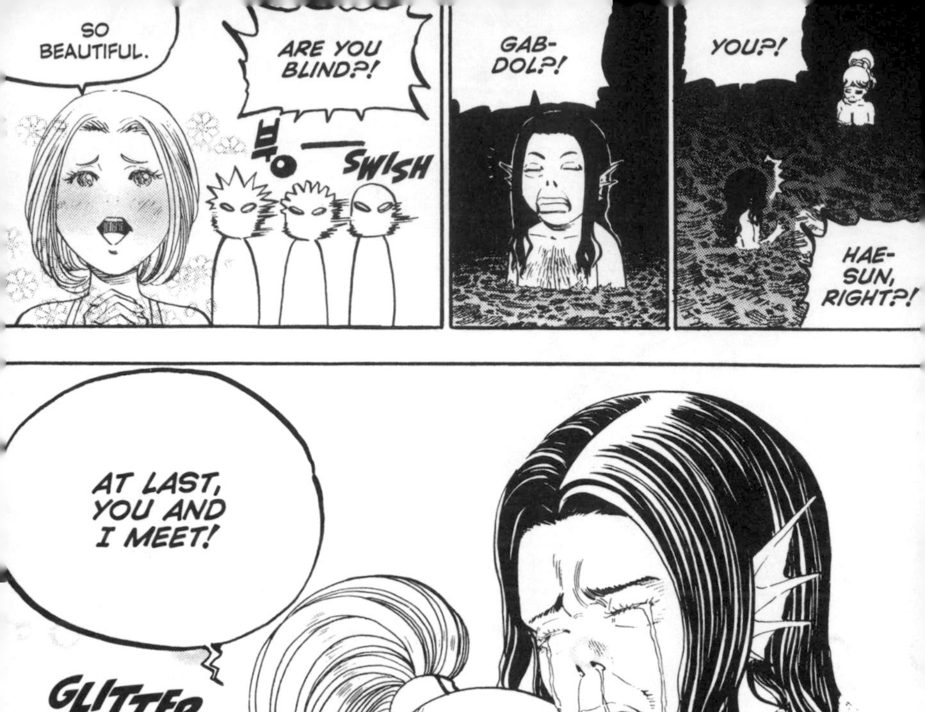
SO BEAUTIFUL.
ARE YOU BLIND?!
SWISH
GAB-DOL?!
YOU?!
HAE-SUN, RIGHT?!
AT LAST, YOU AND I MEET!
GLITTER
YES, YES, HAE-SUN! MY SWEET.

*HANS CHRISTIAN ANDERSEN: THE AUTHOR OF *THE LITTLE MERMAID*

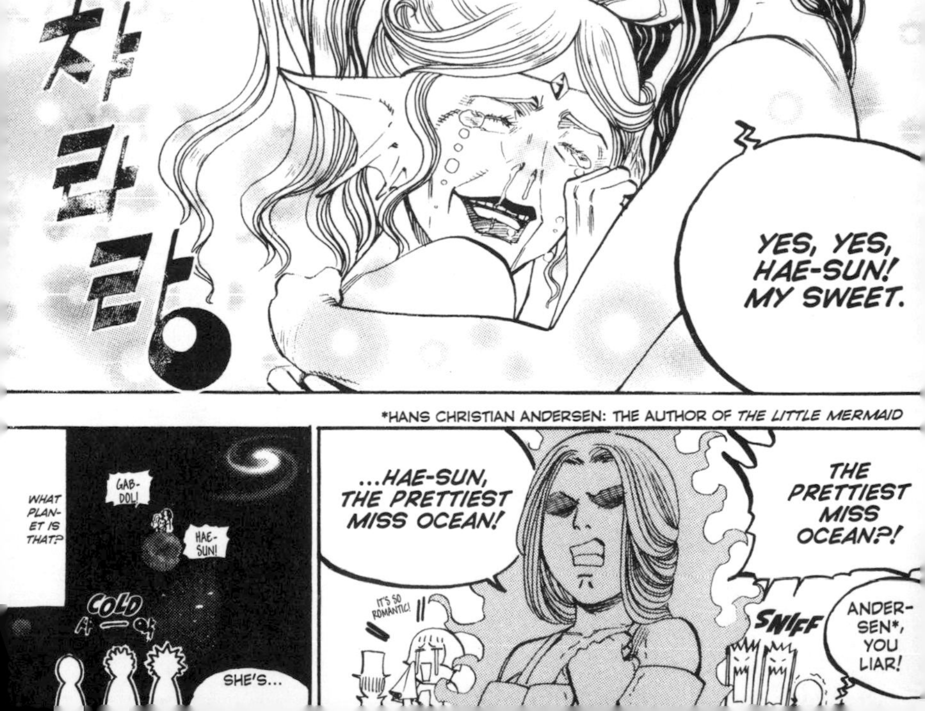
WHAT PLANET IS THAT?
GAB-DOL!
HAE-SUN!
COLD
SHE'S...
...HAE-SUN, THE PRETTIEST MISS OCEAN!
IT'S SO ROMANTIC!
THE PRETTIEST MISS OCEAN?!
SNIFF
ANDERSEN*, YOU LIAR!

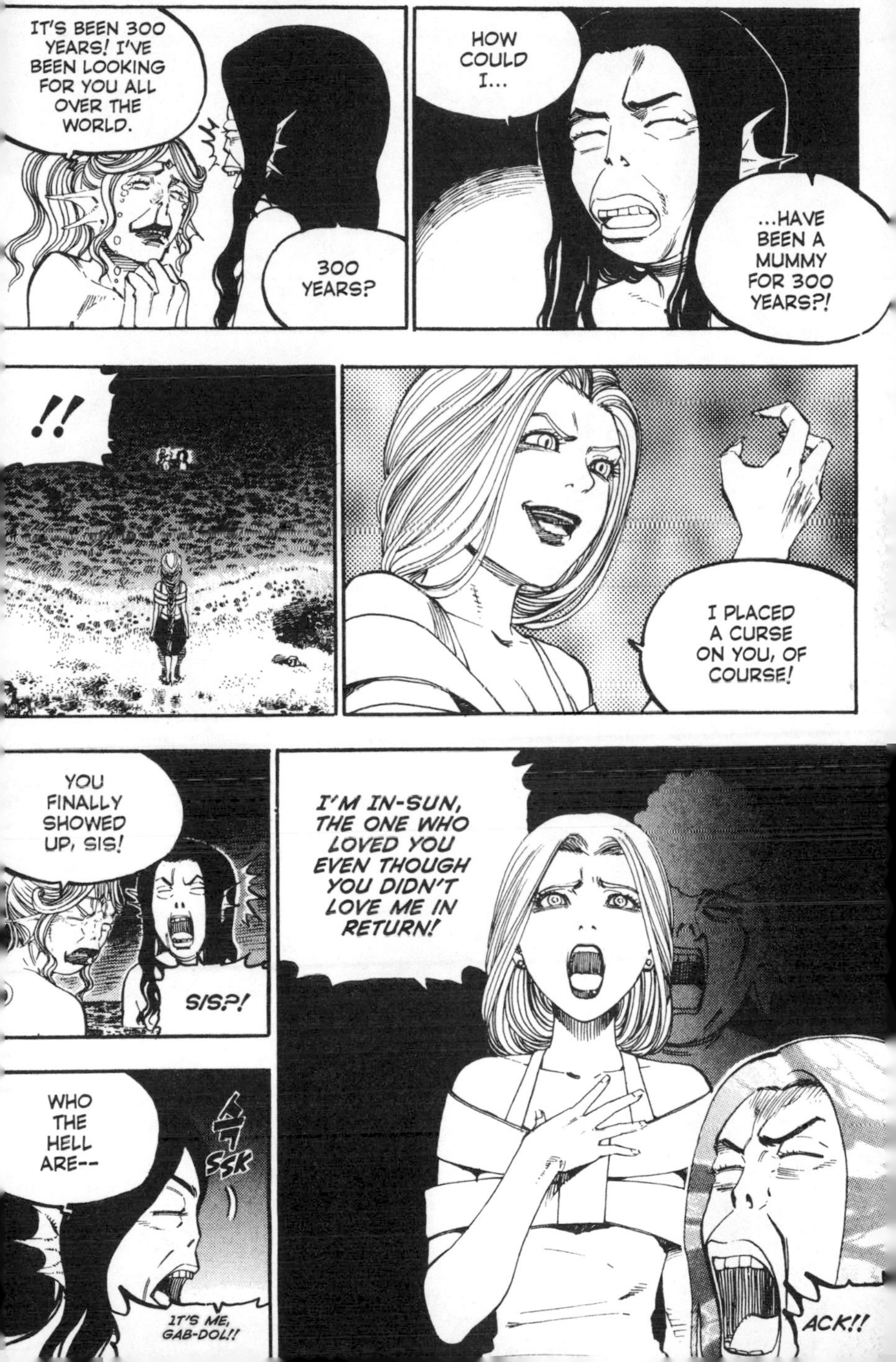
IT'S BEEN 300 YEARS! I'VE BEEN LOOKING FOR YOU ALL OVER THE WORLD.
300 YEARS?
HOW COULD I...
...HAVE BEEN A MUMMY FOR 300 YEARS?!
!!
I PLACED A CURSE ON YOU, OF COURSE!
YOU FINALLY SHOWED UP, SIS!
SIS?!
WHO THE HELL ARE--
SSK
IT'S ME, GAB-DOL!!
I'M IN-SUN, THE ONE WHO LOVED YOU EVEN THOUGH YOU DIDN'T LOVE ME IN RETURN!
ACK!!

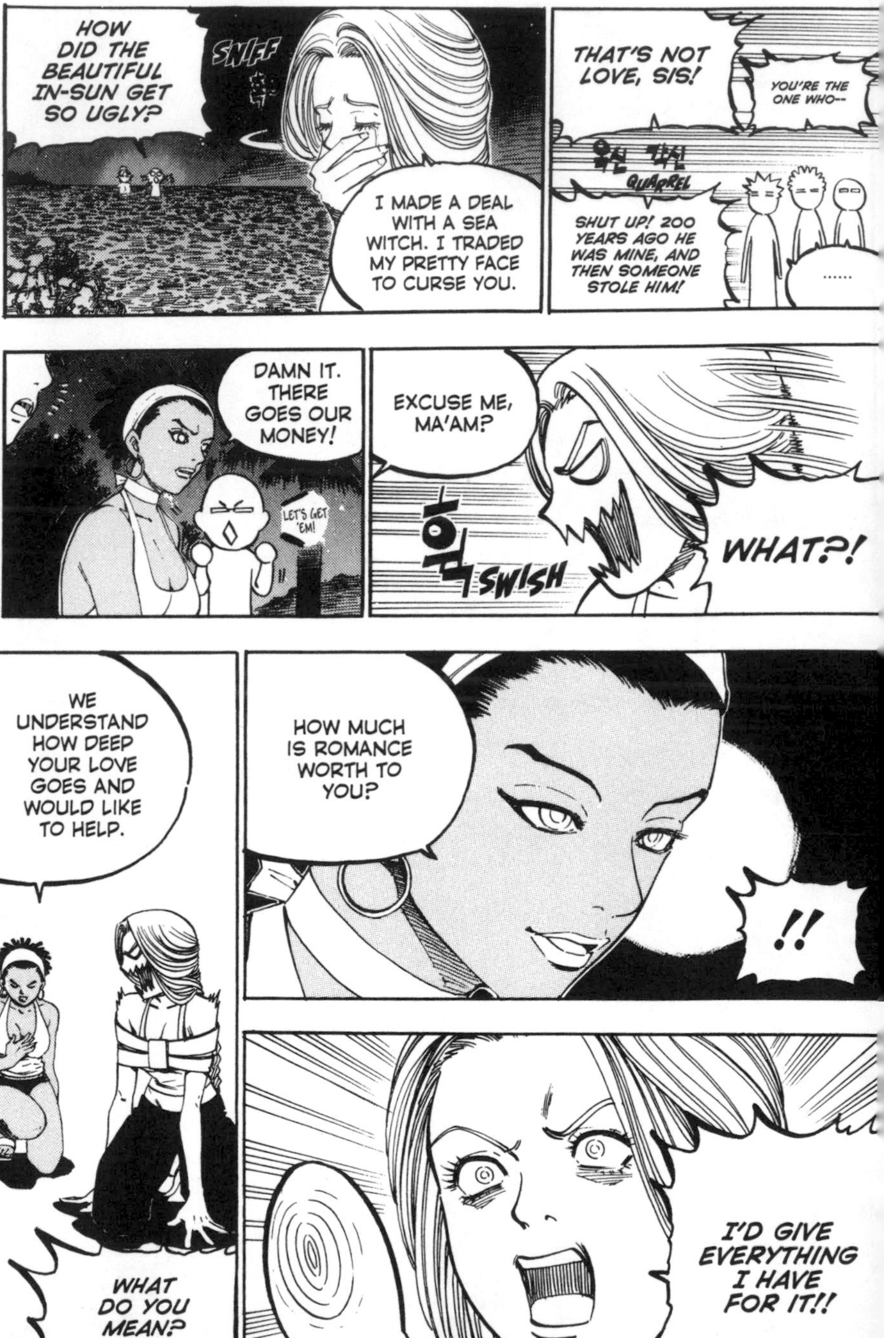
HOW DID THE BEAUTIFUL IN-SUN GET SO UGLY?
SNIFF
I MADE A DEAL WITH A SEA WITCH. I TRADED MY PRETTY FACE TO CURSE YOU.
THAT'S NOT LOVE, SIS!
YOU'RE THE ONE WHO--
QUARREL
SHUT UP! 200 YEARS AGO HE WAS MINE, AND THEN SOMEONE STOLE HIM!
......
DAMN IT. THERE GOES OUR MONEY!
LET'S GET 'EM!
EXCUSE ME, MA'AM?
SWISH
WHAT?!
WE UNDERSTAND HOW DEEP YOUR LOVE GOES AND WOULD LIKE TO HELP.
WHAT DO YOU MEAN?
HOW MUCH IS ROMANCE WORTH TO YOU?
!!
I'D GIVE EVERYTHING I HAVE FOR IT!!

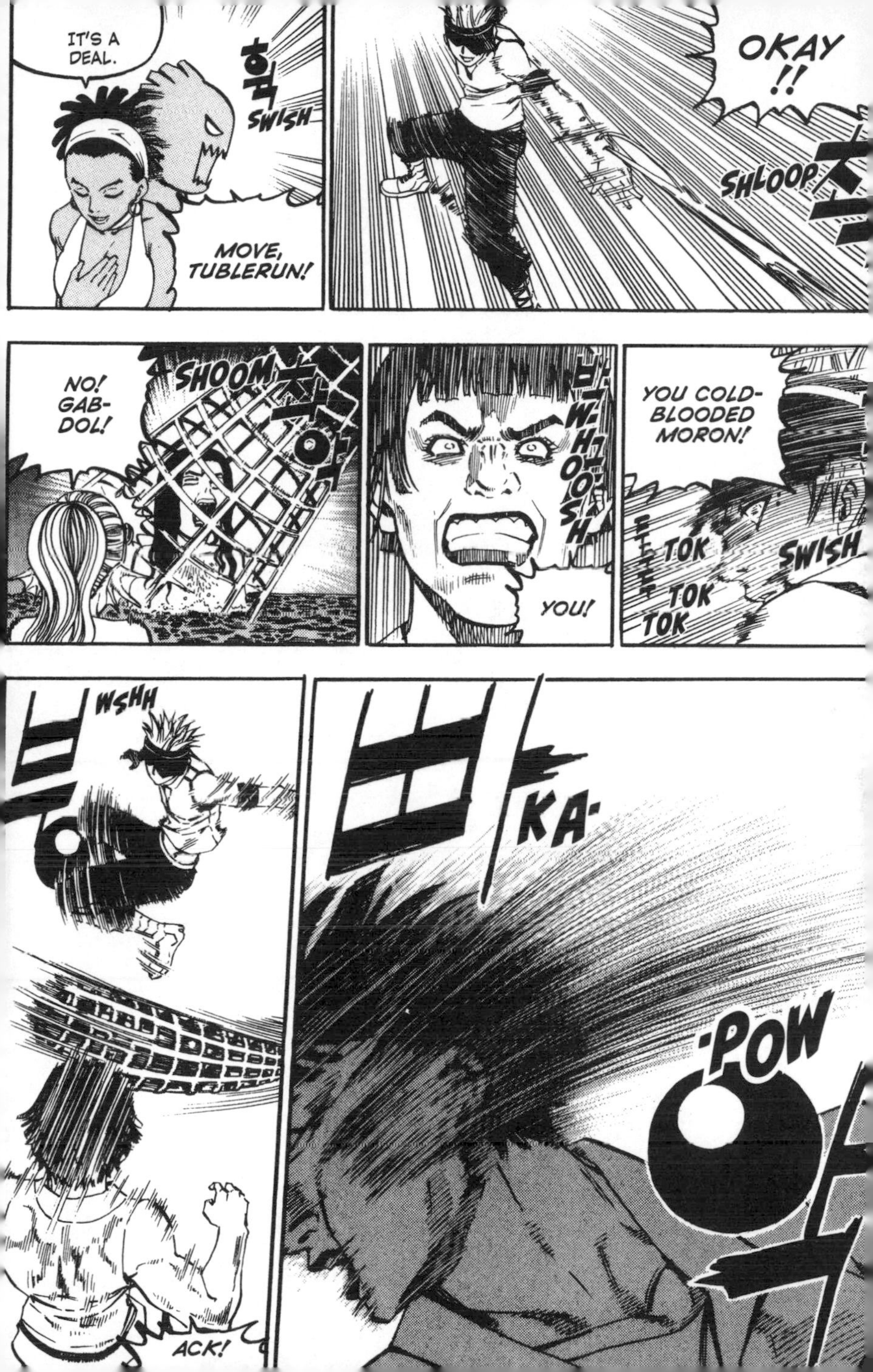
IT'S A DEAL.
SWISH
MOVE, TUBLERUN!
OKAY!!
SHLOOP
NO! GAB-DOL!
SHOOM
WHOOSH
YOU!
YOU COLD-BLOODED MORON!
TOK
TOK
TOK
SWISH
WSHH
ACK!
KA-
-POW

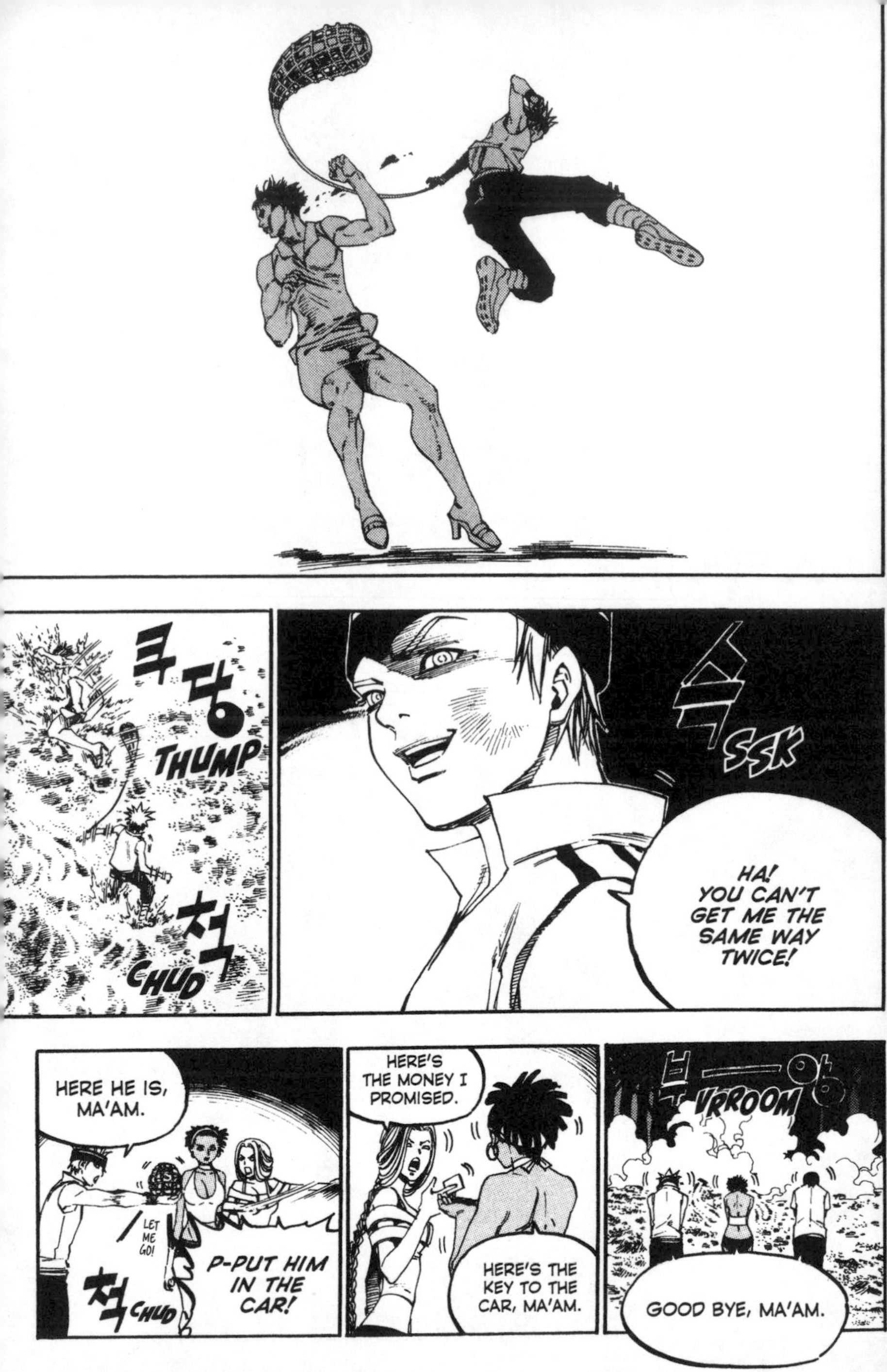

쿠당
THUMP
척
CHUD
슥
SSK
HA! YOU CAN'T GET ME THE SAME WAY TWICE!
HERE HE IS, MA'AM.
LET ME GO!
P-PUT HIM IN THE CAR!
척
CHUD
HERE'S THE MONEY I PROMISED.
HERE'S THE KEY TO THE CAR, MA'AM.
부——앙
VRROOM
GOOD BYE, MA'AM.

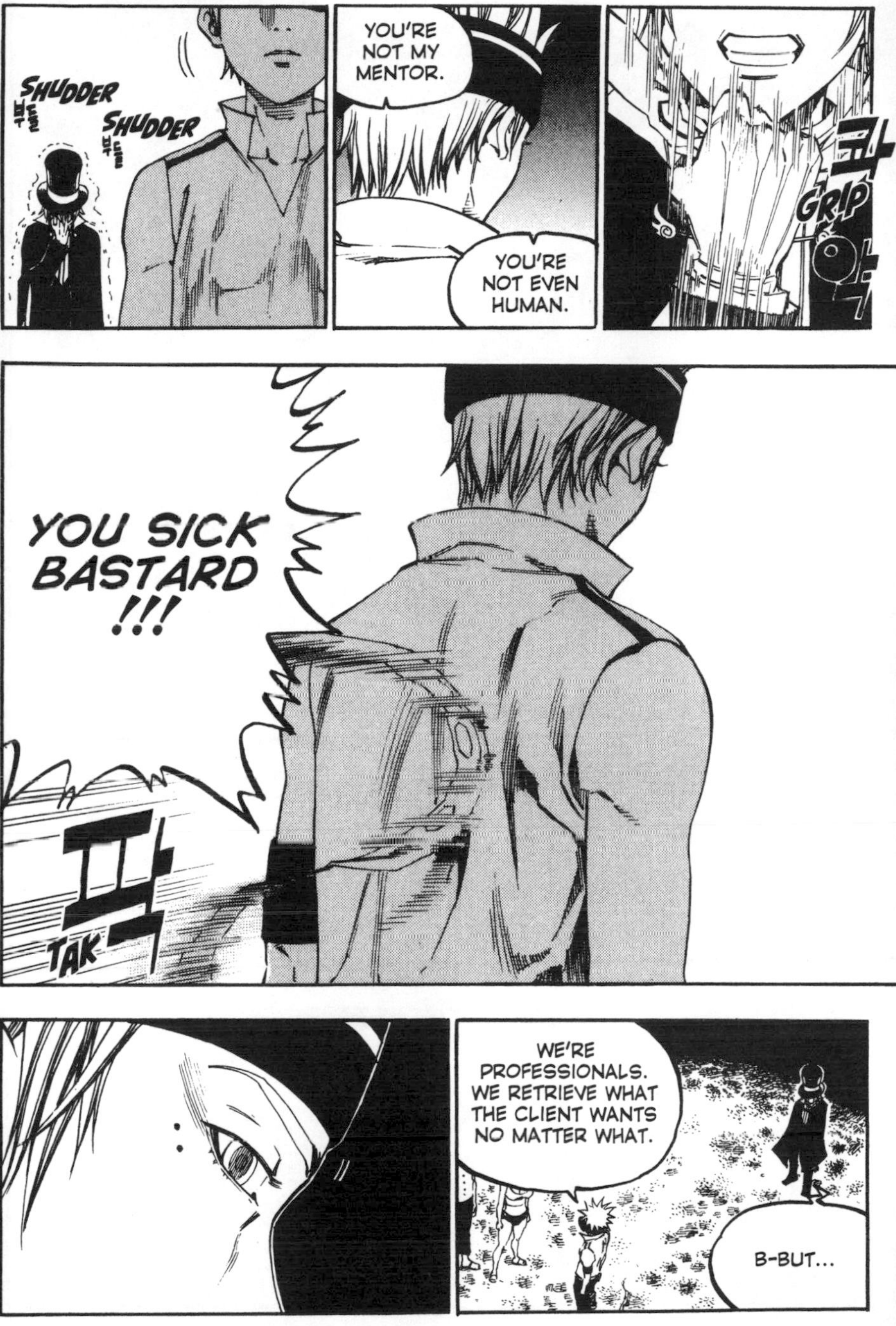
SHUDDER
SHUDDER
YOU'RE NOT MY MENTOR.
YOU'RE NOT EVEN HUMAN.
GRIP
YOU SICK BASTARD !!!
TAK
WE'RE PROFESSIONALS. WE RETRIEVE WHAT THE CLIENT WANTS NO MATTER WHAT.
B-BUT...

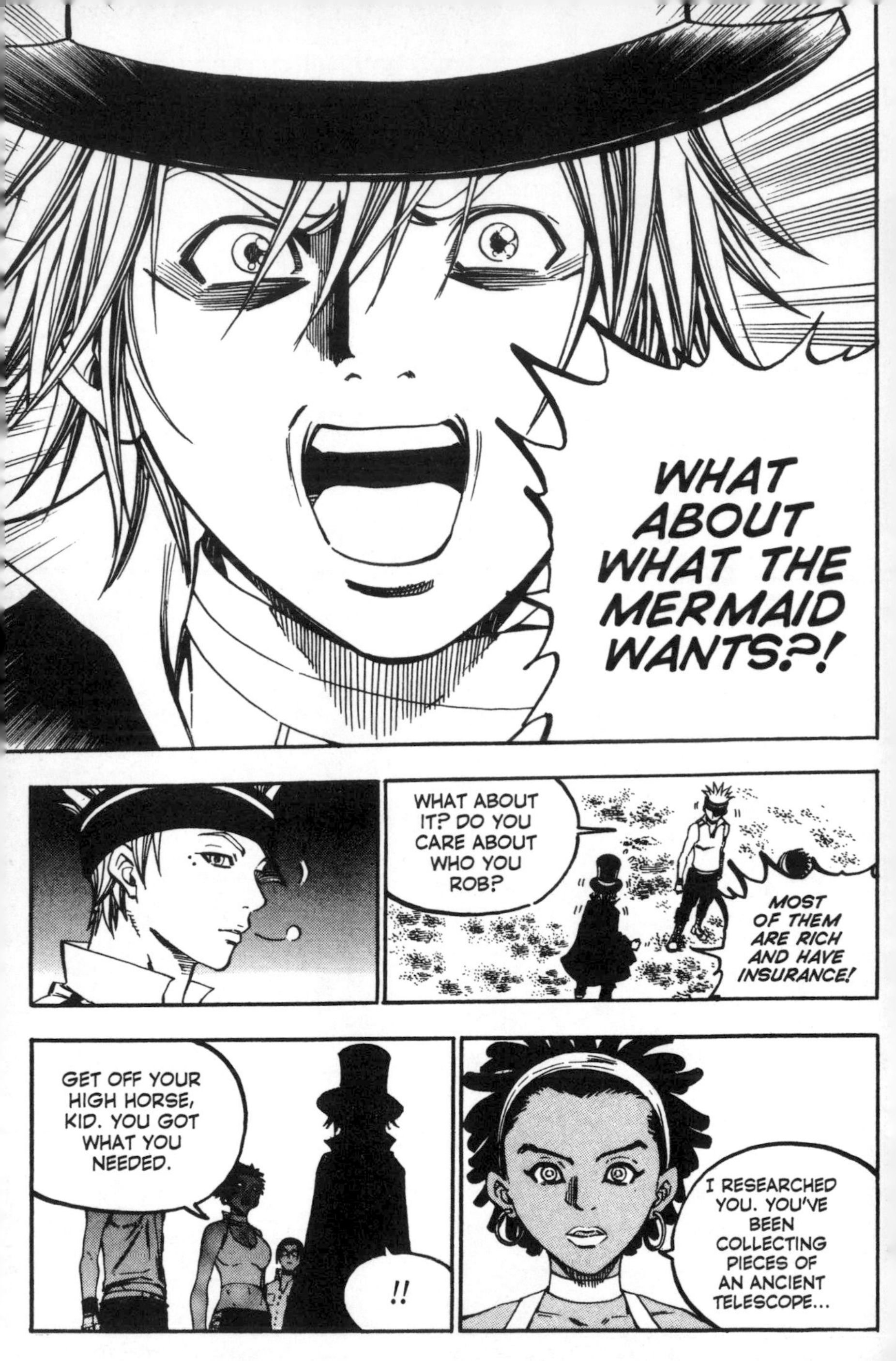
WHAT ABOUT WHAT THE MERMAID WANTS?!
WHAT ABOUT IT? DO YOU CARE ABOUT WHO YOU ROB?
MOST OF THEM ARE RICH AND HAVE INSURANCE!
GET OFF YOUR HIGH HORSE, KID. YOU GOT WHAT YOU NEEDED.
!!
I RESEARCHED YOU. YOU'VE BEEN COLLECTING PIECES OF AN ANCIENT TELESCOPE...

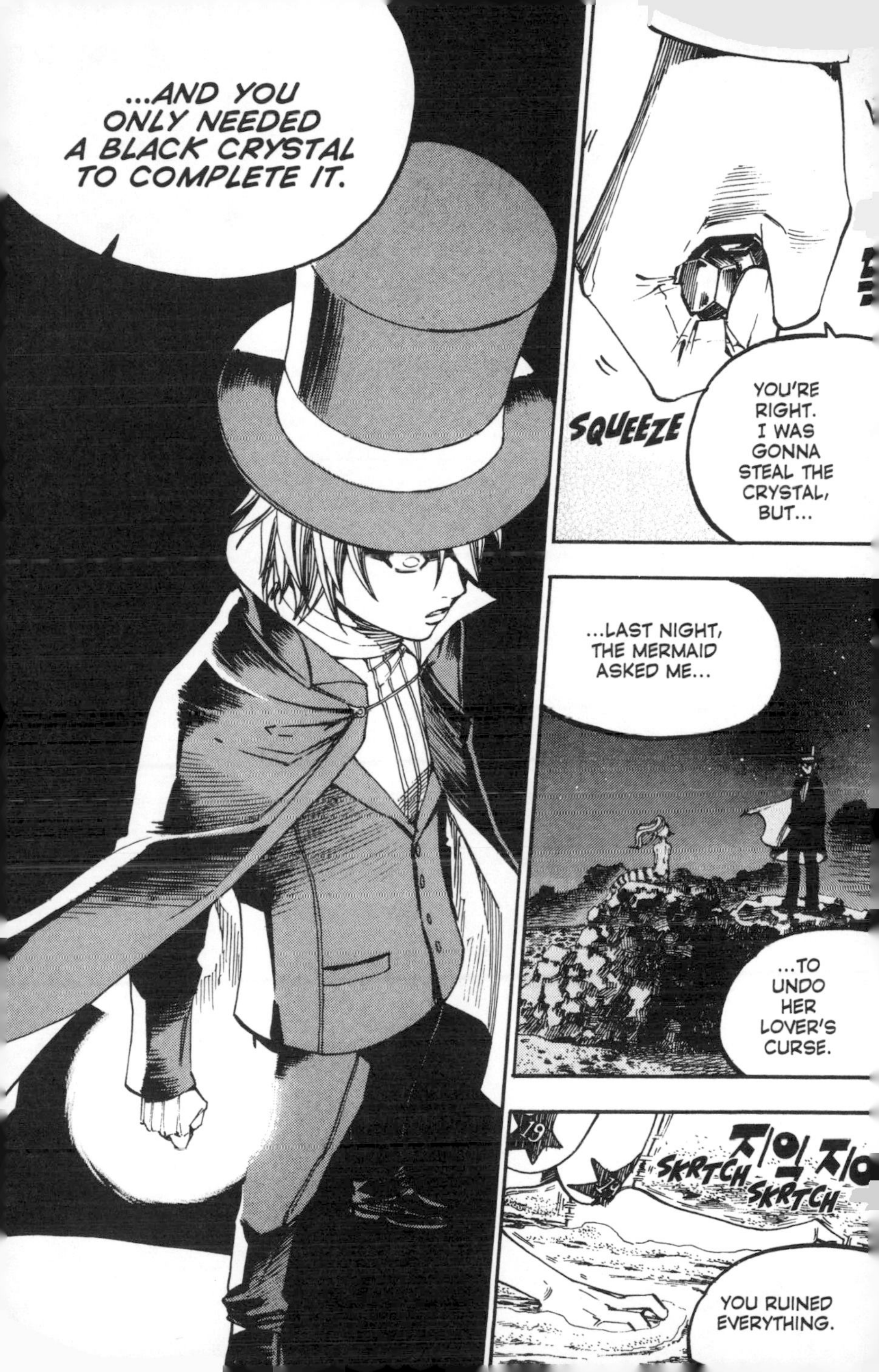
...AND YOU ONLY NEEDED A BLACK CRYSTAL TO COMPLETE IT.
SQUEEZE
YOU'RE RIGHT. I WAS GONNA STEAL THE CRYSTAL, BUT...
...LAST NIGHT, THE MERMAID ASKED ME...
...TO UNDO HER LOVER'S CURSE.
SKRTCH
SKRTCH
YOU RUINED EVERYTHING.

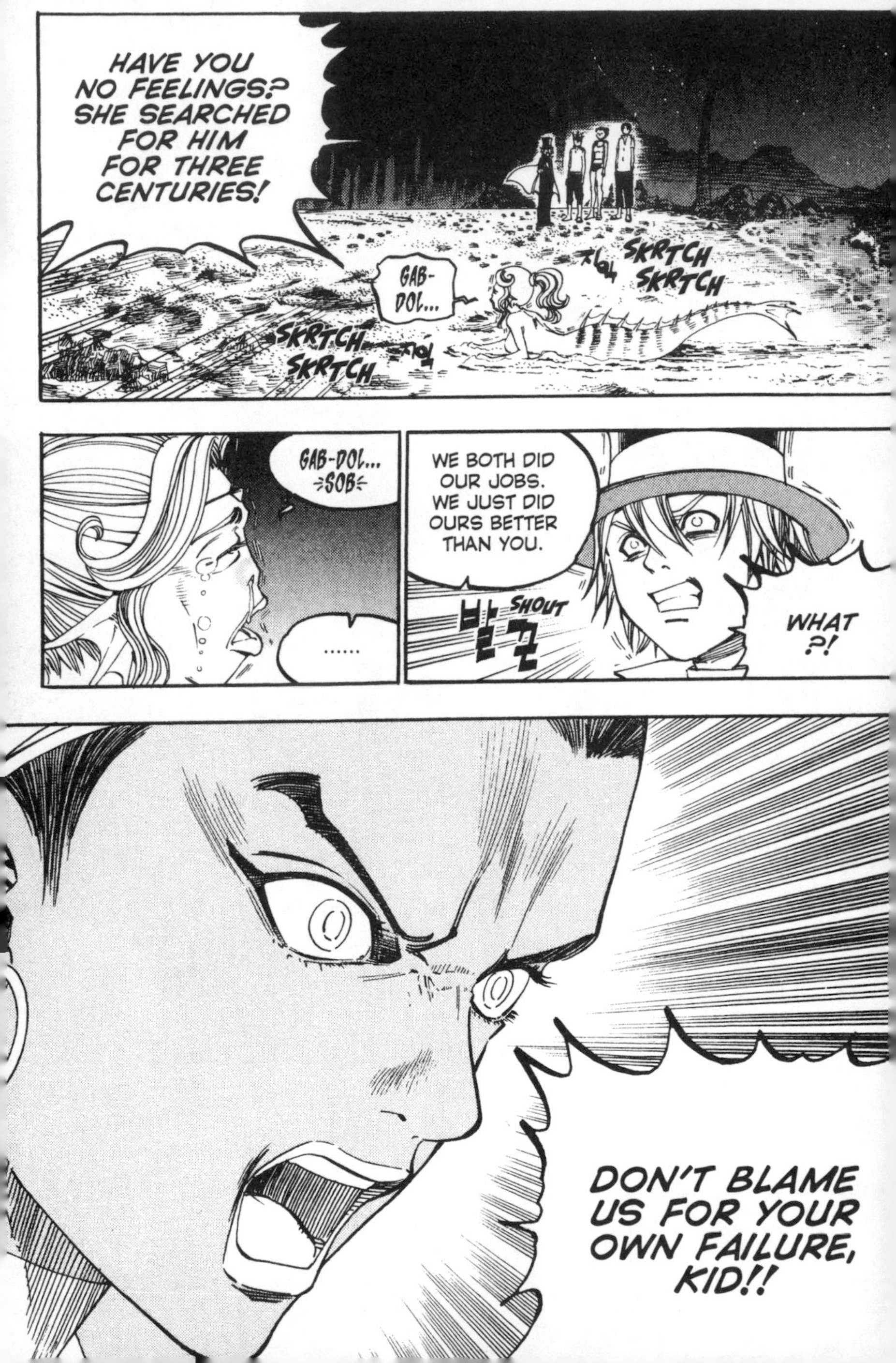
HAVE YOU NO FEELINGS? SHE SEARCHED FOR HIM FOR THREE CENTURIES!
지익
SKRTCH SKRTCH
GAB-DOL...
SKRTCH SKRTCH
지익
GAB-DOL... SOB
......
WE BOTH DID OUR JOBS. WE JUST DID OURS BETTER THAN YOU.
발끈
SHOUT
WHAT?!
DON'T BLAME US FOR YOUR OWN FAILURE, KID!!

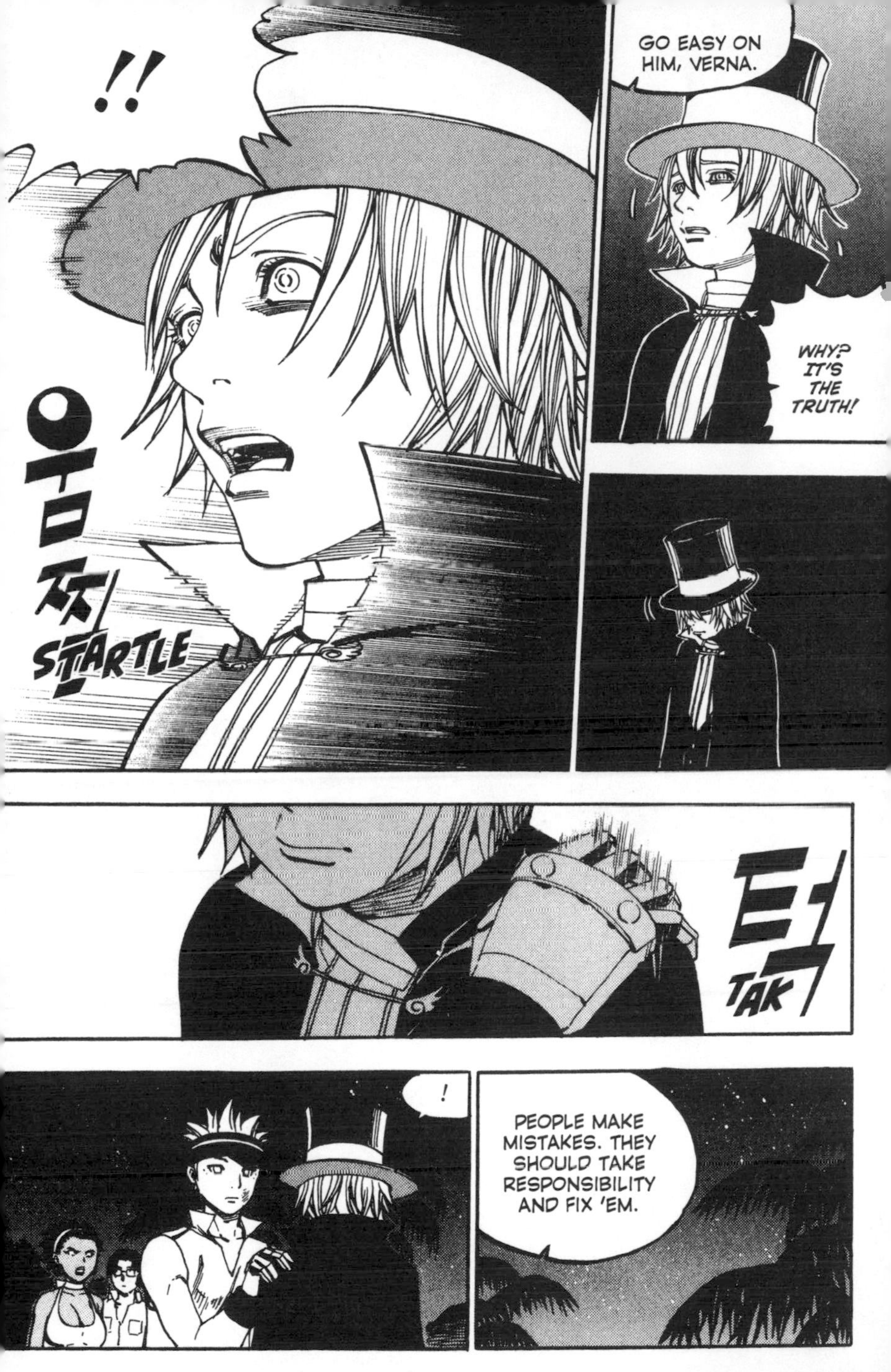
!!
움찔
STARTLE
GO EASY ON HIM, VERNA.
WHY? IT'S THE TRUTH!
탁
TAK
!
PEOPLE MAKE MISTAKES. THEY SHOULD TAKE RESPONSIBILITY AND FIX 'EM.

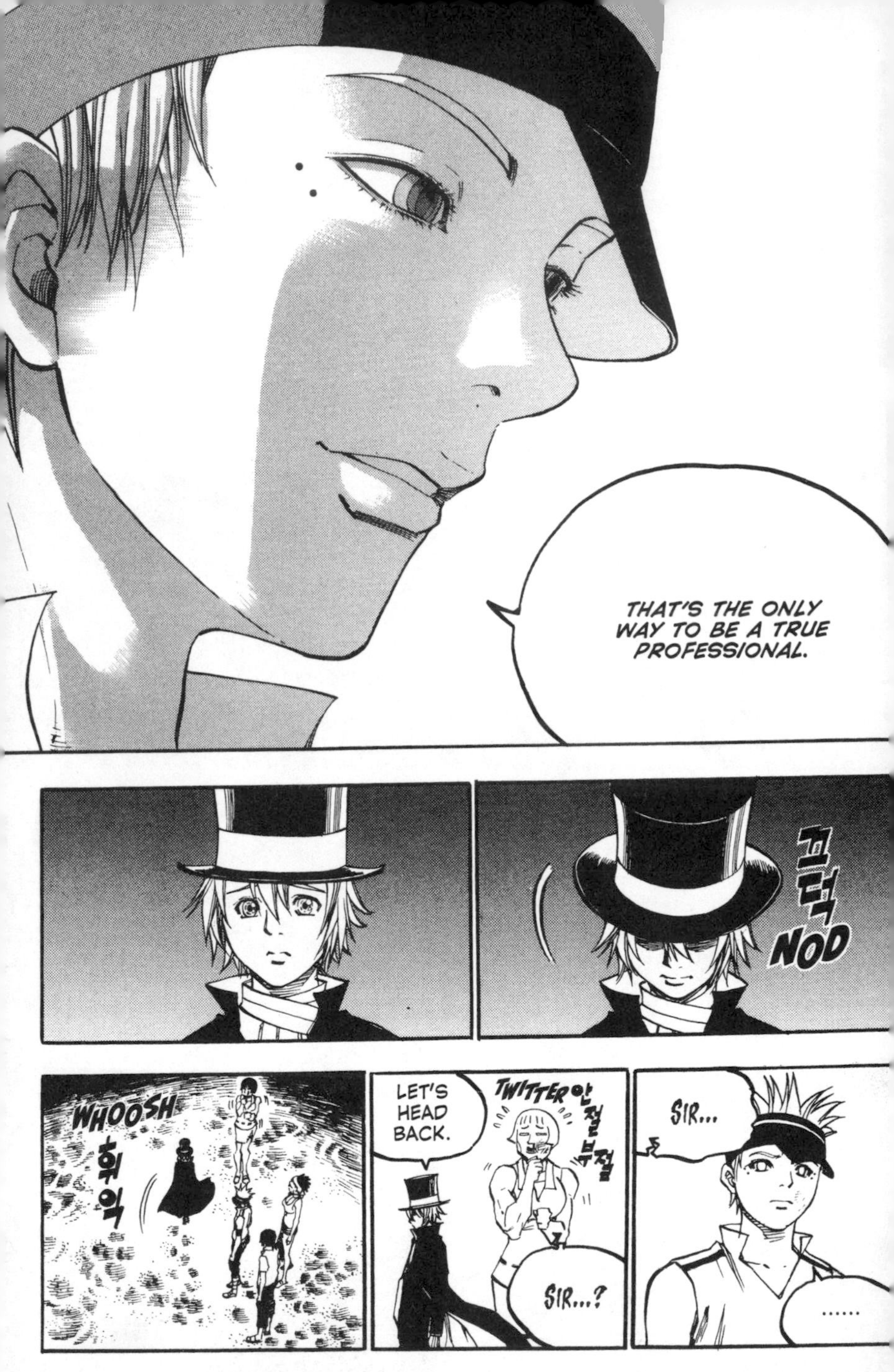
THAT'S THE ONLY WAY TO BE A TRUE PROFESSIONAL.
끄덕
NOD
WHOOSH
훠억
LET'S HEAD BACK.
TWITTER
안절부절
SIR...?
SIR...
......

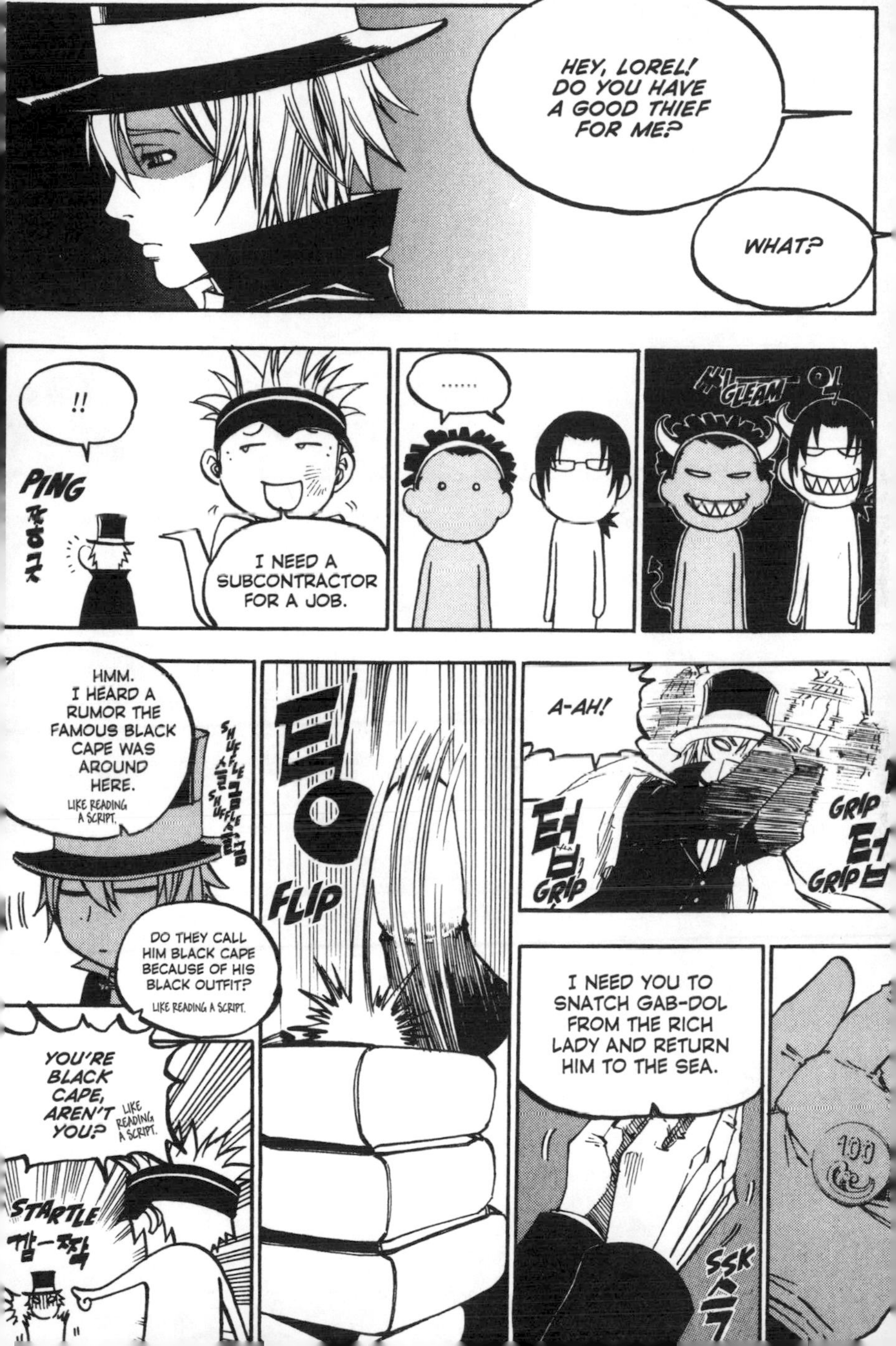
HEY, LOREL! DO YOU HAVE A GOOD THIEF FOR ME?
WHAT?
!!
PING
I NEED A SUBCONTRACTOR FOR A JOB.
......
GLEAM
HMM. I HEARD A RUMOR THE FAMOUS BLACK CAPE WAS AROUND HERE.
LIKE READING A SCRIPT.
SHUFFLE
SHUFFLE
DO THEY CALL HIM BLACK CAPE BECAUSE OF HIS BLACK OUTFIT?
LIKE READING A SCRIPT.
YOU'RE BLACK CAPE, AREN'T YOU?
LIKE READING A SCRIPT.
STARTLE
깜-짝
FLIP
A-AH!
GRIP
GRIP
GRIP
I NEED YOU TO SNATCH GAB-DOL FROM THE RICH LADY AND RETURN HIM TO THE SEA.
SSK
100

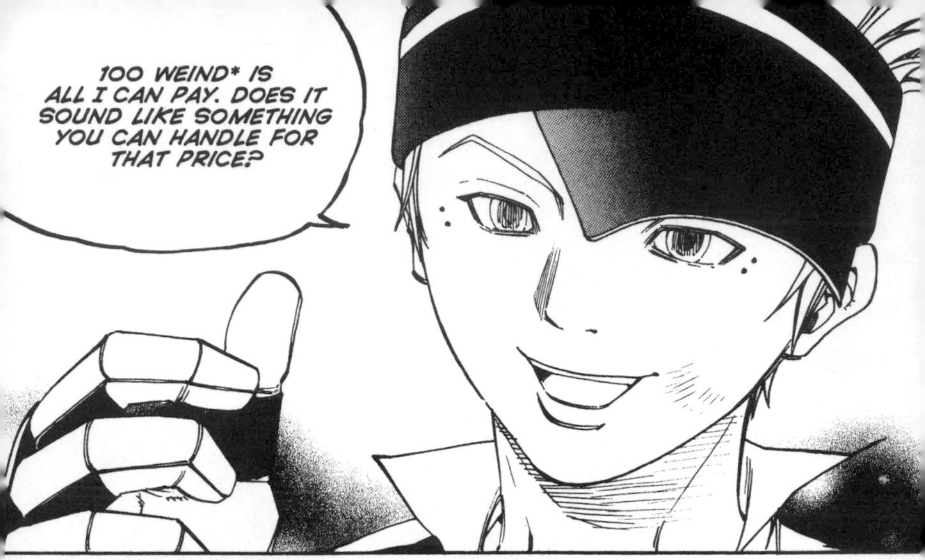
100 WEIND* IS ALL I CAN PAY. DOES IT SOUND LIKE SOMETHING YOU CAN HANDLE FOR THAT PRICE?

*THE CURRENCY OF THE FUTURE

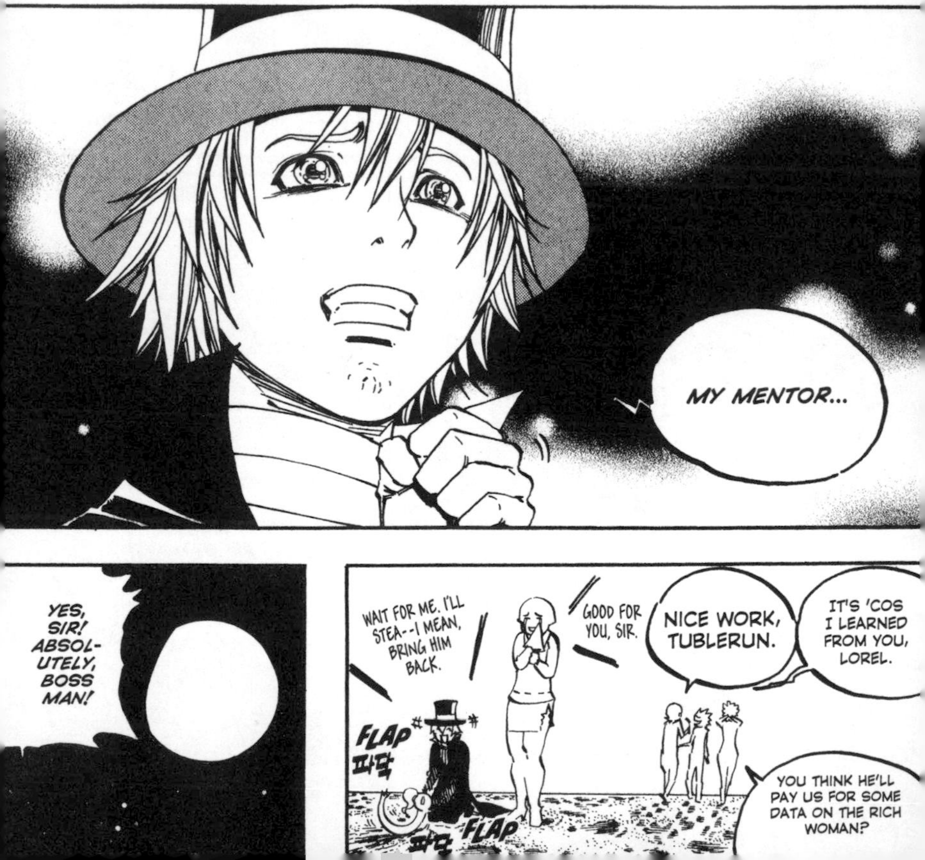
MY MENTOR...
YES, SIR! ABSOL-UTELY, BOSS MAN!
WAIT FOR ME. I'LL STEA--I MEAN, BRING HIM BACK.
GOOD FOR YOU, SIR.
NICE WORK, TUBLERUN.
IT'S 'COS I LEARNED FROM YOU, LOREL.
FLAP
파닥
파닥
FLAP
YOU THINK HE'LL PAY US FOR SOME DATA ON THE RICH WOMAN?

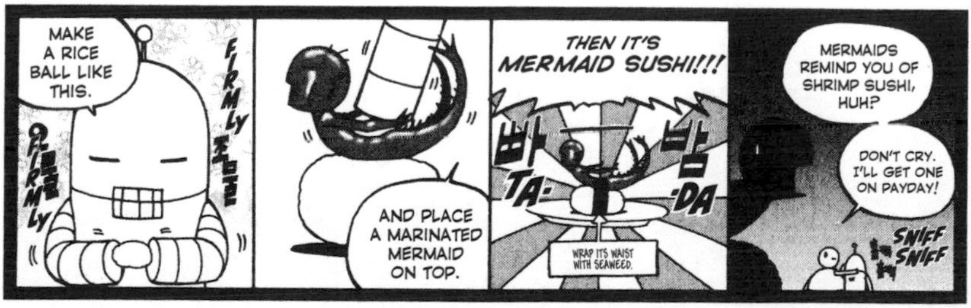
MAKE A RICE BALL LIKE THIS.
FIRMLY
FIRMLY
AND PLACE A MARINATED MERMAID ON TOP.
THEN IT'S MERMAID SUSHI!!!
TA-
-DA
WRAP ITS WAIST WITH SEAWEED.
MERMAIDS REMIND YOU OF SHRIMP SUSHI, HUH?
DON'T CRY. I'LL GET ONE ON PAYDAY!
SNIFF SNIFF

# FREAK

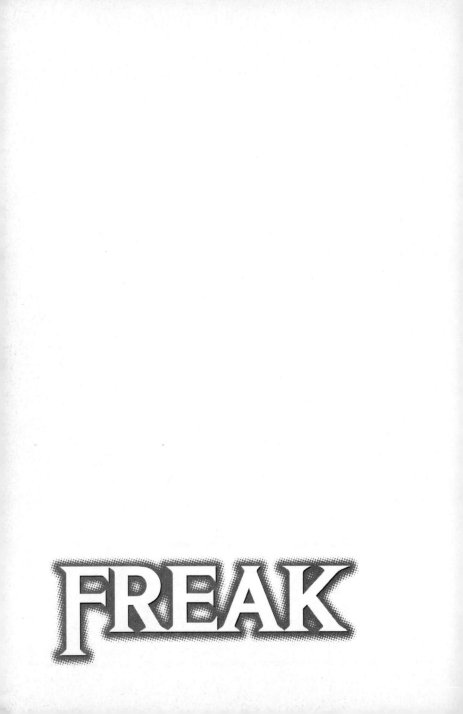

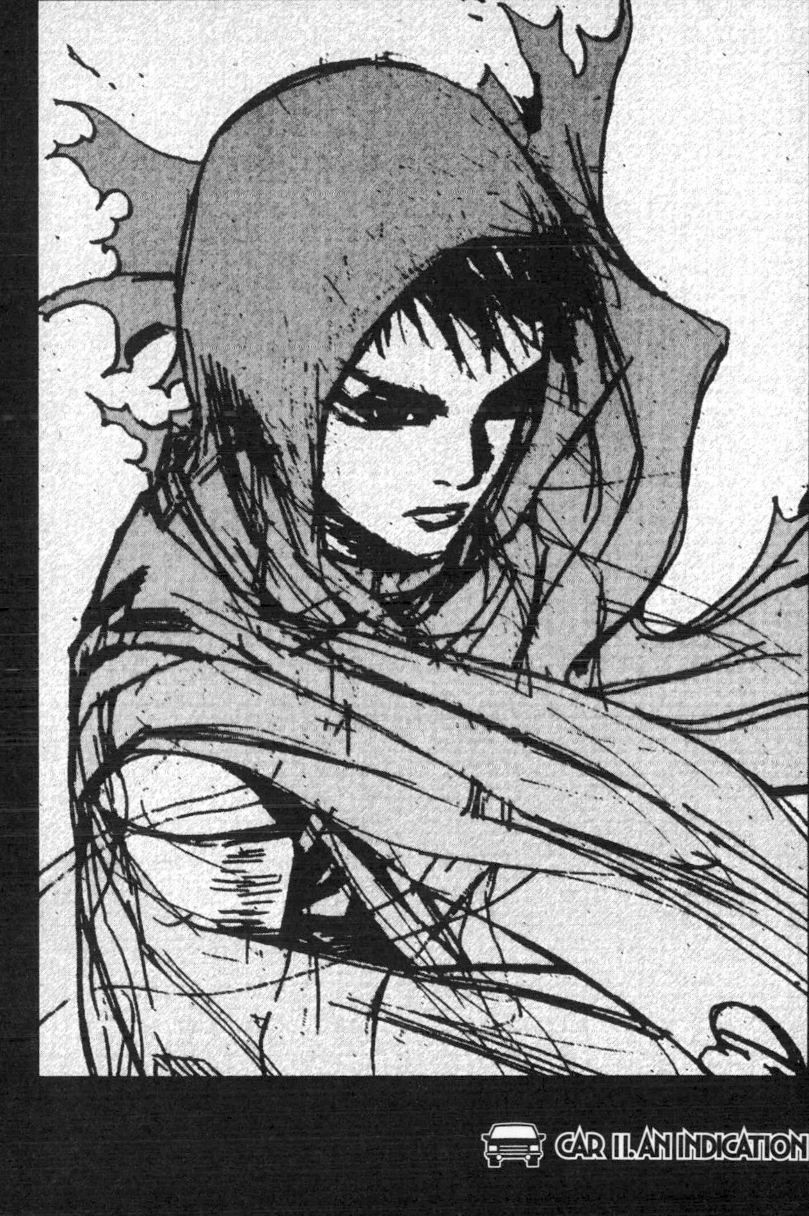

## CAR 11. AN INDICATION

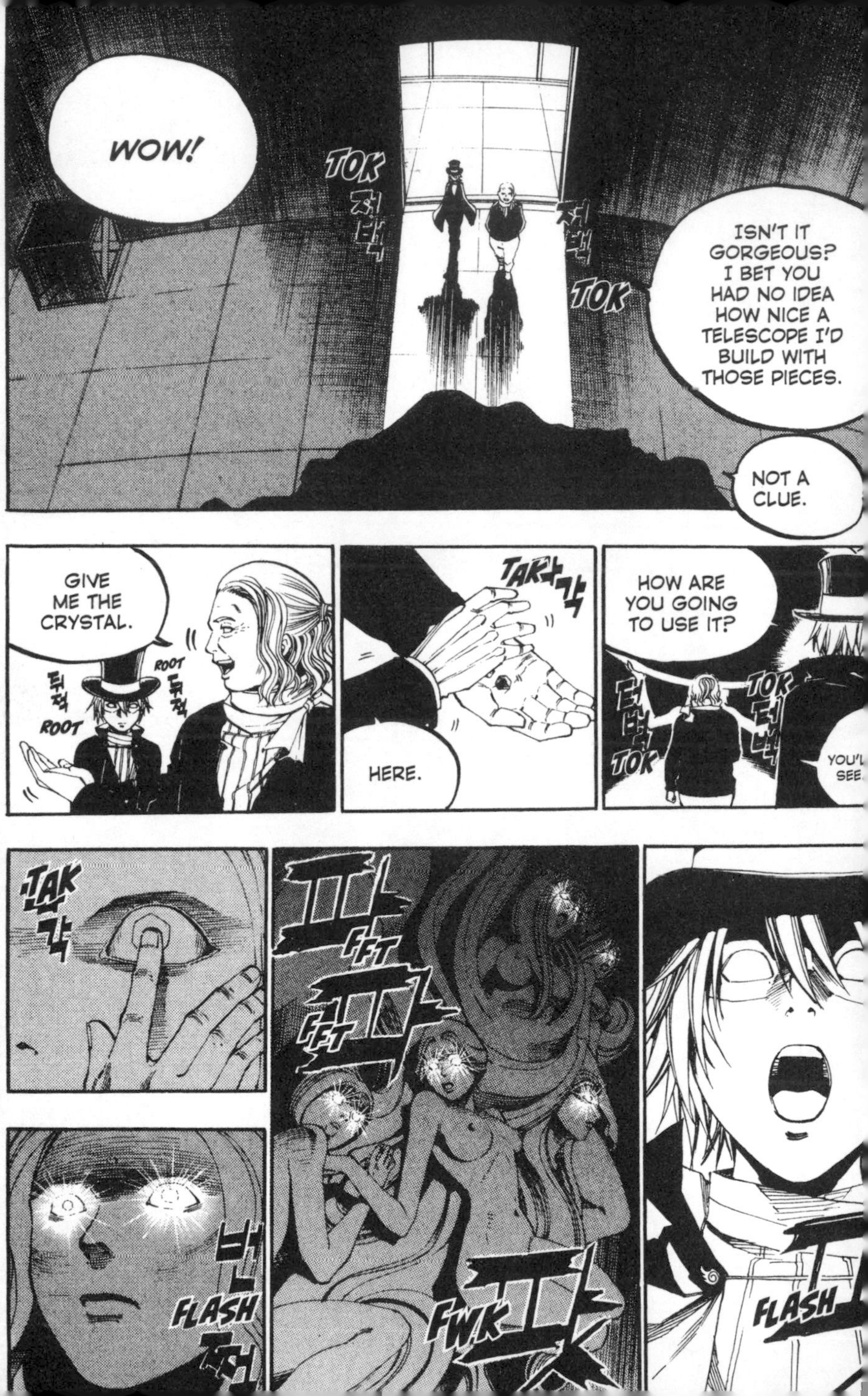
WOW!
TOK 저벅
저벅 TOK
ISN'T IT GORGEOUS? I BET YOU HAD NO IDEA HOW NICE A TELESCOPE I'D BUILD WITH THOSE PIECES.
NOT A CLUE.
GIVE ME THE CRYSTAL.
뒤적 ROOT
ROOT 뒤적
TAK 각
HERE.
HOW ARE YOU GOING TO USE IT?
터벅 TOK
TOK 터벅
YOU'L SEE.
TAK 각
번 FLASH
FFT
FFT
FWK
FLASH

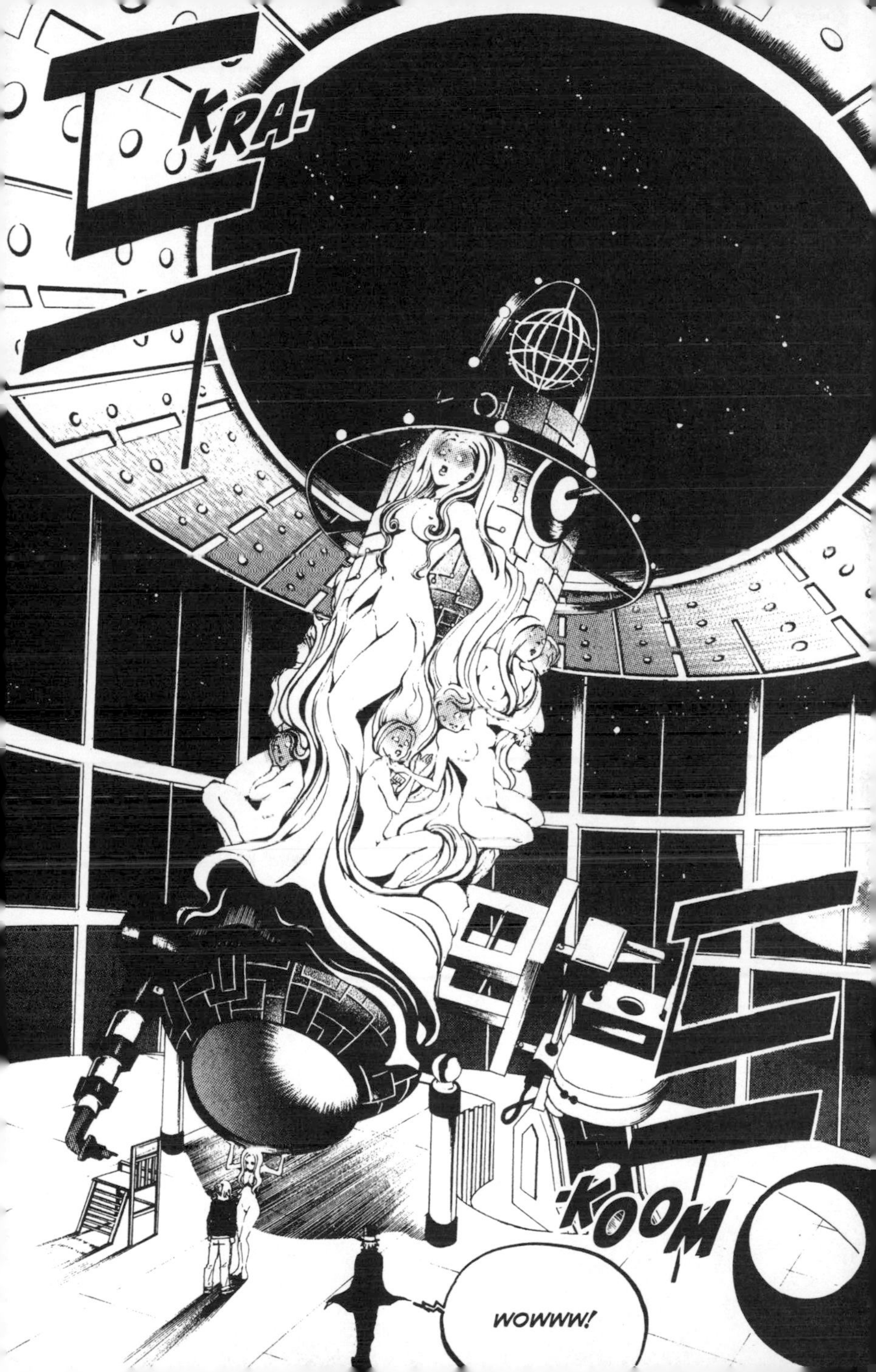
KRA-
-KOOM
WOWWW!

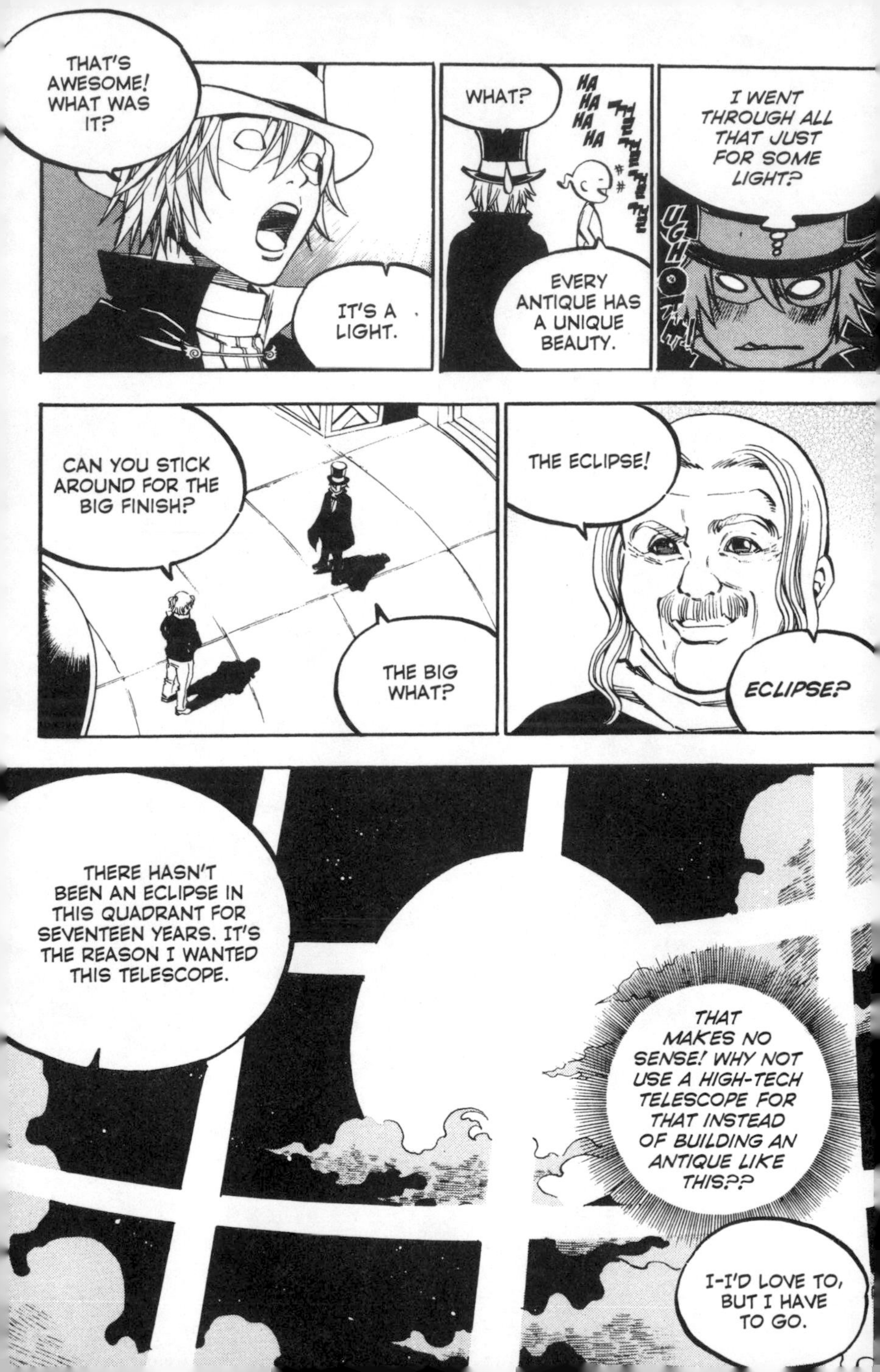

THAT'S AWESOME! WHAT WAS IT?
IT'S A LIGHT.
WHAT?
HA HA HA HA
EVERY ANTIQUE HAS A UNIQUE BEAUTY.
I WENT THROUGH ALL THAT JUST FOR SOME LIGHT?
CAN YOU STICK AROUND FOR THE BIG FINISH?
THE BIG WHAT?
THE ECLIPSE!
ECLIPSE?
THERE HASN'T BEEN AN ECLIPSE IN THIS QUADRANT FOR SEVENTEEN YEARS. IT'S THE REASON I WANTED THIS TELESCOPE.
THAT MAKES NO SENSE! WHY NOT USE A HIGH-TECH TELESCOPE FOR THAT INSTEAD OF BUILDING AN ANTIQUE LIKE THIS??
I-I'D LOVE TO, BUT I HAVE TO GO.

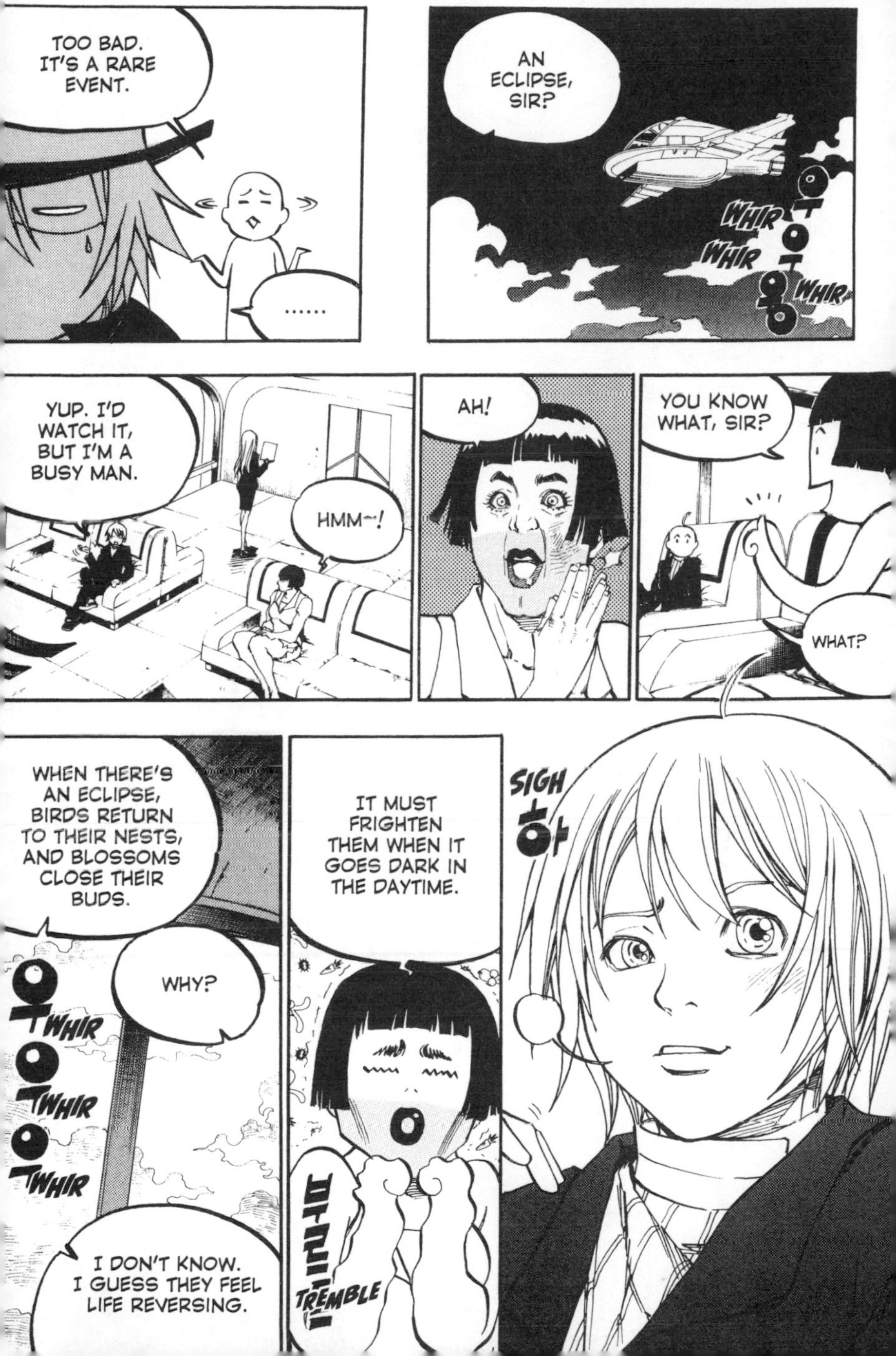

TOO BAD. IT'S A RARE EVENT.
......
AN ECLIPSE, SIR?
WHIR
WHIR
WHIR
YUP. I'D WATCH IT, BUT I'M A BUSY MAN.
HMM~!
AH!
YOU KNOW WHAT, SIR?
WHAT?
WHEN THERE'S AN ECLIPSE, BIRDS RETURN TO THEIR NESTS, AND BLOSSOMS CLOSE THEIR BUDS.
WHY?
WHIR
WHIR
WHIR
I DON'T KNOW. I GUESS THEY FEEL LIFE REVERSING.
IT MUST FRIGHTEN THEM WHEN IT GOES DARK IN THE DAYTIME.
TREMBLE
SIGH
하

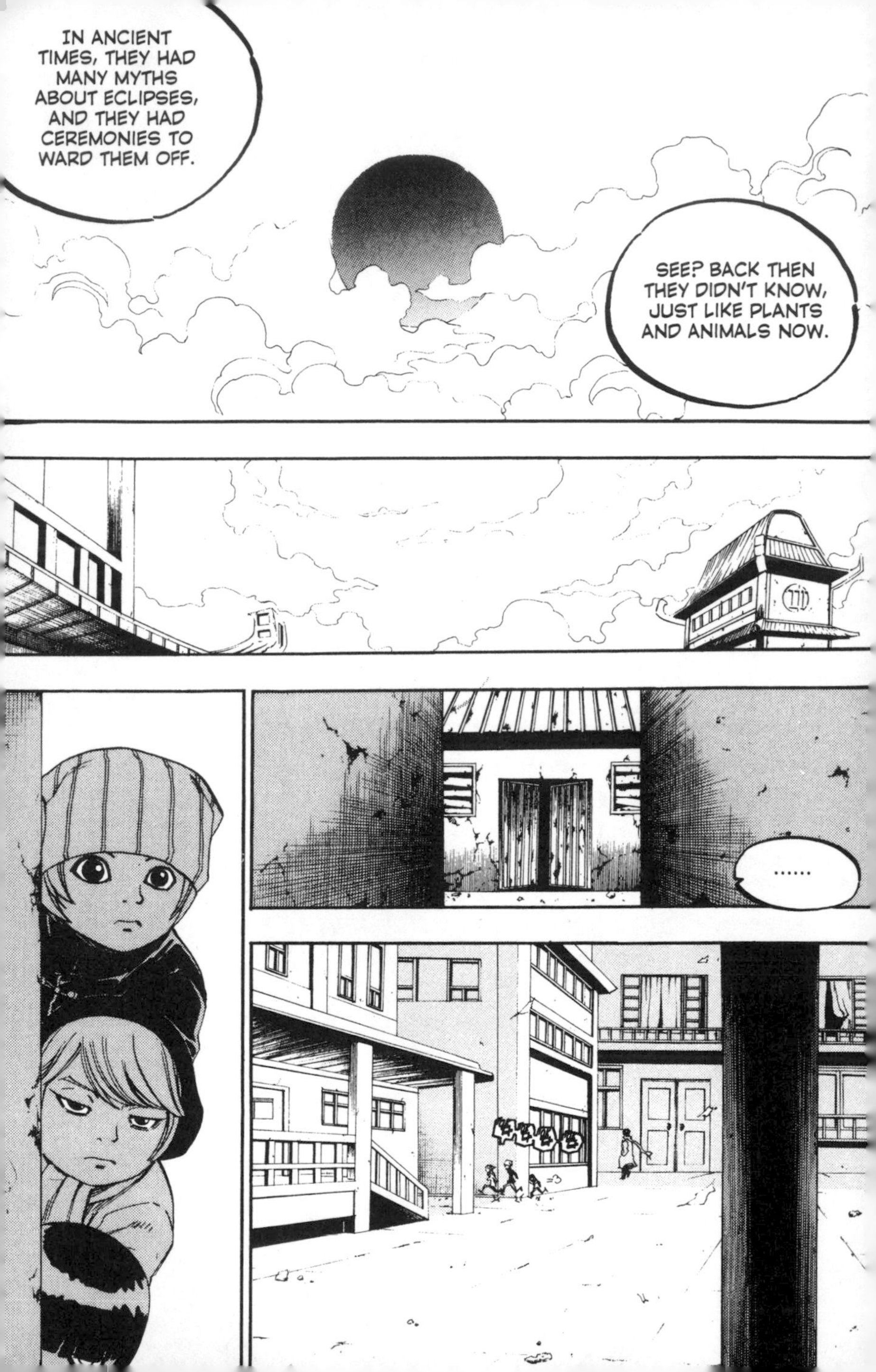
IN ANCIENT TIMES, THEY HAD MANY MYTHS ABOUT ECLIPSES, AND THEY HAD CEREMONIES TO WARD THEM OFF.
SEE? BACK THEN THEY DIDN'T KNOW, JUST LIKE PLANTS AND ANIMALS NOW.
......

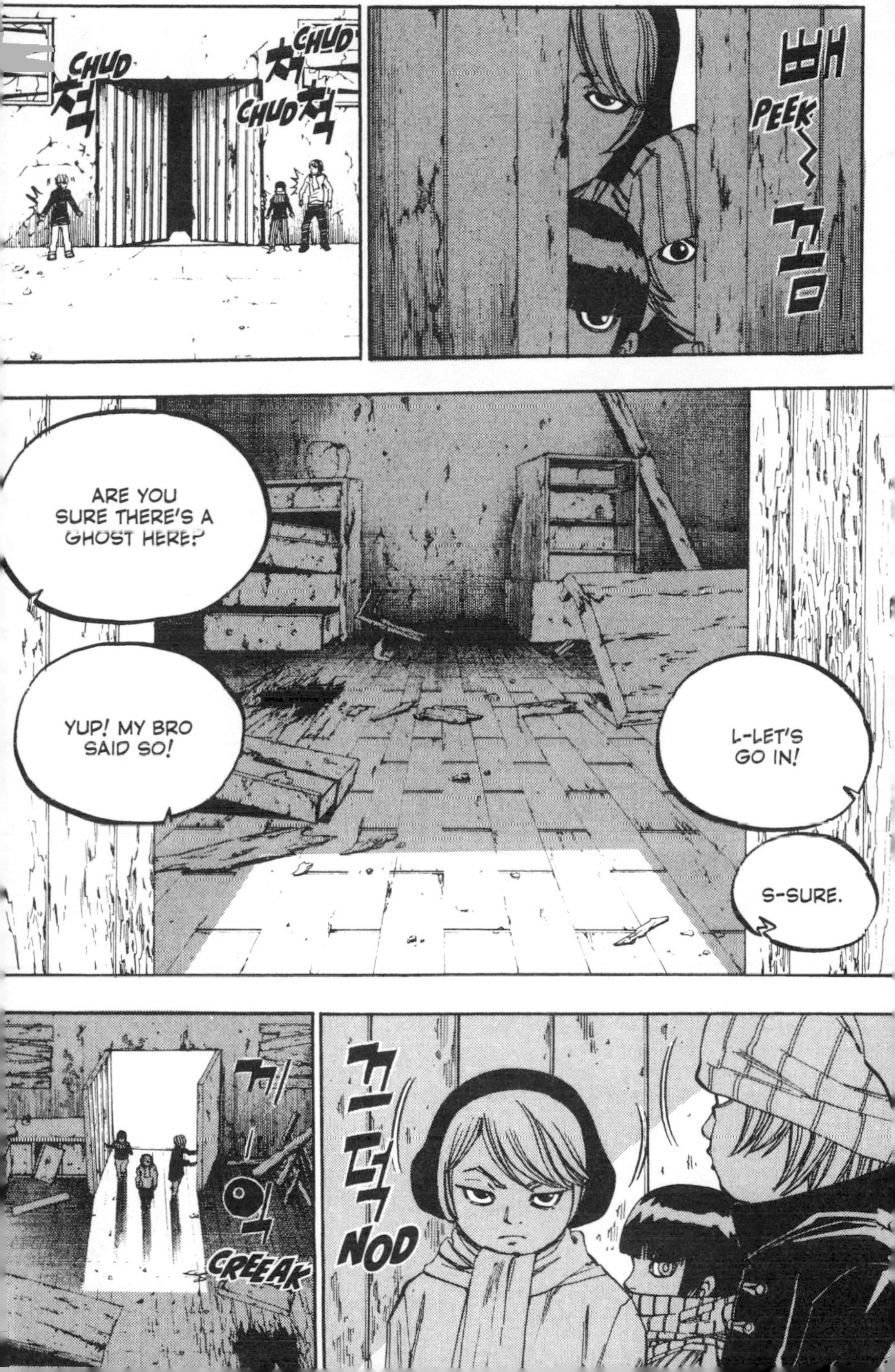
CHUD
척
CHUD
CHUD
척
빼꼼
PEEK~
ARE YOU SURE THERE'S A GHOST HERE?
YUP! MY BRO SAID SO!
L-LET'S GO IN!
S-SURE.
끼익
CREEAK
끄덕
NOD

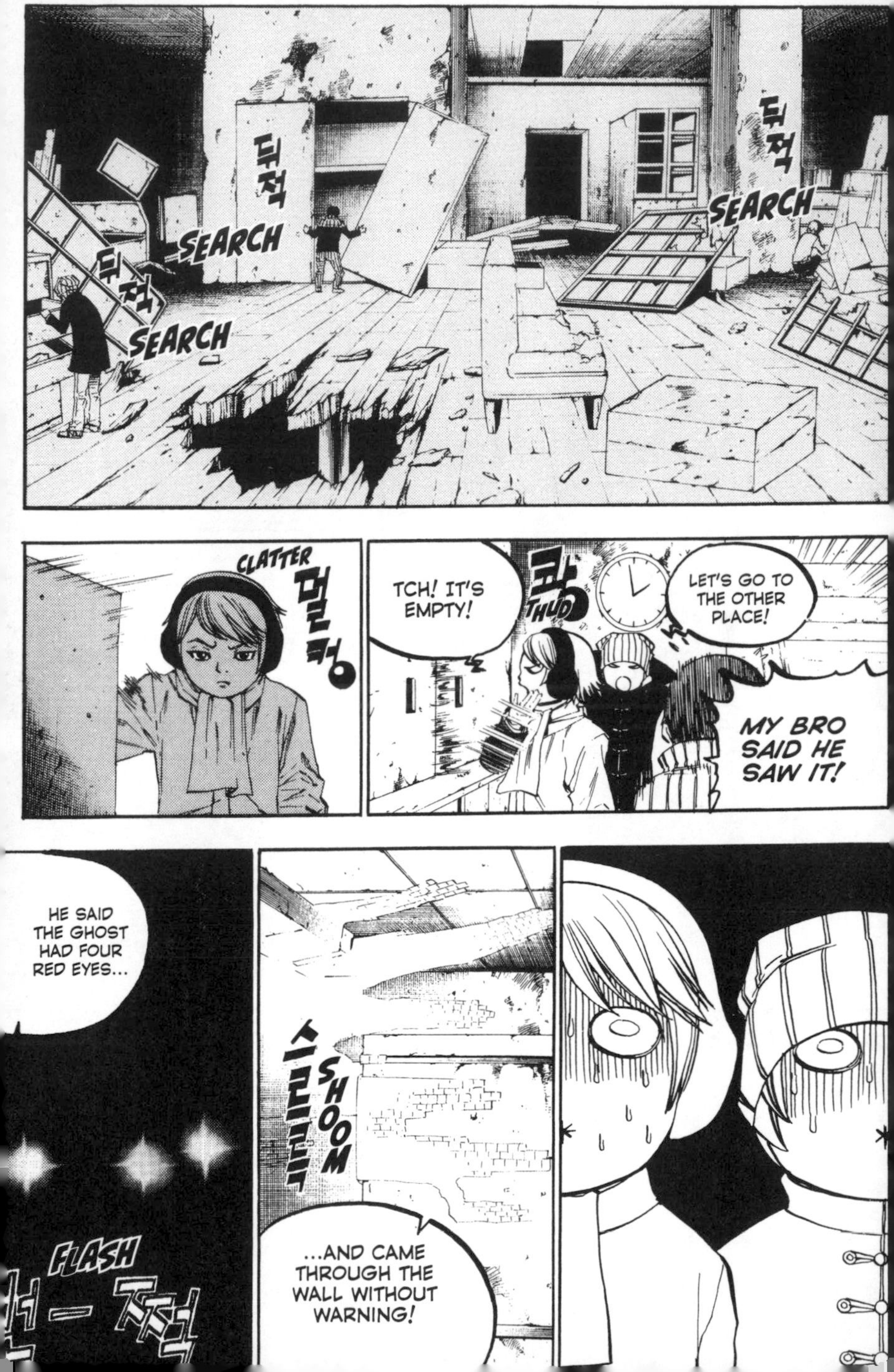
뒤적
SEARCH
뒤적
SEARCH
뒤적
SEARCH
CLATTER
덜컹
TCH! IT'S EMPTY!
쾅
THUD
LET'S GO TO THE OTHER PLACE!
MY BRO SAID HE SAW IT!
HE SAID THE GHOST HAD FOUR RED EYES...
FLASH
번-쩍
스르륵
SHOOM
...AND CAME THROUGH THE WALL WITHOUT WARNING!

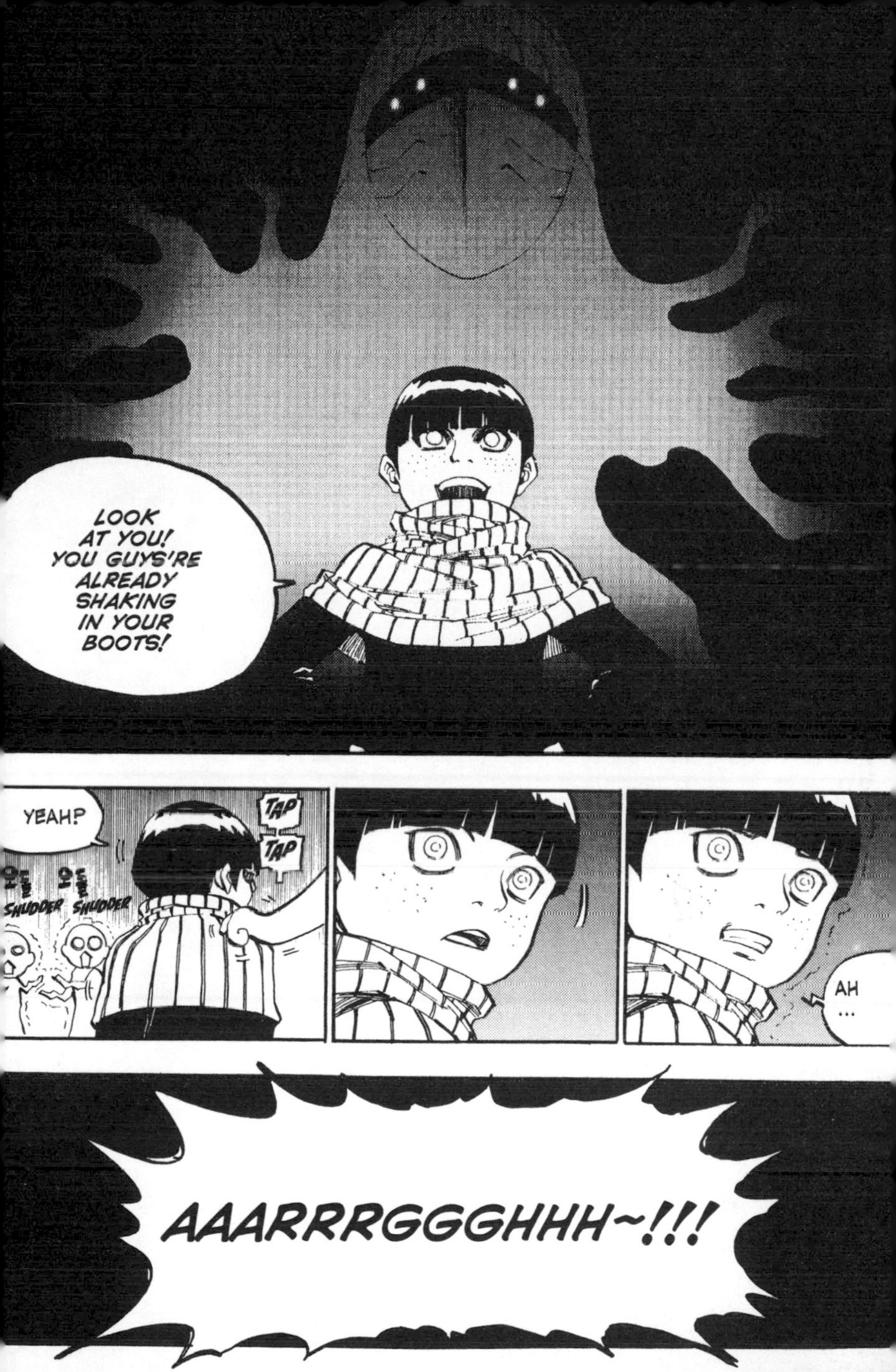
LOOK AT YOU! YOU GUYS'RE ALREADY SHAKING IN YOUR BOOTS!
YEAH?
TAP
TAP
SHUDDER
SHUDDER
AH ...
AAARRRGGGHHH~!!!

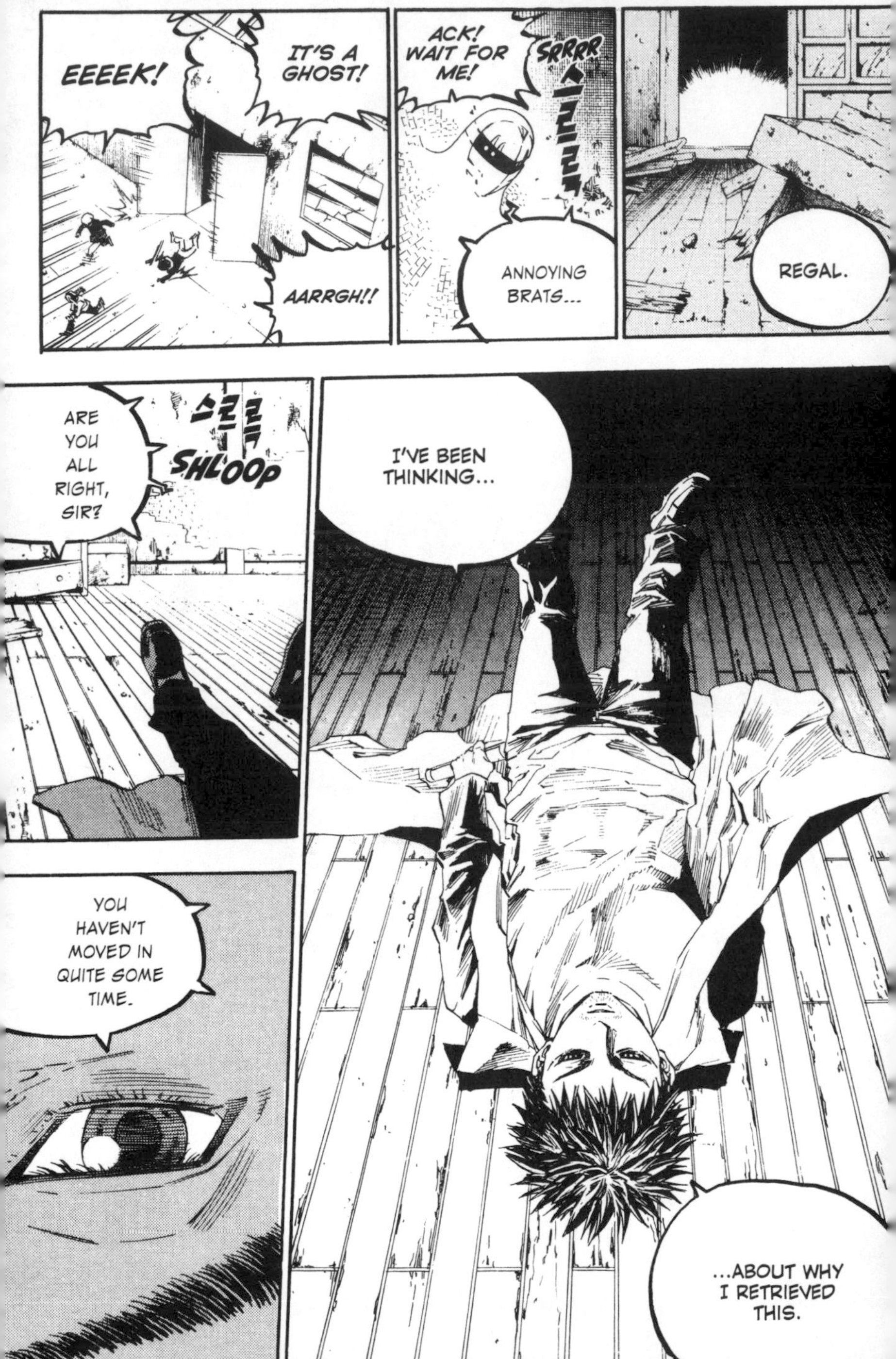
EEEEK!
IT'S A GHOST!
AARRGH!!
ACK! WAIT FOR ME!
SRRRR
스르륵
ANNOYING BRATS...
REGAL.
ARE YOU ALL RIGHT, SIR?
스르륵
SHLOOP
YOU HAVEN'T MOVED IN QUITE SOME TIME.
I'VE BEEN THINKING...
...ABOUT WHY I RETRIEVED THIS.

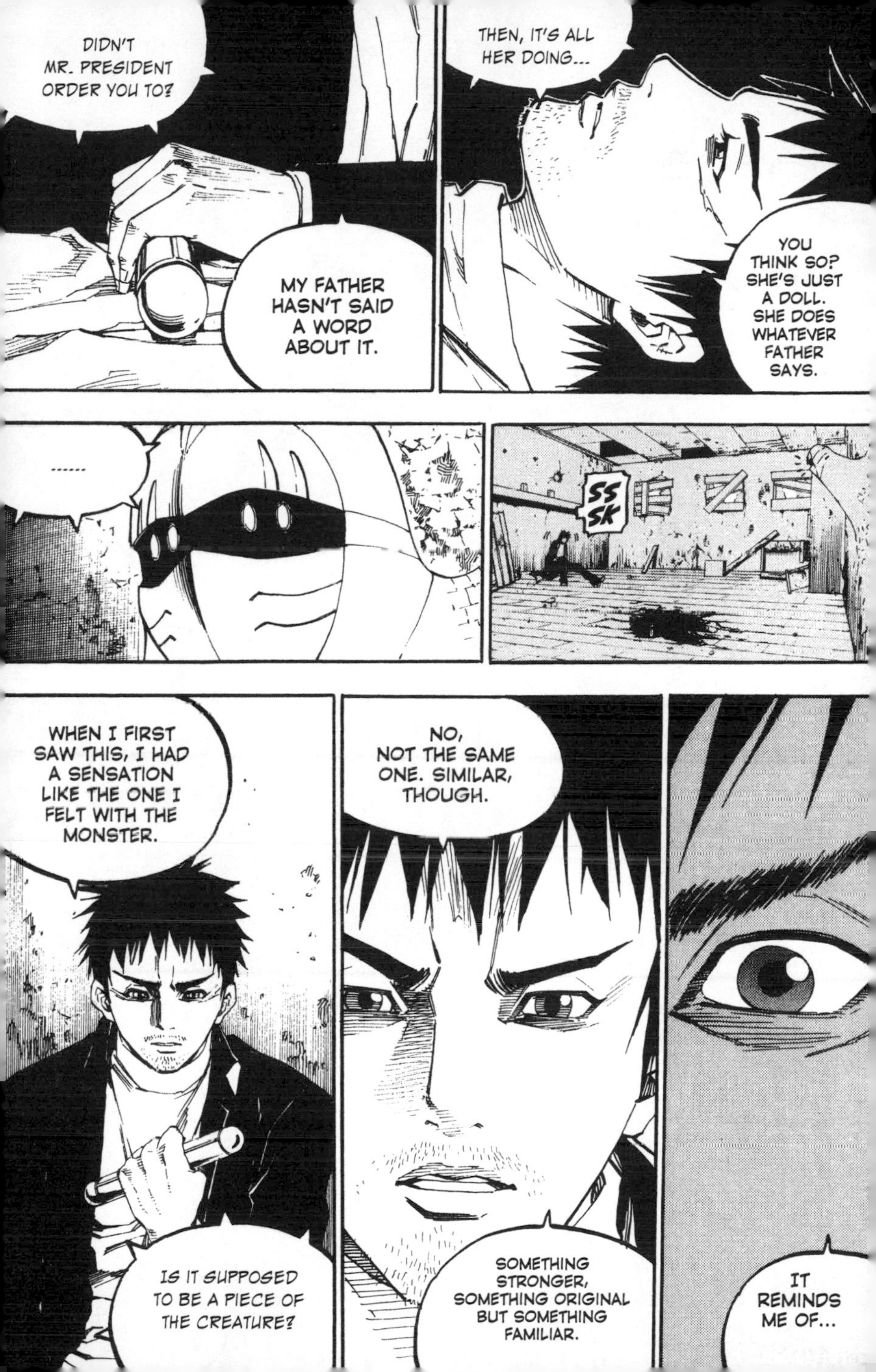
DIDN'T MR. PRESIDENT ORDER YOU TO?
MY FATHER HASN'T SAID A WORD ABOUT IT.
THEN, IT'S ALL HER DOING...
YOU THINK SO? SHE'S JUST A DOLL. SHE DOES WHATEVER FATHER SAYS.
......
SSSK
WHEN I FIRST SAW THIS, I HAD A SENSATION LIKE THE ONE I FELT WITH THE MONSTER.
IS IT SUPPOSED TO BE A PIECE OF THE CREATURE?
NO, NOT THE SAME ONE. SIMILAR, THOUGH.
SOMETHING STRONGER, SOMETHING ORIGINAL BUT SOMETHING FAMILIAR.
IT REMINDS ME OF...

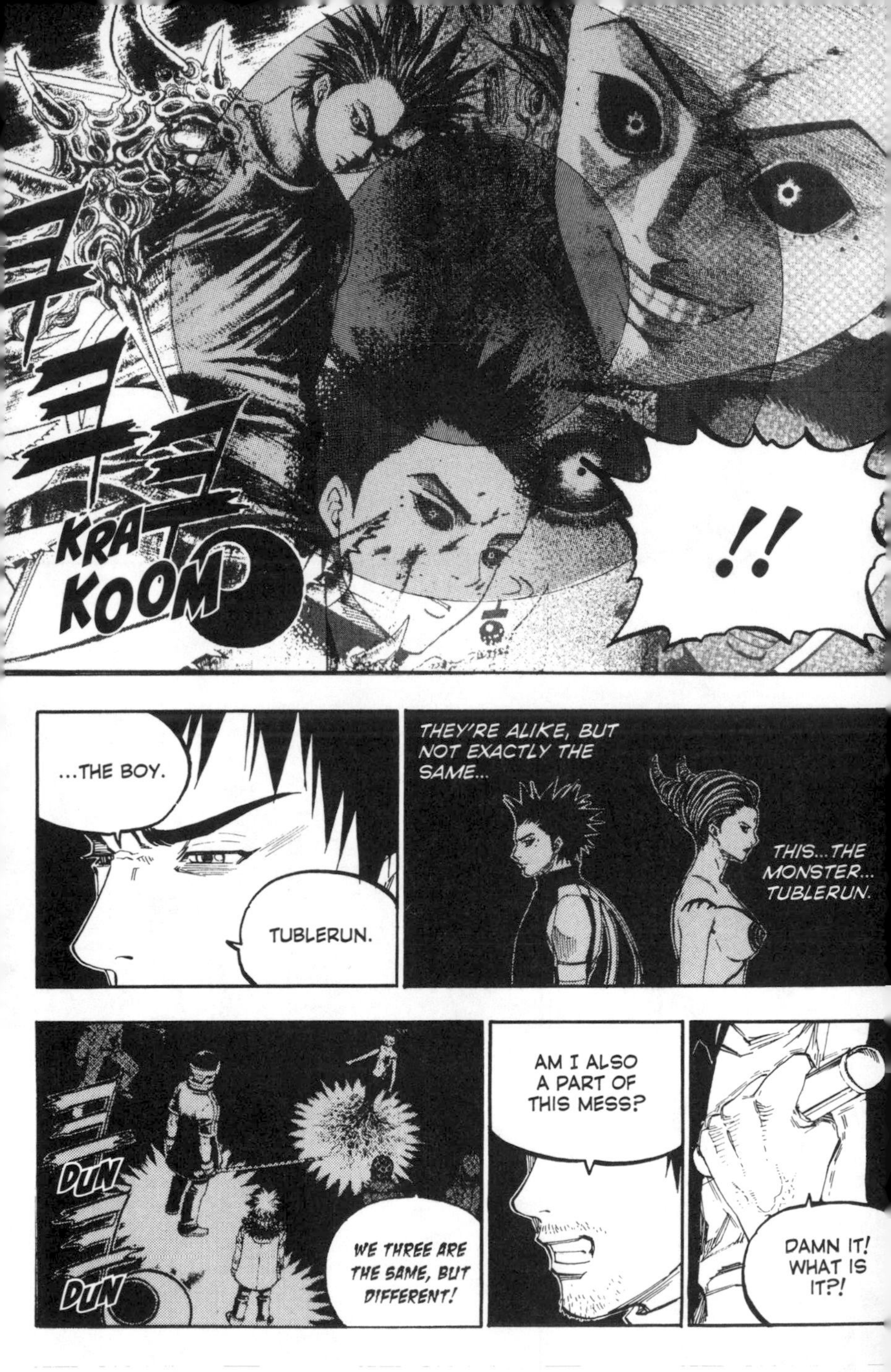
KRA KOOM
!!
...THE BOY.
TUBLERUN.
THEY'RE ALIKE, BUT NOT EXACTLY THE SAME...
THIS...THE MONSTER... TUBLERUN.
DUN
DUN
WE THREE ARE THE SAME, BUT DIFFERENT!
AM I ALSO A PART OF THIS MESS?
DAMN IT! WHAT IS IT?!

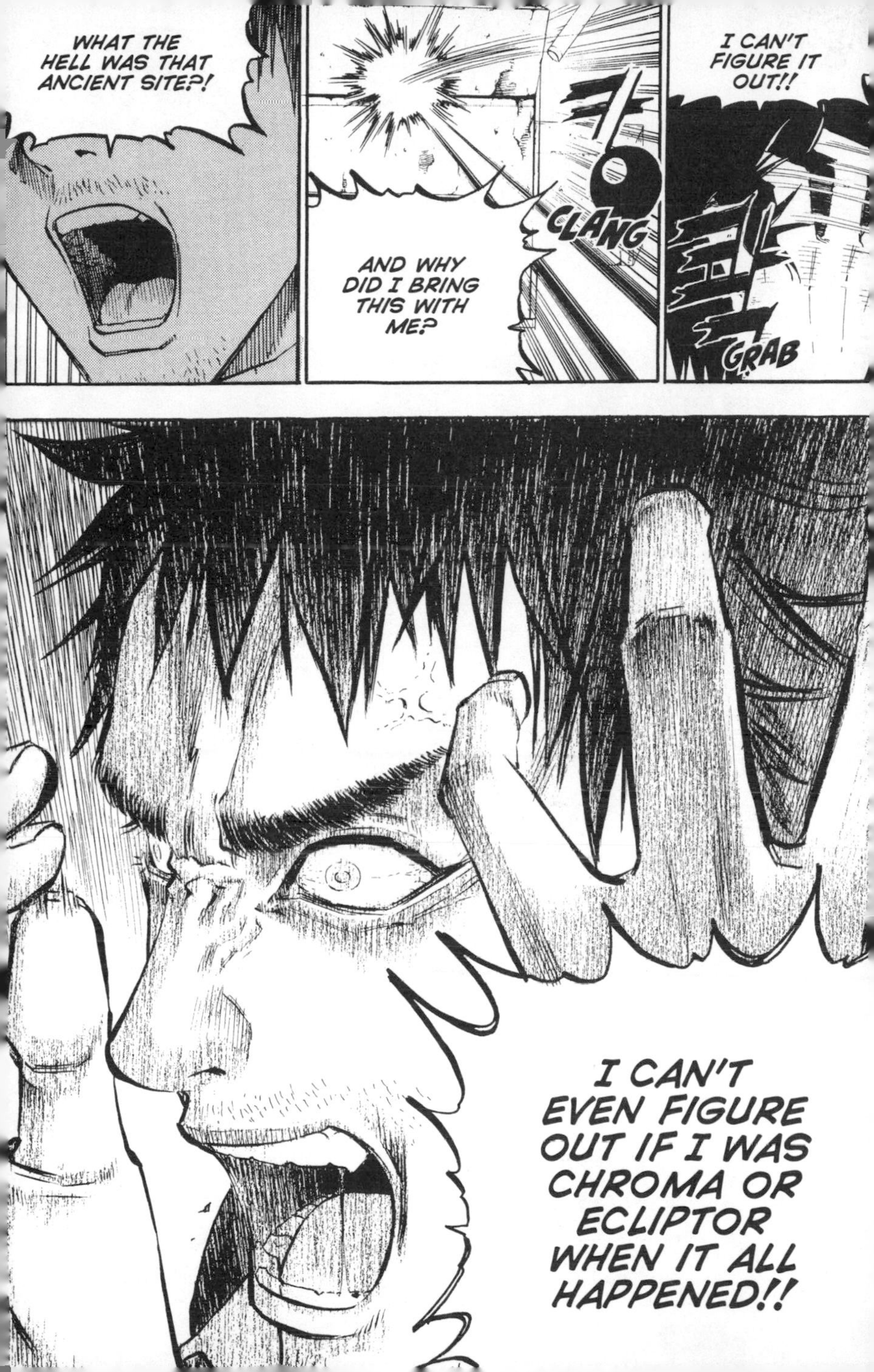
WHAT THE HELL WAS THAT ANCIENT SITE?!
AND WHY DID I BRING THIS WITH ME?
CLANG
I CAN'T FIGURE IT OUT!!
GRAB
I CAN'T EVEN FIGURE OUT IF I WAS CHROMA OR ECLIPTOR WHEN IT ALL HAPPENED!!

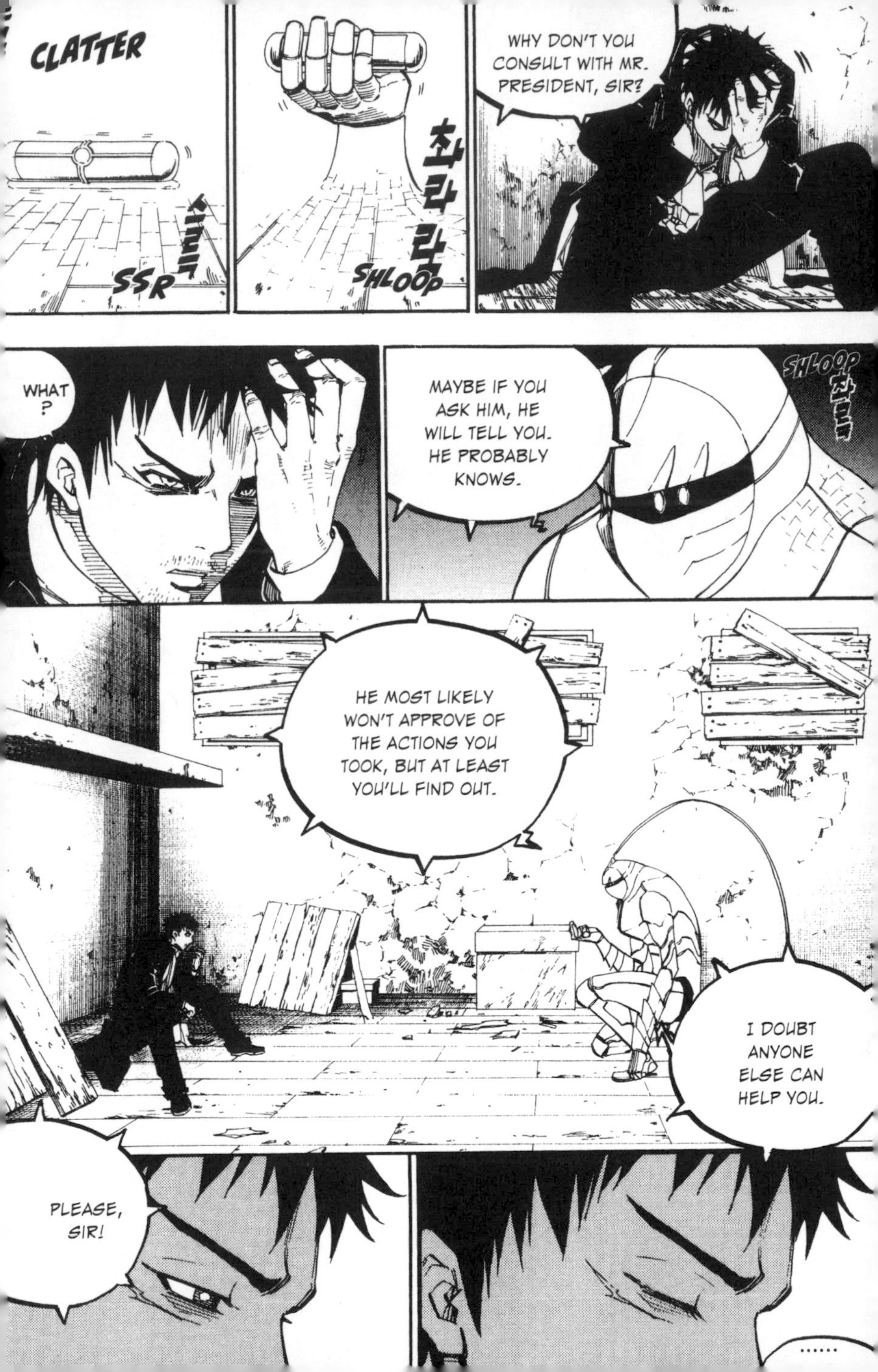
CLATTER
SSR
SHLOOP
WHY DON'T YOU CONSULT WITH MR. PRESIDENT, SIR?
WHAT ?
MAYBE IF YOU ASK HIM, HE WILL TELL YOU. HE PROBABLY KNOWS.
SHLOOP
HE MOST LIKELY WON'T APPROVE OF THE ACTIONS YOU TOOK, BUT AT LEAST YOU'LL FIND OUT.
I DOUBT ANYONE ELSE CAN HELP YOU.
PLEASE, SIR!
......

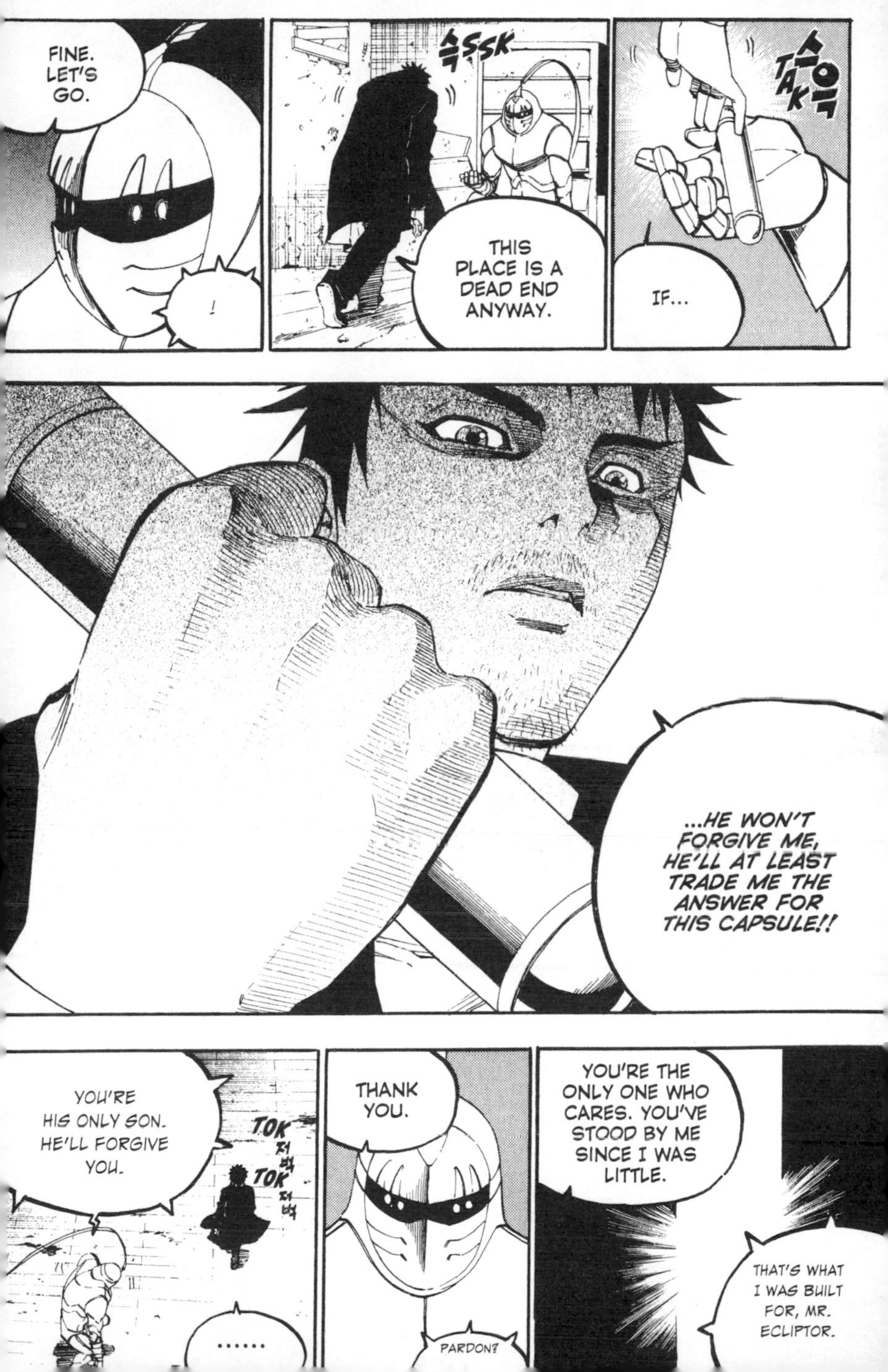
FINE. LET'S GO.
!
슥 SSK
THIS PLACE IS A DEAD END ANYWAY.
스윽 TAK
IF...
...HE WON'T FORGIVE ME, HE'LL AT LEAST TRADE ME THE ANSWER FOR THIS CAPSULE!!
YOU'RE HIS ONLY SON. HE'LL FORGIVE YOU.
TOK 저벅
TOK 저벅
......
THANK YOU.
PARDON?
YOU'RE THE ONLY ONE WHO CARES. YOU'VE STOOD BY ME SINCE I WAS LITTLE.
THAT'S WHAT I WAS BUILT FOR, MR. ECLIPTOR.

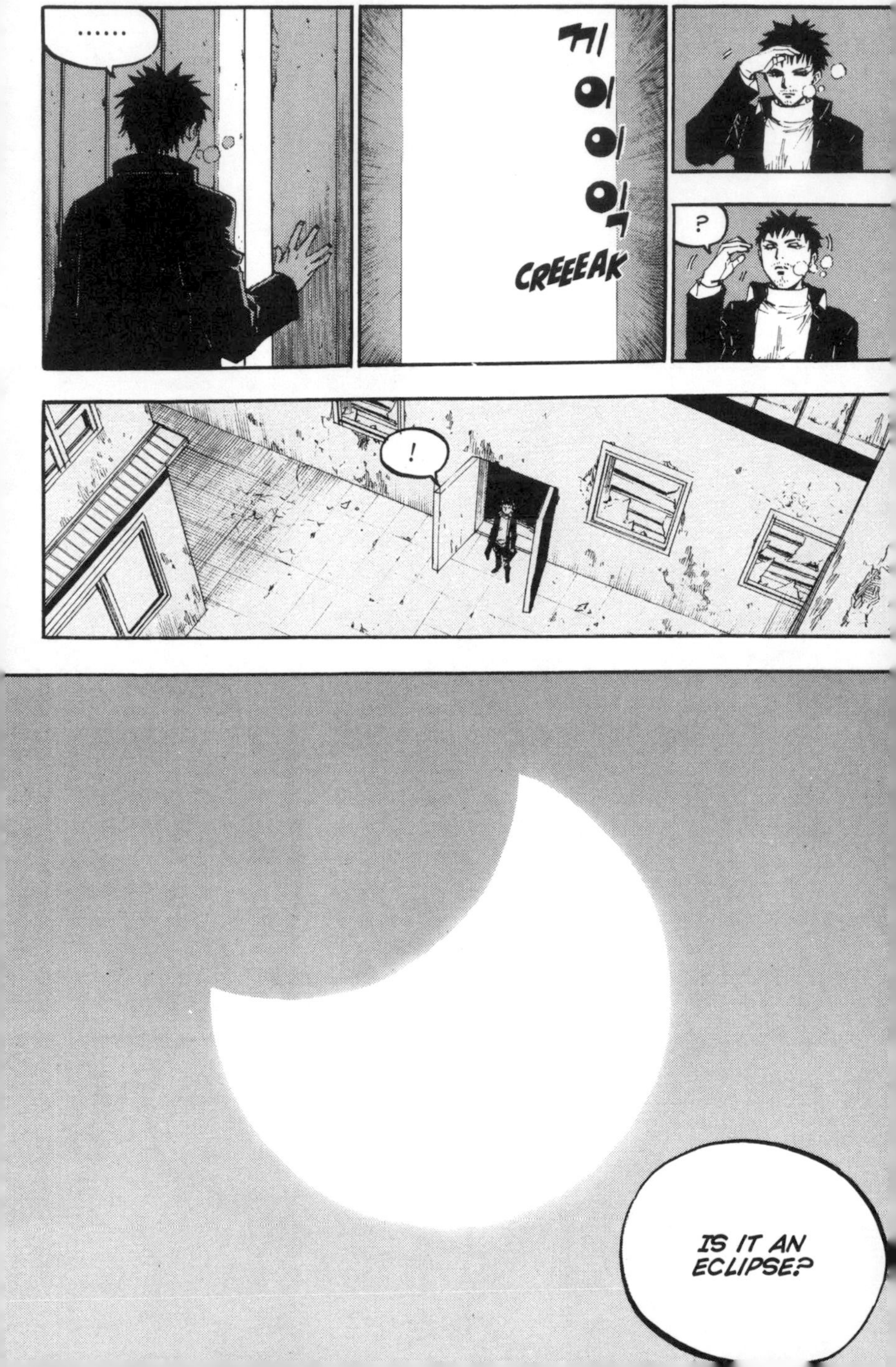
......
끼이이익
CREEEAK
?
!
IS IT AN ECLIPSE?

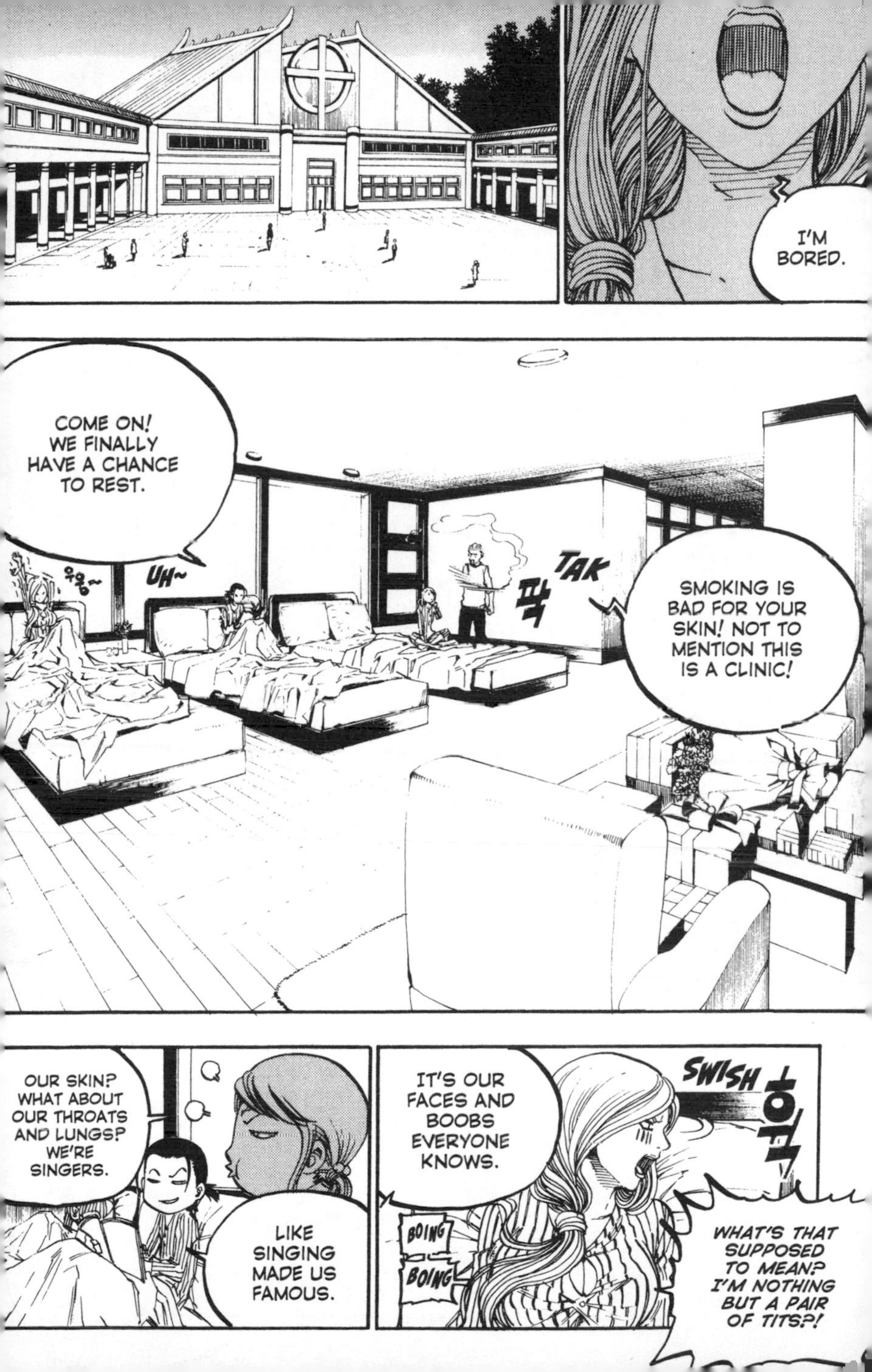
I'M BORED.
COME ON! WE FINALLY HAVE A CHANCE TO REST.
우웅~
UH~
딱
TAK
SMOKING IS BAD FOR YOUR SKIN! NOT TO MENTION THIS IS A CLINIC!
OUR SKIN? WHAT ABOUT OUR THROATS AND LUNGS? WE'RE SINGERS.
LIKE SINGING MADE US FAMOUS.
IT'S OUR FACES AND BOOBS EVERYONE KNOWS.
BOING
BOING
SWISH
WHAT'S THAT SUPPOSED TO MEAN? I'M NOTHING BUT A PAIR OF TITS?!

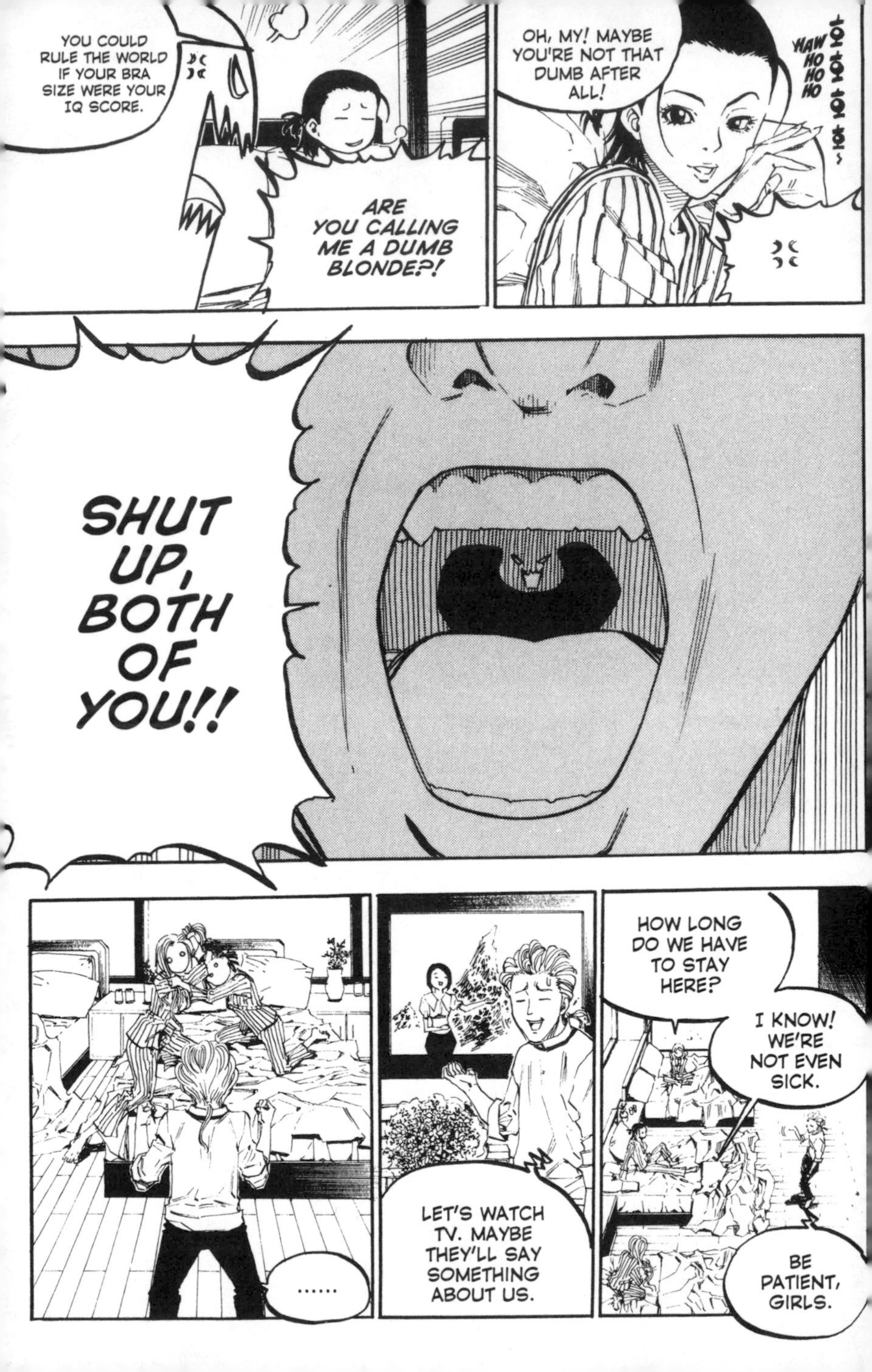
YOU COULD RULE THE WORLD IF YOUR BRA SIZE WERE YOUR IQ SCORE.
ARE YOU CALLING ME A DUMB BLONDE?!
OH, MY! MAYBE YOU'RE NOT THAT DUMB AFTER ALL!
HAW HO HO HO
SHUT UP, BOTH OF YOU!!
......
LET'S WATCH TV. MAYBE THEY'LL SAY SOMETHING ABOUT US.
HOW LONG DO WE HAVE TO STAY HERE?
I KNOW! WE'RE NOT EVEN SICK.
BE PATIENT, GIRLS.

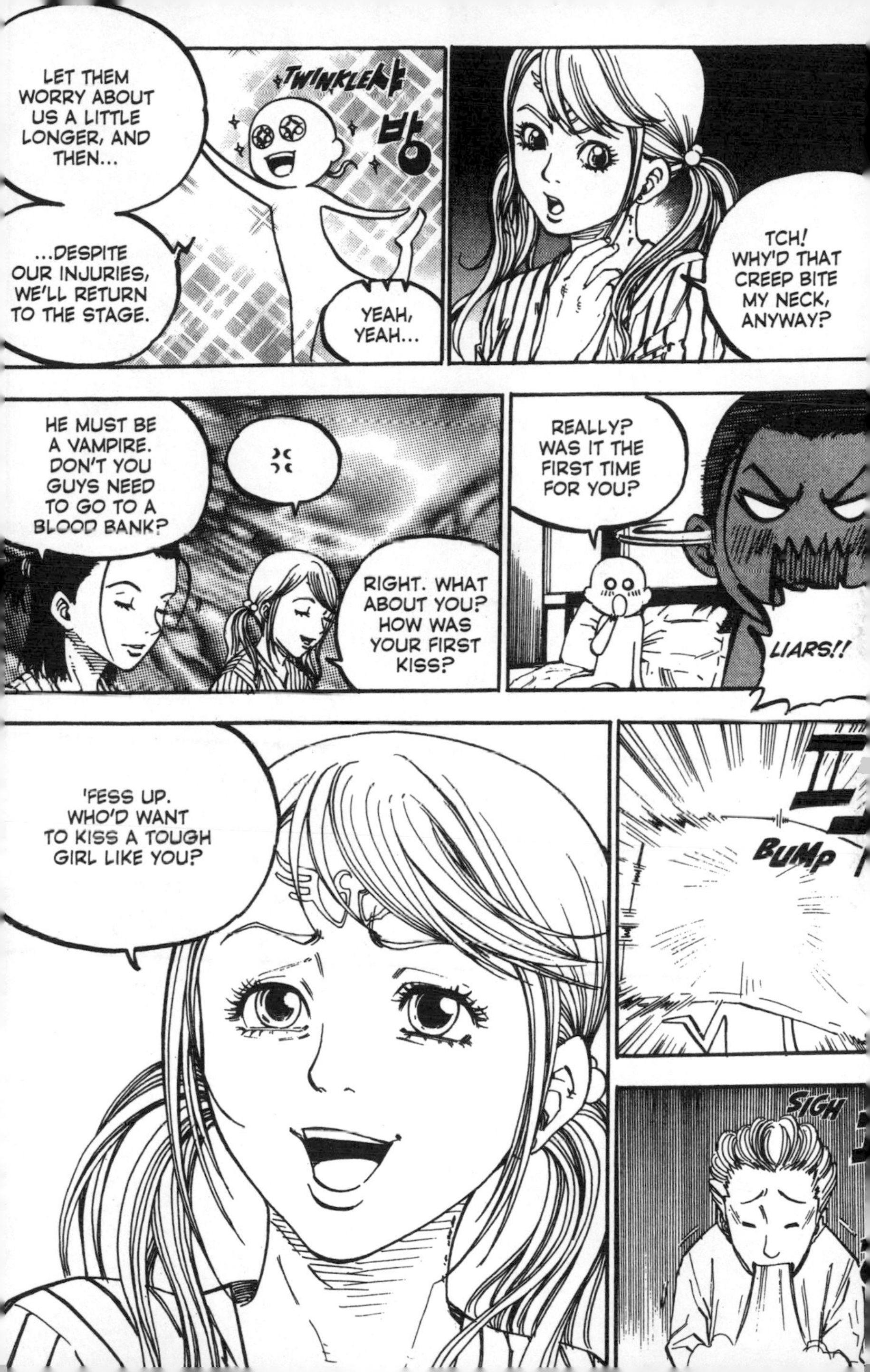
LET THEM WORRY ABOUT US A LITTLE LONGER, AND THEN...
TWINKLE
...DESPITE OUR INJURIES, WE'LL RETURN TO THE STAGE.
YEAH, YEAH...
TCH! WHY'D THAT CREEP BITE MY NECK, ANYWAY?
HE MUST BE A VAMPIRE. DON'T YOU GUYS NEED TO GO TO A BLOOD BANK?
RIGHT. WHAT ABOUT YOU? HOW WAS YOUR FIRST KISS?
REALLY? WAS IT THE FIRST TIME FOR YOU?
LIARS!!
'FESS UP. WHO'D WANT TO KISS A TOUGH GIRL LIKE YOU?
BUMP
SIGH

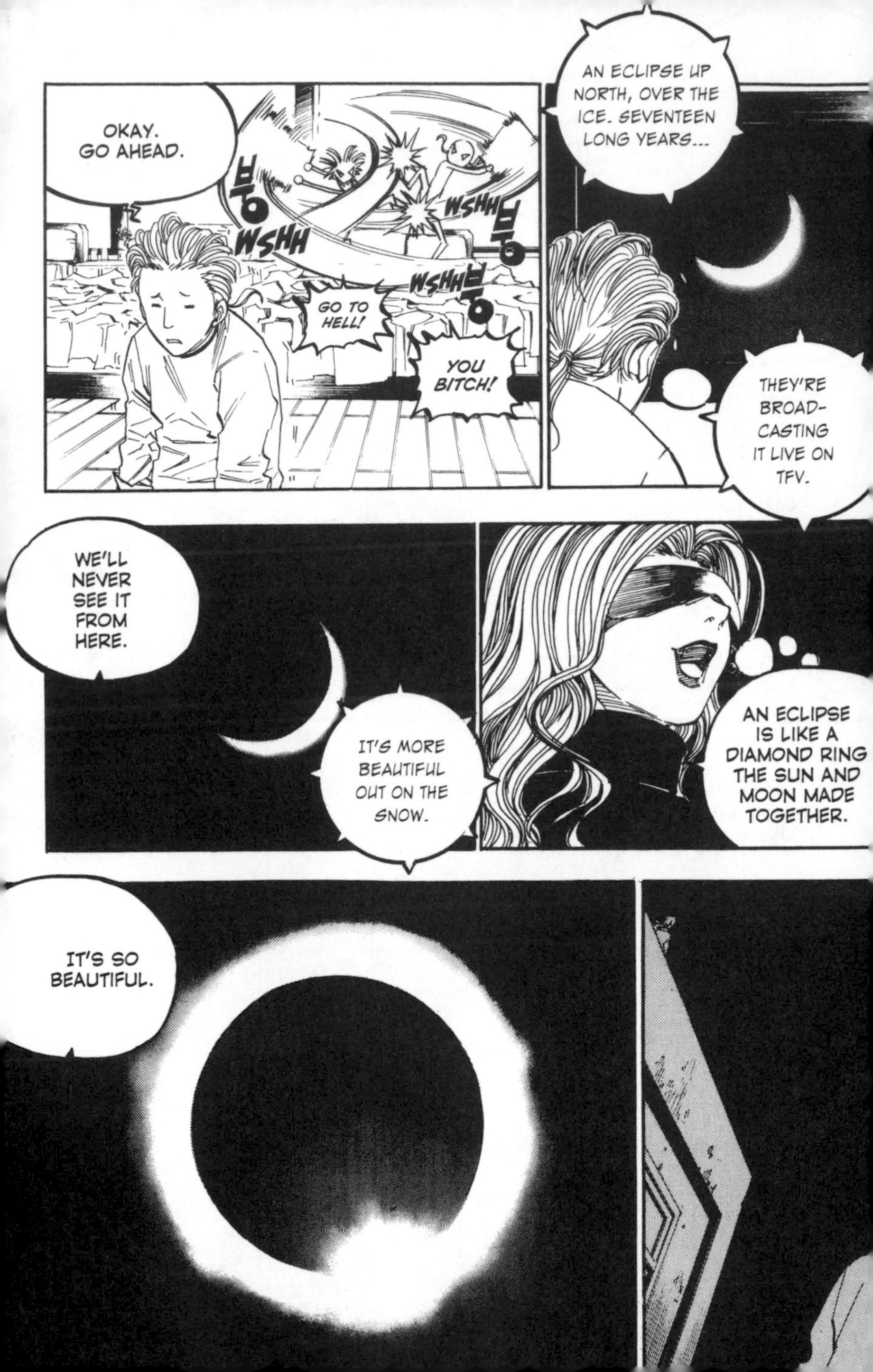
OKAY. GO AHEAD.
붕
WSHH
WSHH
붕
WSHH
붕
GO TO HELL!
YOU BITCH!
AN ECLIPSE UP NORTH, OVER THE ICE. SEVENTEEN LONG YEARS...
THEY'RE BROAD-CASTING IT LIVE ON TFV.
WE'LL NEVER SEE IT FROM HERE.
IT'S MORE BEAUTIFUL OUT ON THE SNOW.
AN ECLIPSE IS LIKE A DIAMOND RING THE SUN AND MOON MADE TOGETHER.
IT'S SO BEAUTIFUL.

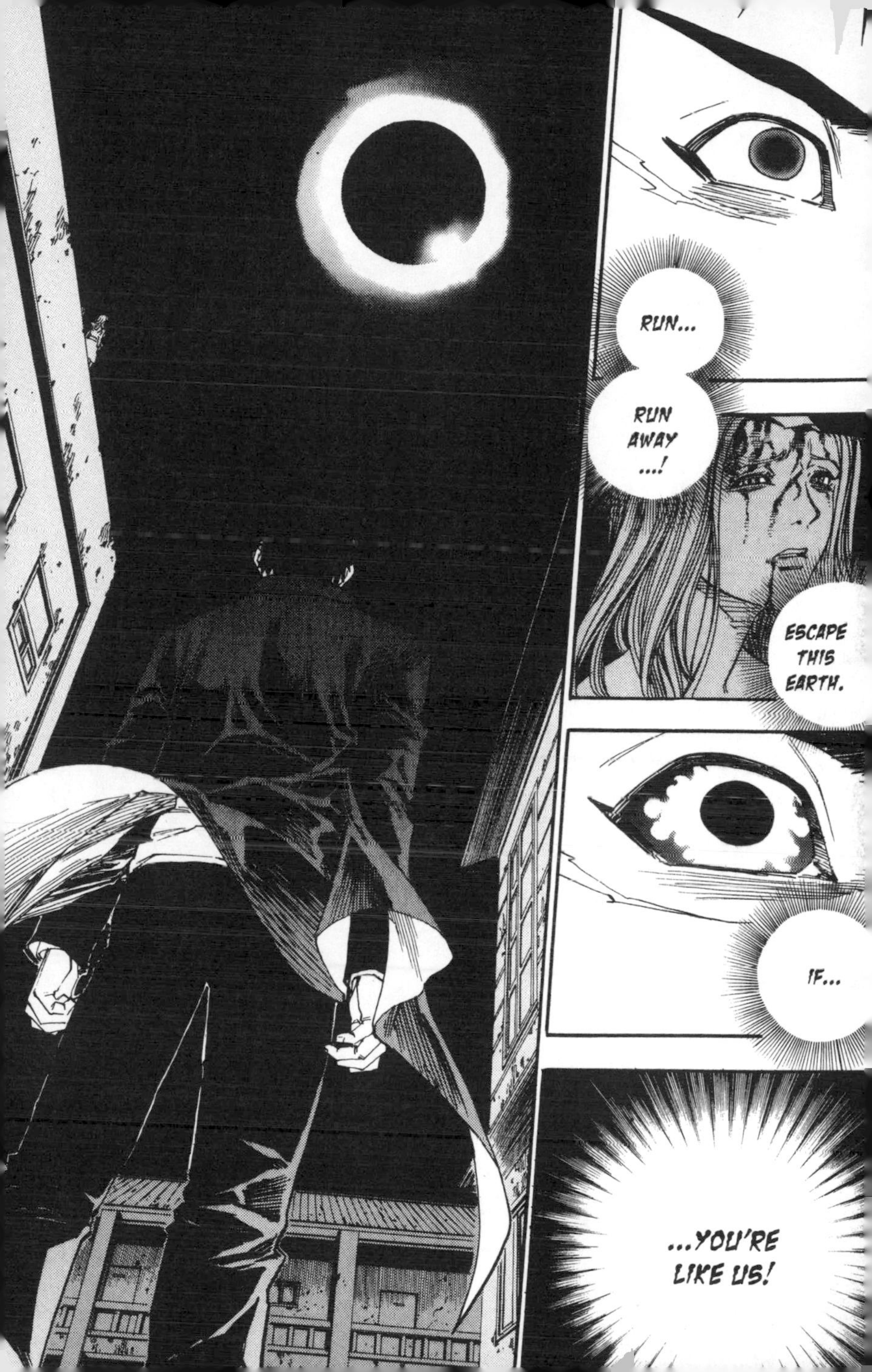
RUN...
RUN AWAY ...!
ESCAPE THIS EARTH.
IF...
...YOU'RE LIKE US!

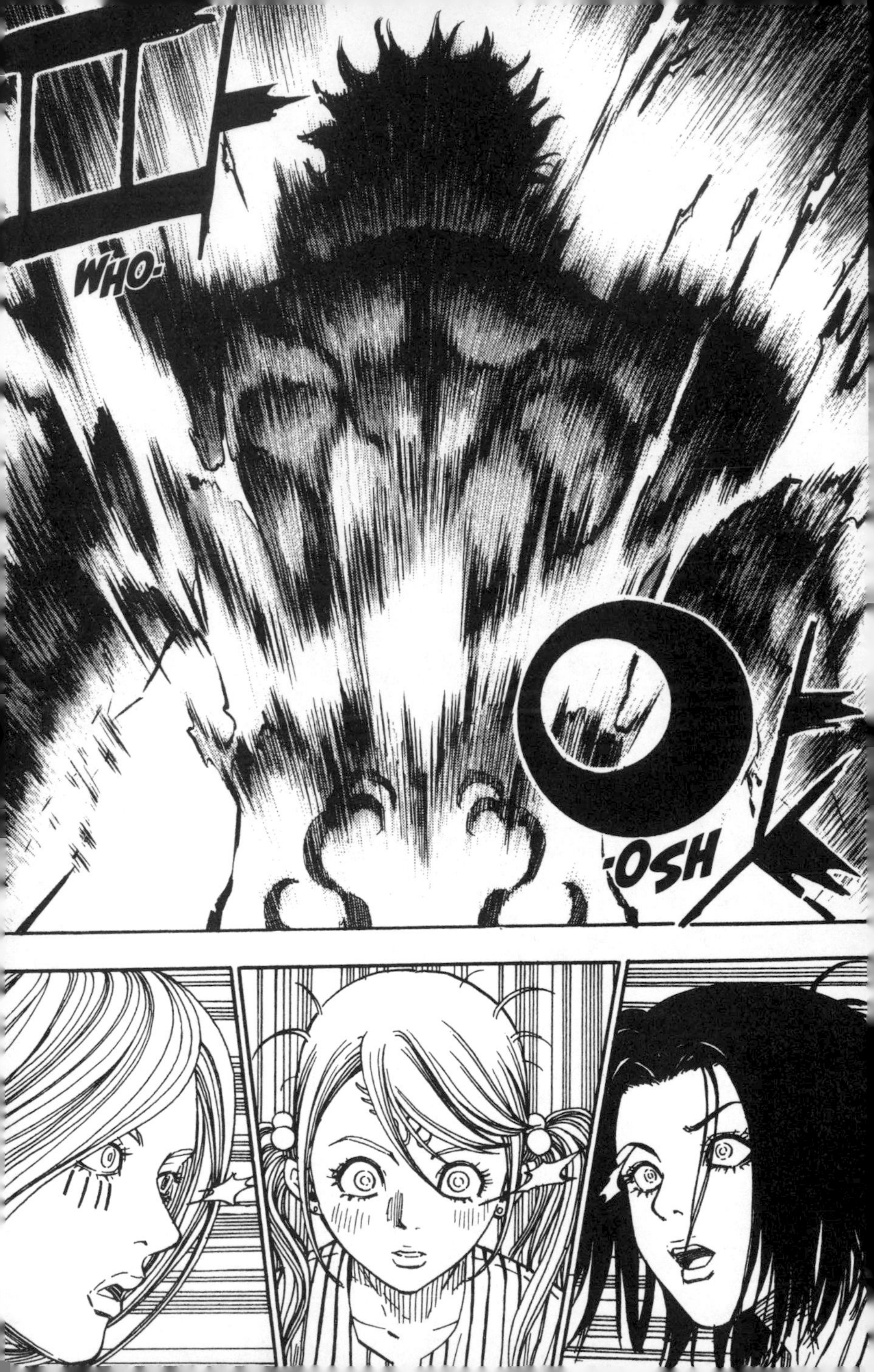
WHO-
-OSH

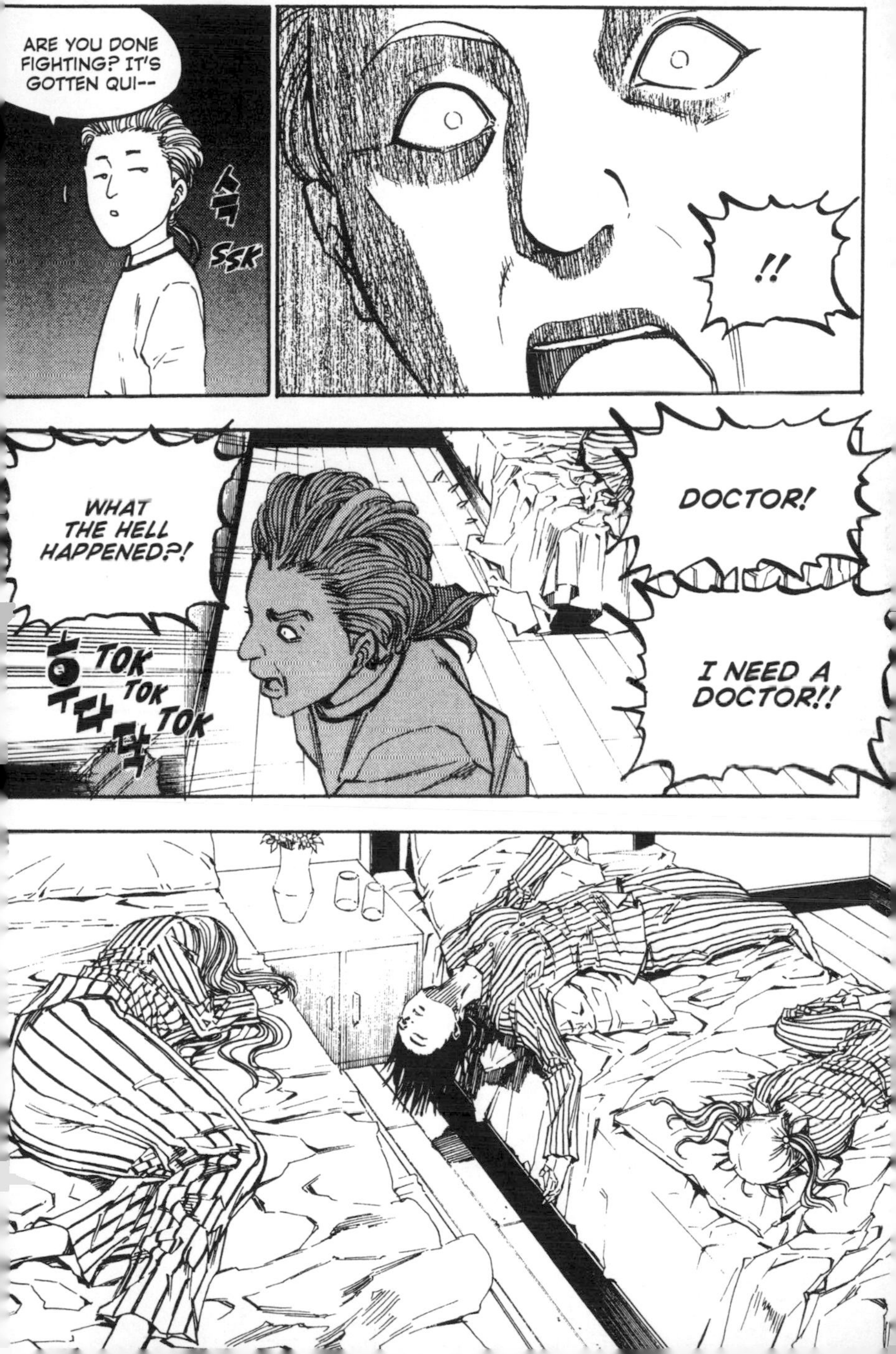
ARE YOU DONE FIGHTING? IT'S GOTTEN QUI--
SSK
!!
WHAT THE HELL HAPPENED?!
TOK TOK TOK
DOCTOR!
I NEED A DOCTOR!!

# FREAK

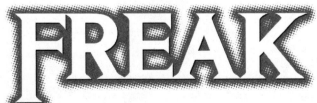

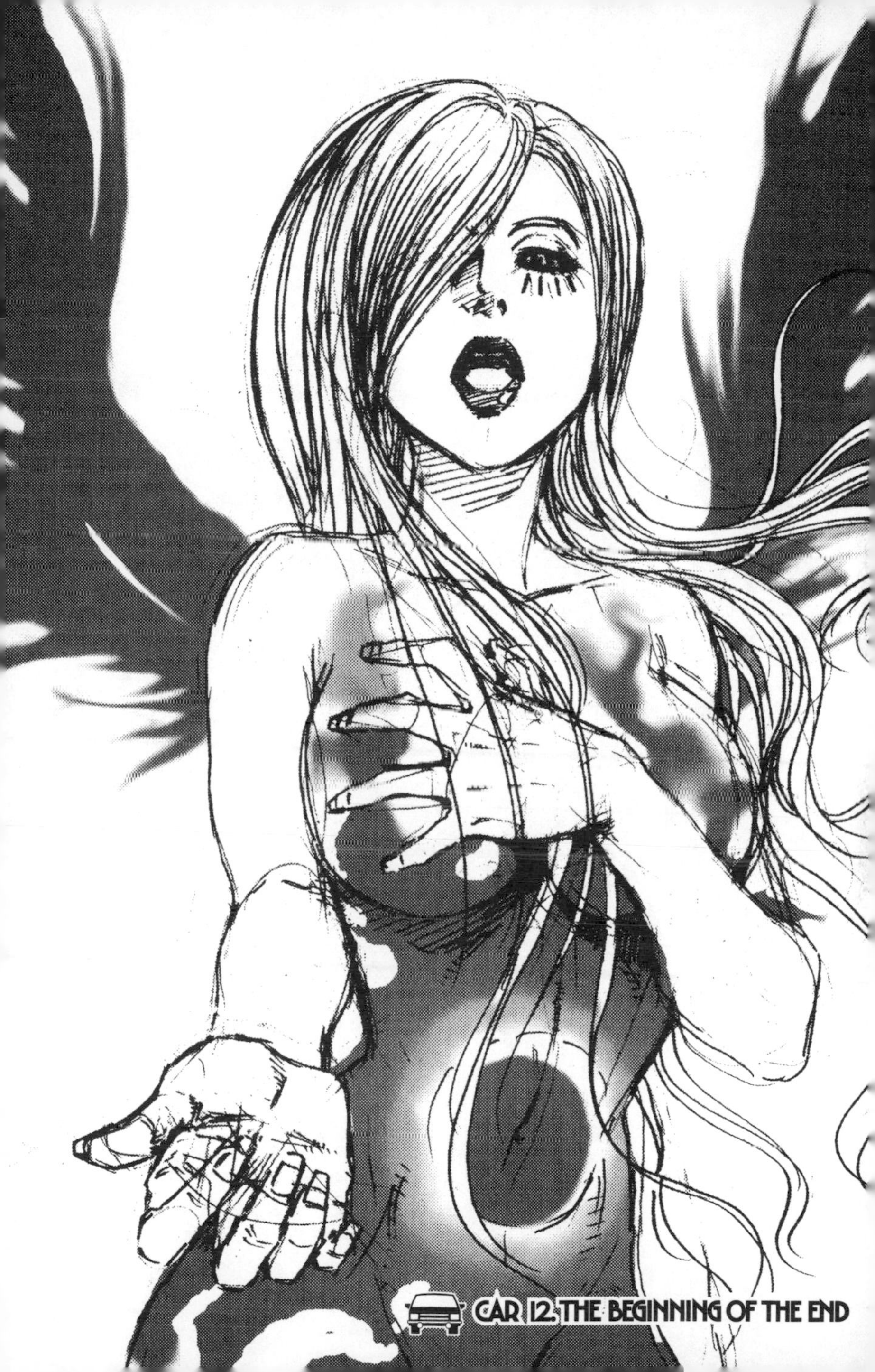
CAR 12: THE BEGINNING OF THE END

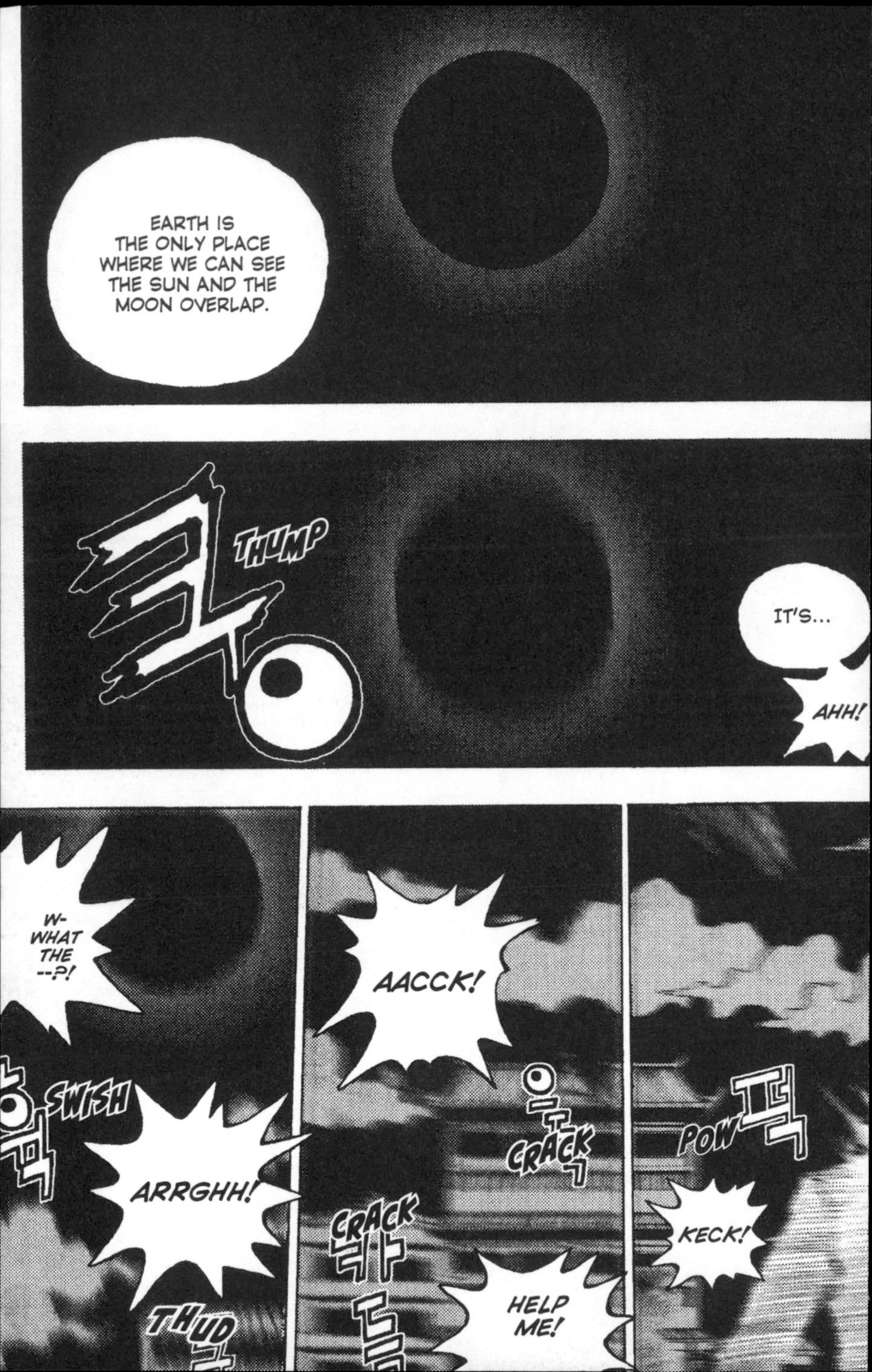
EARTH IS THE ONLY PLACE WHERE WE CAN SEE THE SUN AND THE MOON OVERLAP.
THUMP
IT'S...
AHH!
W-WHAT THE --?!
SWISH
ARRGHH!
THUD
AACCK!
CRACK
CRACK
HELP ME!
POW
KECK!

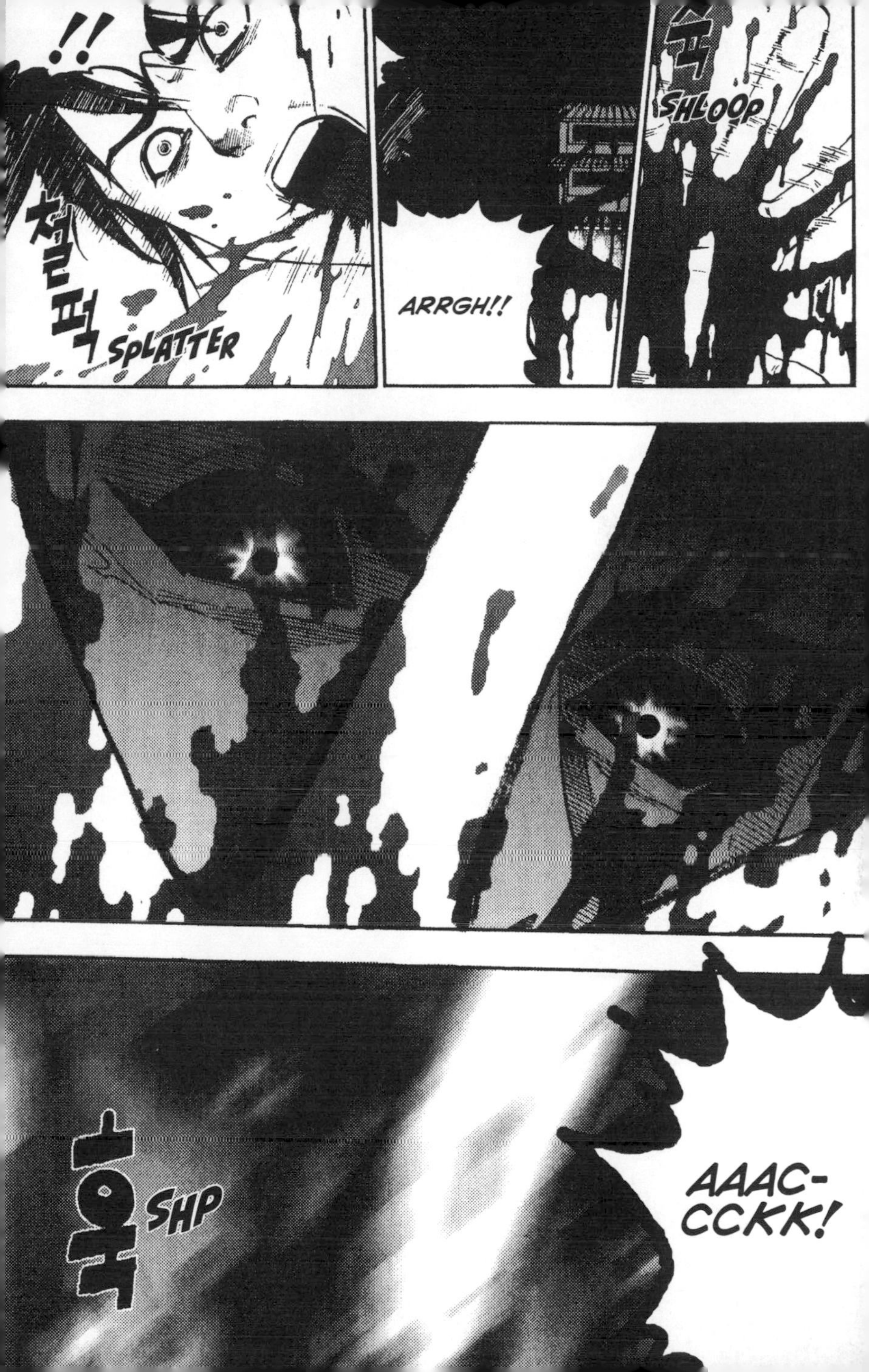
!!
SPLATTER
ARRGH!!
SHLOOP
SHP
AAAC-
CCKK!

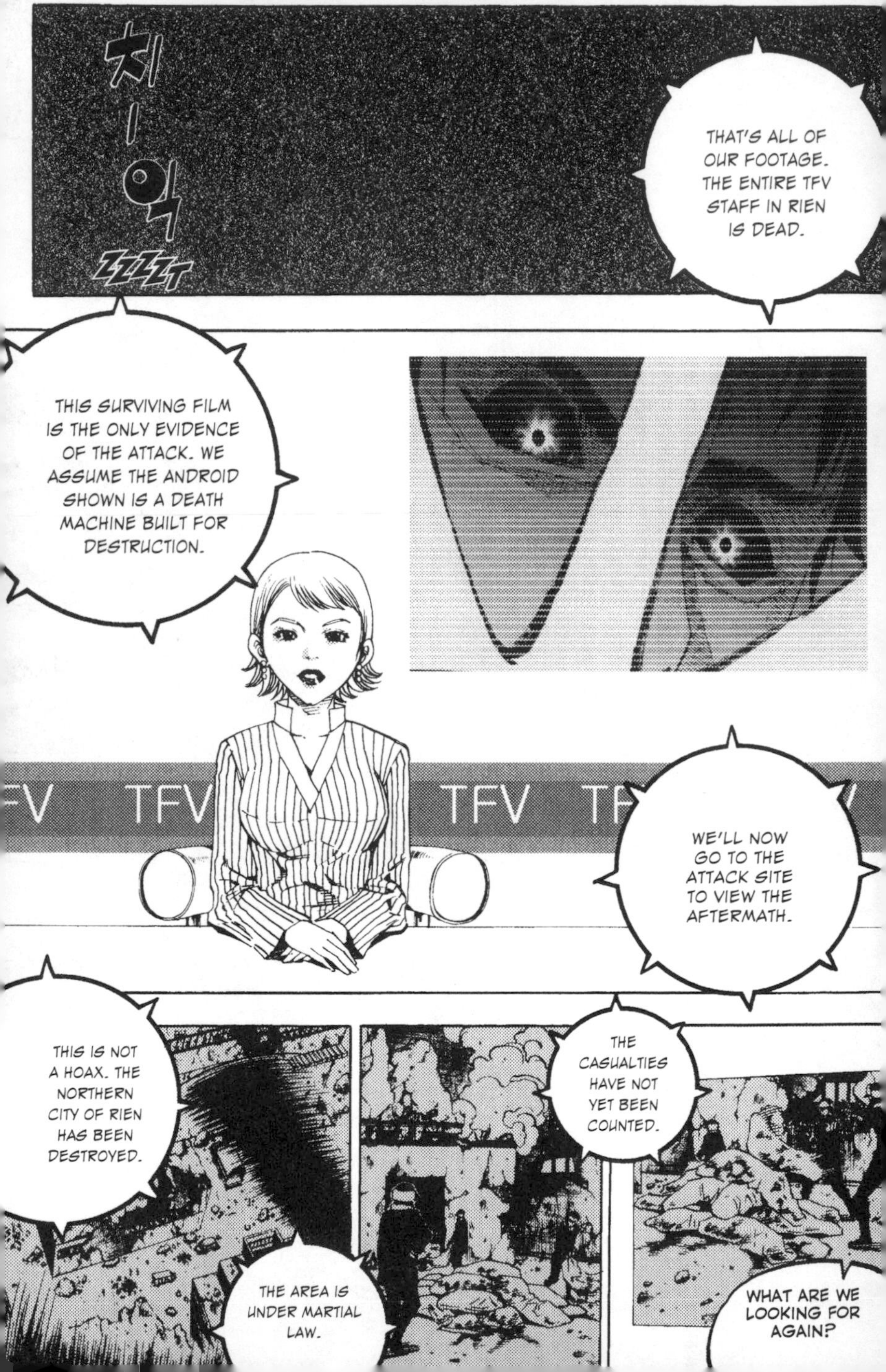
치—익
ZZZZT
THAT'S ALL OF OUR FOOTAGE. THE ENTIRE TFV STAFF IN RIEN IS DEAD.
THIS SURVIVING FILM IS THE ONLY EVIDENCE OF THE ATTACK. WE ASSUME THE ANDROID SHOWN IS A DEATH MACHINE BUILT FOR DESTRUCTION.
TFV TFV TFV
WE'LL NOW GO TO THE ATTACK SITE TO VIEW THE AFTERMATH.
THIS IS NOT A HOAX. THE NORTHERN CITY OF RIEN HAS BEEN DESTROYED.
THE AREA IS UNDER MARTIAL LAW.
THE CASUALTIES HAVE NOT YET BEEN COUNTED.
WHAT ARE WE LOOKING FOR AGAIN?

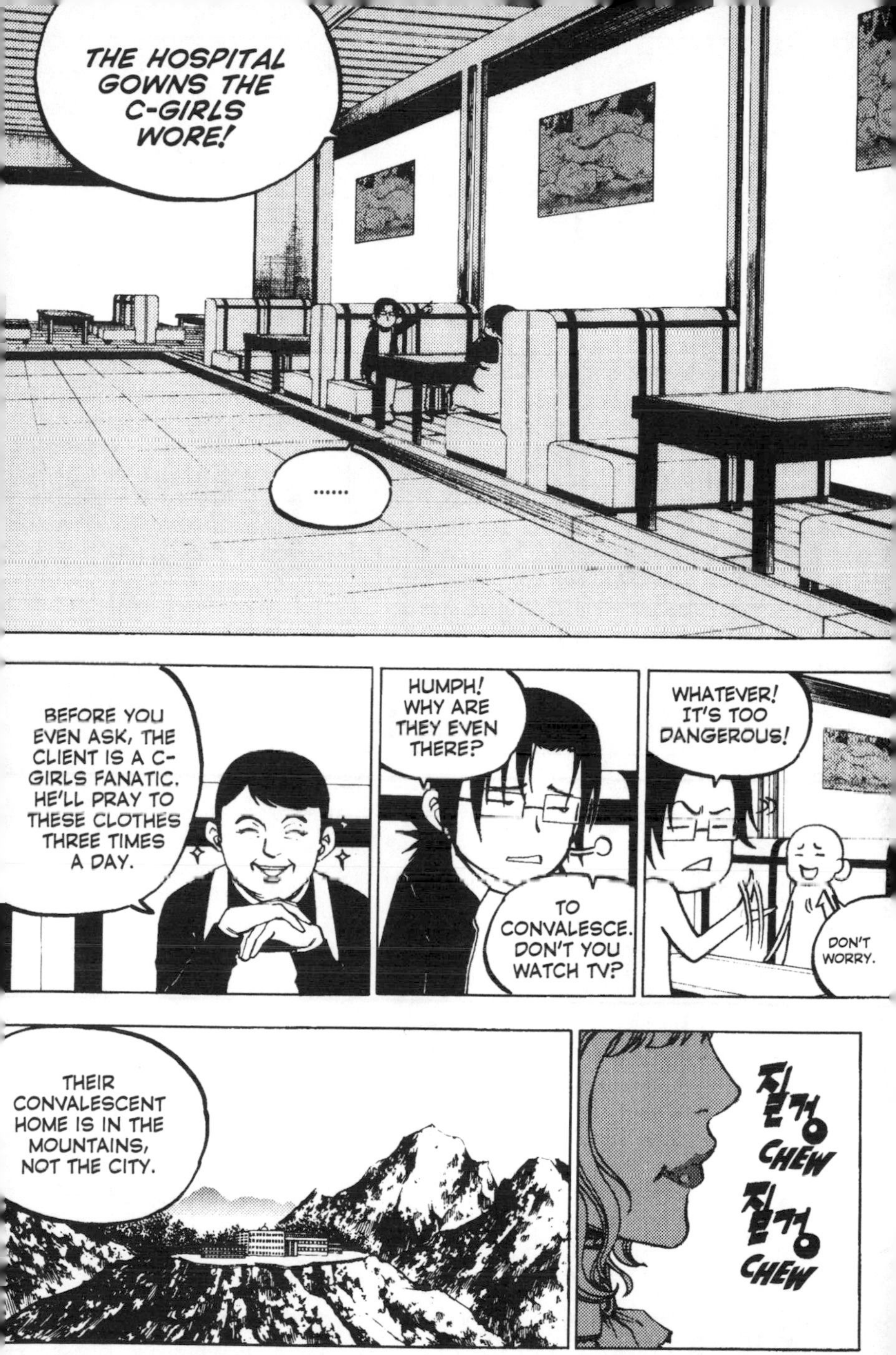
THE HOSPITAL GOWNS THE C-GIRLS WORE!
......
BEFORE YOU EVEN ASK, THE CLIENT IS A C-GIRLS FANATIC. HE'LL PRAY TO THESE CLOTHES THREE TIMES A DAY.
HUMPH! WHY ARE THEY EVEN THERE?
TO CONVALESCE. DON'T YOU WATCH TV?
WHATEVER! IT'S TOO DANGEROUS!
DON'T WORRY.
THEIR CONVALESCENT HOME IS IN THE MOUNTAINS, NOT THE CITY.
질겅
CHEW
질겅
CHEW

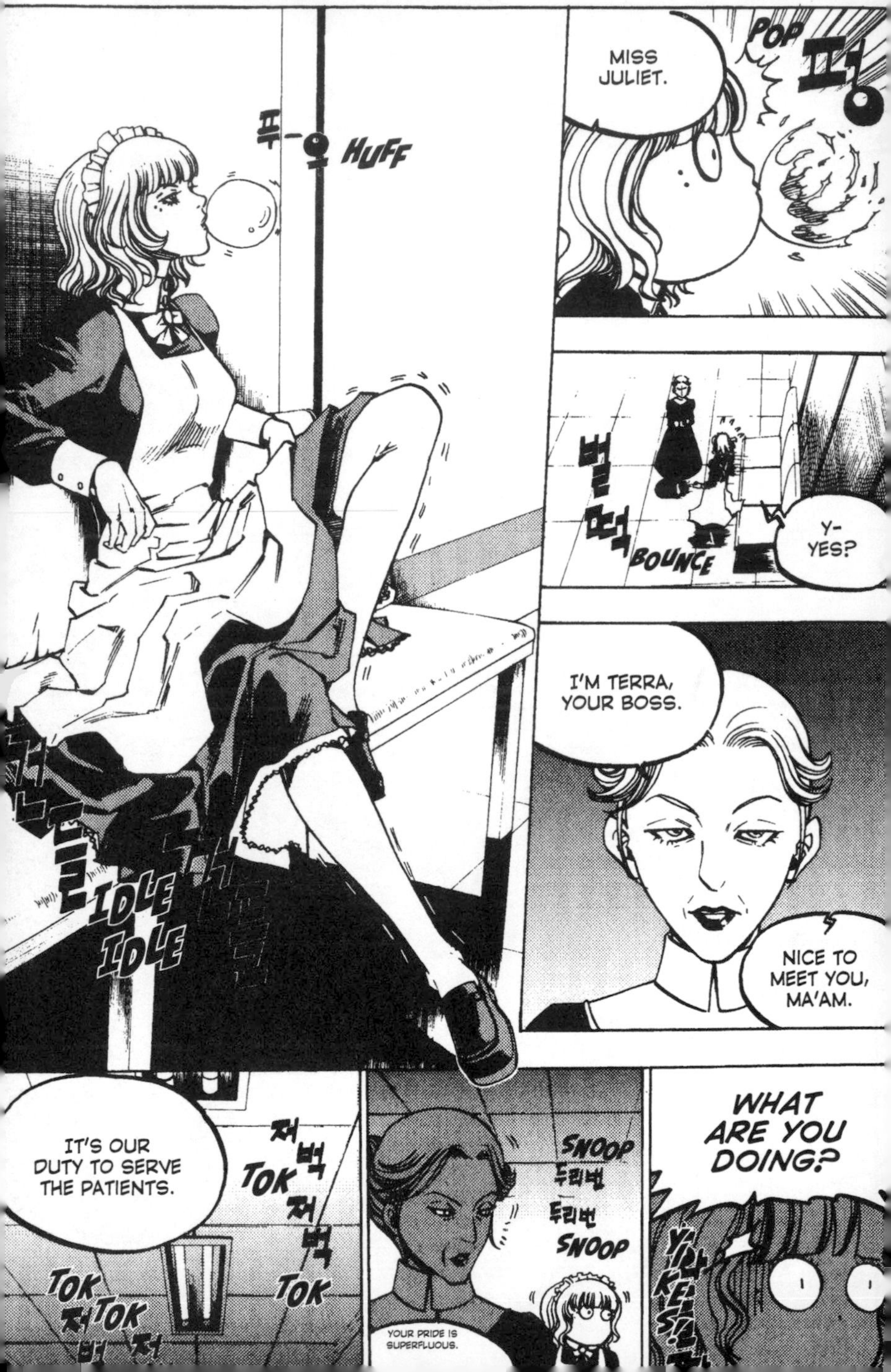
HUFF
IDLE
IDLE
MISS JULIET.
POP
펑
벌떡
BOUNCE
Y-YES?
I'M TERRA, YOUR BOSS.
NICE TO MEET YOU, MA'AM.
IT'S OUR DUTY TO SERVE THE PATIENTS.
저벅
TOK
저벅
TOK
TOK
TOK
YOUR PRIDE IS SUPERFLUOUS.
SNOOP
두리번
두리번
SNOOP
WHAT ARE YOU DOING?
YIKES!

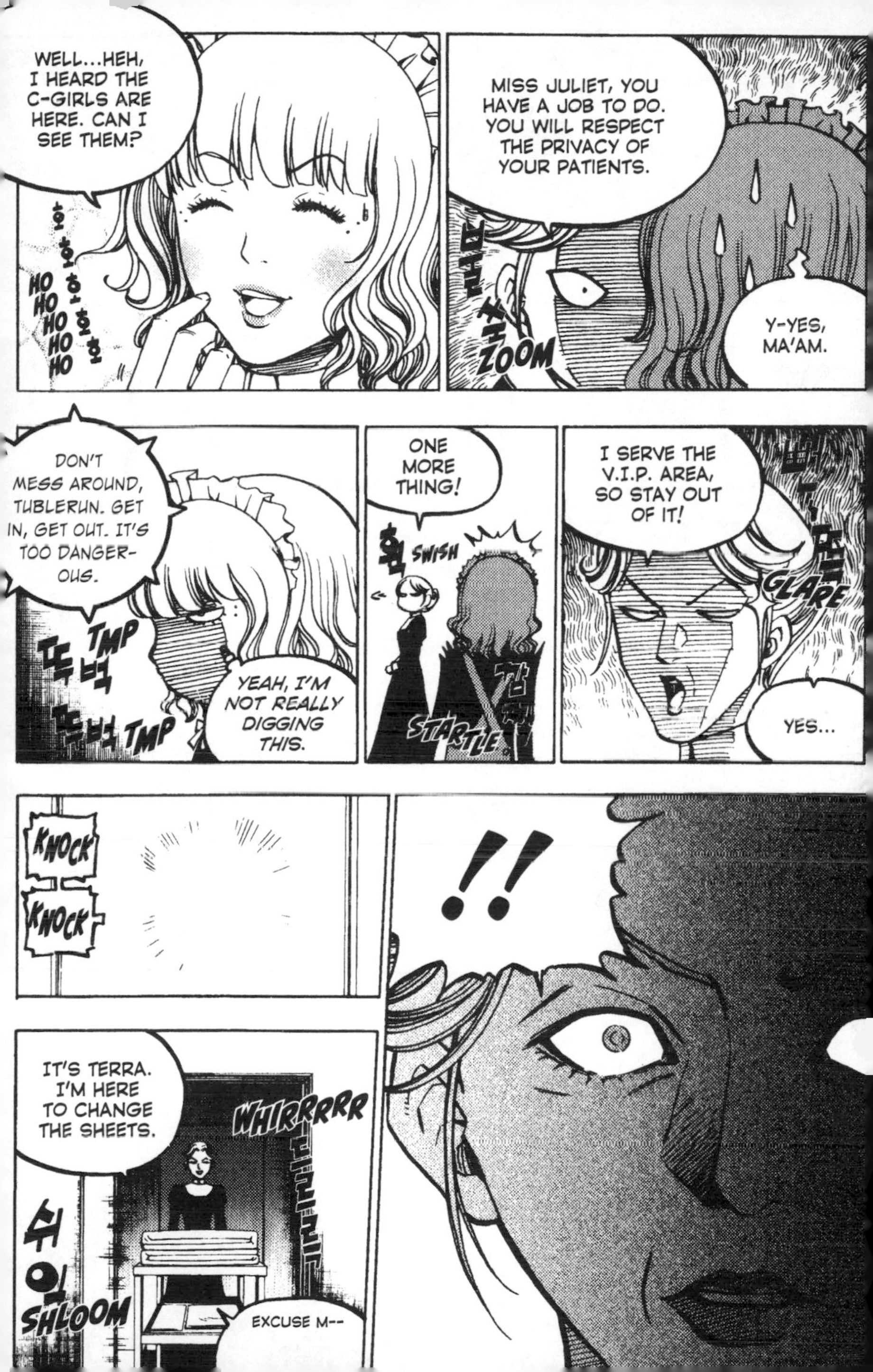

WELL...HEH, I HEARD THE C-GIRLS ARE HERE. CAN I SEE THEM?
HO HO HO HO HO
MISS JULIET, YOU HAVE A JOB TO DO. YOU WILL RESPECT THE PRIVACY OF YOUR PATIENTS.
ZOOM
Y-YES, MA'AM.
DON'T MESS AROUND, TUBLERUN. GET IN, GET OUT. IT'S TOO DANGER-OUS.
TMP TMP
YEAH, I'M NOT REALLY DIGGING THIS.
ONE MORE THING!
SWISH
STARTLE
I SERVE THE V.I.P. AREA, SO STAY OUT OF IT!
GLARE
YES...
KNOCK
KNOCK
IT'S TERRA. I'M HERE TO CHANGE THE SHEETS.
WHIRRRRR
SHLOOM
EXCUSE M--
!!

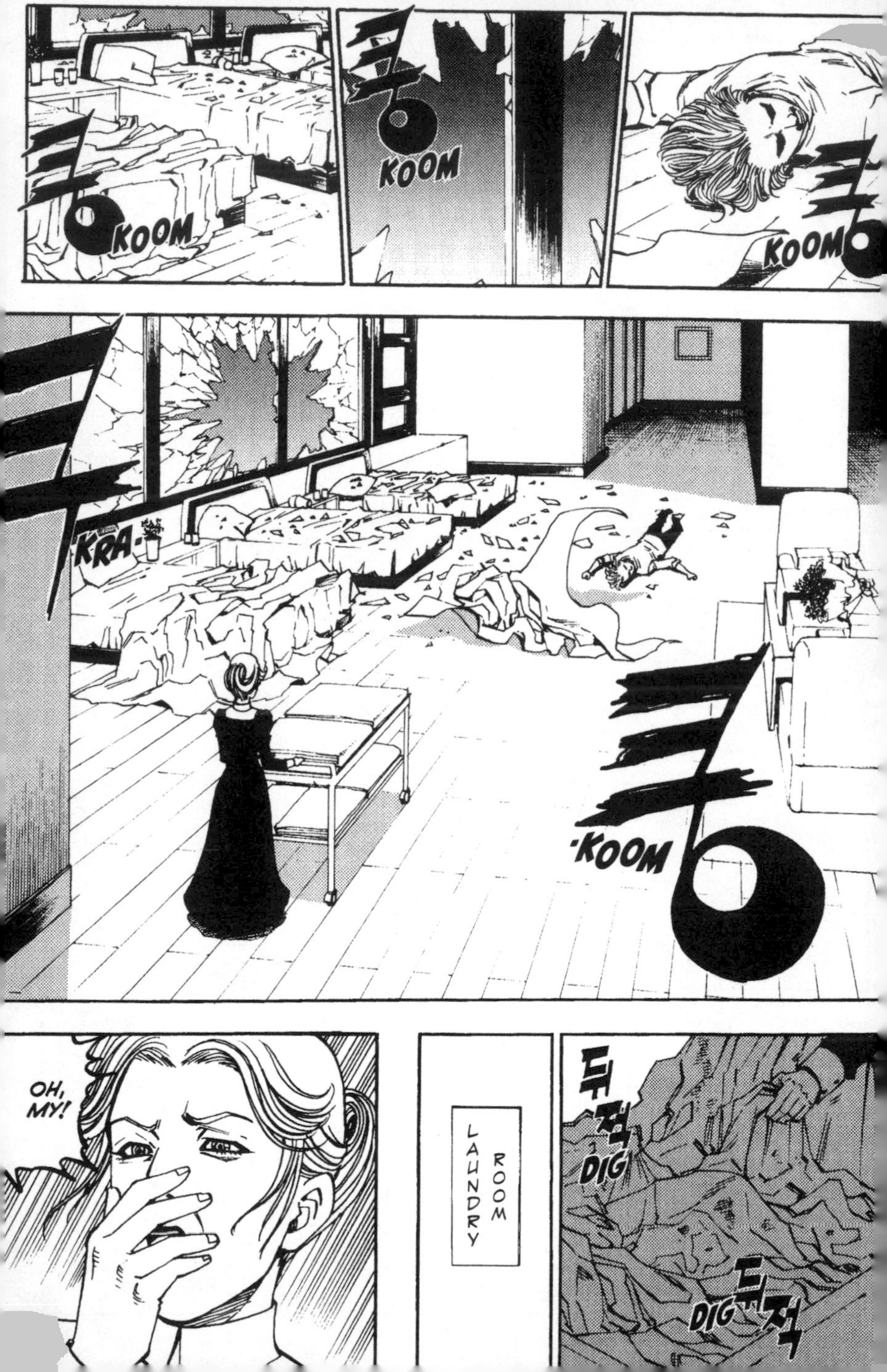

KOOM
KOOM
KOOM
KRA-
-KOOM
OH, MY!
LAUNDRY ROOM
뒤적
DIG
DIG
뒤적

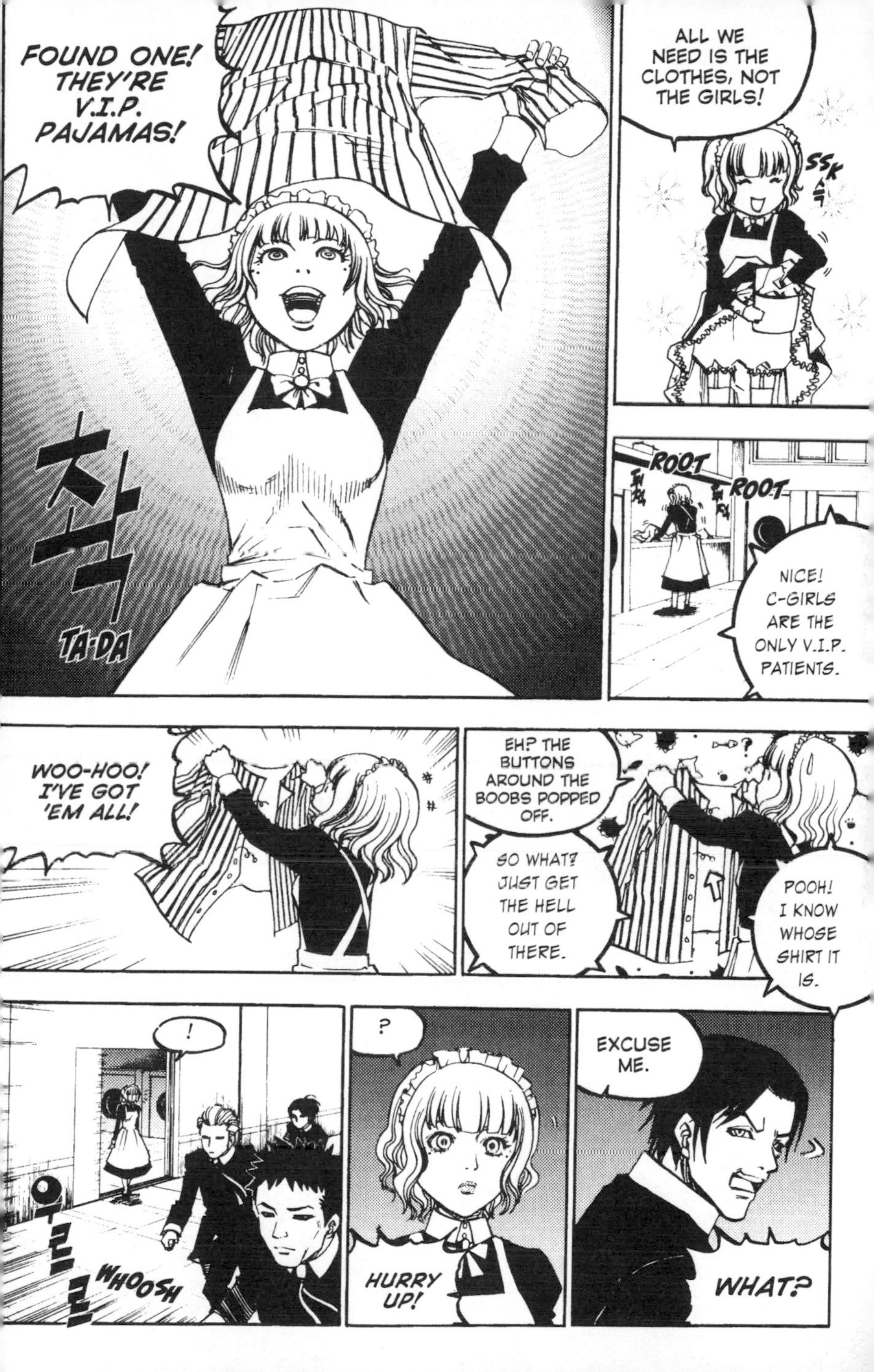
FOUND ONE! THEY'RE V.I.P. PAJAMAS!
TA-DA
ALL WE NEED IS THE CLOTHES, NOT THE GIRLS!
SSK
ROOT
ROOT
NICE! C-GIRLS ARE THE ONLY V.I.P. PATIENTS.
WOO-HOO! I'VE GOT 'EM ALL!
EH? THE BUTTONS AROUND THE BOOBS POPPED OFF.
SO WHAT? JUST GET THE HELL OUT OF THERE.
POOH! I KNOW WHOSE SHIRT IT IS.
!
WHOOSH
?
HURRY UP!
EXCUSE ME.
WHAT?

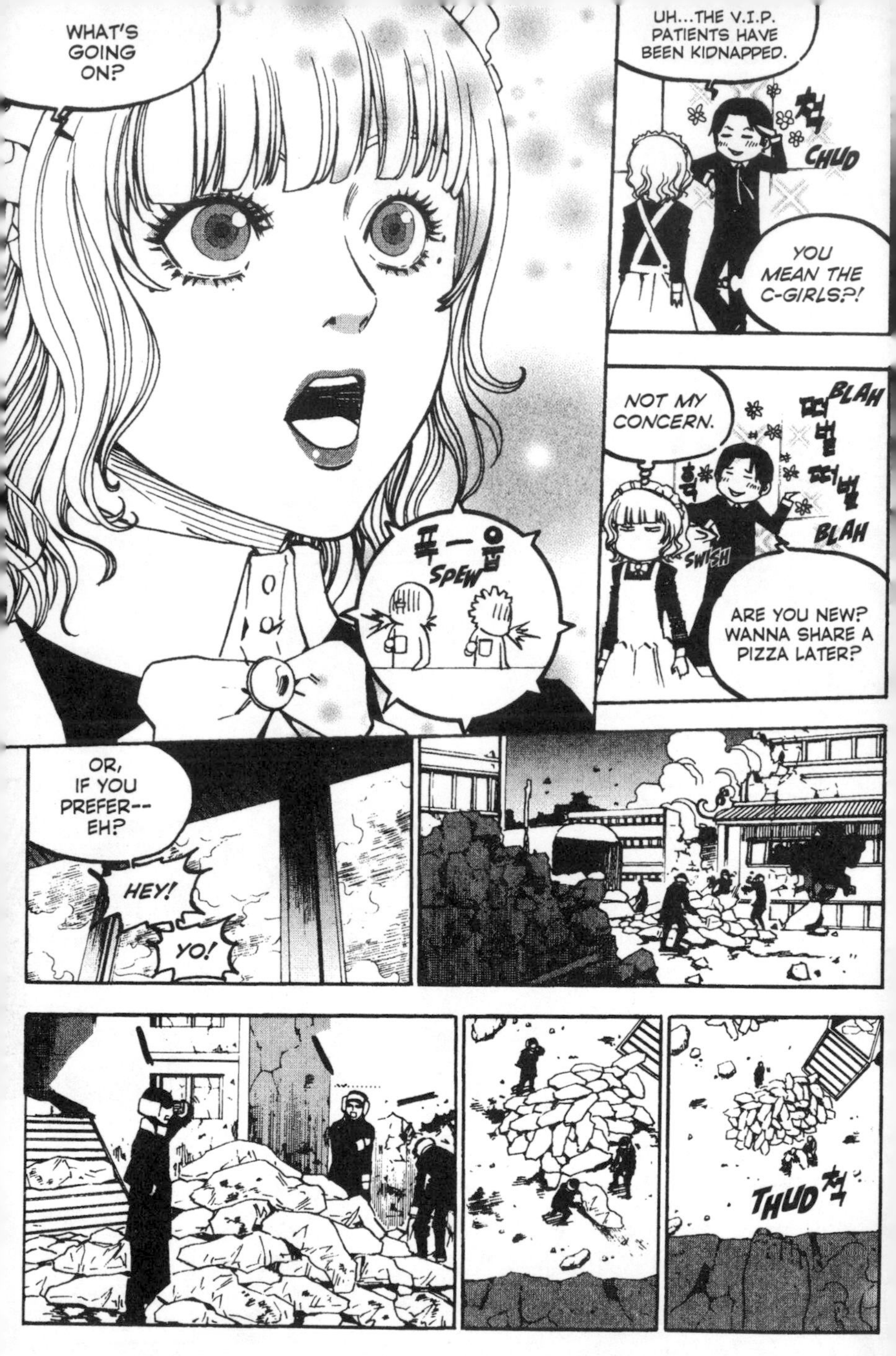
WHAT'S GOING ON?
SPEW
UH...THE V.I.P. PATIENTS HAVE BEEN KIDNAPPED.
척
CHUD
YOU MEAN THE C-GIRLS?!
NOT MY CONCERN.
떠벌 떠벌
BLAH
BLAH
SWISH
ARE YOU NEW? WANNA SHARE A PIZZA LATER?
OR, IF YOU PREFER-- EH?
HEY!
YO!
THUD 척

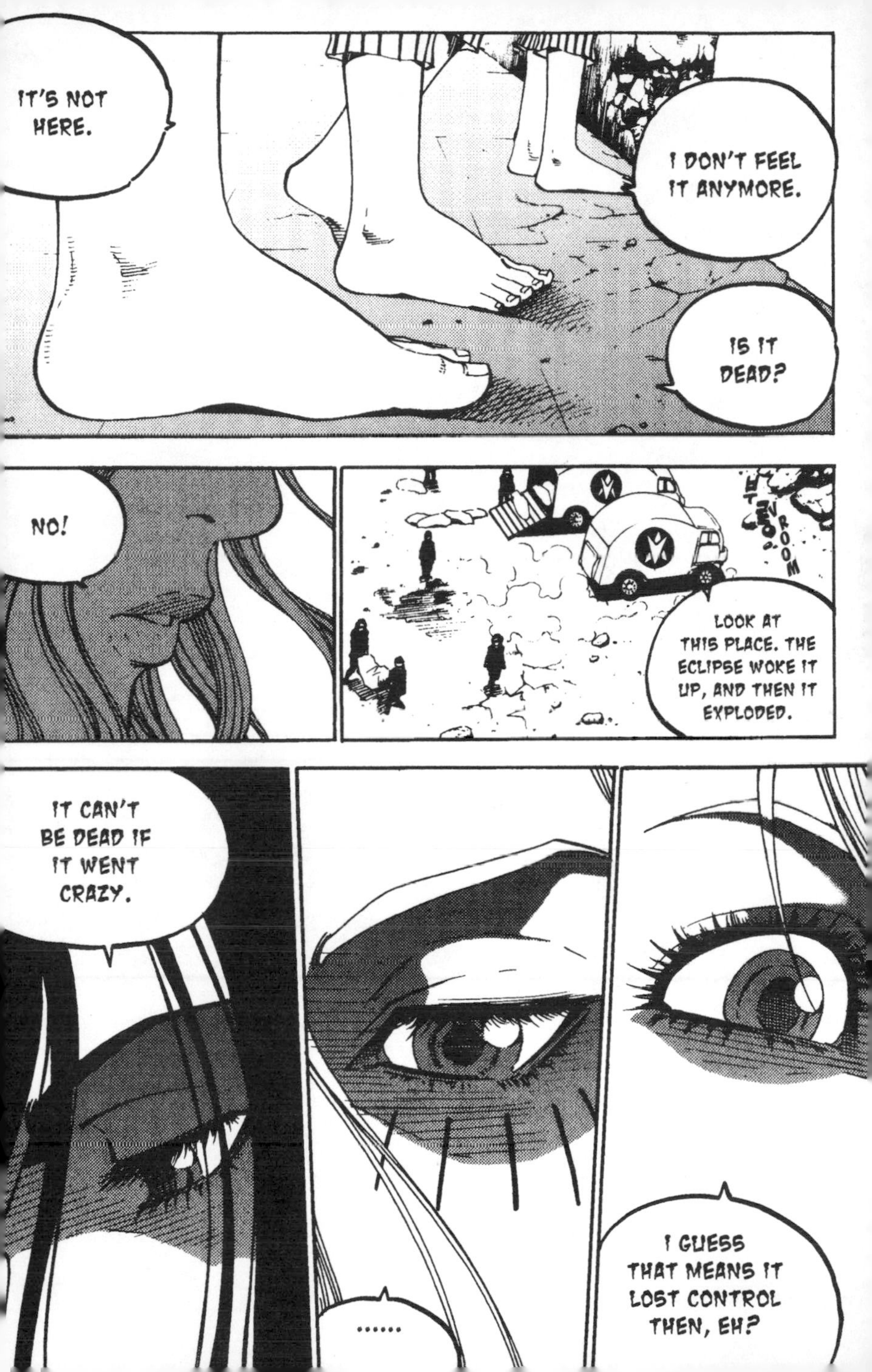
IT'S NOT HERE.
I DON'T FEEL IT ANYMORE.
IS IT DEAD?
NO!
VROOM
LOOK AT THIS PLACE. THE ECLIPSE WOKE IT UP, AND THEN IT EXPLODED.
IT CAN'T BE DEAD IF IT WENT CRAZY.
......
I GUESS THAT MEANS IT LOST CONTROL THEN, EH?

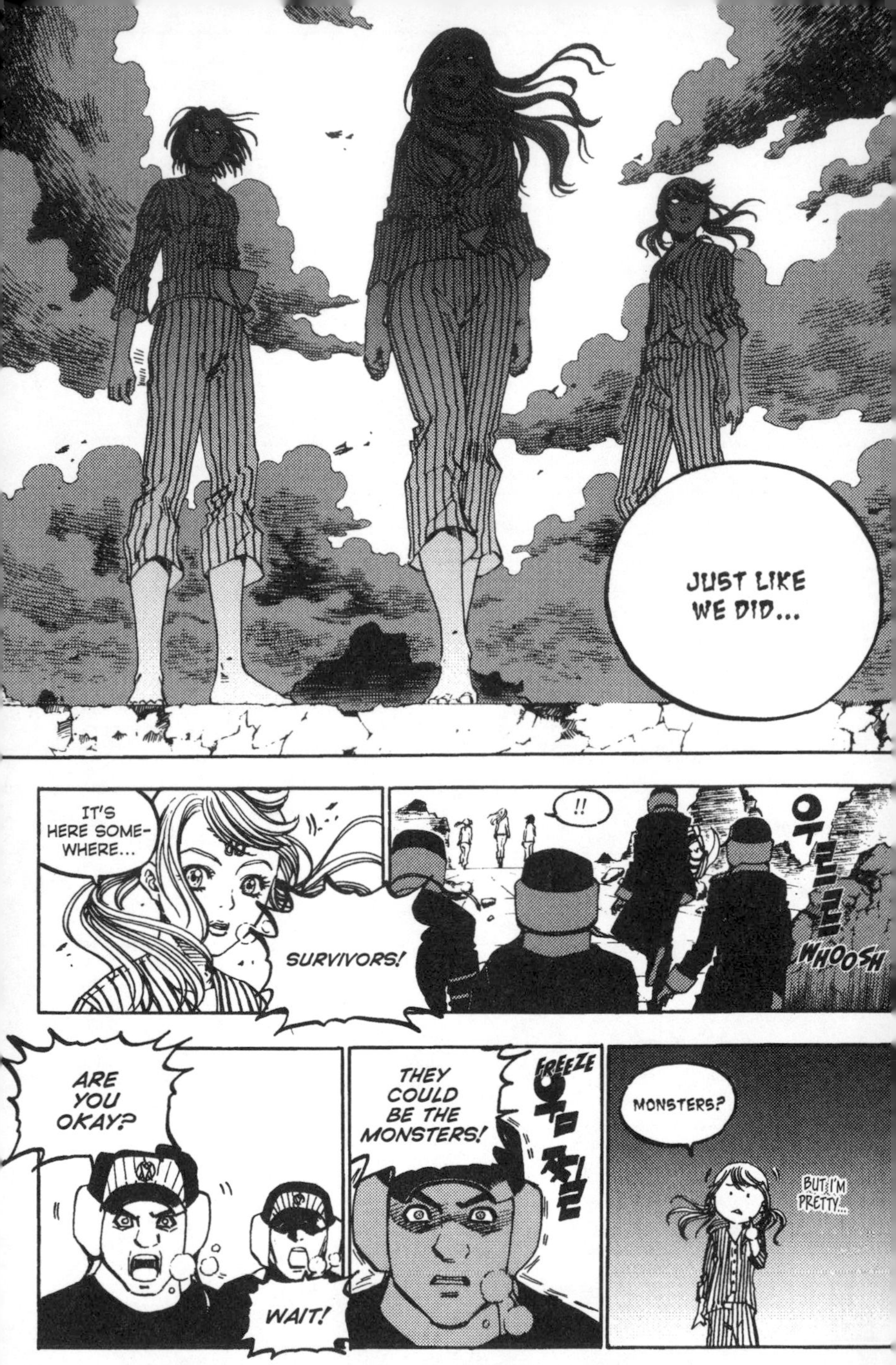
JUST LIKE WE DID...
IT'S HERE SOME-WHERE...
SURVIVORS!
!!
우르르
WHOOSH
ARE YOU OKAY?
WAIT!
THEY COULD BE THE MONSTERS!
FREEZE
움찔
MONSTERS?
BUT I'M PRETTY...

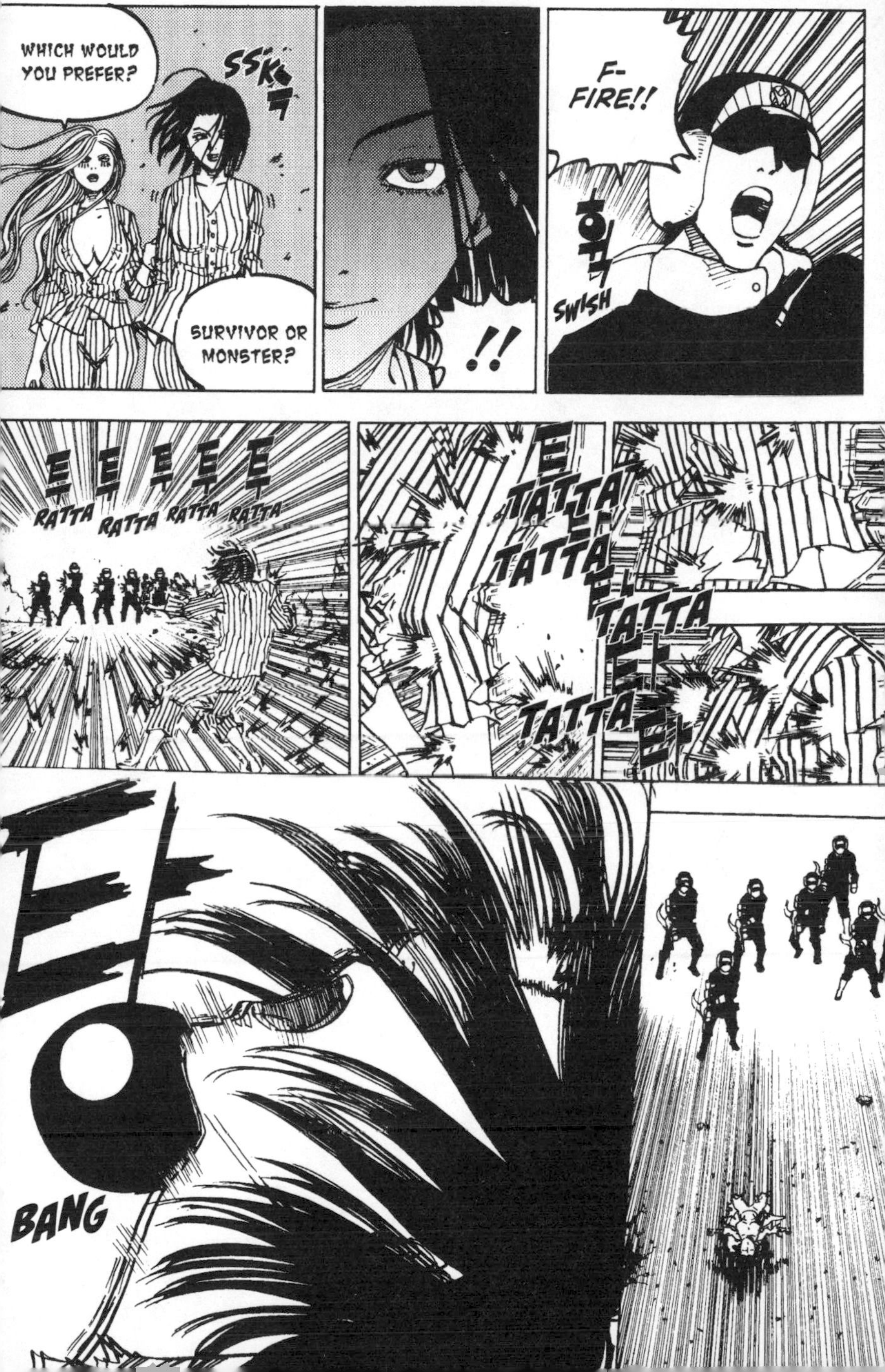
WHICH WOULD YOU PREFER?
SSK
SURVIVOR OR MONSTER?
!!
F- FIRE!!
SWISH
RATTA RATTA RATTA RATTA
TATTA TATTA TATTA TATTA
BANG

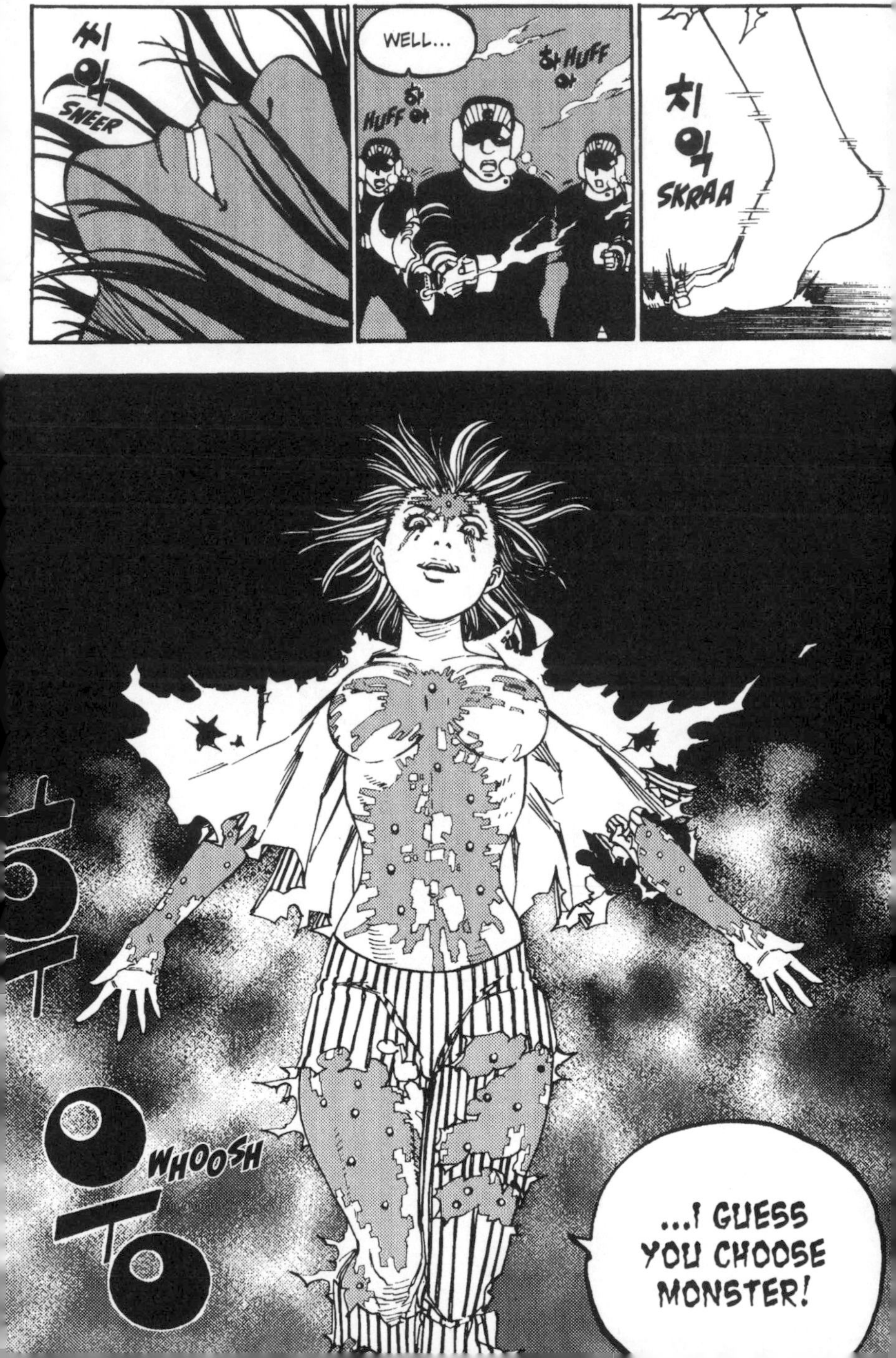

씨익
SNEER
WELL...
하 HUFF 아
하 HUFF 아
치익
SKRAA
WHOOSH
...I GUESS YOU CHOOSE MONSTER!

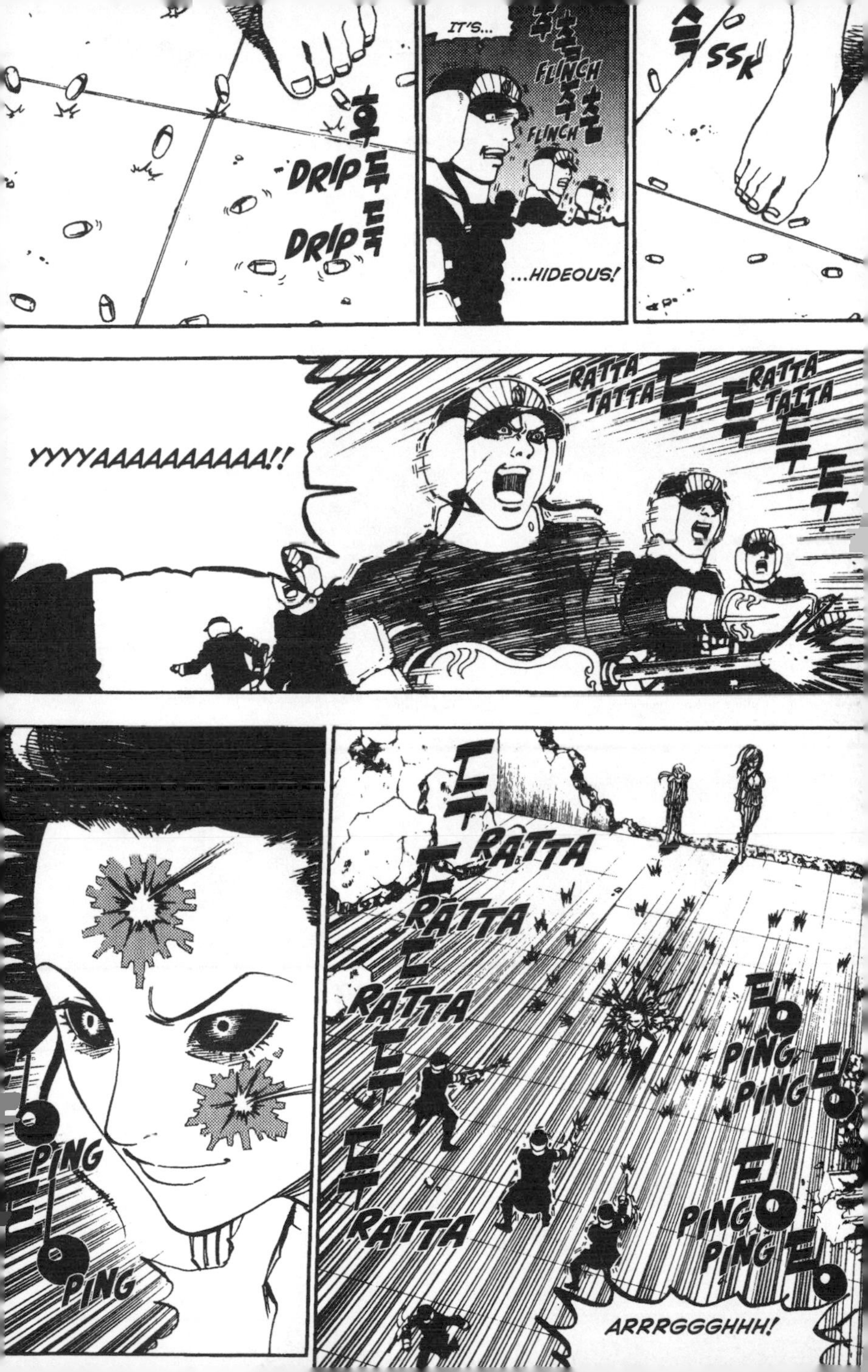
DRIP
DRIP
IT'S...
FLINCH
FLINCH
...HIDEOUS!
SSK
YYYYAAAAAAAAAA!!
RATTA TATTA
RATTA TATTA
PING
PING
RATTA
RATTA
RATTA
RATTA
PING
PING
PING
PING
ARRRGGGHHH!

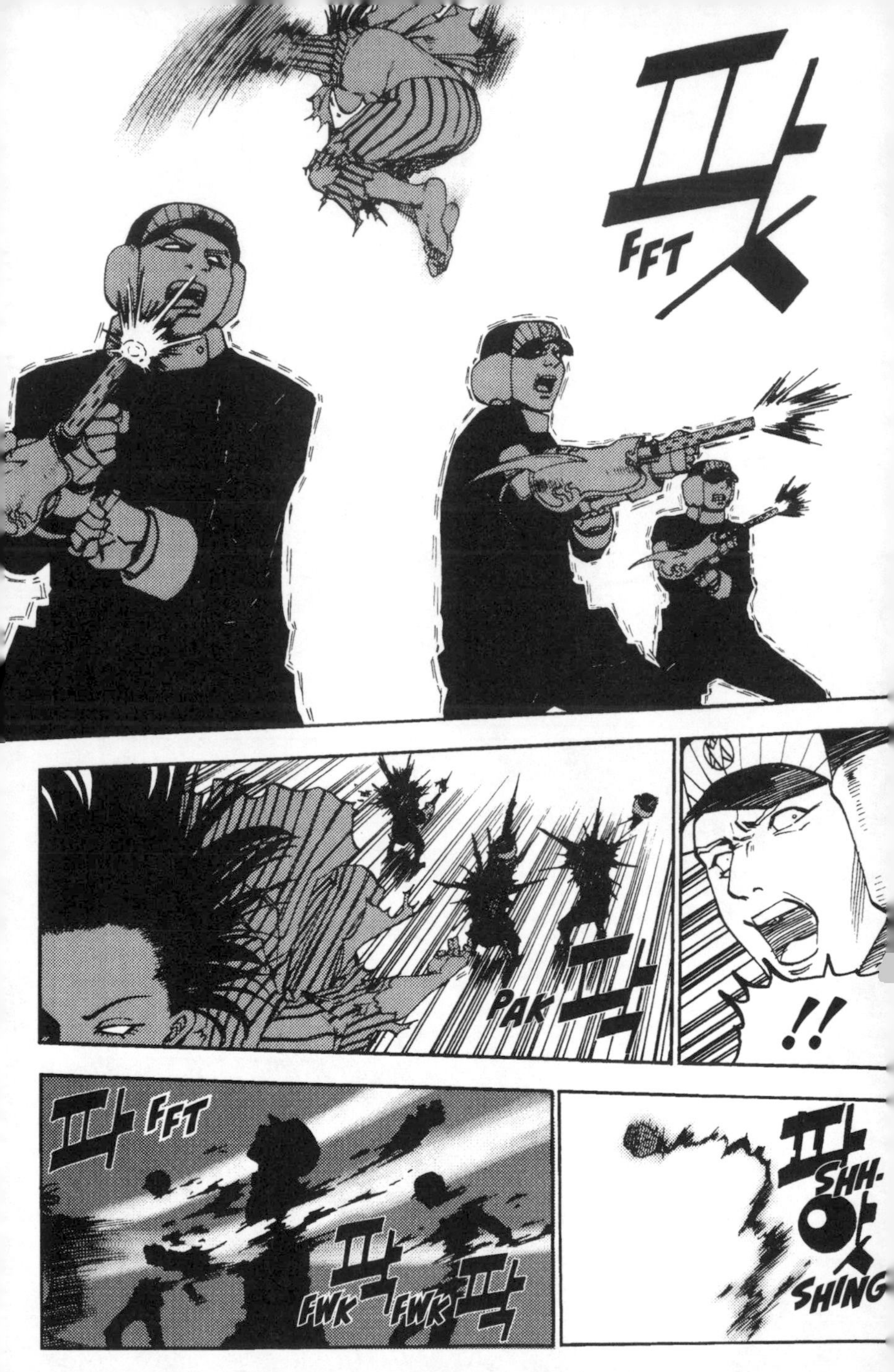
팟
FFT
PAK
팍
!!
파
FFT
퍽
FWK
FWK
퍽
파
SHH-
앗
SHING

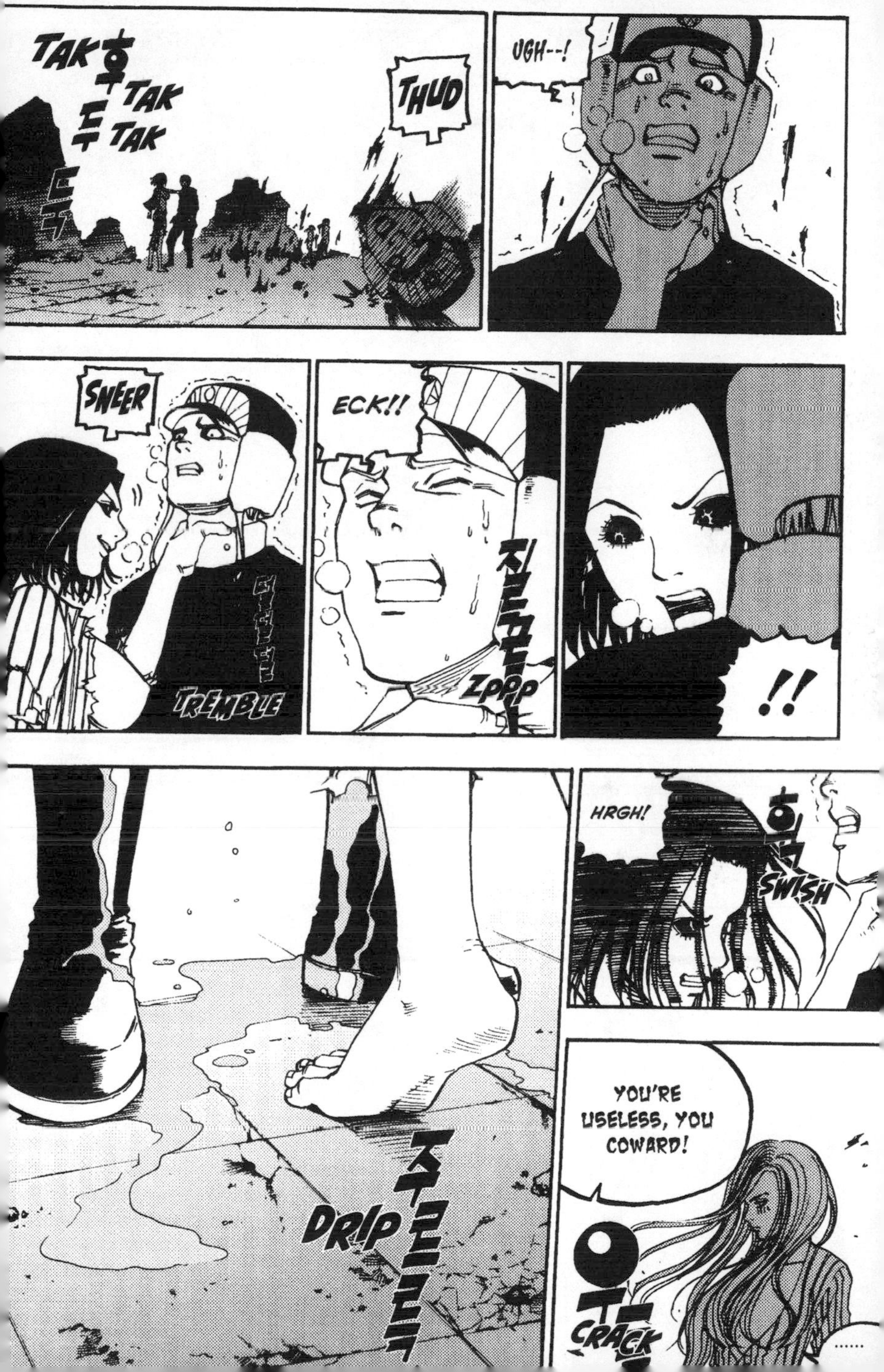

TAK TAK TAK TAK
THUD
UGH--!
SNEER
TREMBLE
ECK!!
ZPPP
!!
DRIP
HRGH!
SWISH
YOU'RE USELESS, YOU COWARD!
CRACK
......

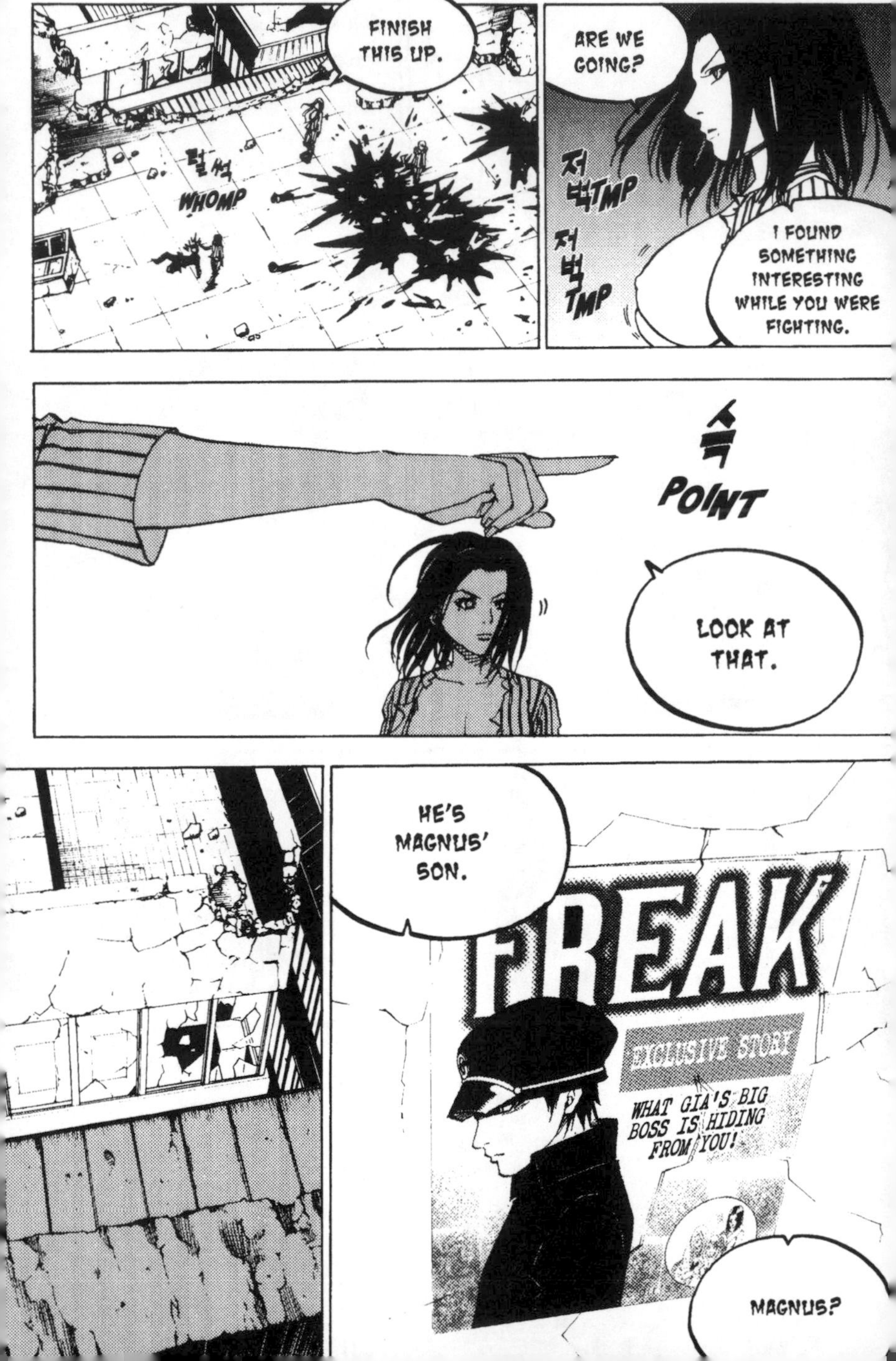
FINISH THIS UP.
털썩
WHOMP
ARE WE GOING?
저벅
TMP
저벅
TMP
I FOUND SOMETHING INTERESTING WHILE YOU WERE FIGHTING.
슥
POINT
LOOK AT THAT.
HE'S MAGNUS' SON.
FREAK
EXCLUSIVE STORY
WHAT GIA'S BIG BOSS IS HIDING FROM YOU!
MAGNUS?

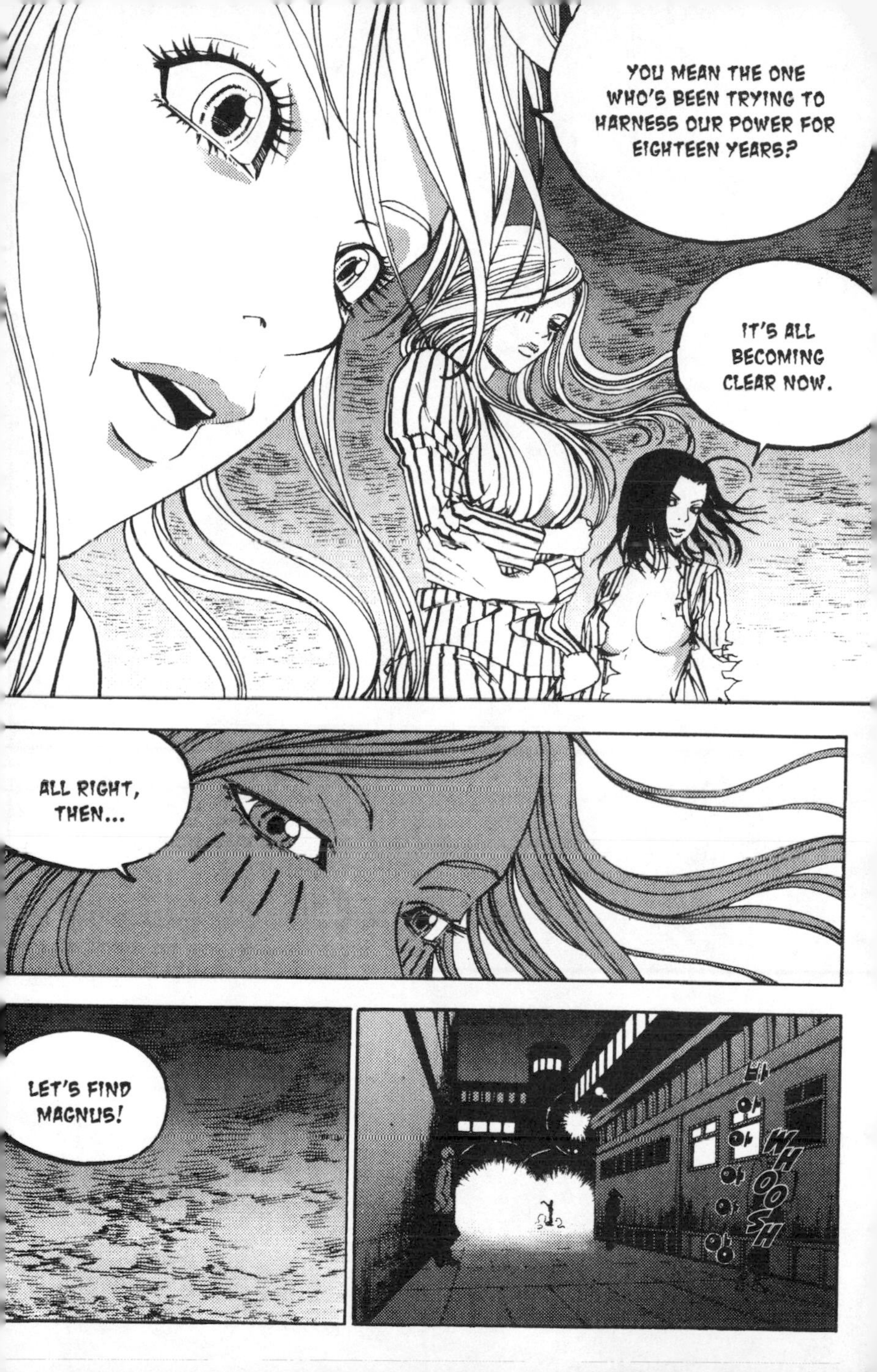
YOU MEAN THE ONE WHO'S BEEN TRYING TO HARNESS OUR POWER FOR EIGHTEEN YEARS?
IT'S ALL BECOMING CLEAR NOW.
ALL RIGHT, THEN...
LET'S FIND MAGNUS!
WHOOOSH

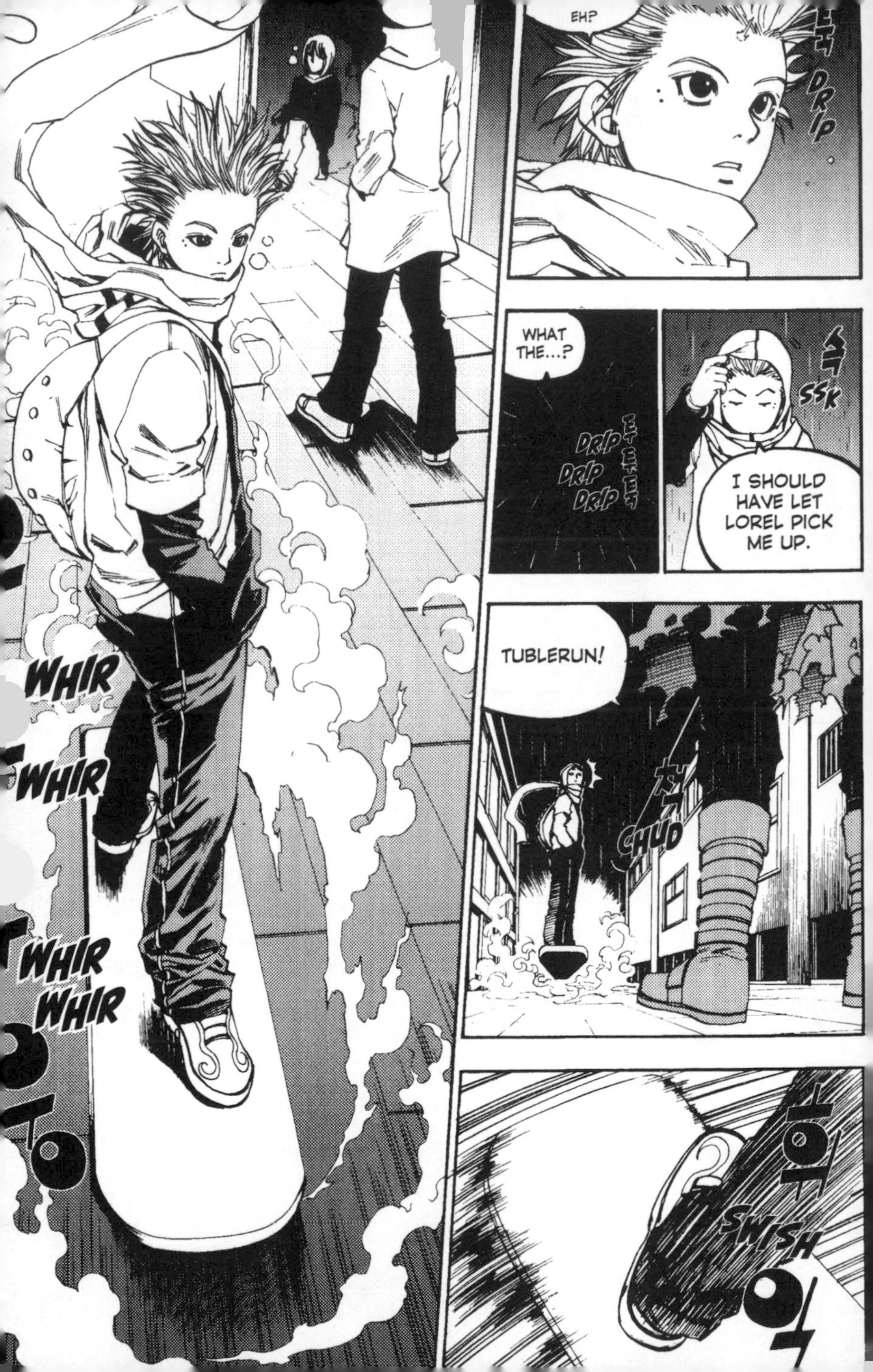
WHIR
WHIR
WHIR
WHIR
EH?
DRIP
WHAT THE...?
DRIP
DRIP
DRIP
SSK
I SHOULD HAVE LET LOREL PICK ME UP.
TUBLERUN!
CHUD
SWISH

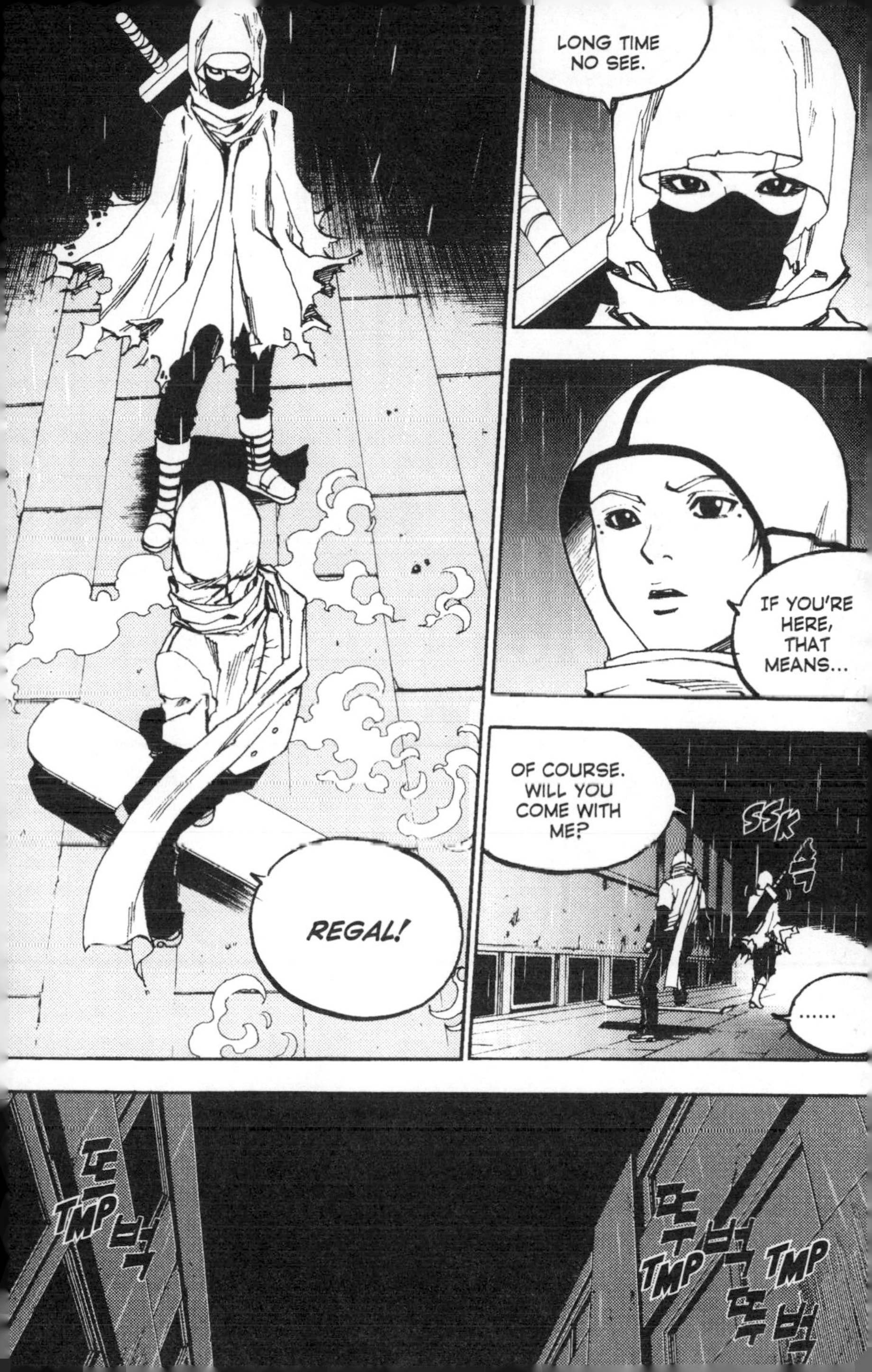
REGAL!
LONG TIME NO SEE.
IF YOU'RE HERE, THAT MEANS...
OF COURSE. WILL YOU COME WITH ME?
SSK
슥
......
TMP
뚜벅
TMP
뚜벅
TMP
뚜벅

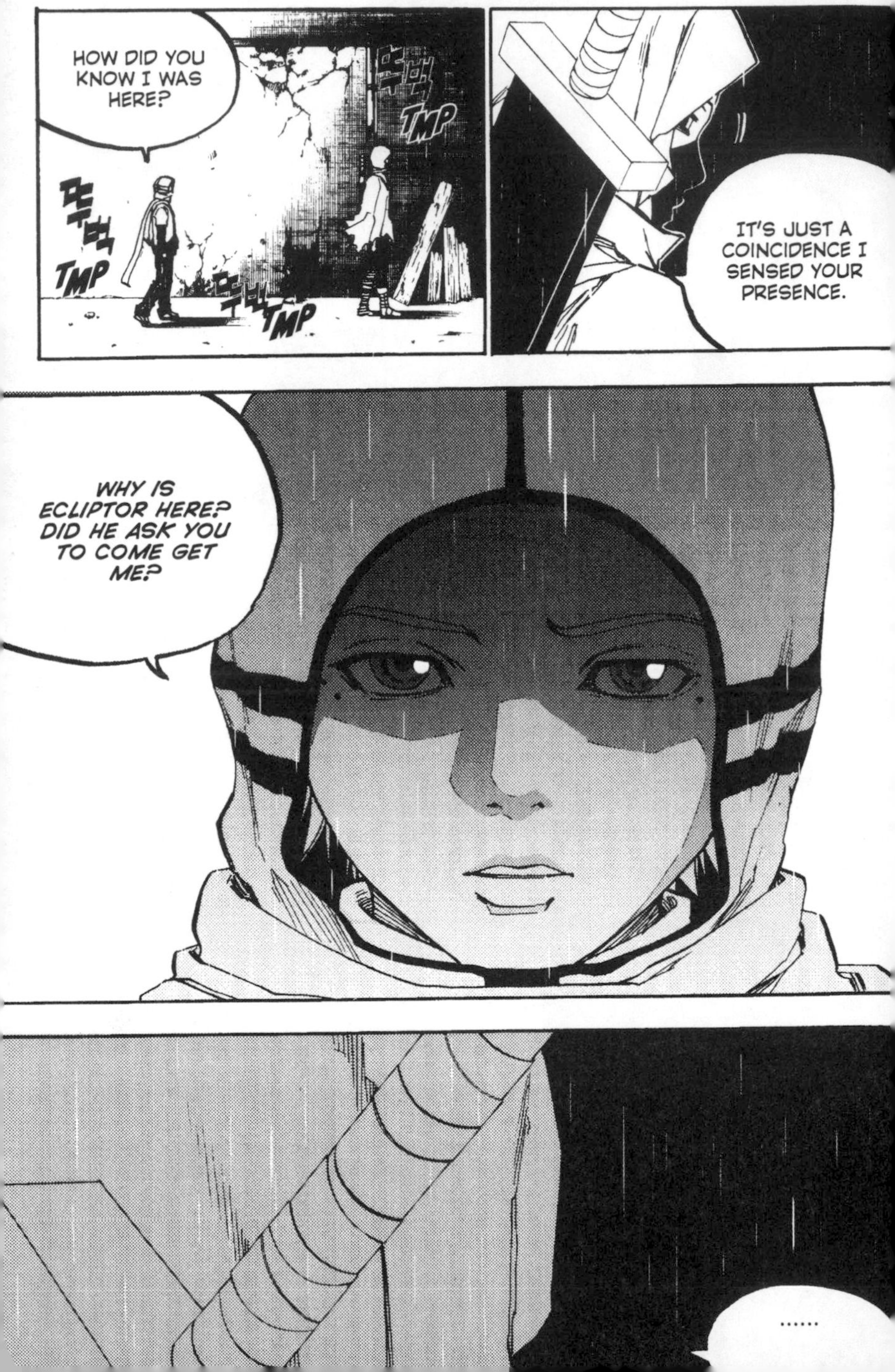

HOW DID YOU KNOW I WAS HERE?
TMP
TMP
TMP
IT'S JUST A COINCIDENCE I SENSED YOUR PRESENCE.
*WHY IS ECLIPTOR HERE? DID HE ASK YOU TO COME GET ME?*
......

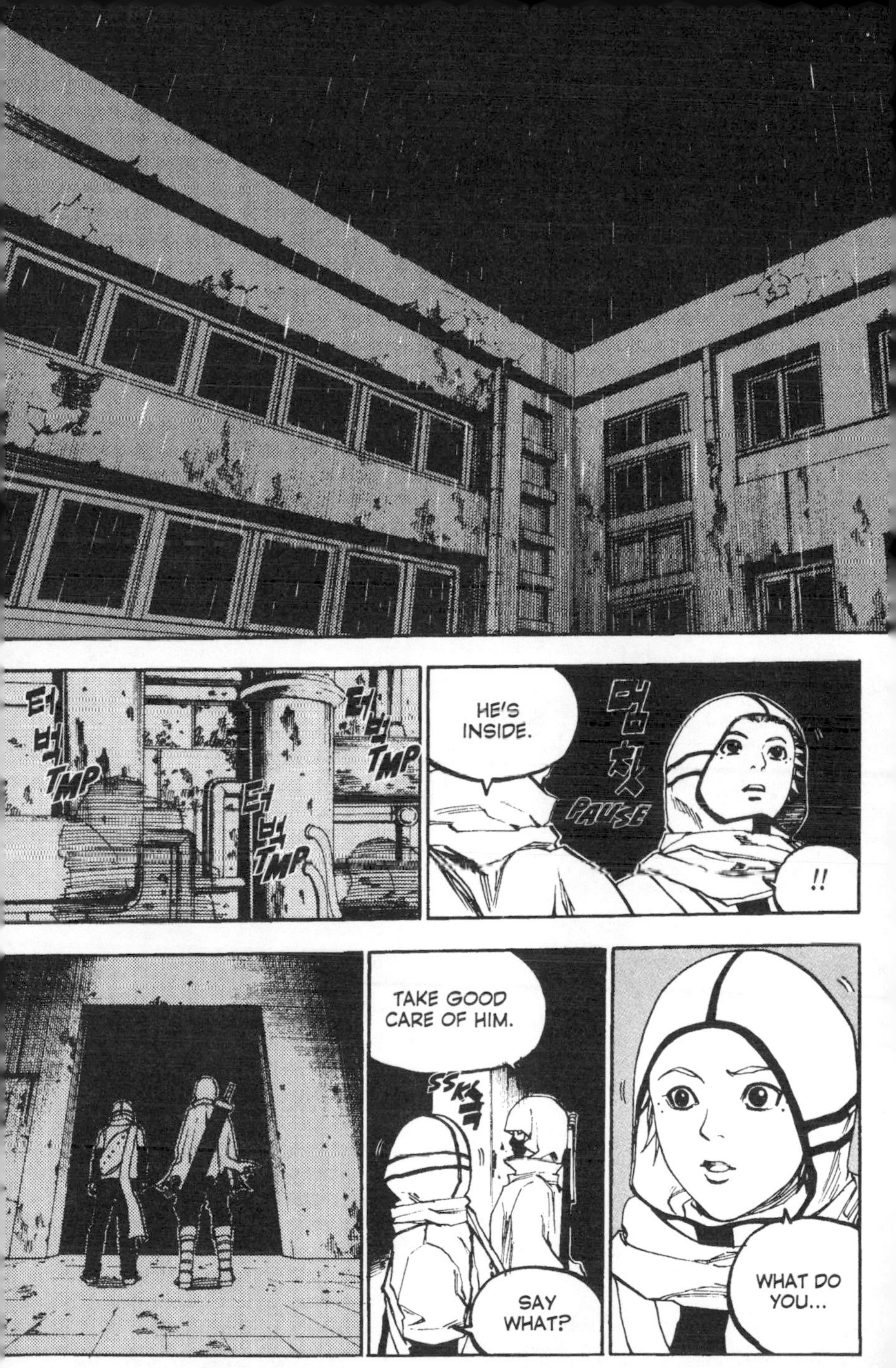

터벅
TMP
터벅
TMP
터벅
TMP
HE'S INSIDE.
멈칫
PAUSE
!!
TAKE GOOD CARE OF HIM.
SSK
슥
SAY WHAT?
WHAT DO YOU...

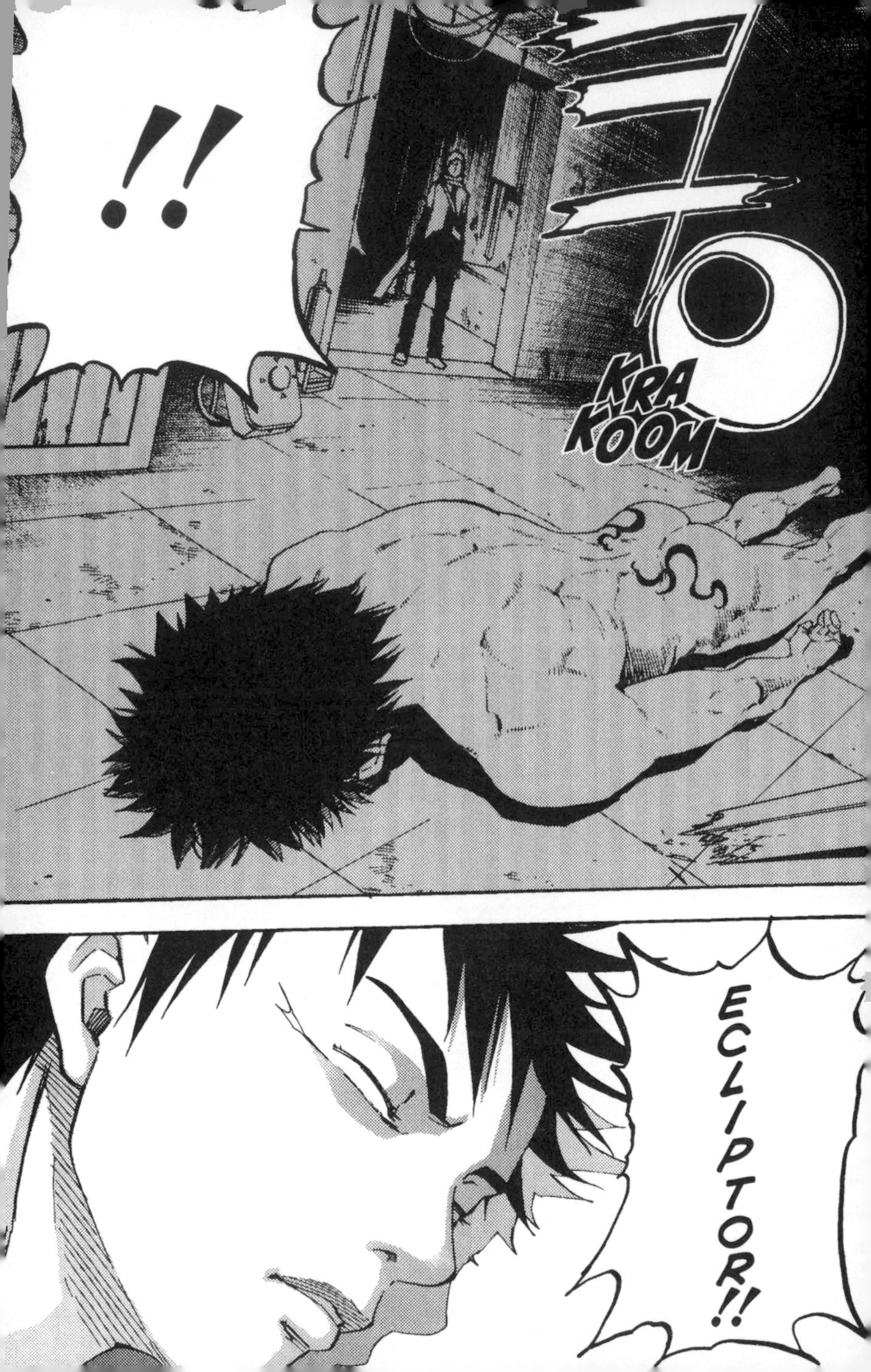
!!
KRA KOOM
ECLIPTOR!!

# CAR 13. THE SECOND STAGE OF THE END

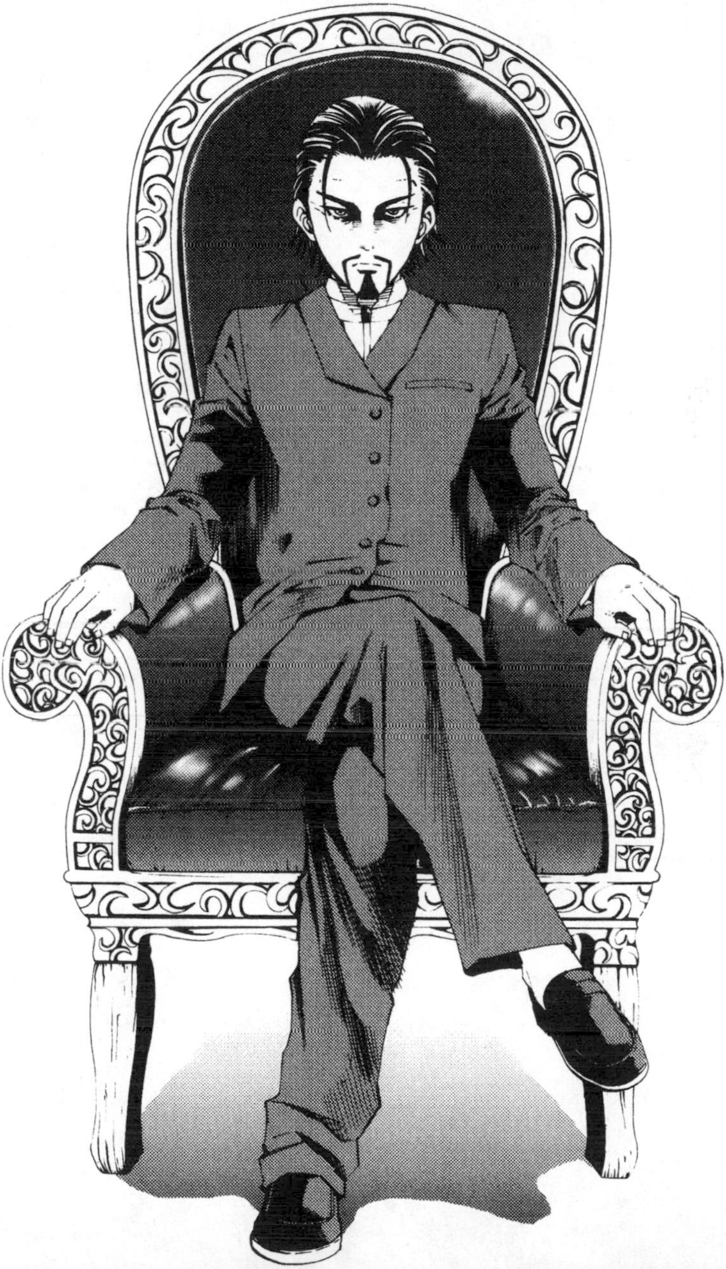

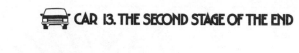

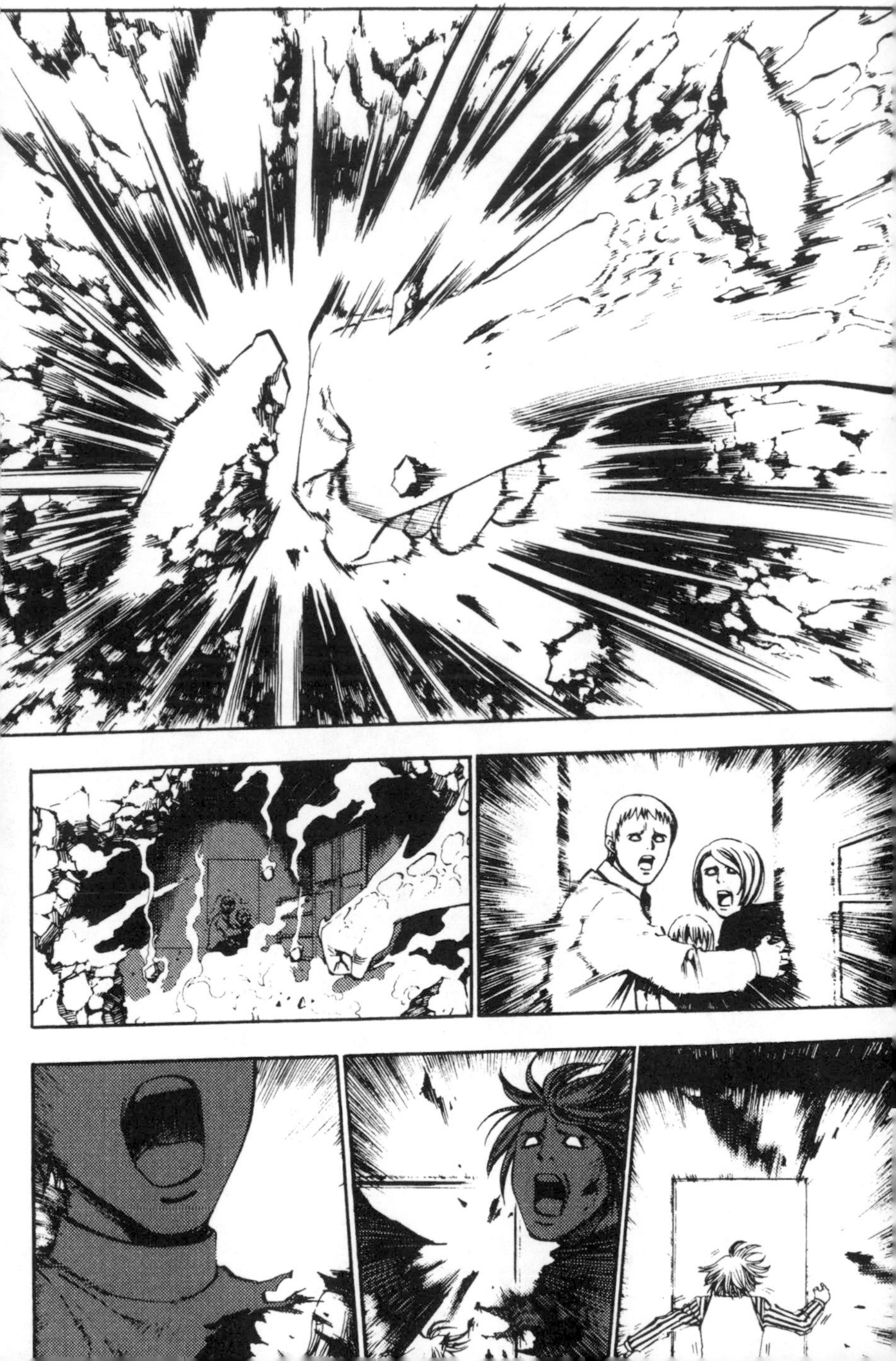

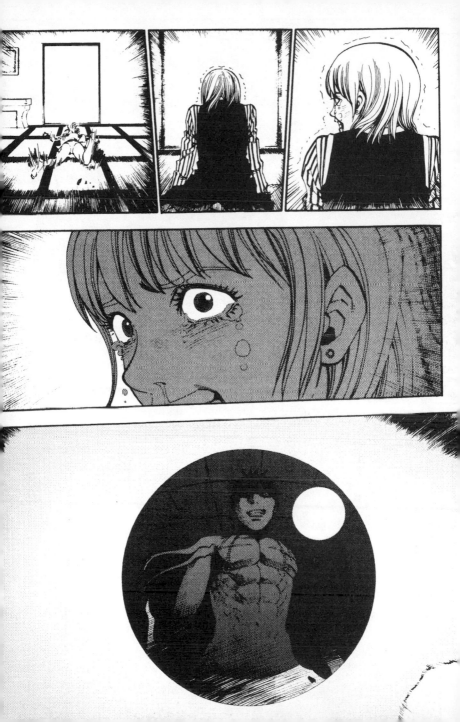

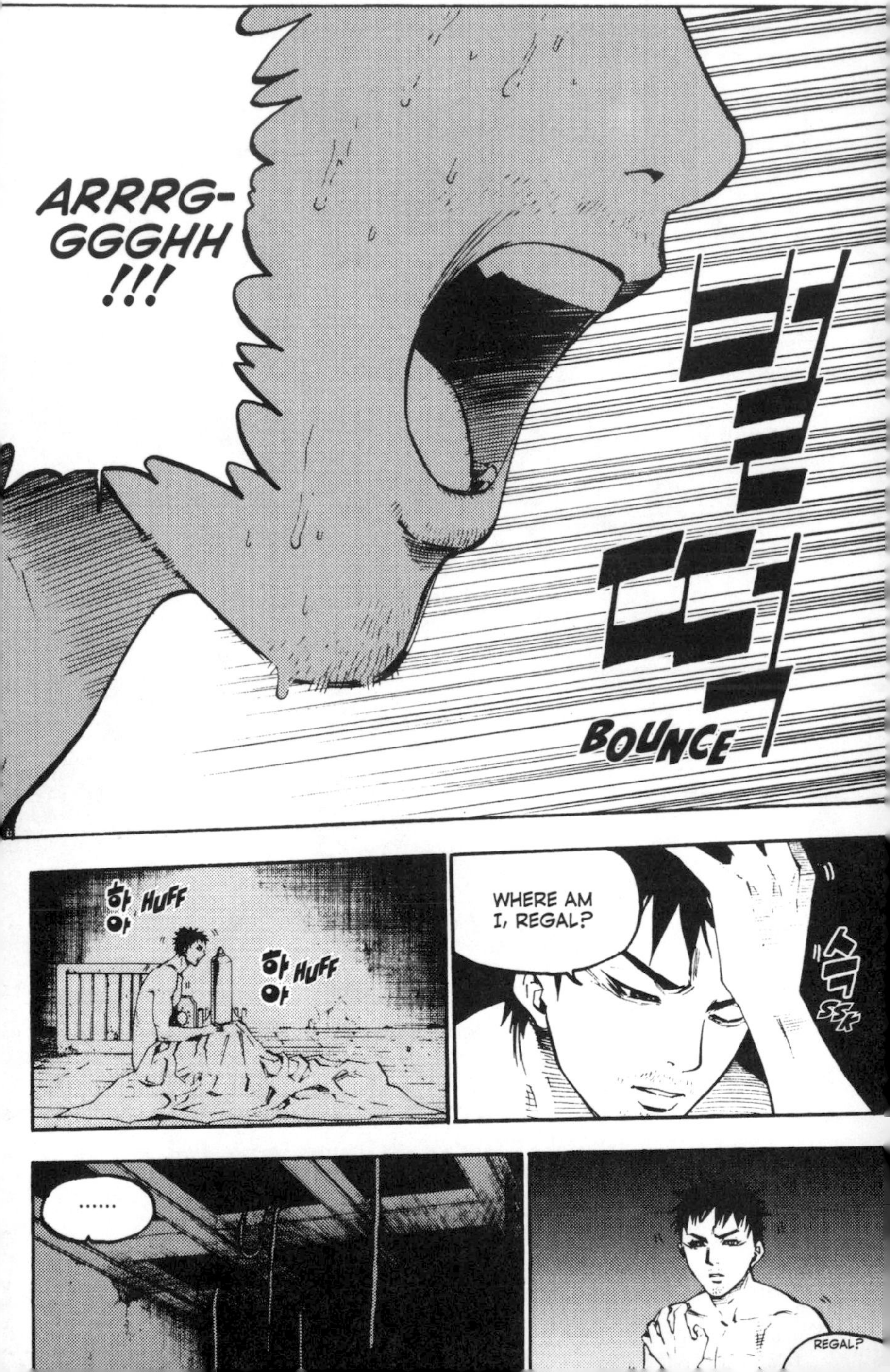
ARRRG-GGGHH !!!
벌떡
BOUNCE
하아 HUFF
하아 HUFF
WHERE AM I, REGAL?
슥 SSK
......
REGAL?

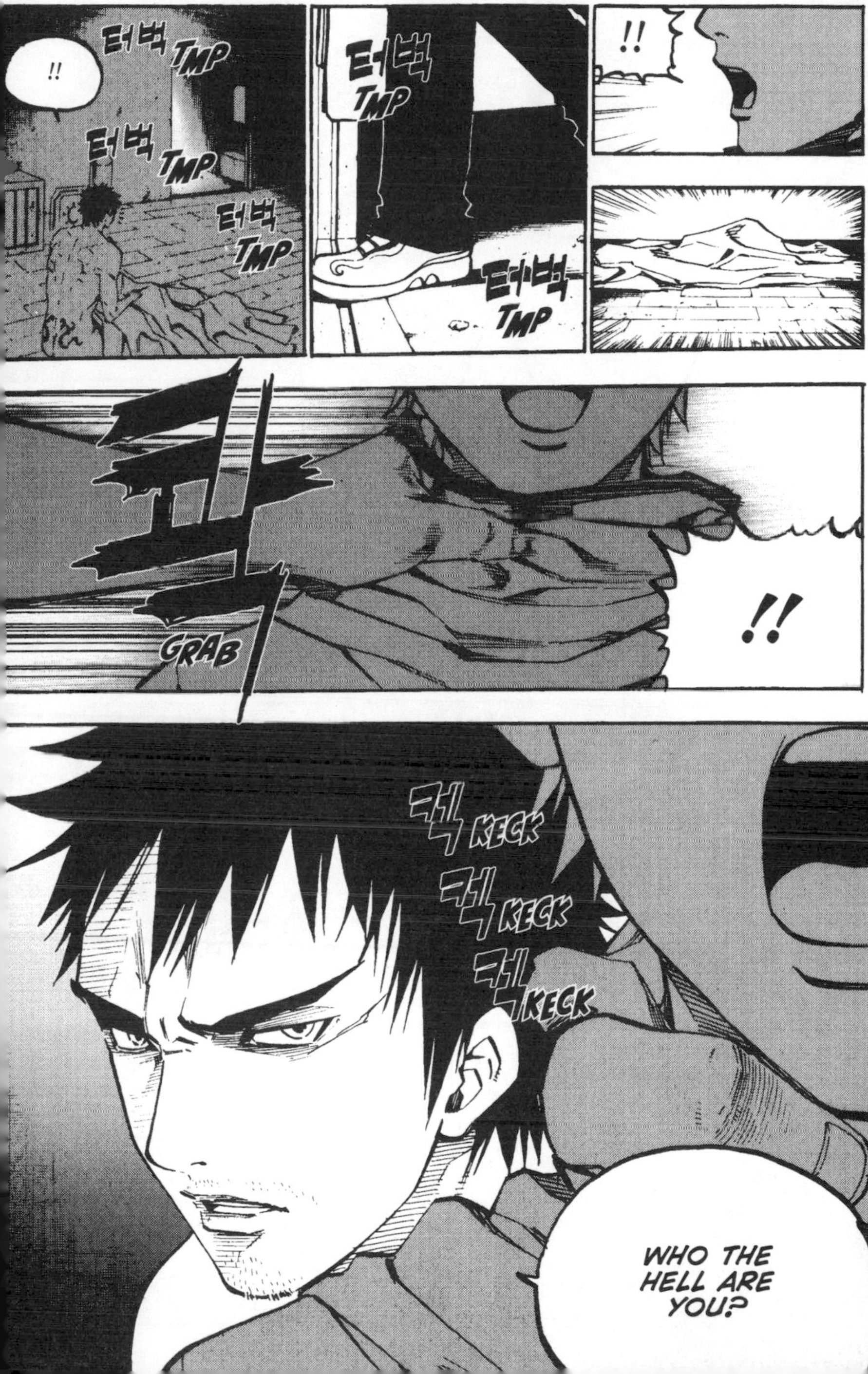
!!
터벅 TMP
터벅 TMP
터벅 TMP
터벅 TMP
터벅 TMP
!!
콱 GRAB
!!
켁 KECK
켁 KECK
켁 KECK
WHO THE HELL ARE YOU?

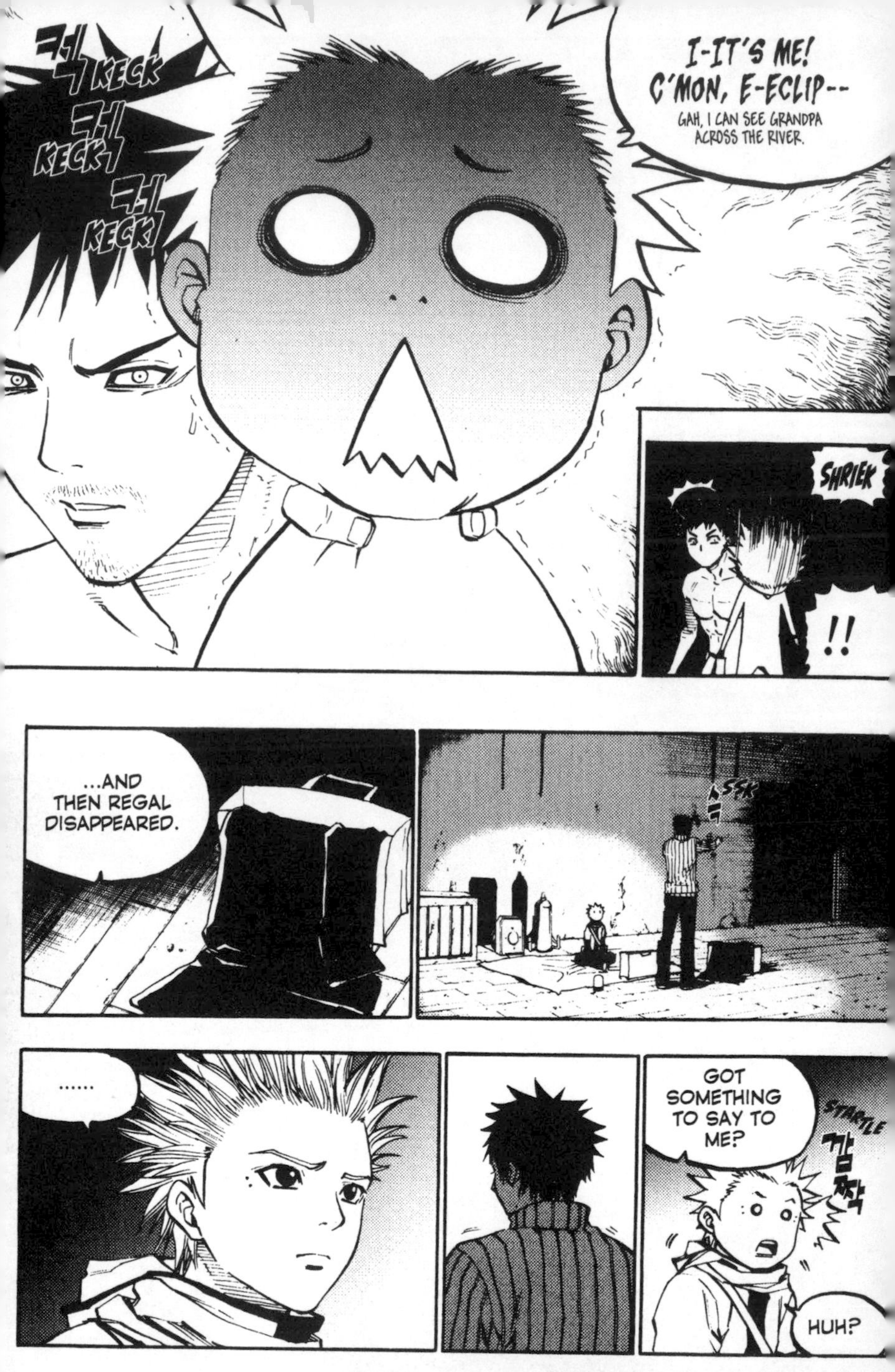

I-IT'S ME! C'MON, E-ECLIP--
GAH, I CAN SEE GRANDPA ACROSS THE RIVER.
켁 KECK
켁 KECK
켁 KECK
SHRIEK
!!
...AND THEN REGAL DISAPPEARED.
SSK
GOT SOMETHING TO SAY TO ME?
깜짝 STARTLE
HUH?
......

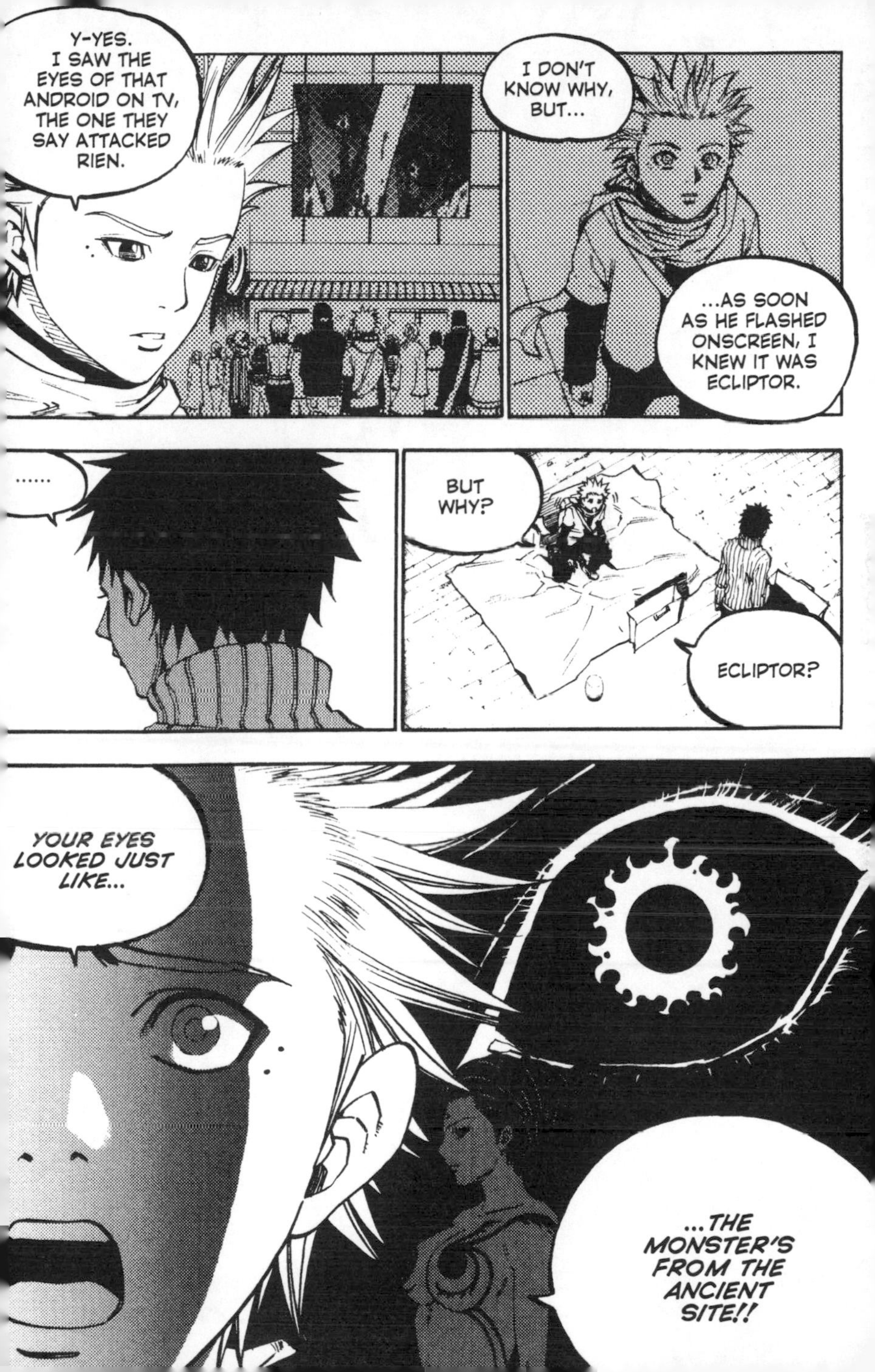
Y-YES. I SAW THE EYES OF THAT ANDROID ON TV, THE ONE THEY SAY ATTACKED RIEN.
I DON'T KNOW WHY, BUT...
...AS SOON AS HE FLASHED ONSCREEN, I KNEW IT WAS ECLIPTOR.
......
BUT WHY?
ECLIPTOR?
YOUR EYES LOOKED JUST LIKE...
...THE MONSTER'S FROM THE ANCIENT SITE!!

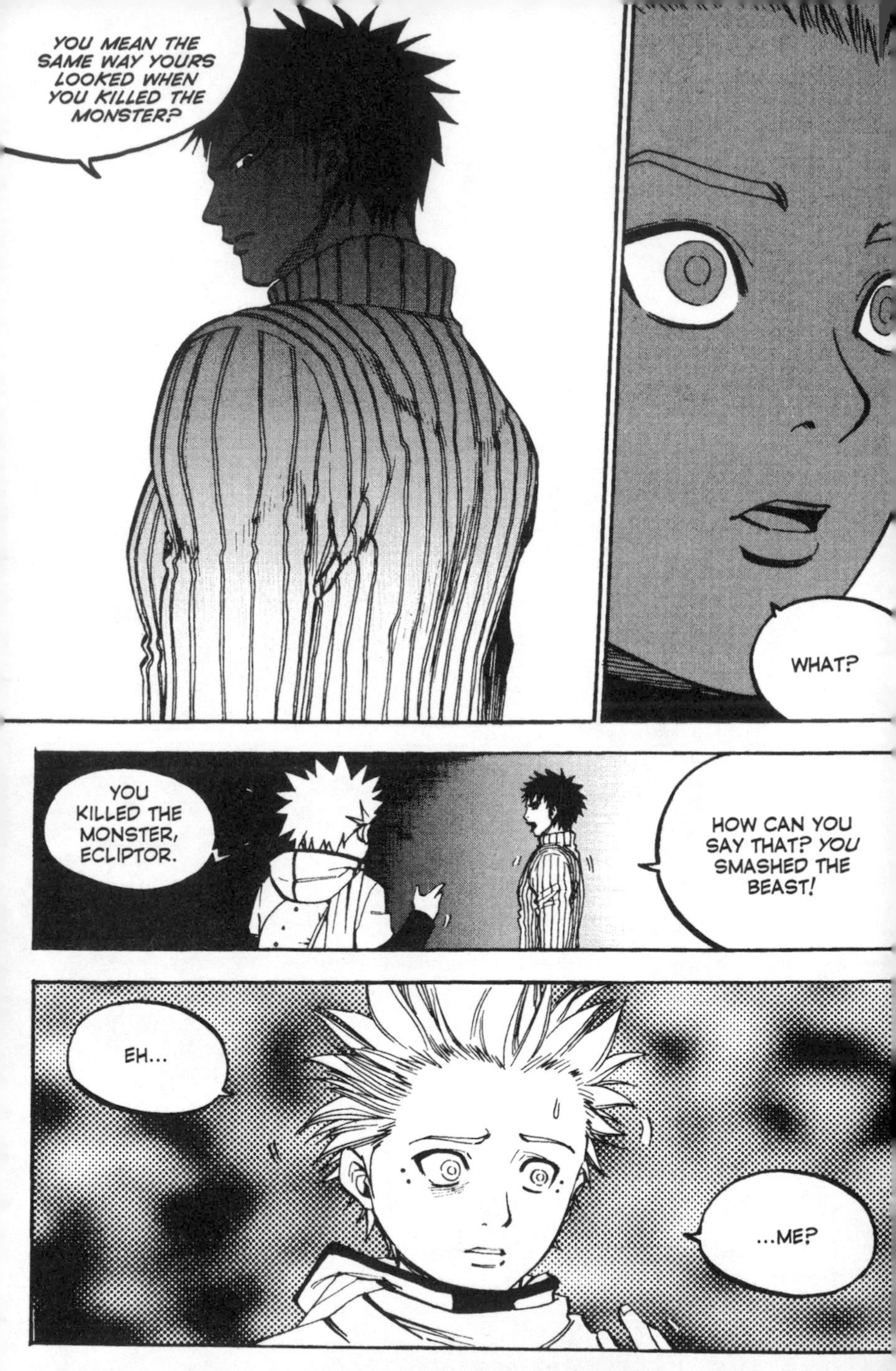
YOU MEAN THE SAME WAY YOURS LOOKED WHEN YOU KILLED THE MONSTER?
WHAT?
YOU KILLED THE MONSTER, ECLIPTOR.
HOW CAN YOU SAY THAT? YOU SMASHED THE BEAST!
EH...
...ME?

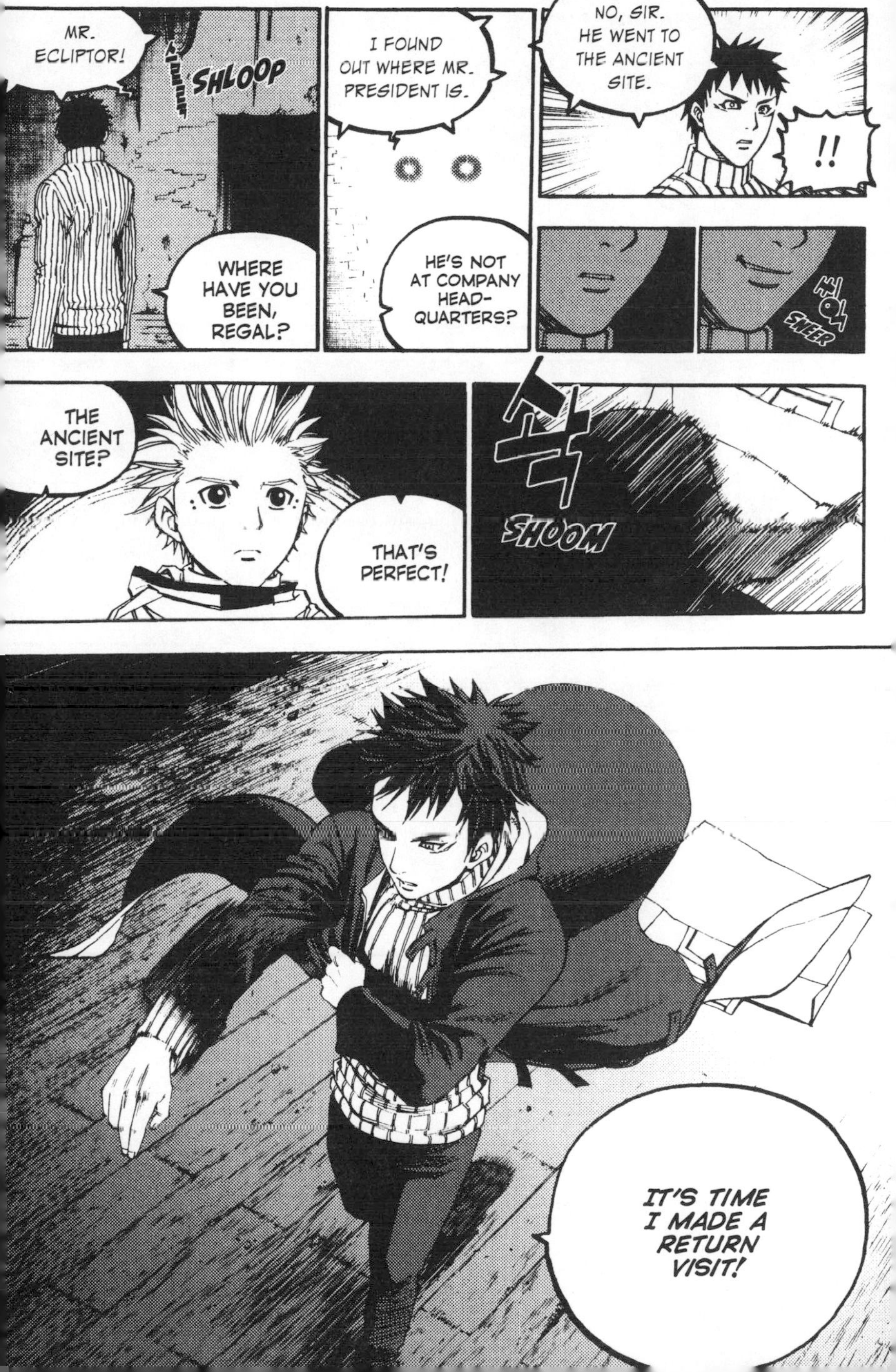
MR. ECLIPTOR!
SHLOOP
WHERE HAVE YOU BEEN, REGAL?
I FOUND OUT WHERE MR. PRESIDENT IS.
HE'S NOT AT COMPANY HEAD-QUARTERS?
NO, SIR. HE WENT TO THE ANCIENT SITE.
!!
SNEER
THE ANCIENT SITE?
THAT'S PERFECT!
SHOOM
IT'S TIME I MADE A RETURN VISIT!

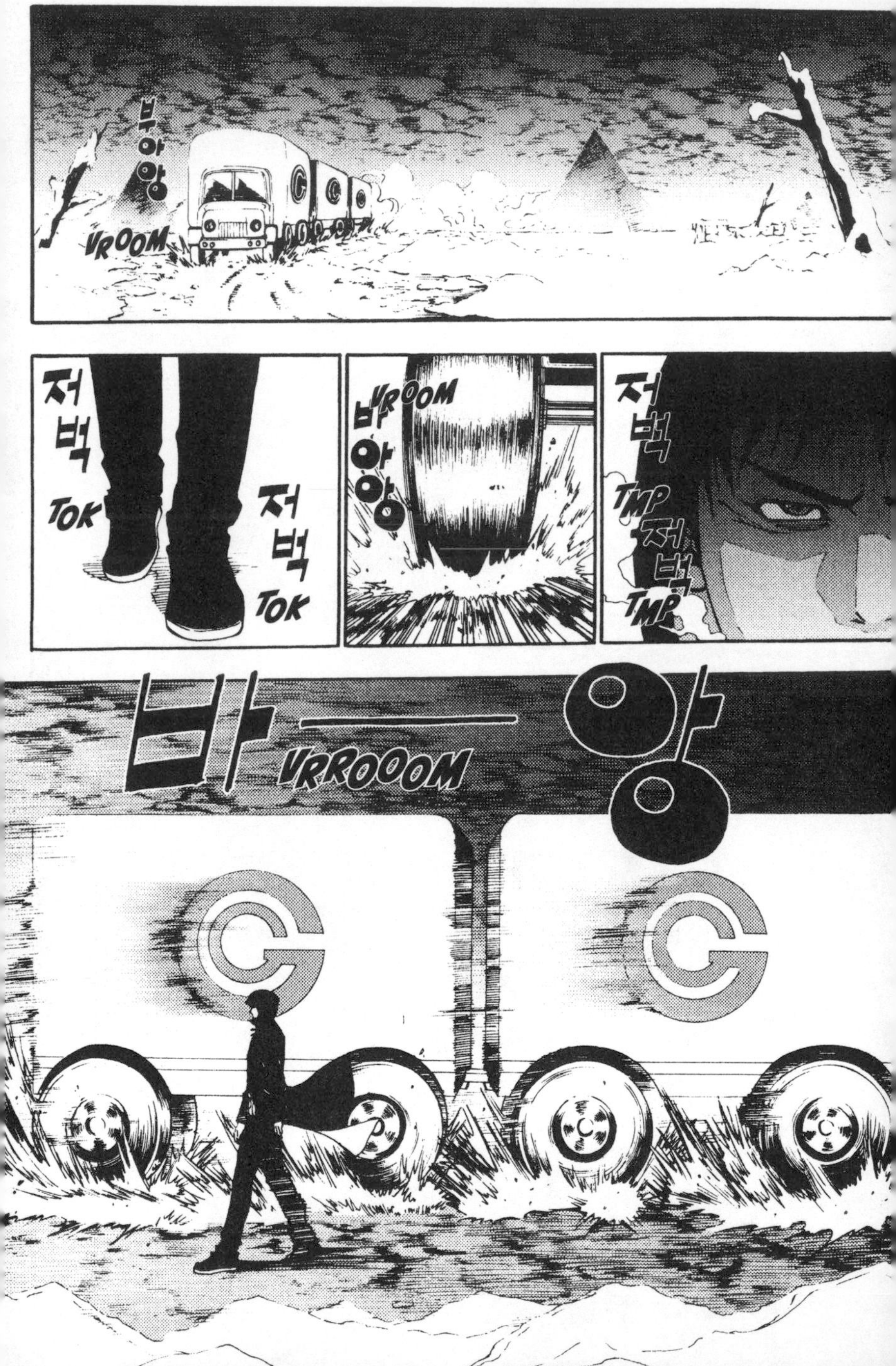
부아앙
VROOM
저벅
TOK
저벅
TOK
바아앙
VROOM
저벅
TMP
저벅
TMP
바—앙
VRROOOM

AH-CHOO!
WOW, WHAT A BIG TRUCK! DID IT COME FROM THE SITE?
SNUFF
......
WHY ARE YOU FOLLOWING ME?
YOU THINK I WAS JUST GONNA STAY HOME?
I NEED TO KNOW...
...TO FILL IN THE GAPS IN MY MEMORY AND...
...REMEMBER WHAT I DID THERE.

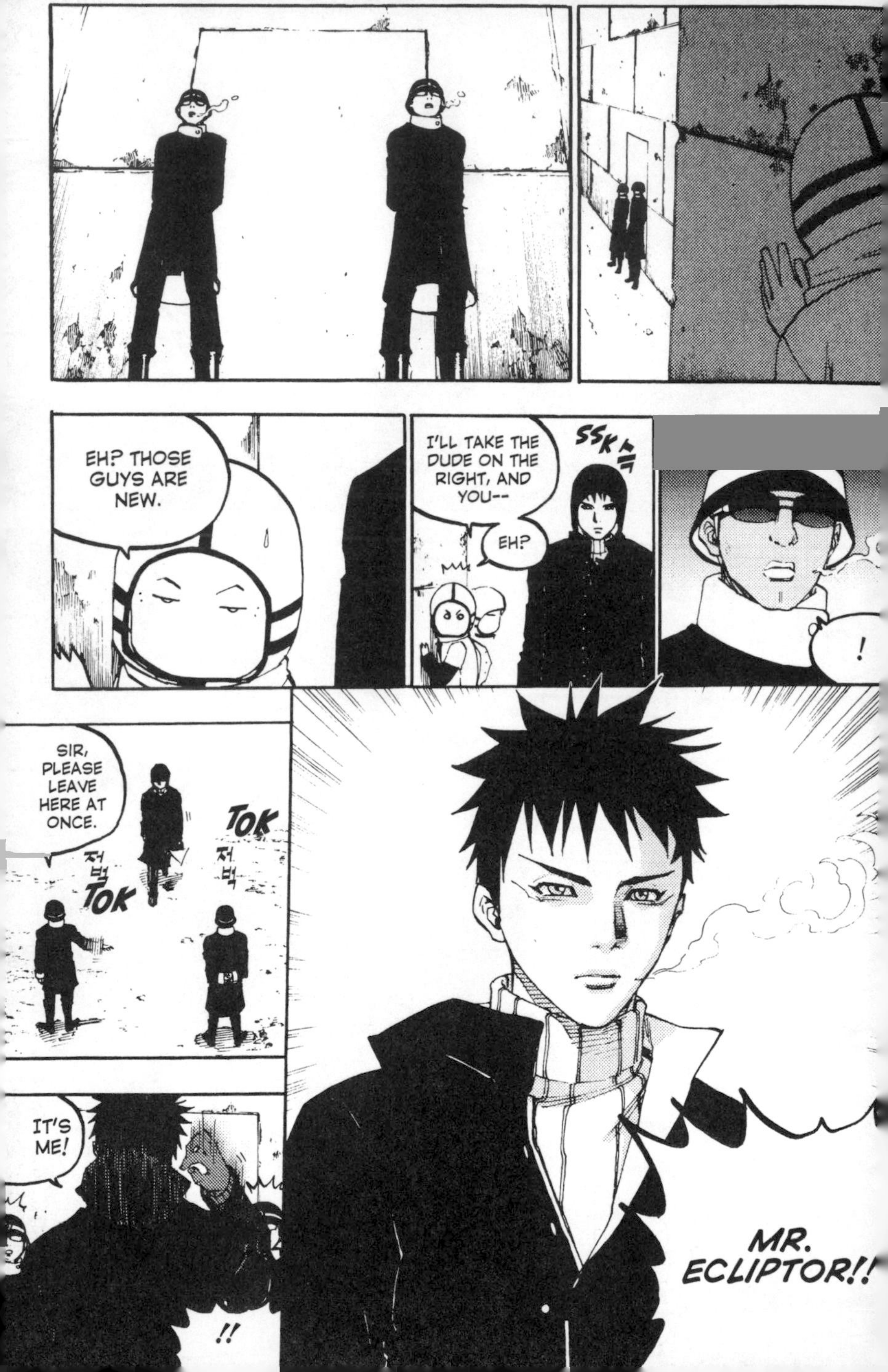
EH? THOSE GUYS ARE NEW.
I'LL TAKE THE DUDE ON THE RIGHT, AND YOU--
SSK
EH?
!
SIR, PLEASE LEAVE HERE AT ONCE.
TOK
저벅
TOK
저벅
IT'S ME!
!!
MR. ECLIPTOR!!

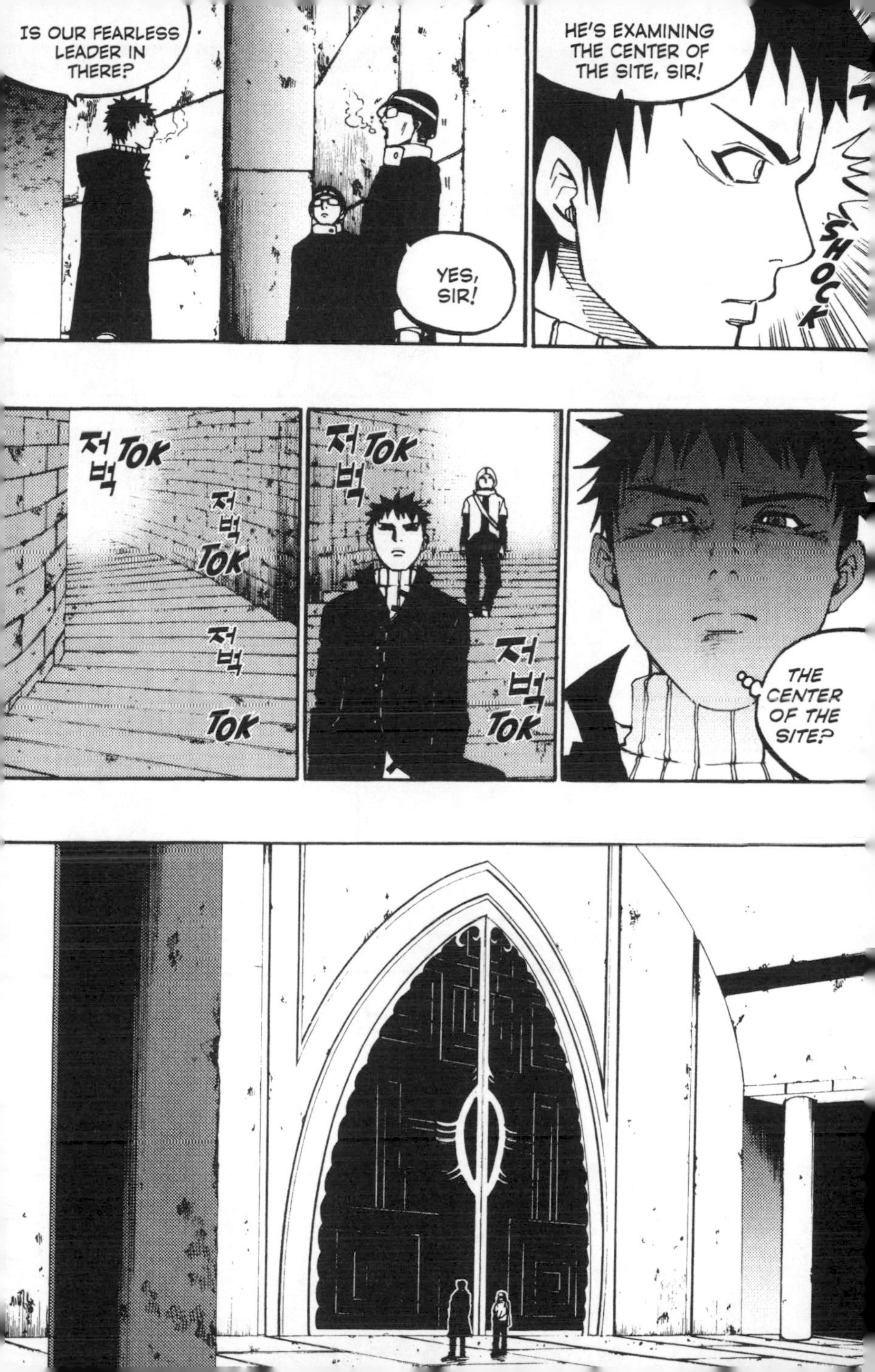
IS OUR FEARLESS LEADER IN THERE?
YES, SIR!
HE'S EXAMINING THE CENTER OF THE SITE, SIR!
SHOCK
저벅 TOK
저벅 TOK
저벅
TOK
저벅 TOK
저벅 TOK
THE CENTER OF THE SITE?

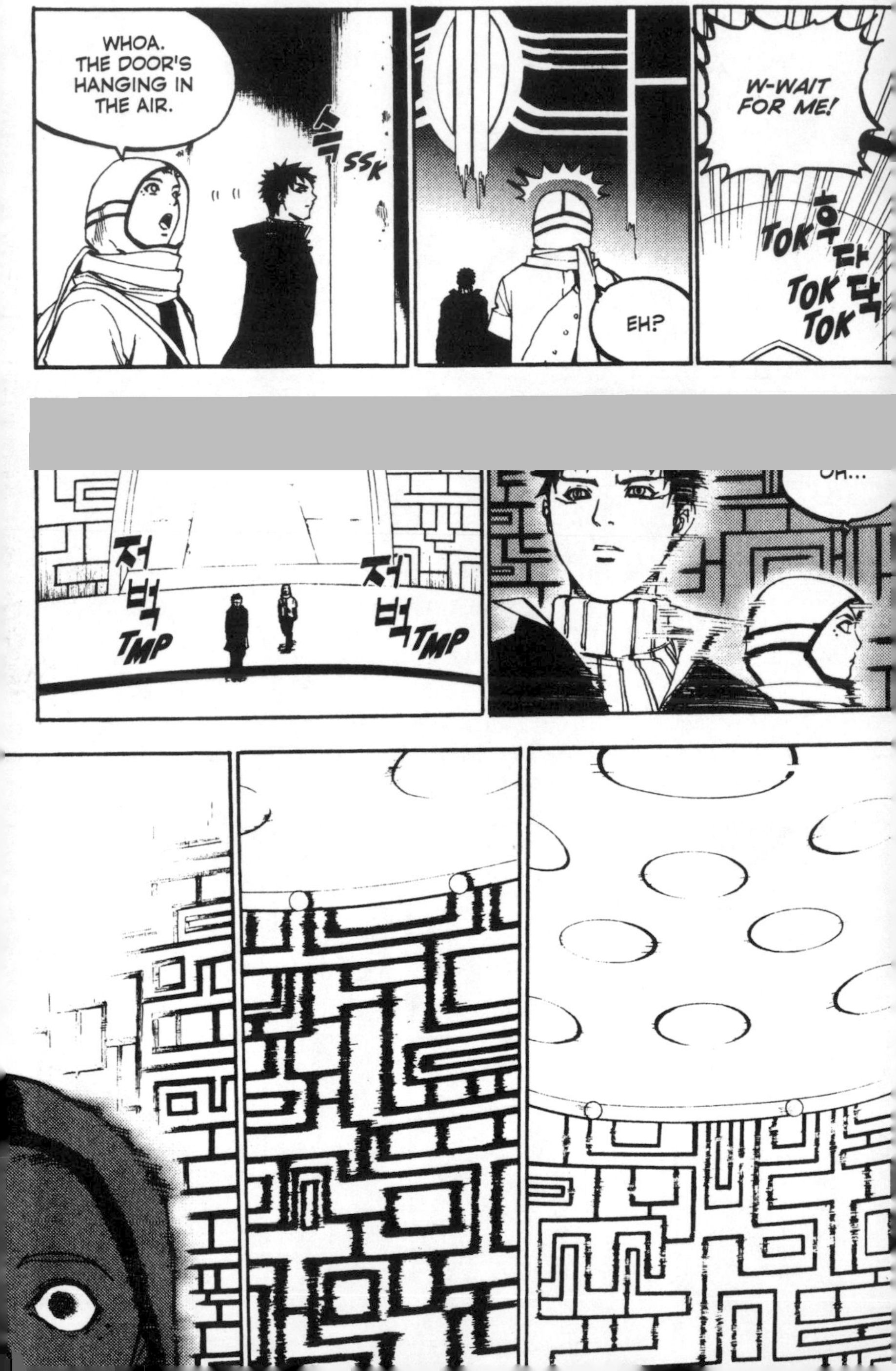
WHOA. THE DOOR'S HANGING IN THE AIR.
슥
SSK
EH?
W-WAIT FOR ME!
후다닥
TOK TOK TOK
저벅
TMP
저벅
TMP
UH...

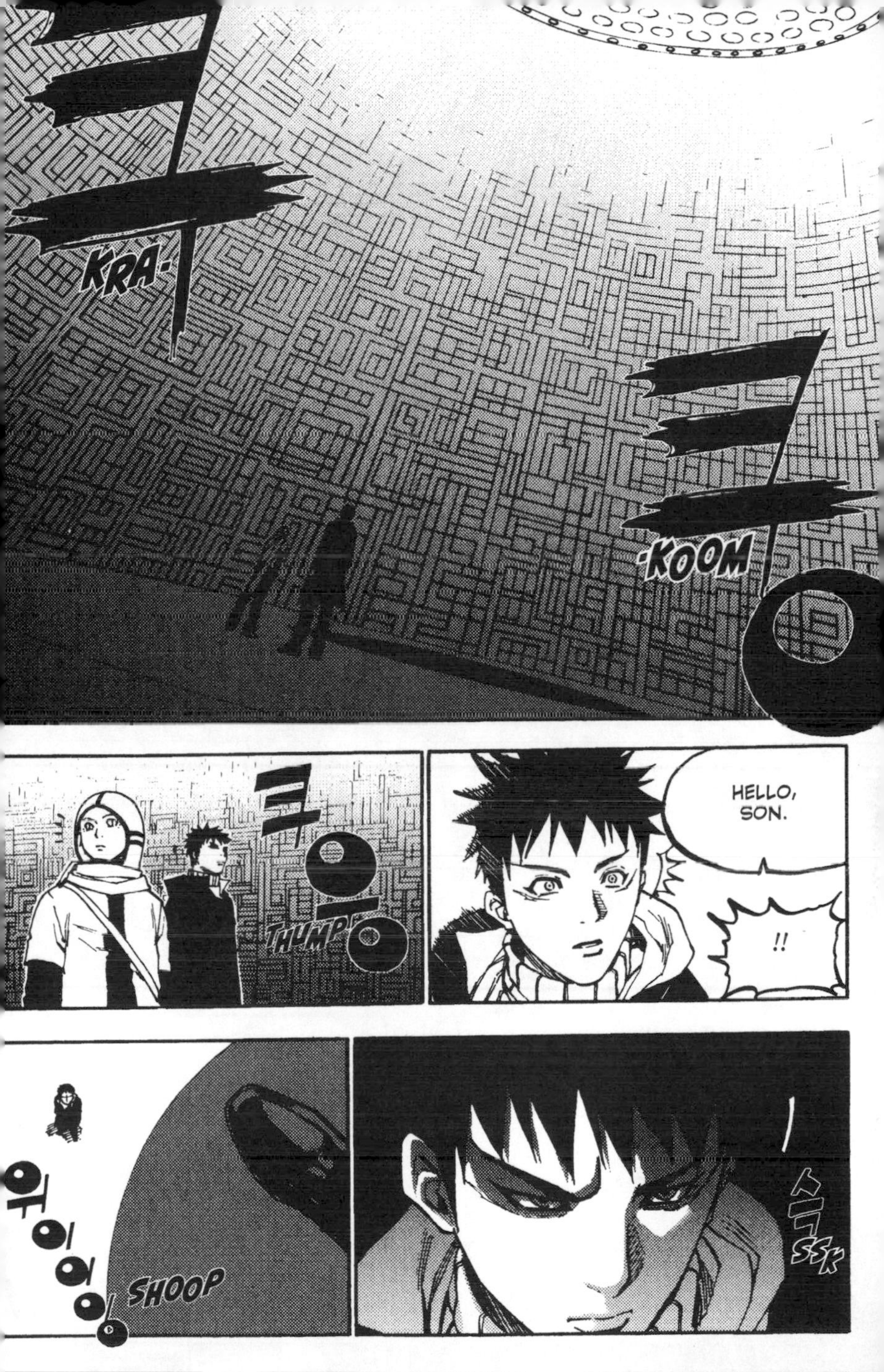

KRA-
-KOOM
THUMP
HELLO, SON.
!!
SHOOP
SSK

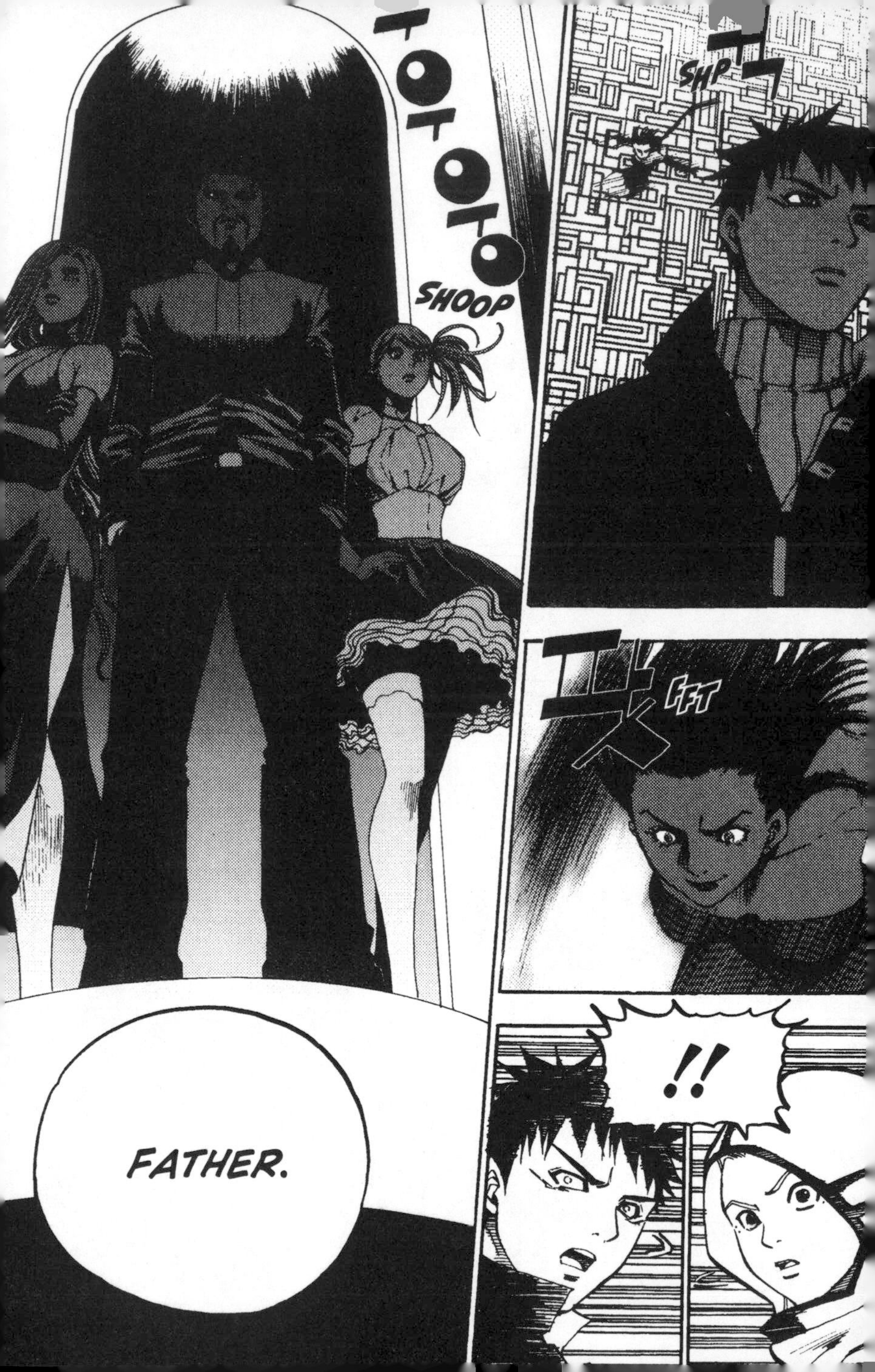
TOTOTO
SHOOP
FATHER.
SHP
FFT
!!

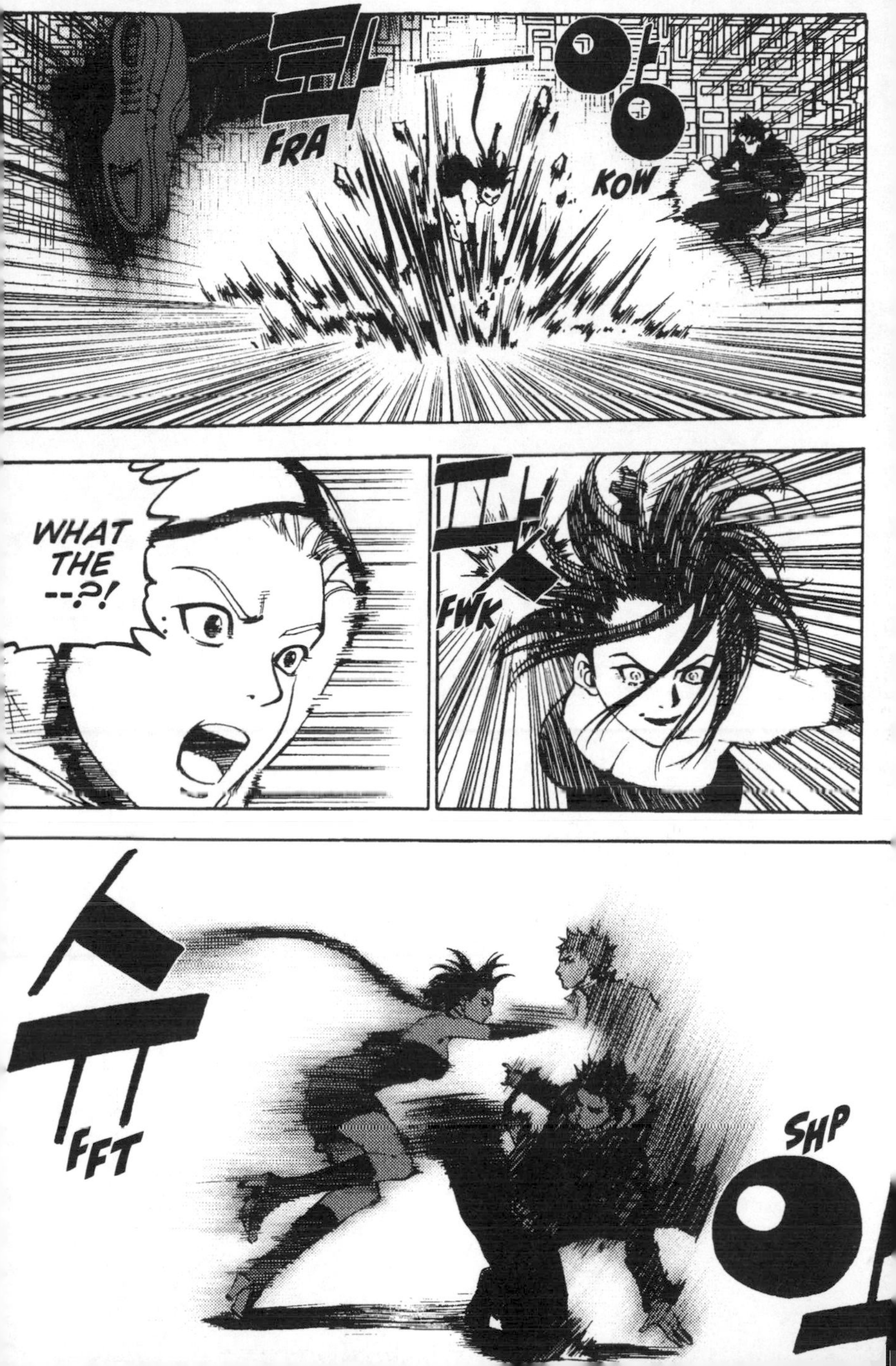
FRA
KOW
WHAT THE --?!
FWK
FFT
SHP

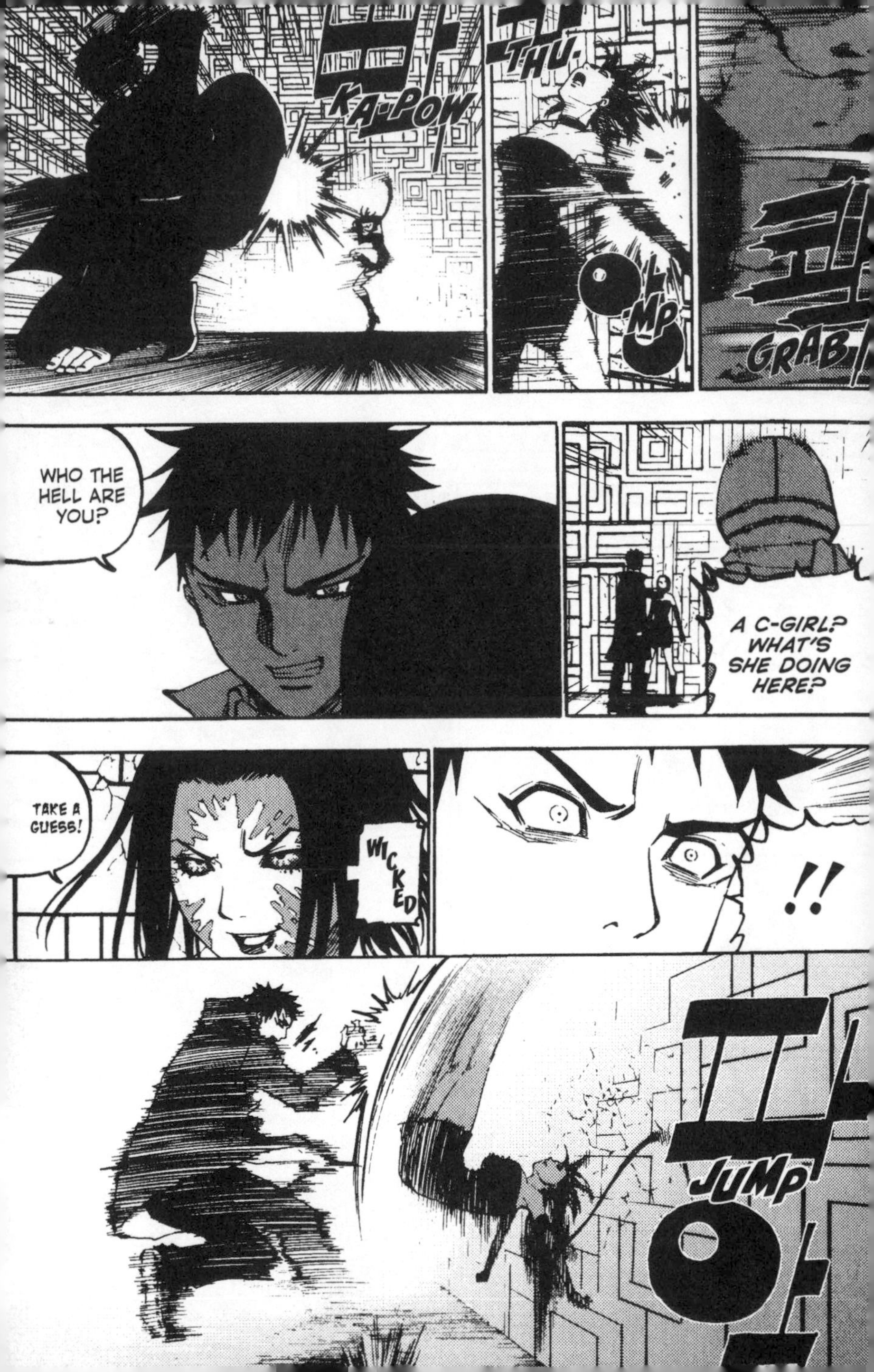
KA-POW
THU-
JUMP
GRAB
WHO THE HELL ARE YOU?
A C-GIRL? WHAT'S SHE DOING HERE?
TAKE A GUESS!
WICKED
!!
JUMP

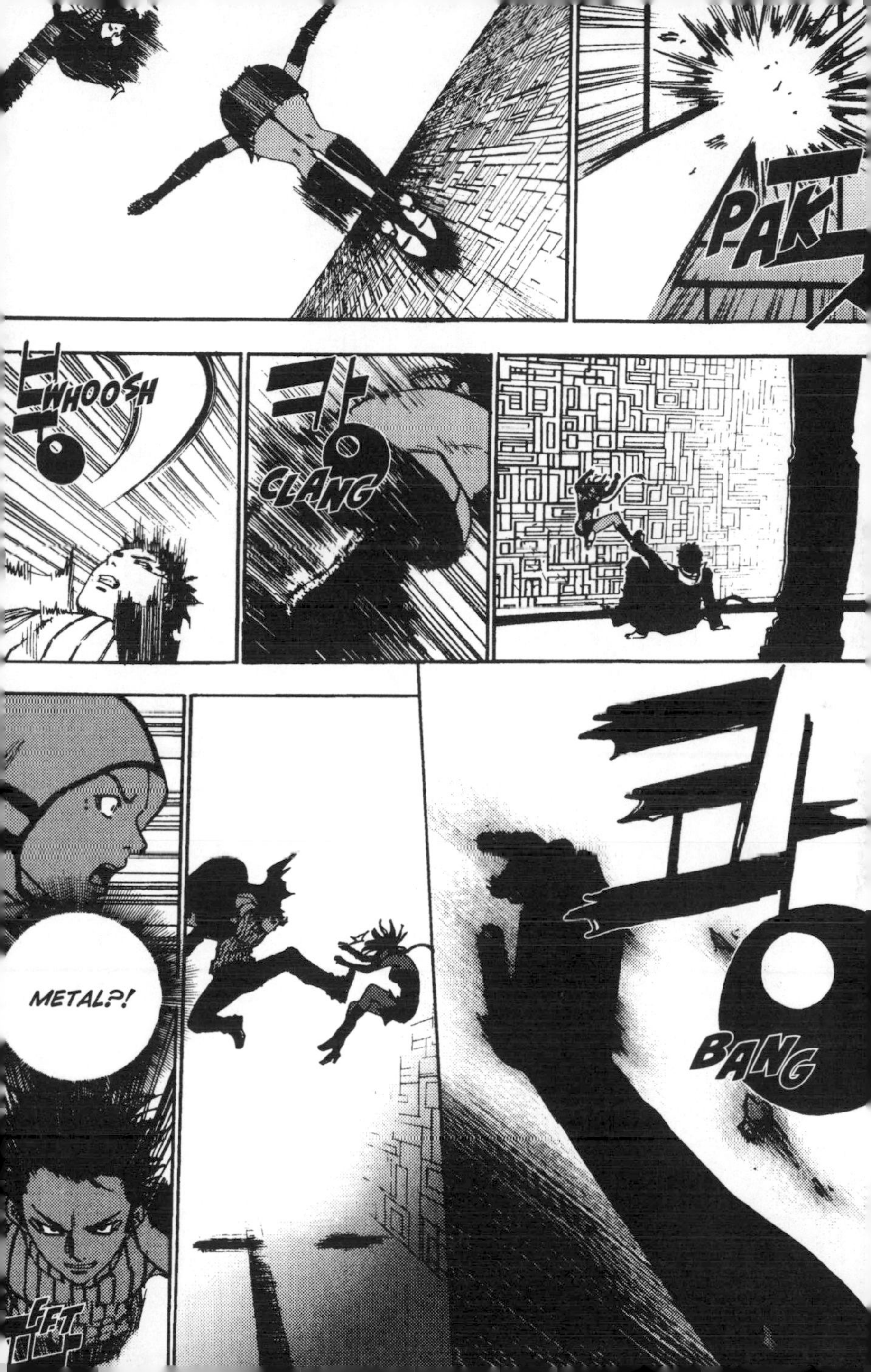
PAK
WHOOSH
CLANG
METAL?!
FFT
BANG

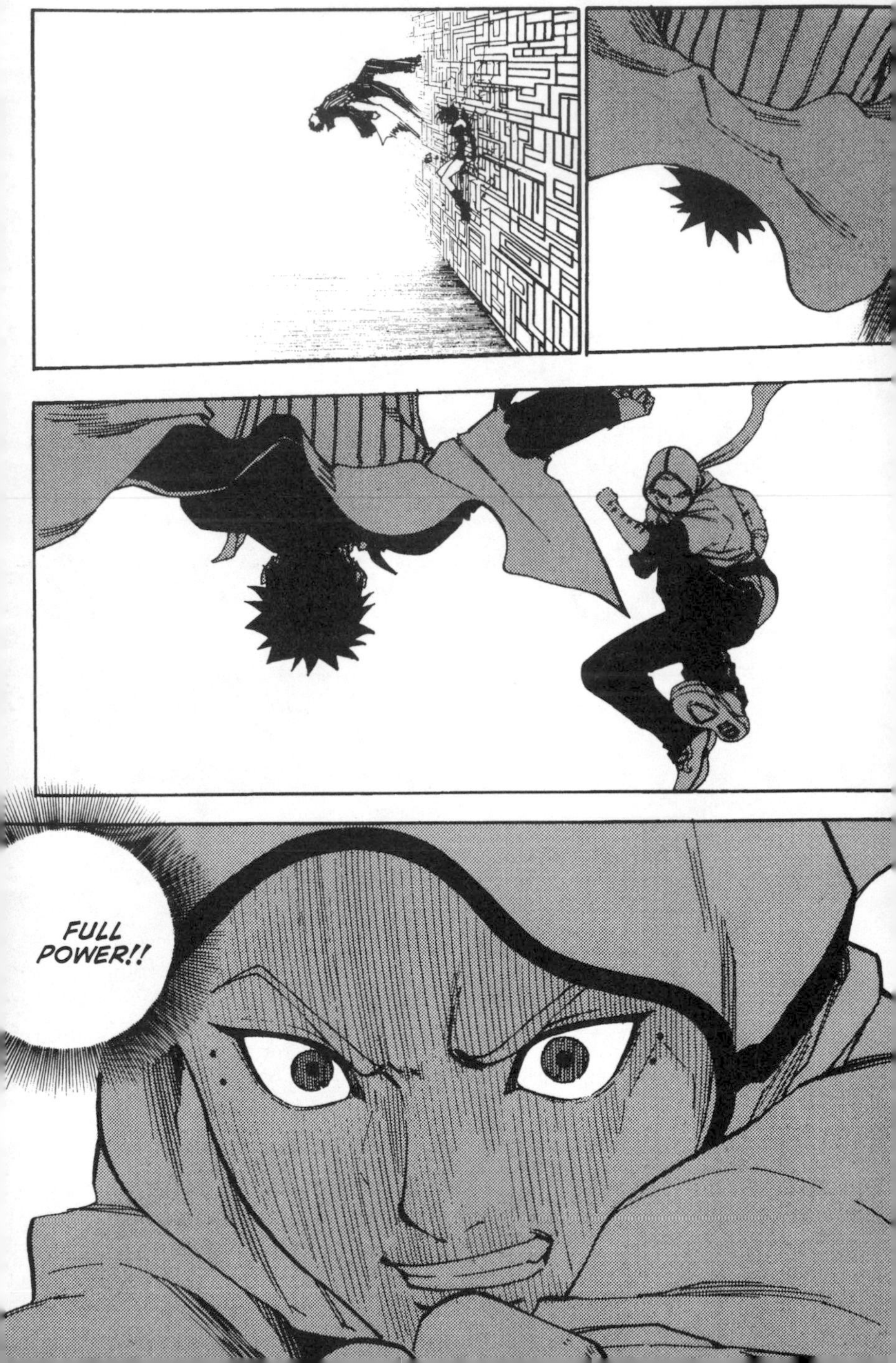
FULL POWER!!

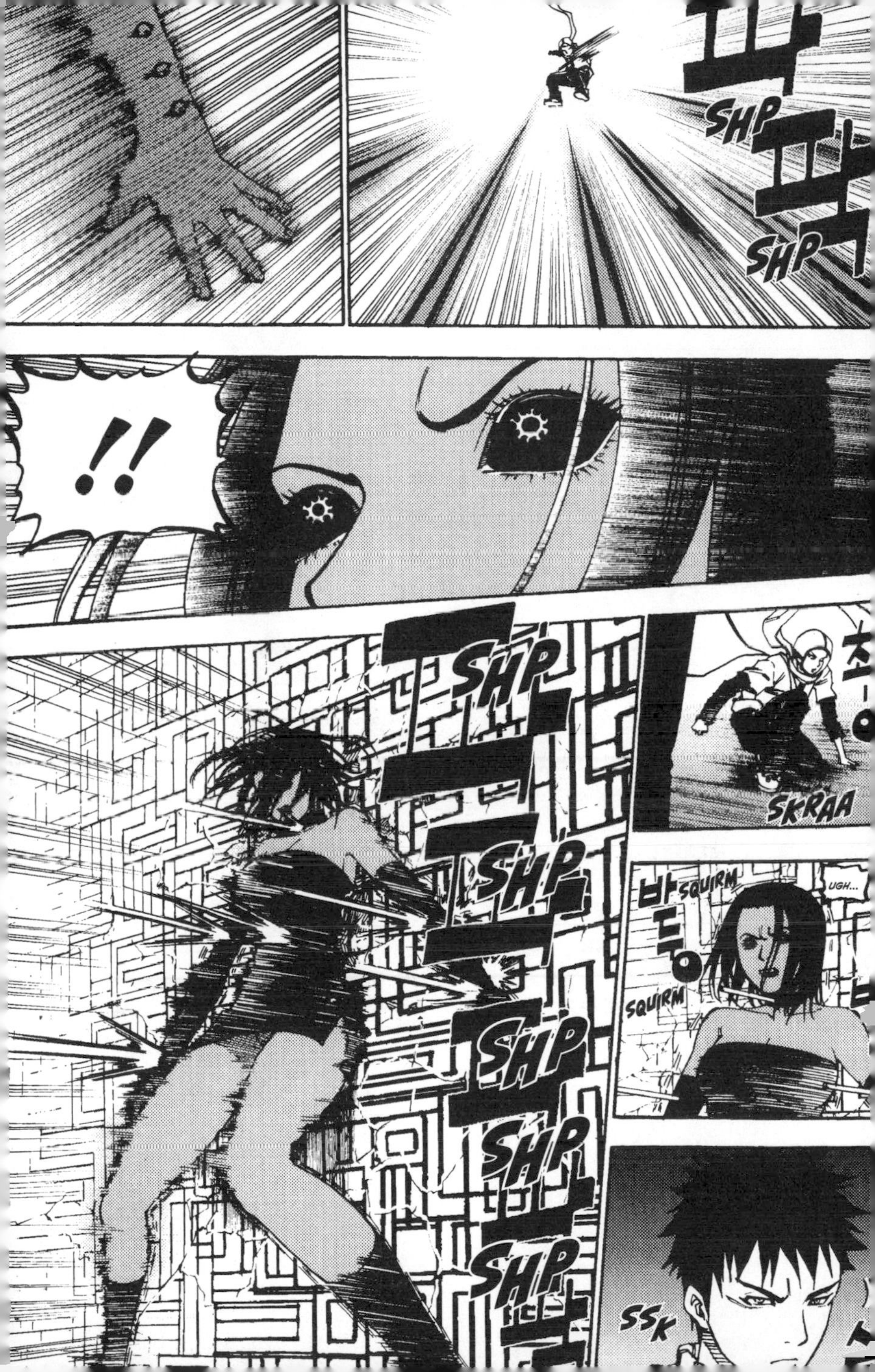
SHP
SHP
!!
SHP
SHP
SHP
SHP
SHP
SKRAA
SQUIRM
UGH...
SQUIRM
SSK

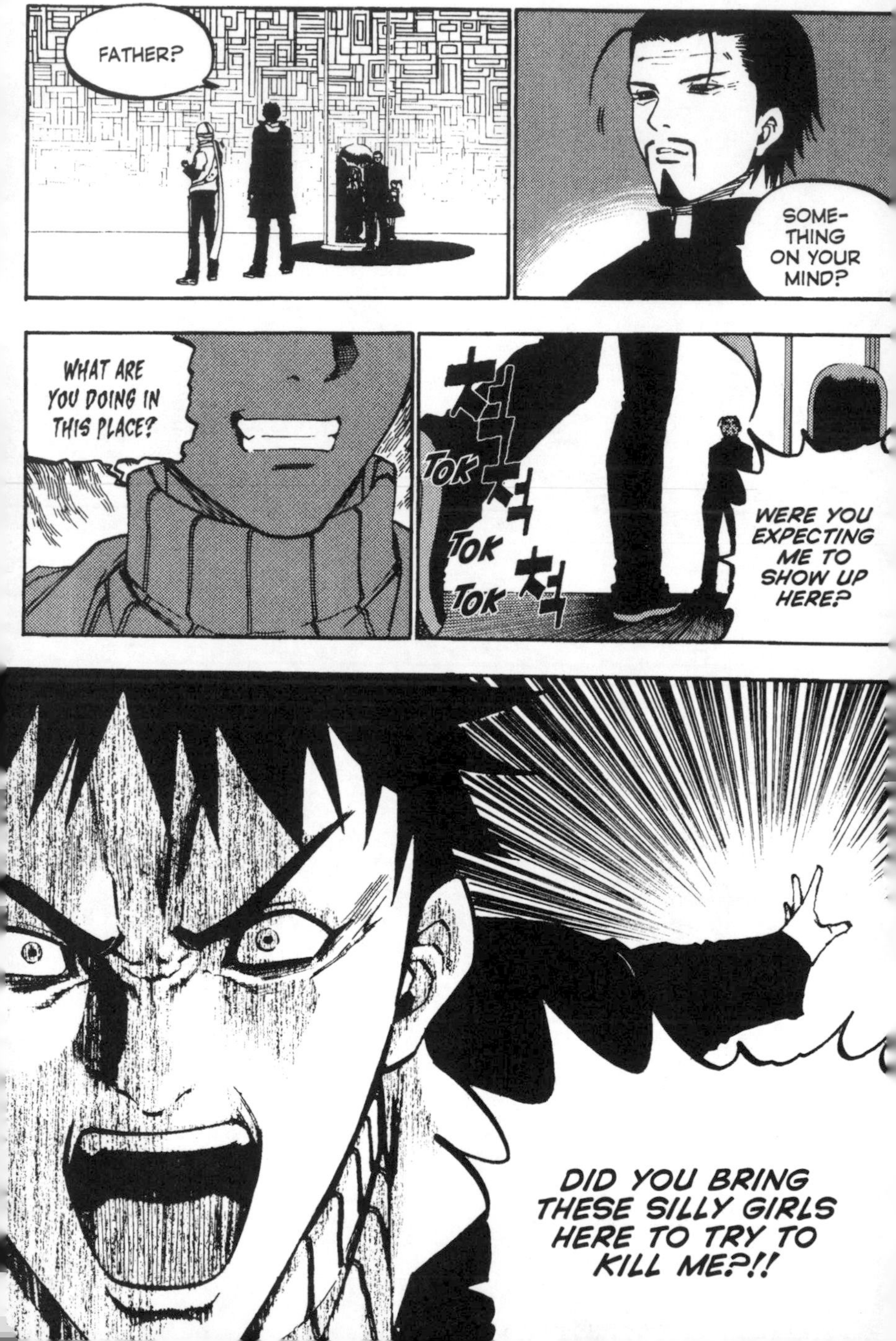
FATHER?
SOME-THING ON YOUR MIND?
WHAT ARE YOU DOING IN THIS PLACE?
척
TOK
척
TOK
척
TOK
WERE YOU EXPECTING ME TO SHOW UP HERE?
DID YOU BRING THESE SILLY GIRLS HERE TO TRY TO KILL ME?!!

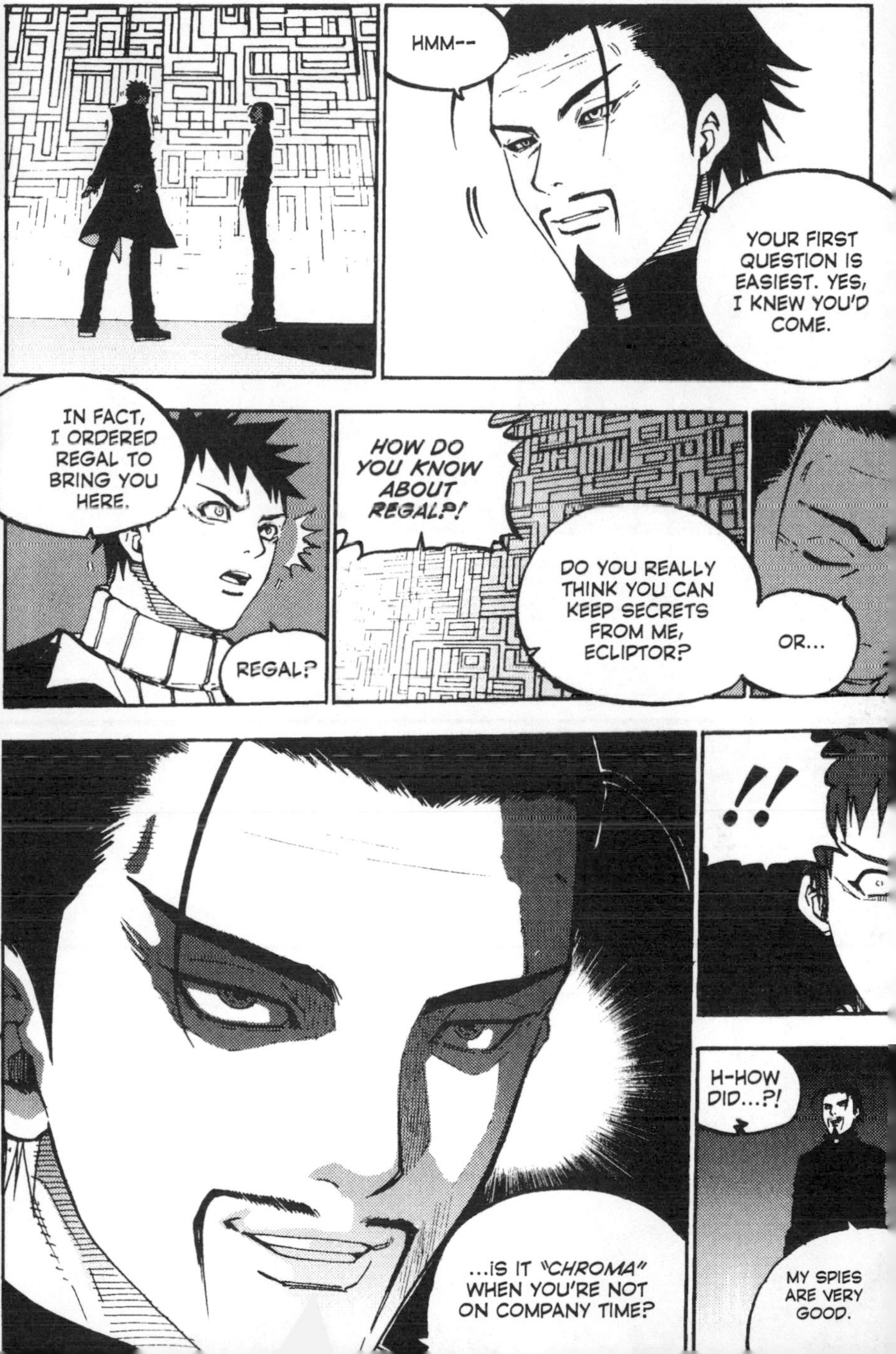
HMM--
YOUR FIRST QUESTION IS EASIEST. YES, I KNEW YOU'D COME.
IN FACT, I ORDERED REGAL TO BRING YOU HERE.
REGAL?
HOW DO YOU KNOW ABOUT REGAL?!
DO YOU REALLY THINK YOU CAN KEEP SECRETS FROM ME, ECLIPTOR?
OR...
...IS IT "CHROMA" WHEN YOU'RE NOT ON COMPANY TIME?
!!
H-HOW DID...?!
MY SPIES ARE VERY GOOD.

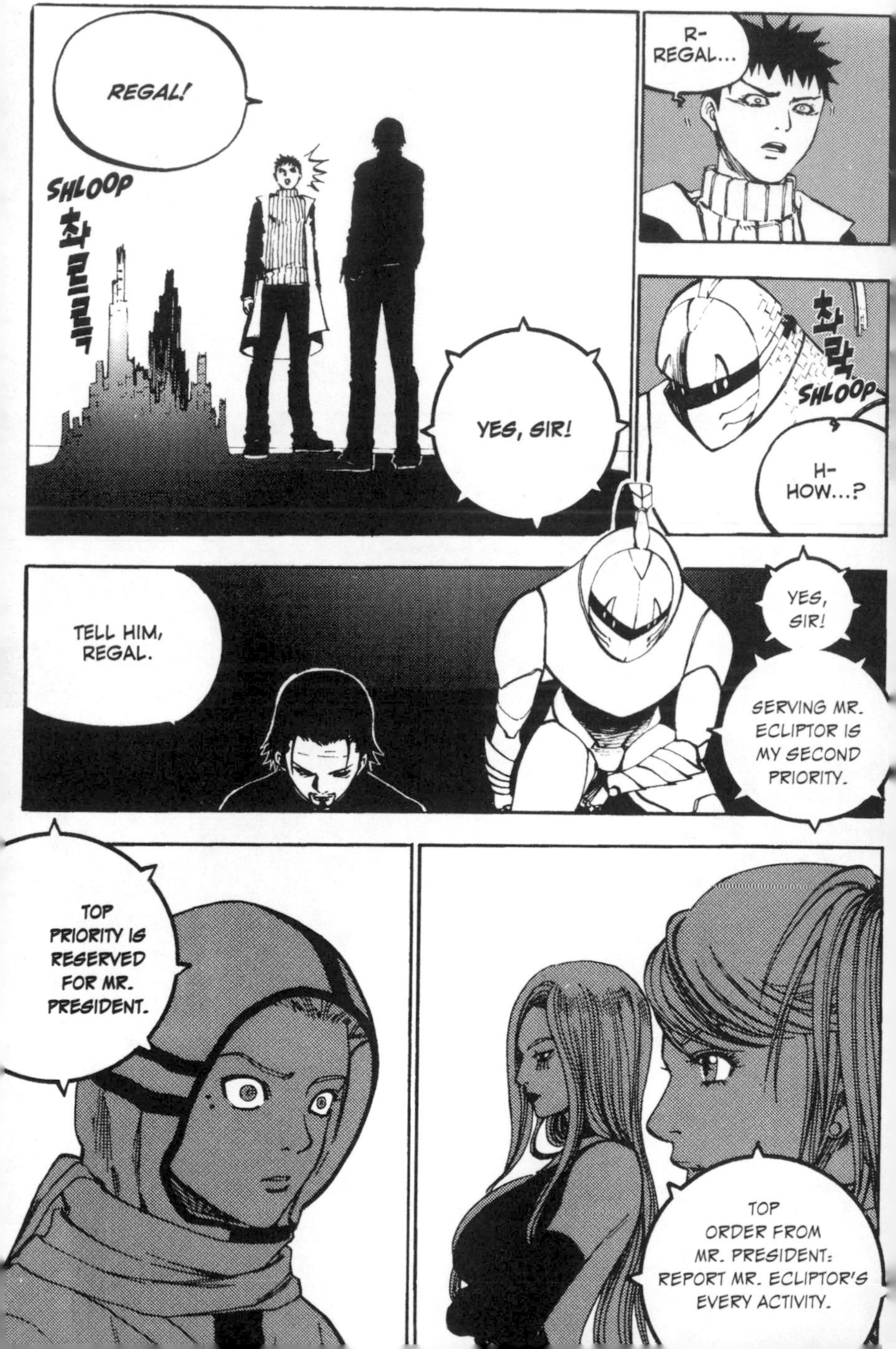
REGAL!
SHLOOP
좌르륵
YES, SIR!
R-
REGAL...
좌락
SHLOOP
H-
HOW...?
TELL HIM,
REGAL.
YES,
SIR!
SERVING MR. ECLIPTOR IS MY SECOND PRIORITY.
TOP PRIORITY IS RESERVED FOR MR. PRESIDENT.
TOP ORDER FROM MR. PRESIDENT: REPORT MR. ECLIPTOR'S EVERY ACTIVITY.

MY MAKER SET MY PRIORITY STATUS, AND HIS WORD IS LAW.

WHAT...

WHAT THE HELL ARE YOU TALKING ABOUT, REGAL?

I MADE YOU. I MAINTAINED YOU.

I'M THE ONE WHO PROGRAMMED YOU!

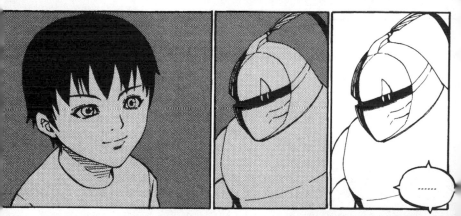

......

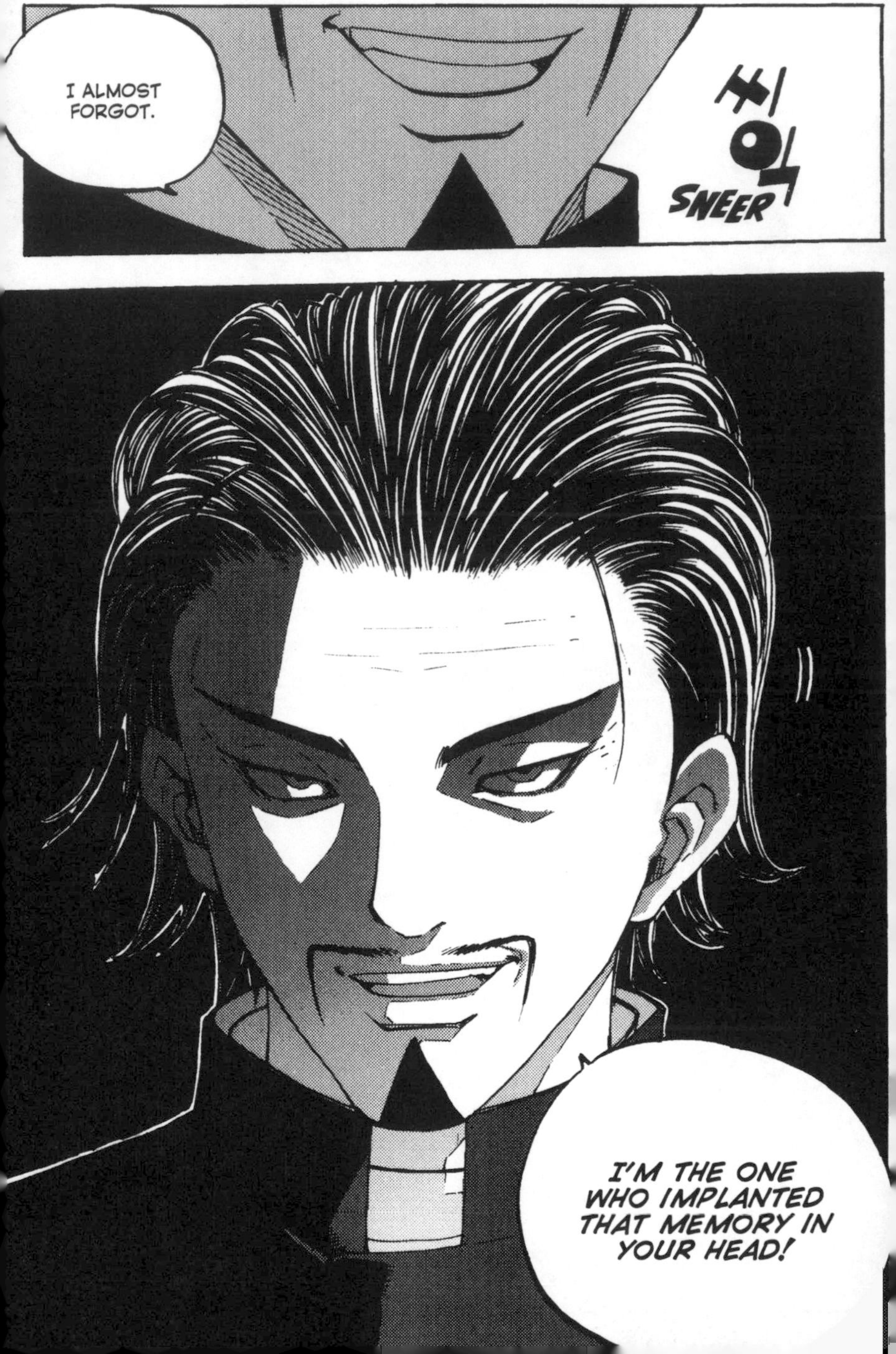
I ALMOST FORGOT.
씨익
SNEER
I'M THE ONE WHO IMPLANTED THAT MEMORY IN YOUR HEAD!

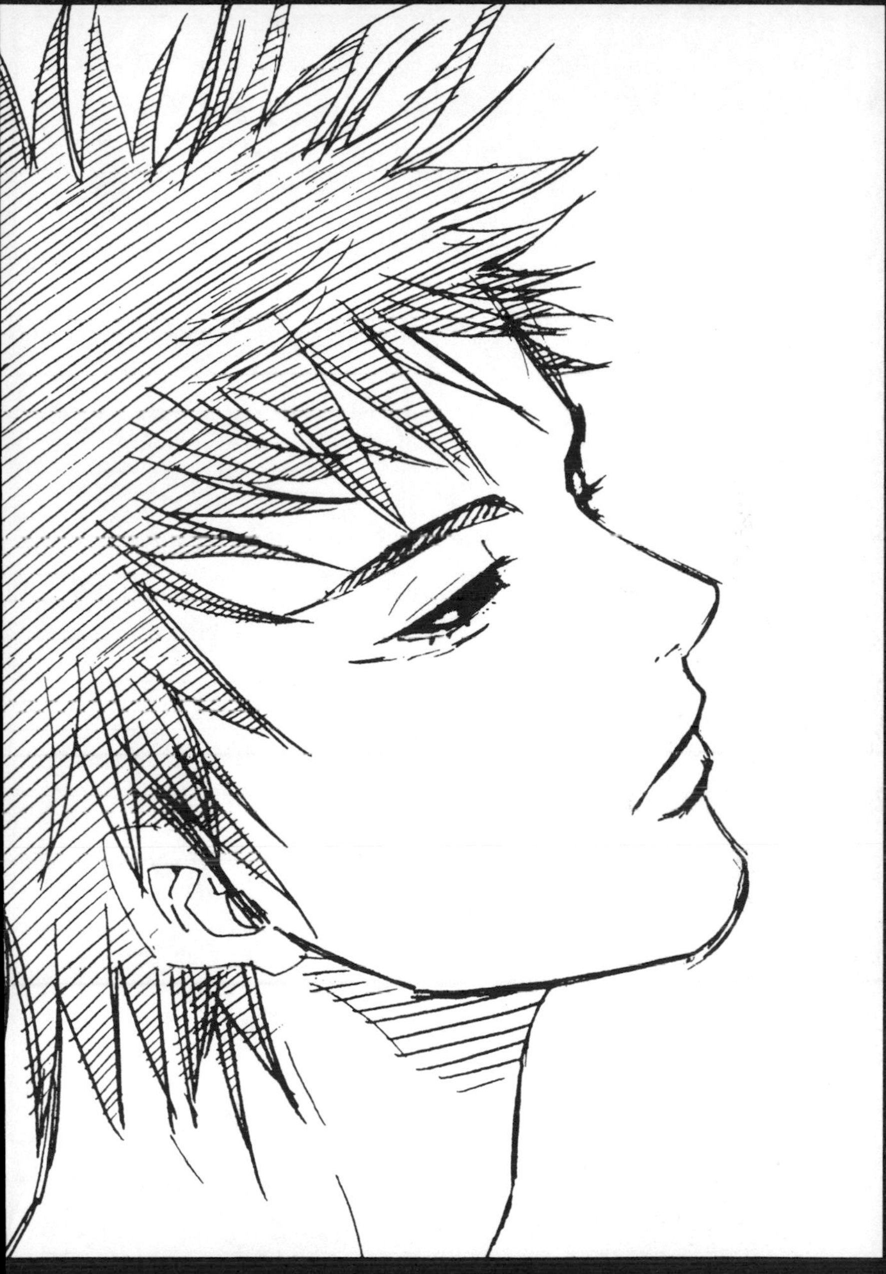

CAR 14. THE CONTINUATION OF THE END

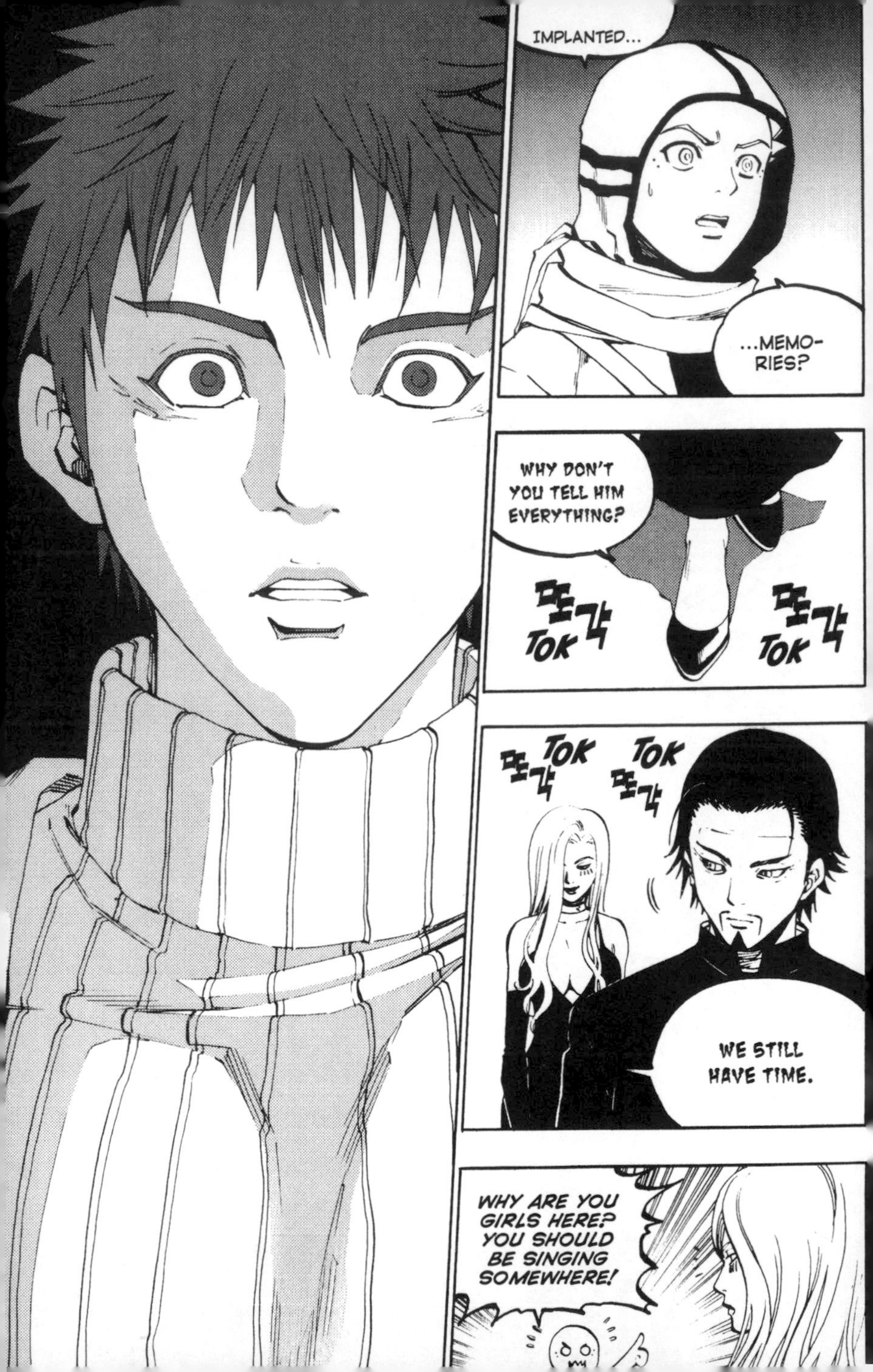
IMPLANTED...
...MEMORIES?
WHY DON'T YOU TELL HIM EVERYTHING?
또각 TOK
또각 TOK
또각 TOK
또각 TOK
WE STILL HAVE TIME.
WHY ARE YOU GIRLS HERE? YOU SHOULD BE SINGING SOMEWHERE!

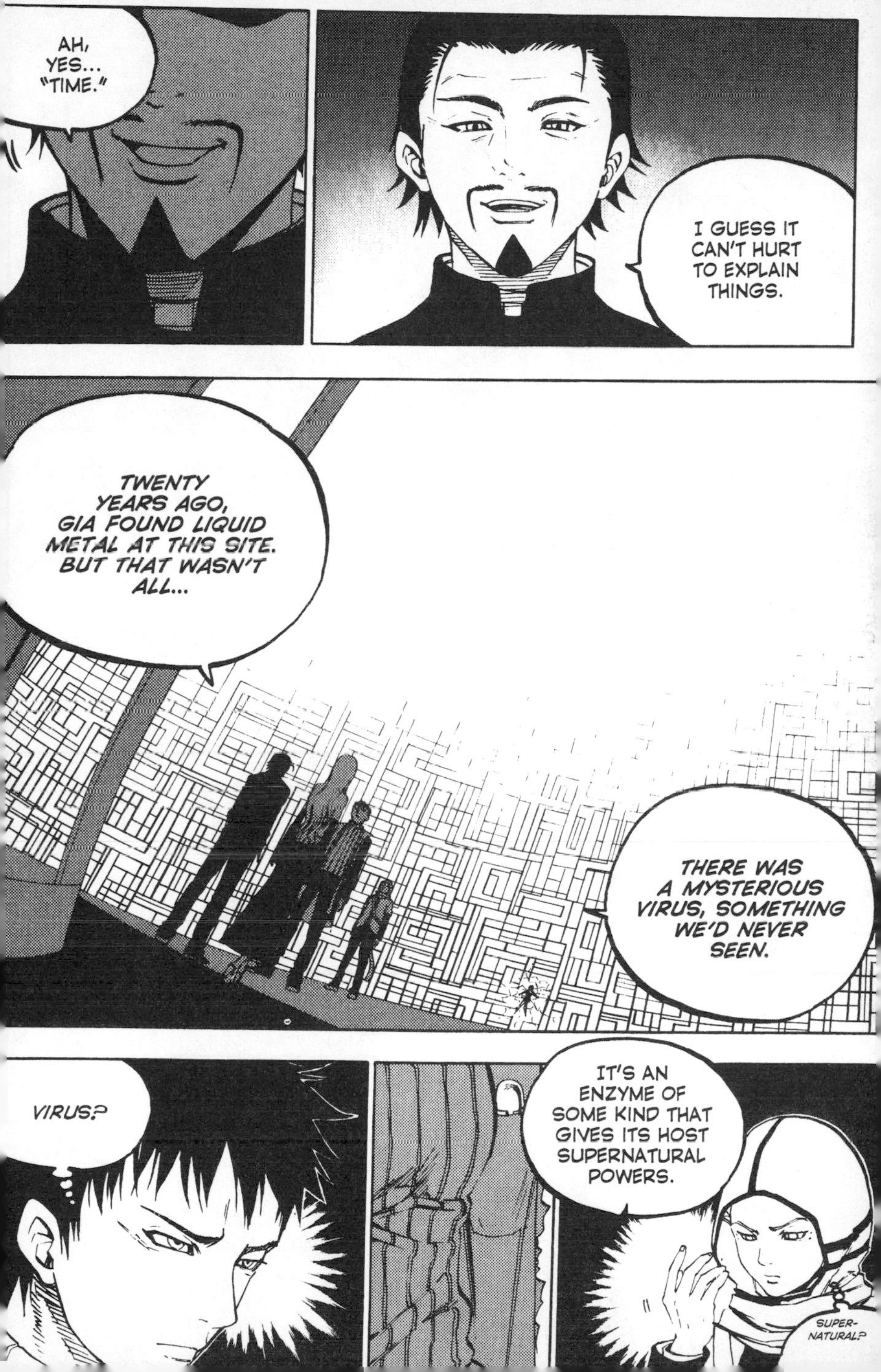
AH, YES... "TIME."
I GUESS IT CAN'T HURT TO EXPLAIN THINGS.
TWENTY YEARS AGO, GIA FOUND LIQUID METAL AT THIS SITE. BUT THAT WASN'T ALL...
THERE WAS A MYSTERIOUS VIRUS, SOMETHING WE'D NEVER SEEN.
VIRUS?
IT'S AN ENZYME OF SOME KIND THAT GIVES ITS HOST SUPERNATURAL POWERS.
SUPER-NATURAL?

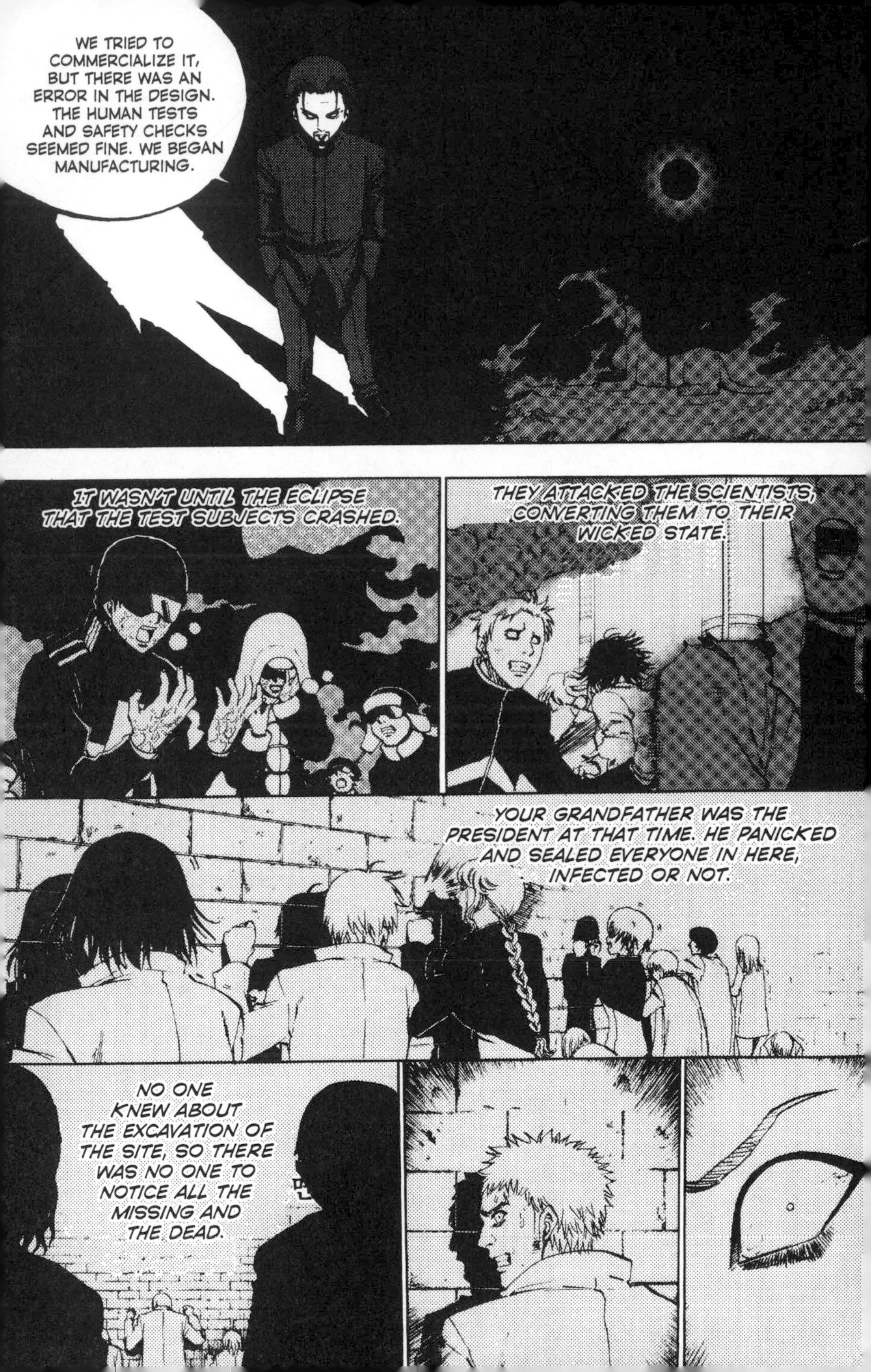
WE TRIED TO COMMERCIALIZE IT, BUT THERE WAS AN ERROR IN THE DESIGN. THE HUMAN TESTS AND SAFETY CHECKS SEEMED FINE. WE BEGAN MANUFACTURING.
IT WASN'T UNTIL THE ECLIPSE THAT THE TEST SUBJECTS CRASHED.
THEY ATTACKED THE SCIENTISTS, CONVERTING THEM TO THEIR WICKED STATE.
YOUR GRANDFATHER WAS THE PRESIDENT AT THAT TIME. HE PANICKED AND SEALED EVERYONE IN HERE, INFECTED OR NOT.
NO ONE KNEW ABOUT THE EXCAVATION OF THE SITE, SO THERE WAS NO ONE TO NOTICE ALL THE MISSING AND THE DEAD.

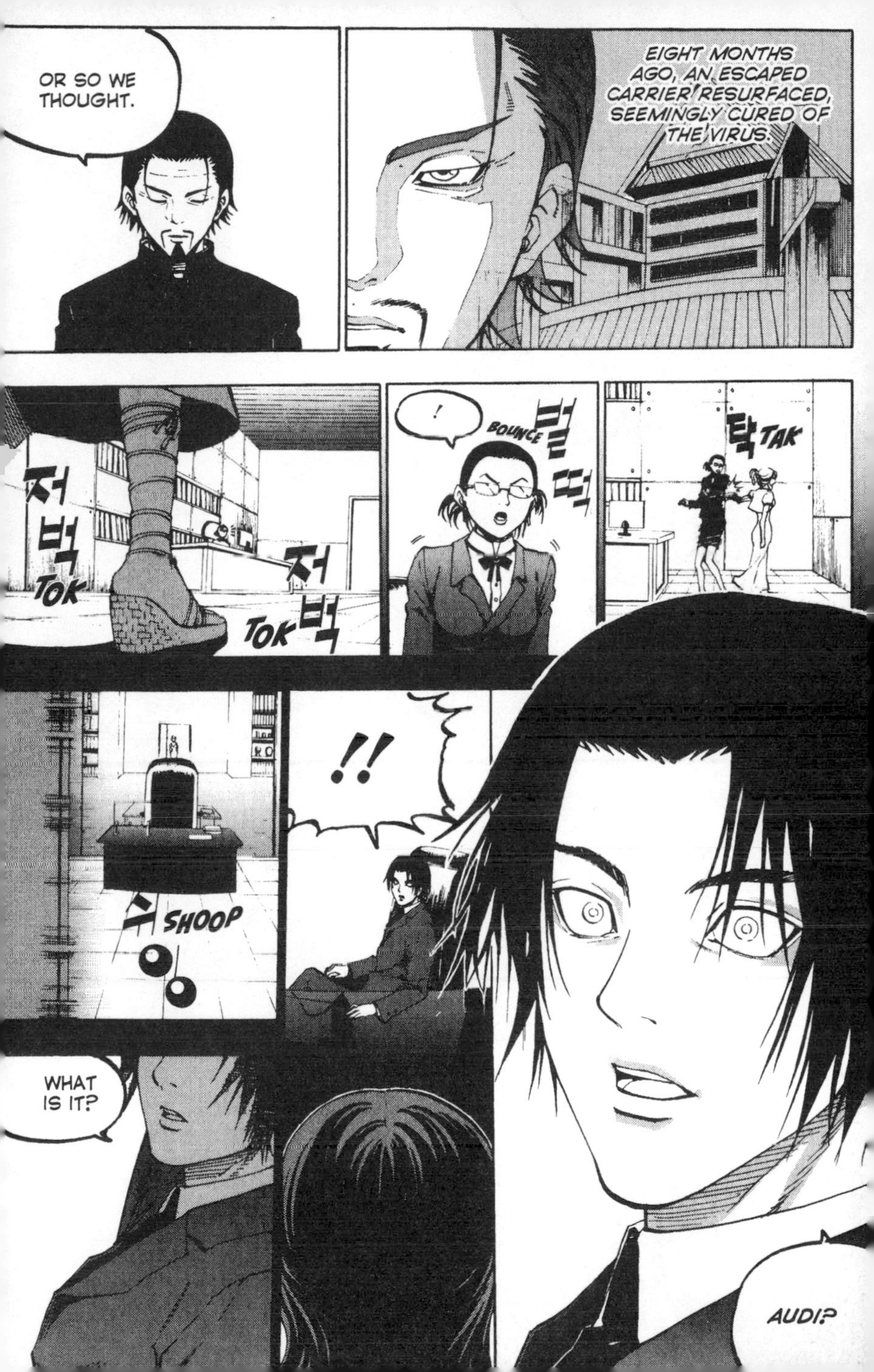
OR SO WE THOUGHT.
EIGHT MONTHS AGO, AN ESCAPED CARRIER RESURFACED, SEEMINGLY CURED OF THE VIRUS.
저벅 TOK
저벅 TOK
!
BOUNCE 벌떡
탁 TAK
슉 SHOOP
!!
WHAT IS IT?
AUDI?

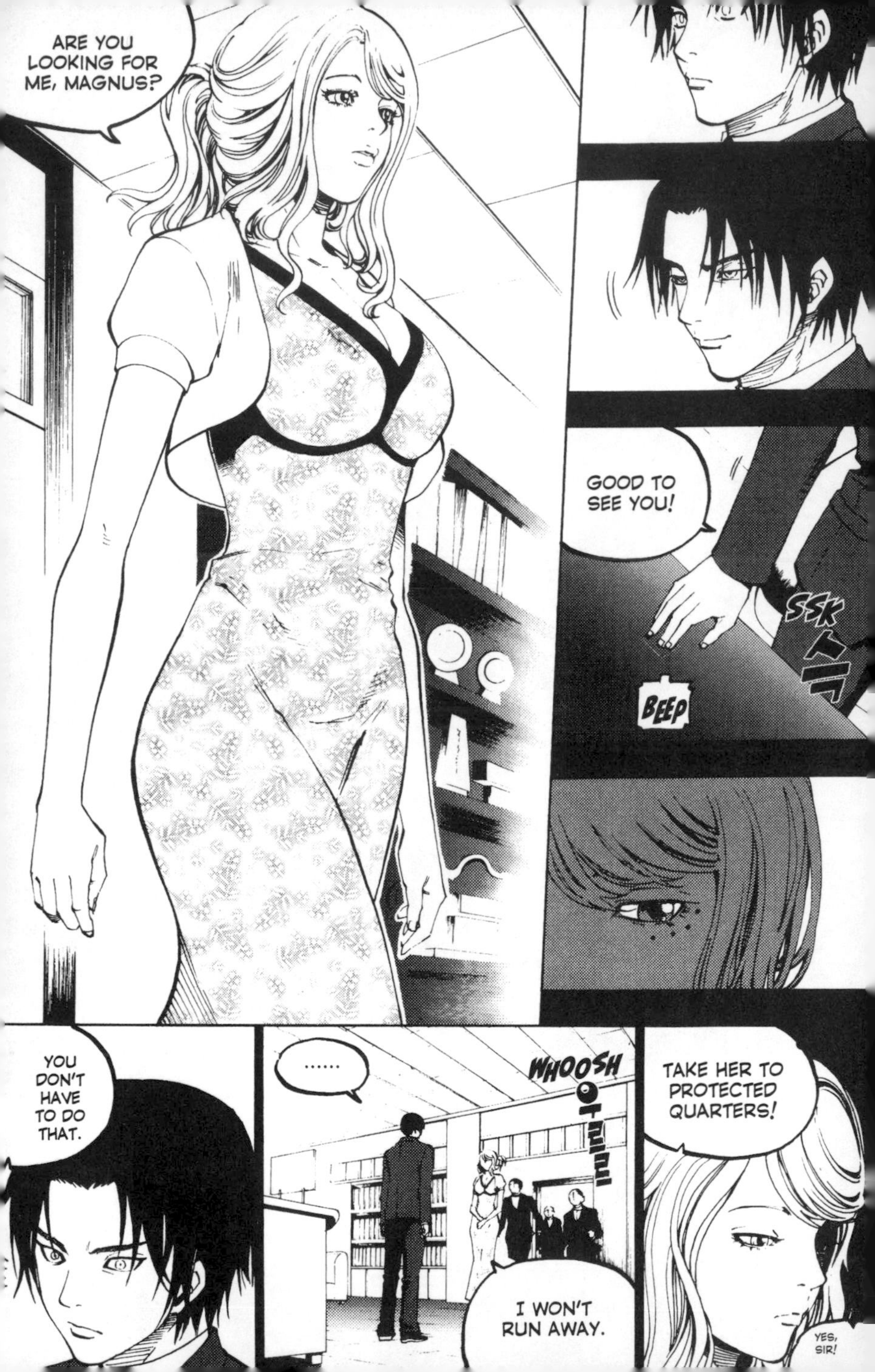
ARE YOU LOOKING FOR ME, MAGNUS?
GOOD TO SEE YOU!
SSK
BEEP
YOU DON'T HAVE TO DO THAT.
......
WHOOSH
I WON'T RUN AWAY.
TAKE HER TO PROTECTED QUARTERS!
YES, SIR!

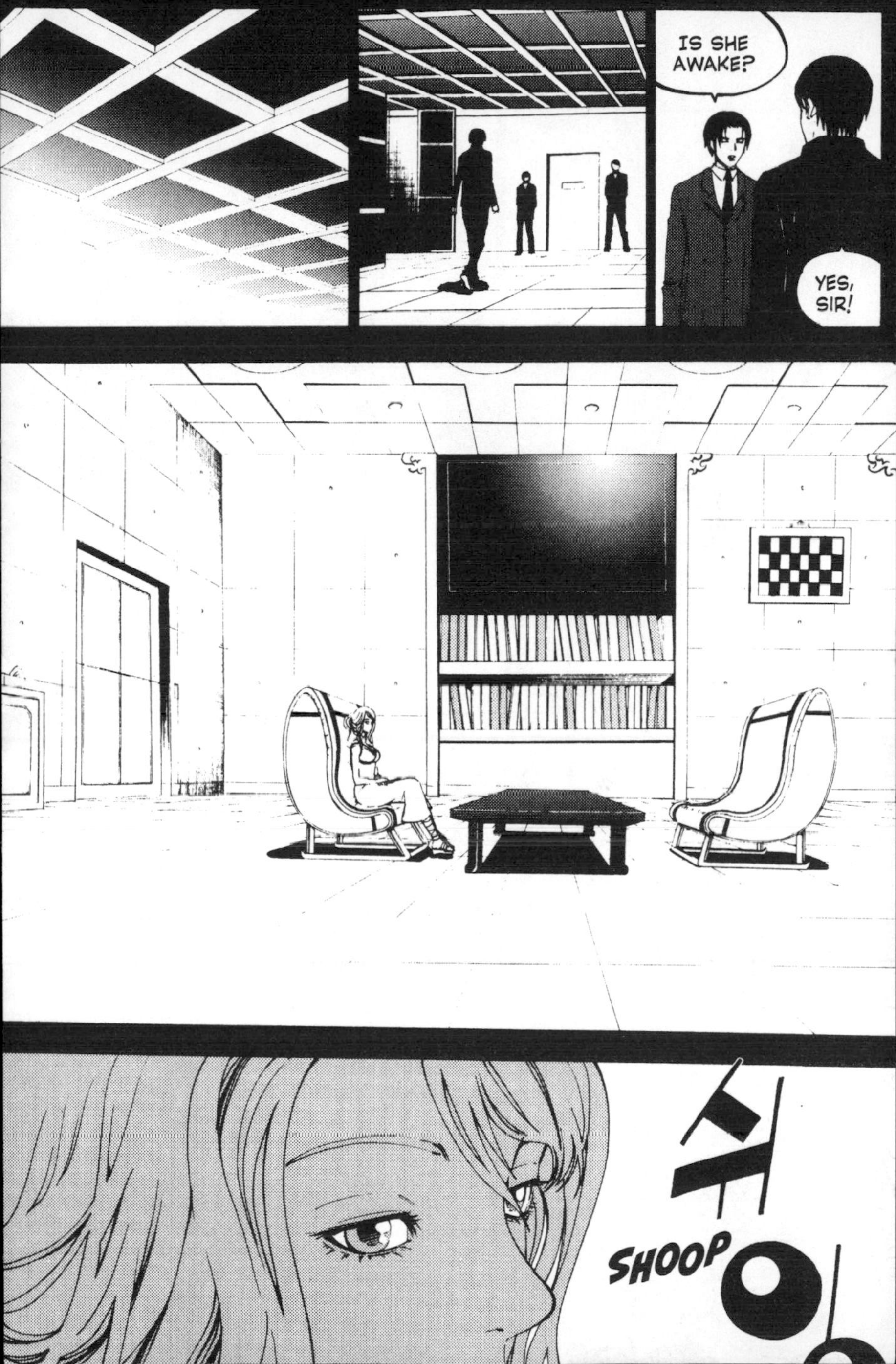
IS SHE AWAKE?
YES, SIR!
SHOOP

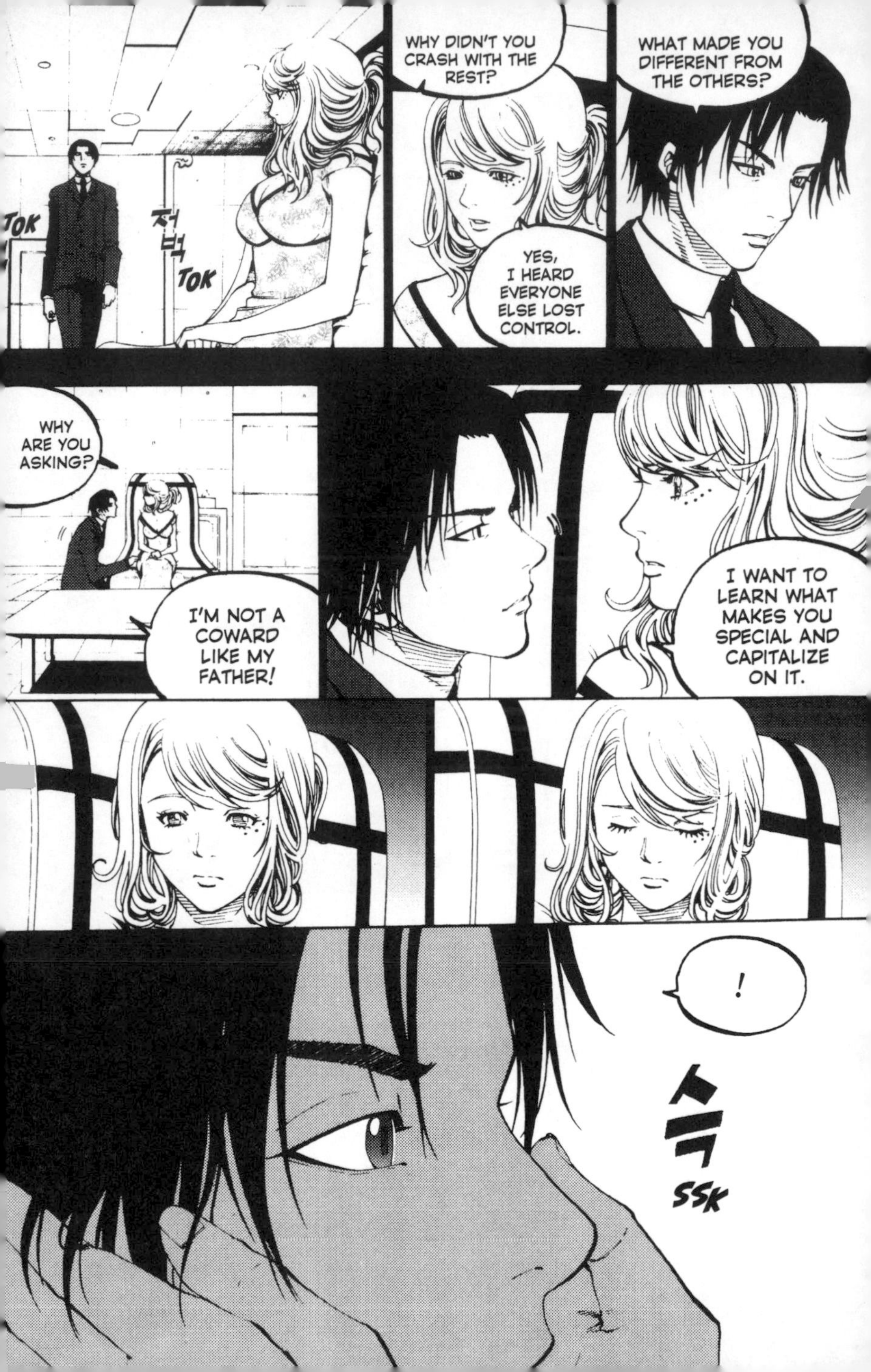
TOK
저벅
TOK
WHY DIDN'T YOU CRASH WITH THE REST?
YES, I HEARD EVERYONE ELSE LOST CONTROL.
WHAT MADE YOU DIFFERENT FROM THE OTHERS?
WHY ARE YOU ASKING?
I'M NOT A COWARD LIKE MY FATHER!
I WANT TO LEARN WHAT MAKES YOU SPECIAL AND CAPITALIZE ON IT.
!
SSK

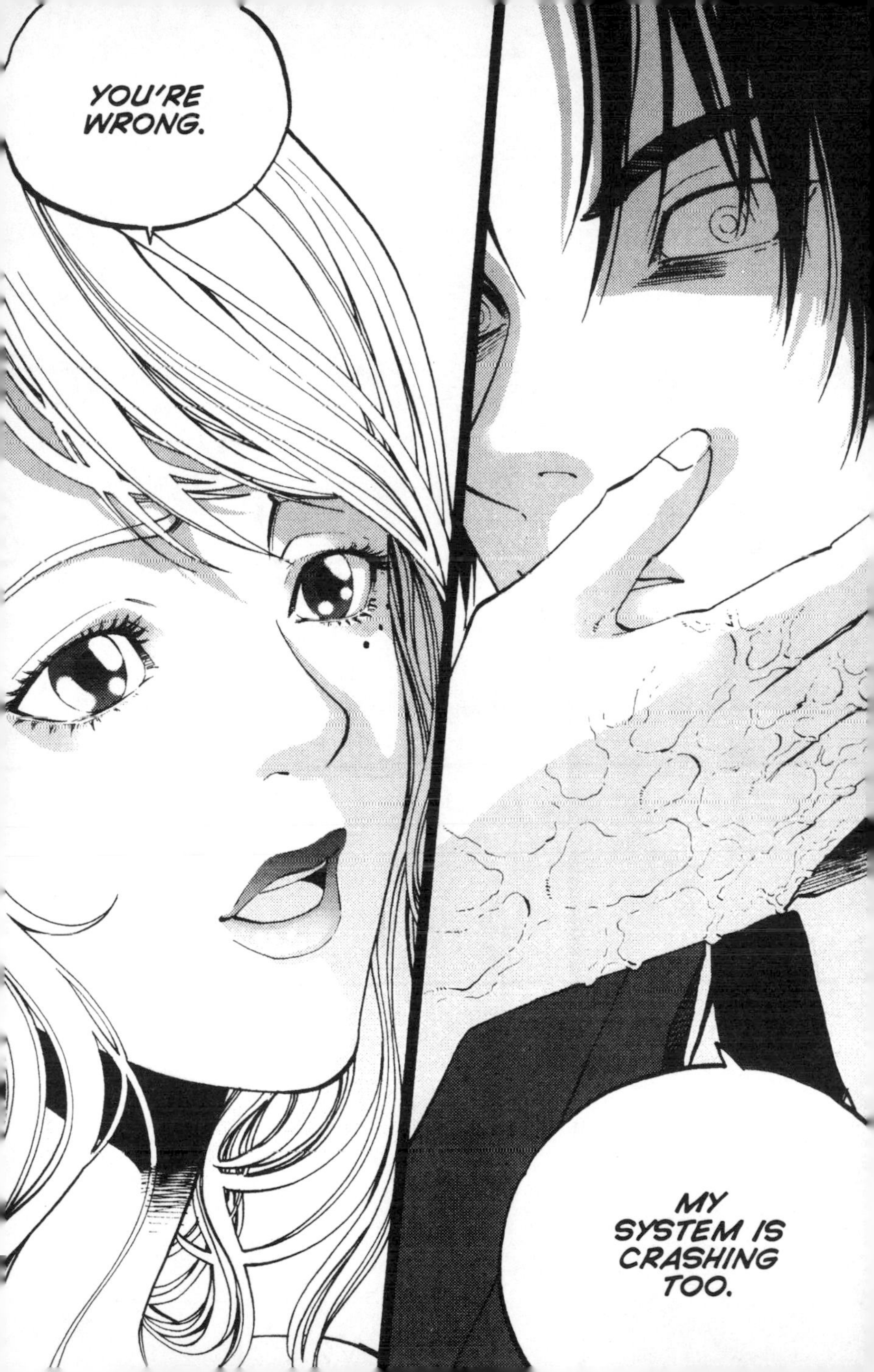
YOU'RE WRONG.
MY SYSTEM IS CRASHING TOO.

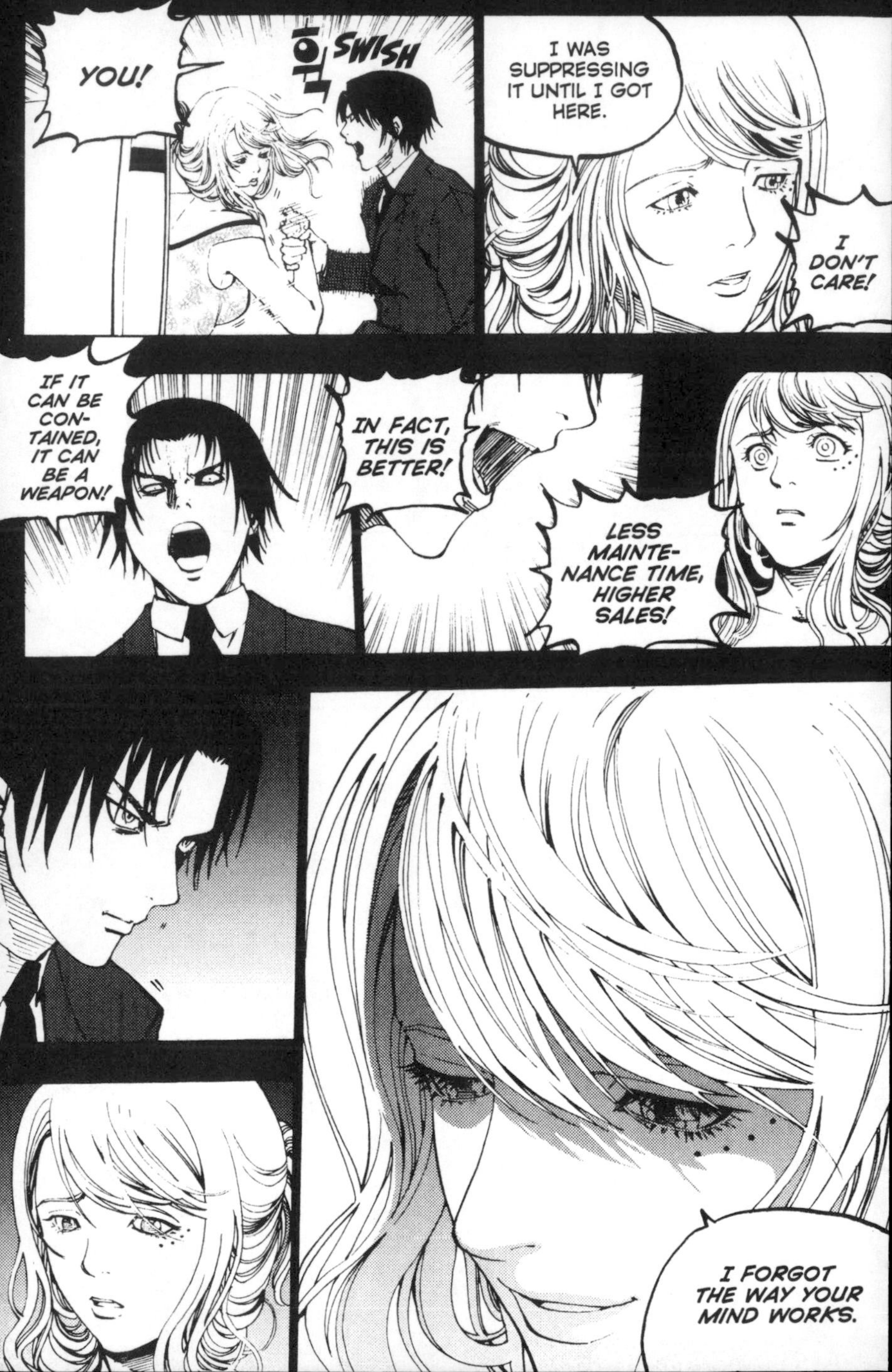
YOU!
SWISH
I WAS SUPPRESSING IT UNTIL I GOT HERE.
I DON'T CARE!
IF IT CAN BE CON-TAINED, IT CAN BE A WEAPON!
IN FACT, THIS IS BETTER!
LESS MAINTE-NANCE TIME, HIGHER SALES!
I FORGOT THE WAY YOUR MIND WORKS.

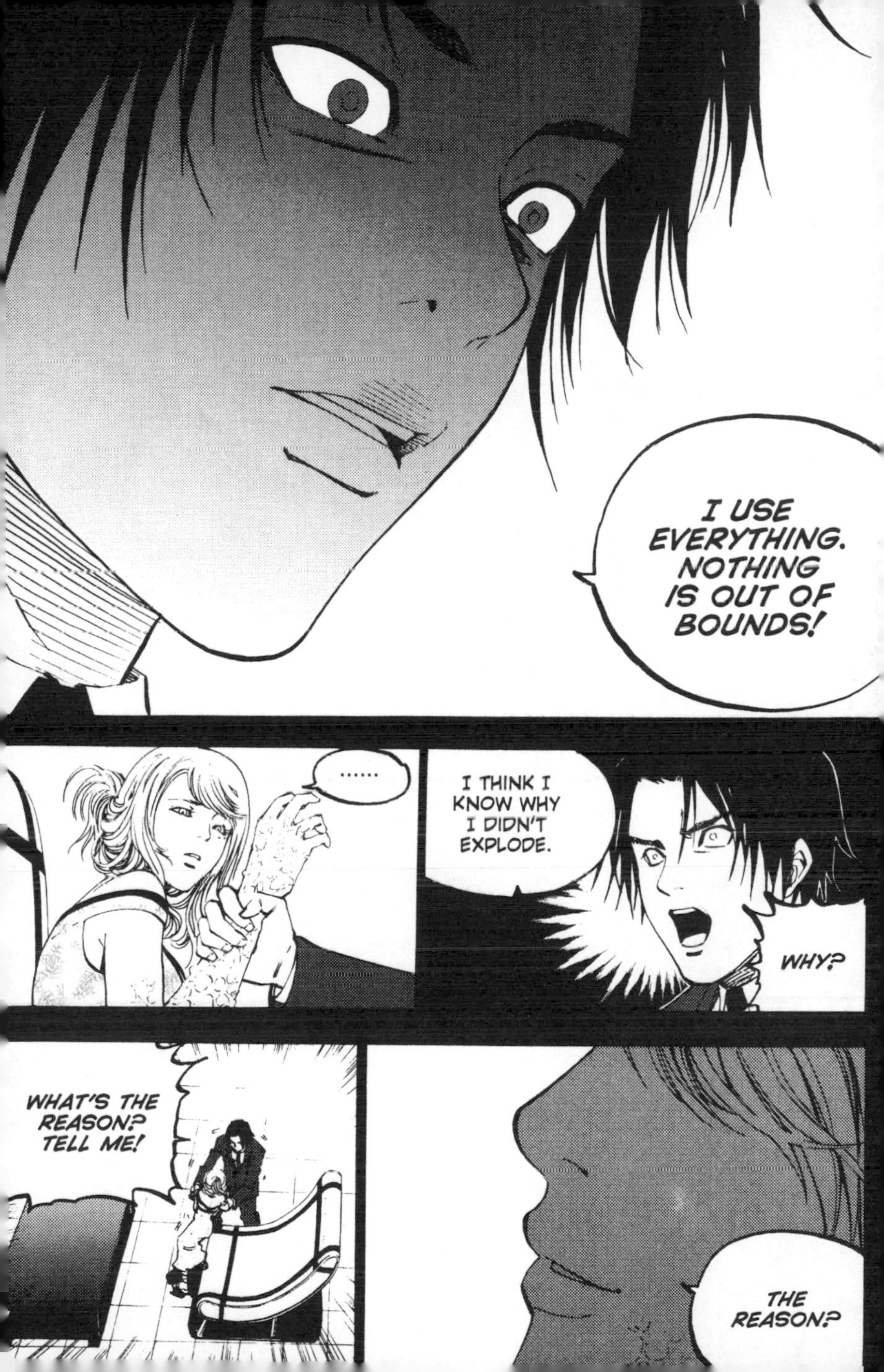
I USE EVERYTHING. NOTHING IS OUT OF BOUNDS!
......
I THINK I KNOW WHY I DIDN'T EXPLODE.
WHY?
WHAT'S THE REASON? TELL ME!
THE REASON?

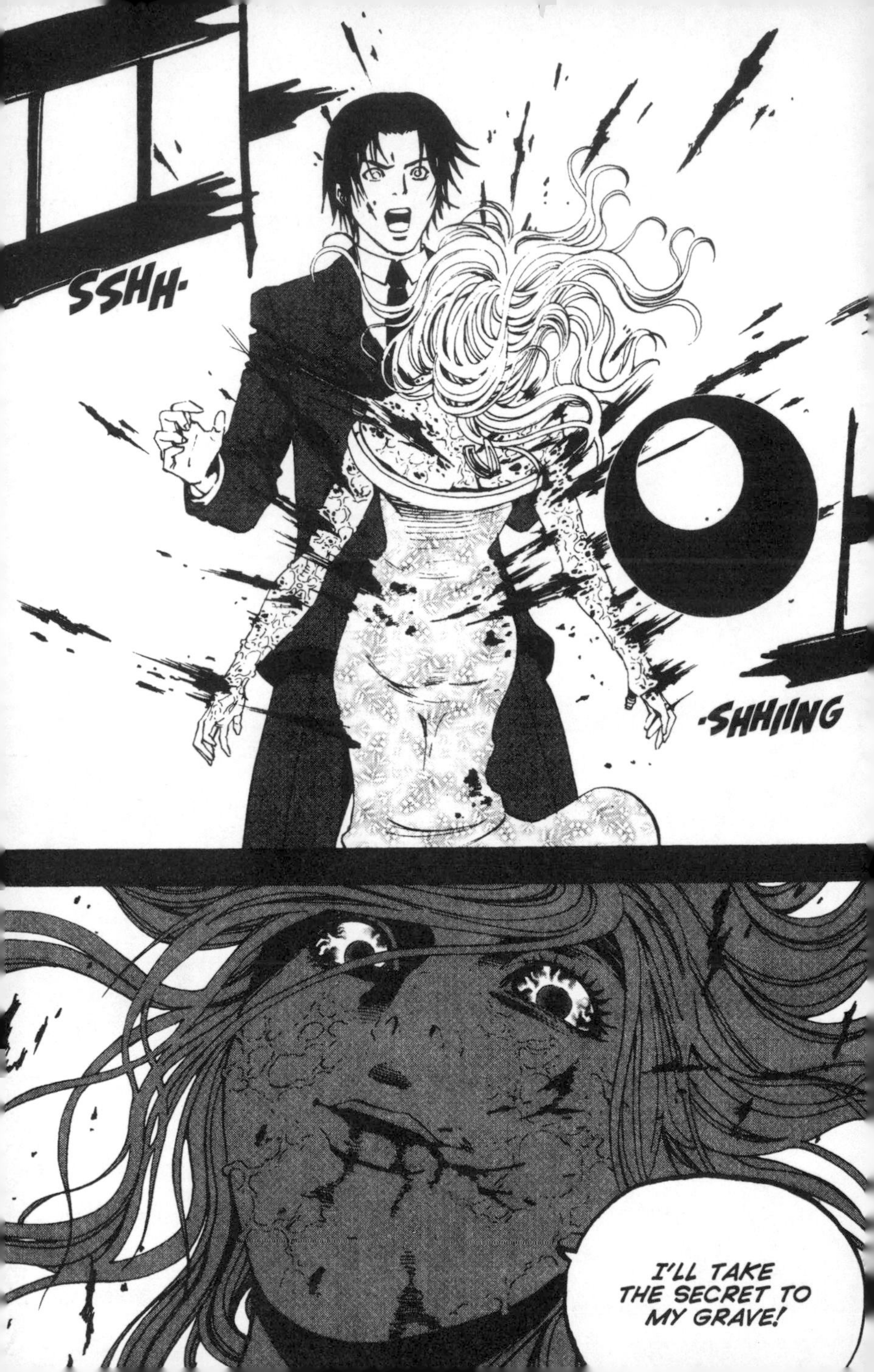
SSHH-
-SHHIING
I'LL TAKE THE SECRET TO MY GRAVE!

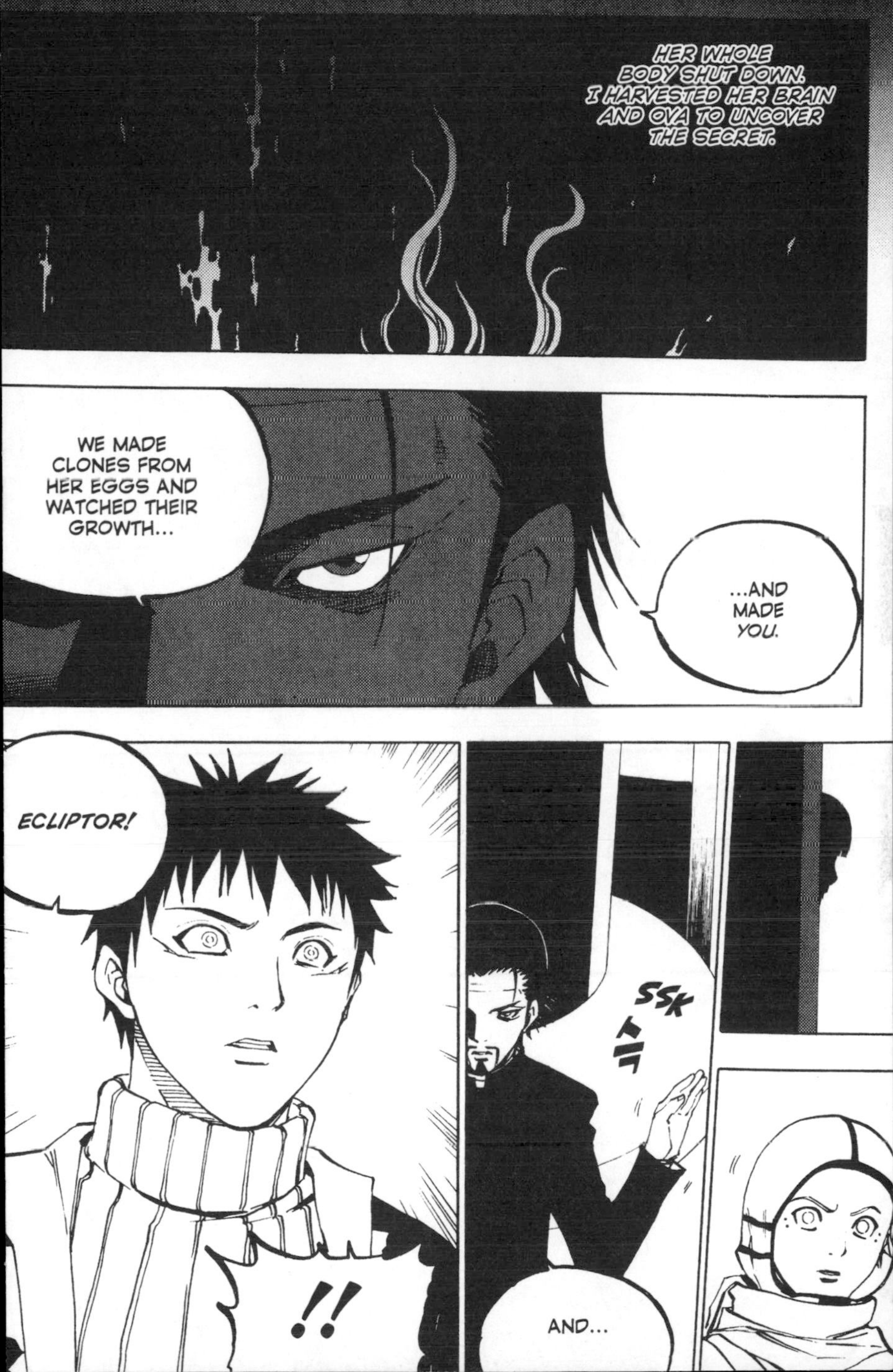
HER WHOLE BODY SHUT DOWN. I HARVESTED HER BRAIN AND OVA TO UNCOVER THE SECRET.
WE MADE CLONES FROM HER EGGS AND WATCHED THEIR GROWTH...
...AND MADE YOU.
ECLIPTOR!
!!
SSK
AND...

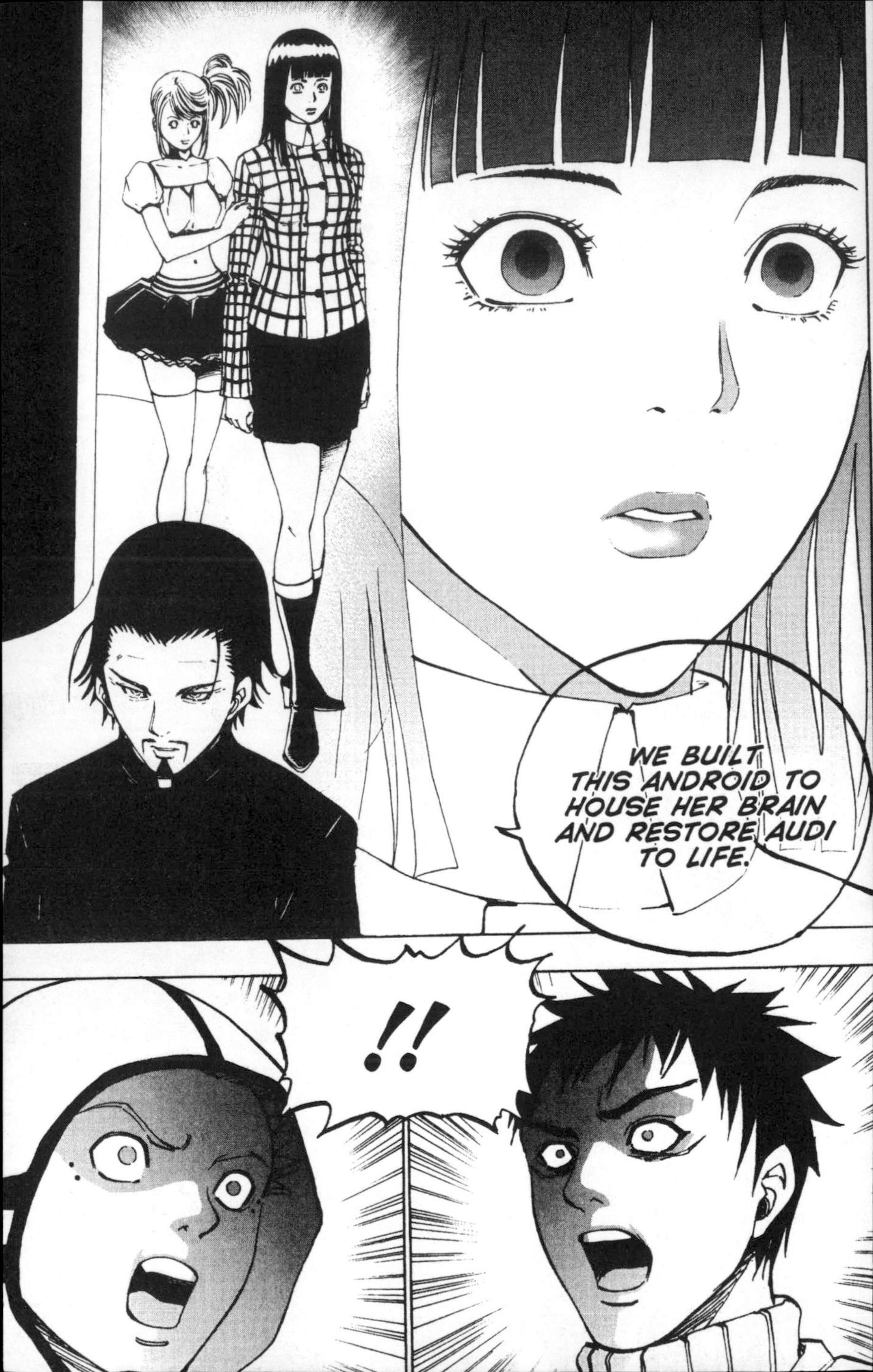
WE BUILT THIS ANDROID TO HOUSE HER BRAIN AND RESTORE AUDI TO LIFE.
!!

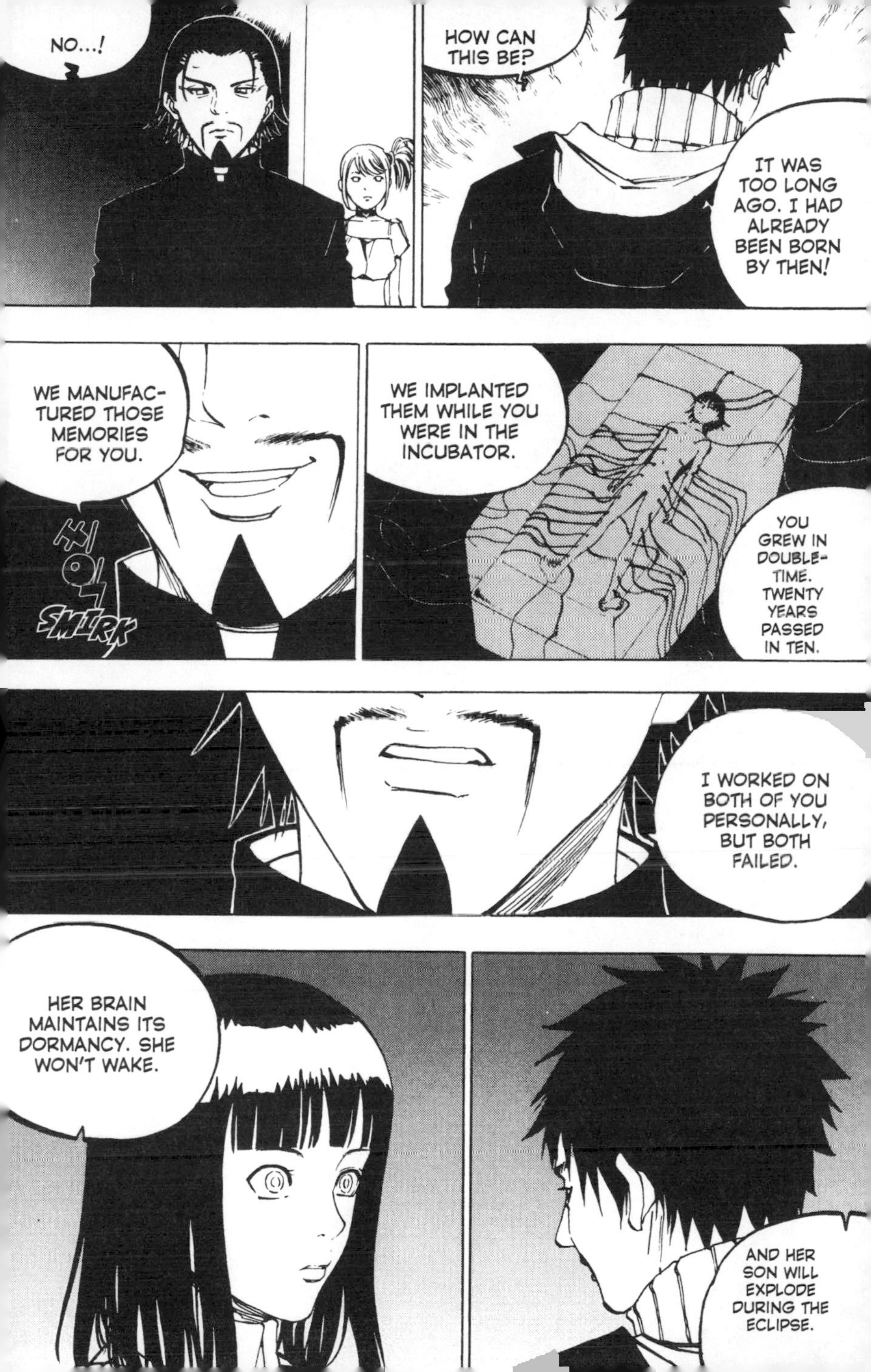
NO...!
HOW CAN THIS BE?
IT WAS TOO LONG AGO. I HAD ALREADY BEEN BORN BY THEN!
WE MANUFACTURED THOSE MEMORIES FOR YOU.
SMIRK
WE IMPLANTED THEM WHILE YOU WERE IN THE INCUBATOR.
YOU GREW IN DOUBLE-TIME. TWENTY YEARS PASSED IN TEN.
I WORKED ON BOTH OF YOU PERSONALLY, BUT BOTH FAILED.
HER BRAIN MAINTAINS ITS DORMANCY. SHE WON'T WAKE.
AND HER SON WILL EXPLODE DURING THE ECLIPSE.

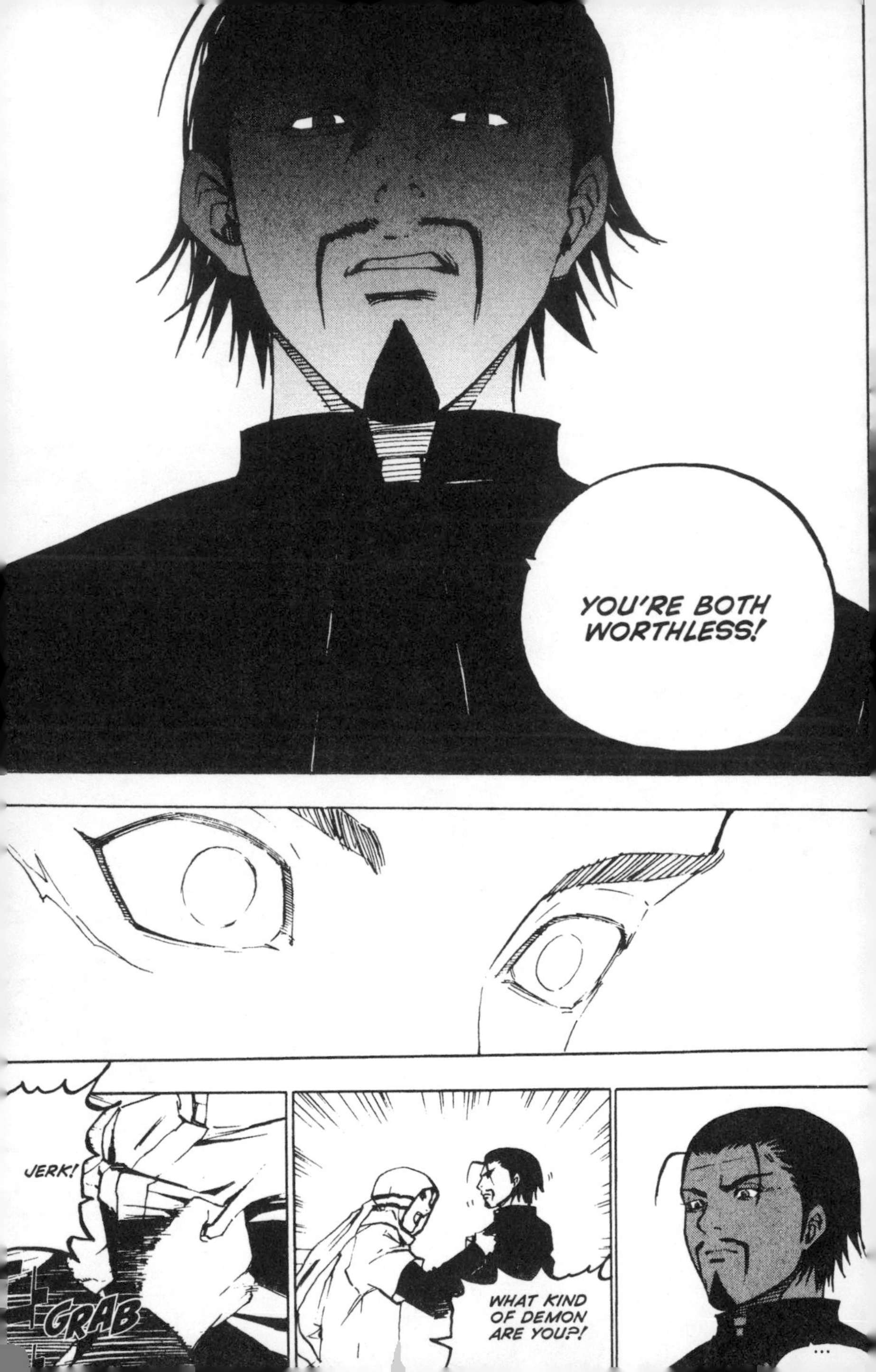
YOU'RE BOTH WORTHLESS!
JERK!
GRAB
WHAT KIND OF DEMON ARE YOU?!
...

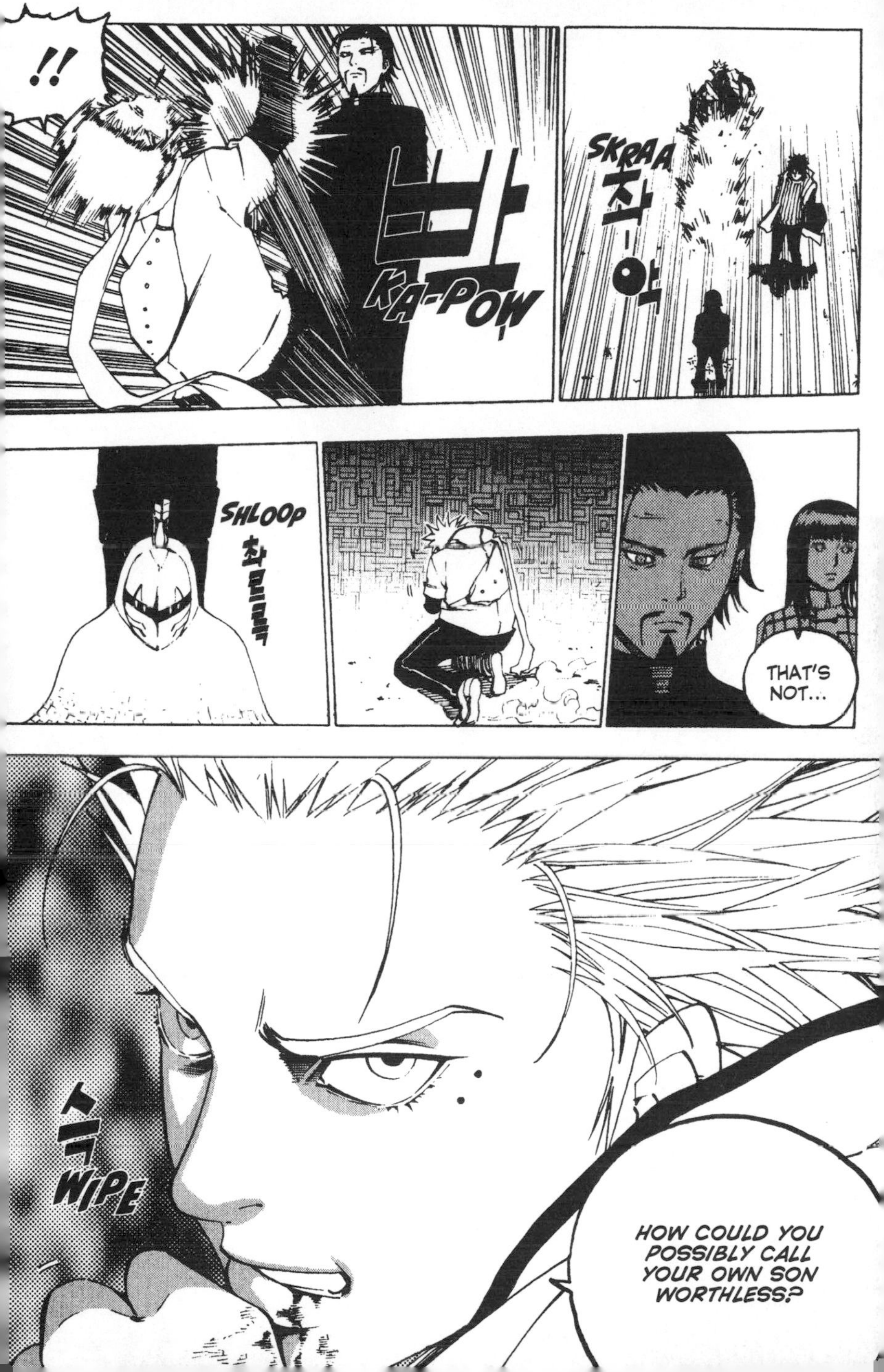
!!
빠
KA-POW
SKRAA
촤-악
SHLOOP
촤르륵
THAT'S NOT...
WIPE
HOW COULD YOU POSSIBLY CALL YOUR OWN SON WORTHLESS?

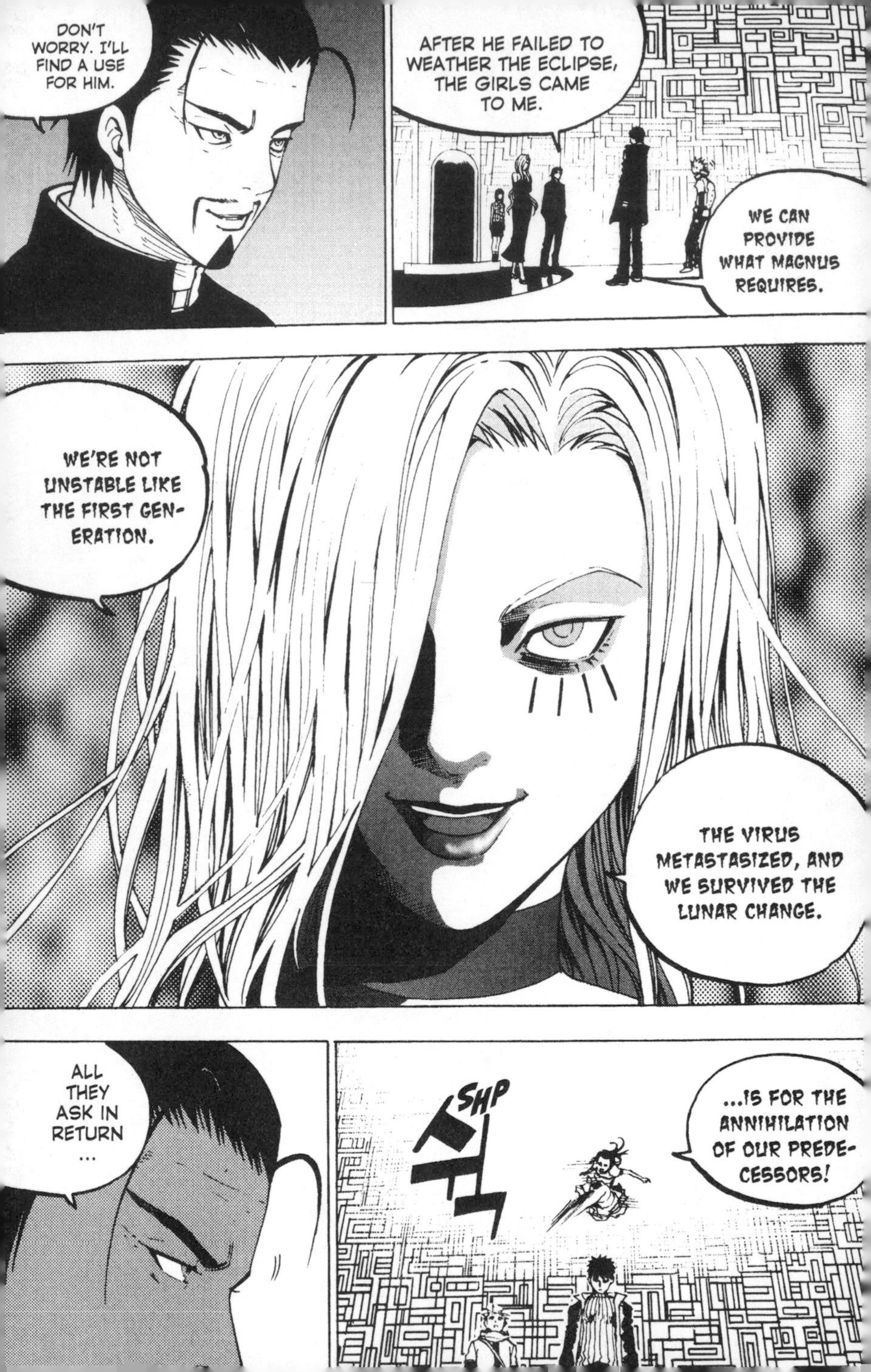
DON'T WORRY. I'LL FIND A USE FOR HIM.
AFTER HE FAILED TO WEATHER THE ECLIPSE, THE GIRLS CAME TO ME.
WE CAN PROVIDE WHAT MAGNUS REQUIRES.
WE'RE NOT UNSTABLE LIKE THE FIRST GEN-ERATION.
THE VIRUS METASTASIZED, AND WE SURVIVED THE LUNAR CHANGE.
ALL THEY ASK IN RETURN ...
SHP
...IS FOR THE ANNIHILATION OF OUR PREDE-CESSORS!

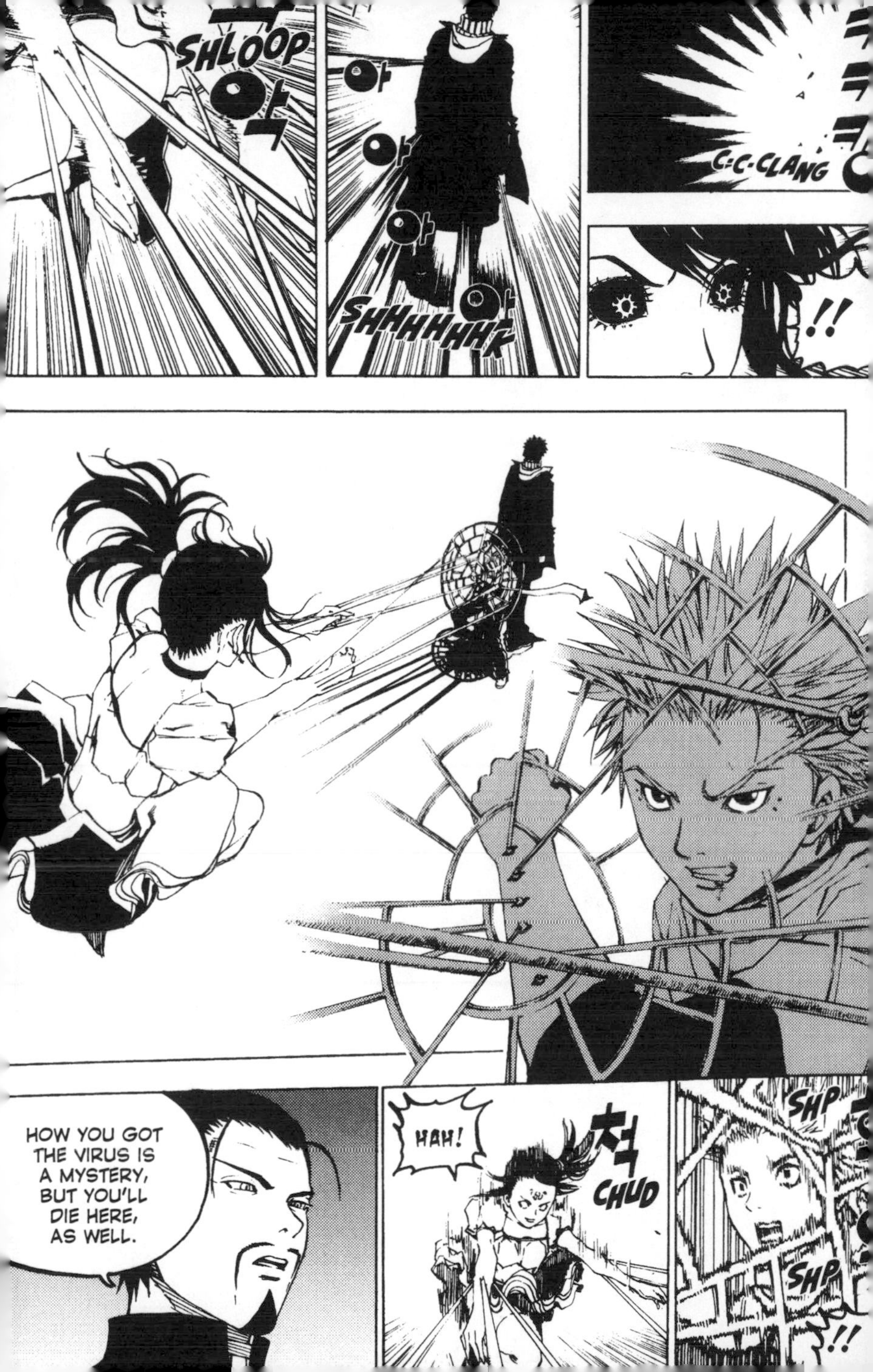
SHLOOP
SHHHHHHK
C-C-CLANG
!!
HOW YOU GOT THE VIRUS IS A MYSTERY, BUT YOU'LL DIE HERE, AS WELL.
HAH!
CHUD
SHP
SHP
!!

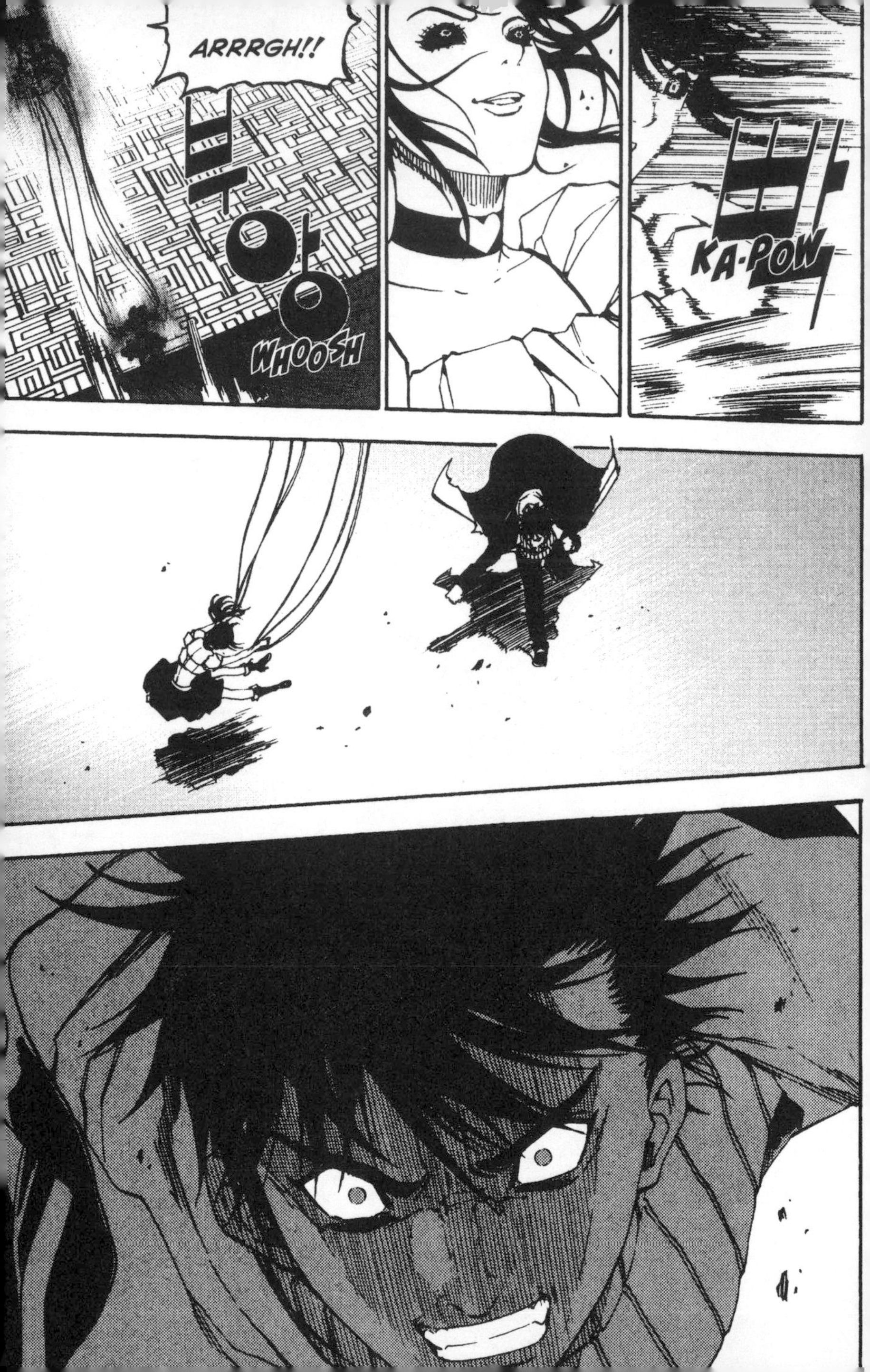
ARRRGH!!
WHOOSH
KA-POW

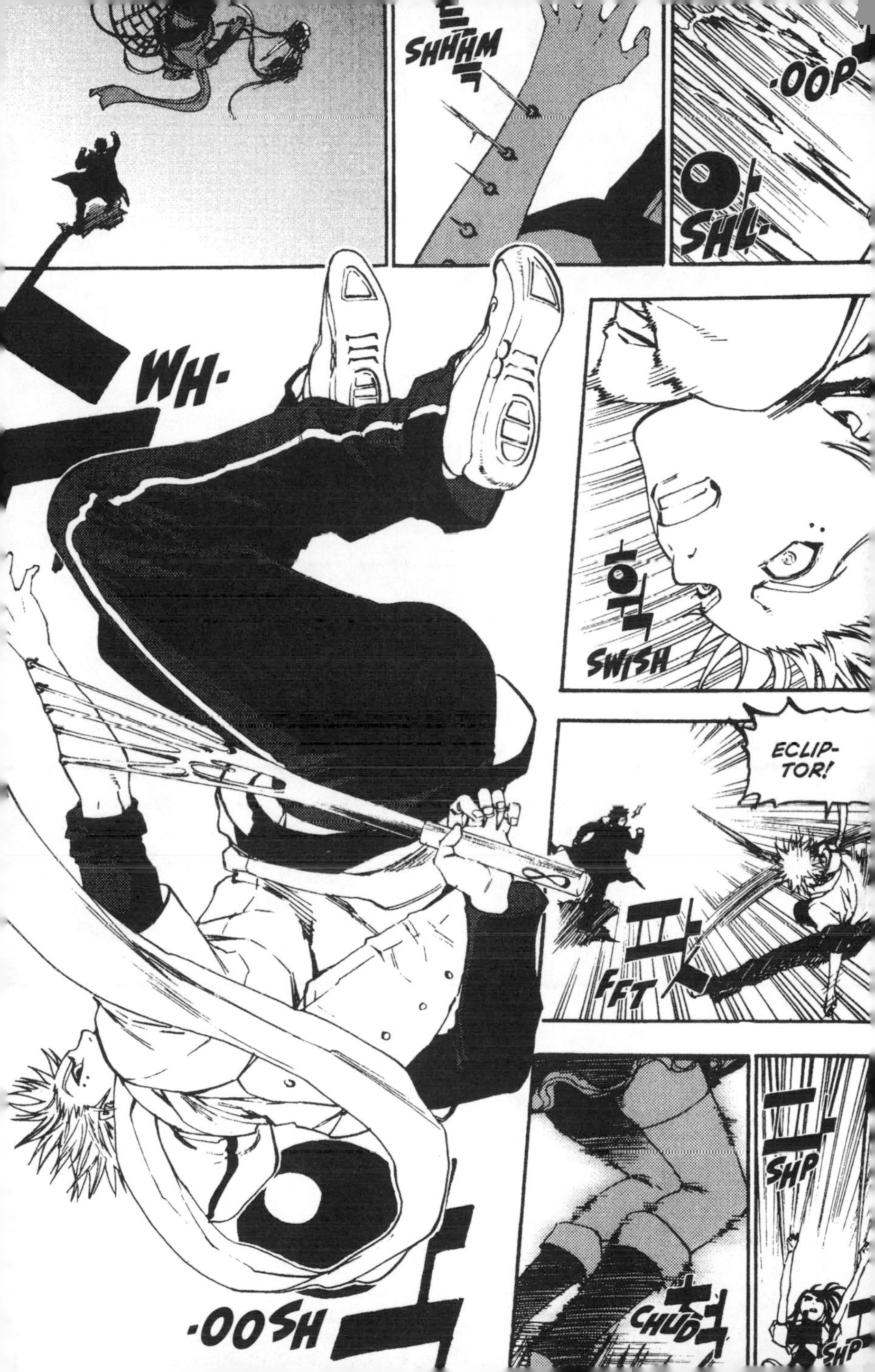
SHHHM
-OOP
SHL-
WH-
SWISH
ECLIP-
TOR!
FFT
-OOSH
SHP
CHUD
SHP

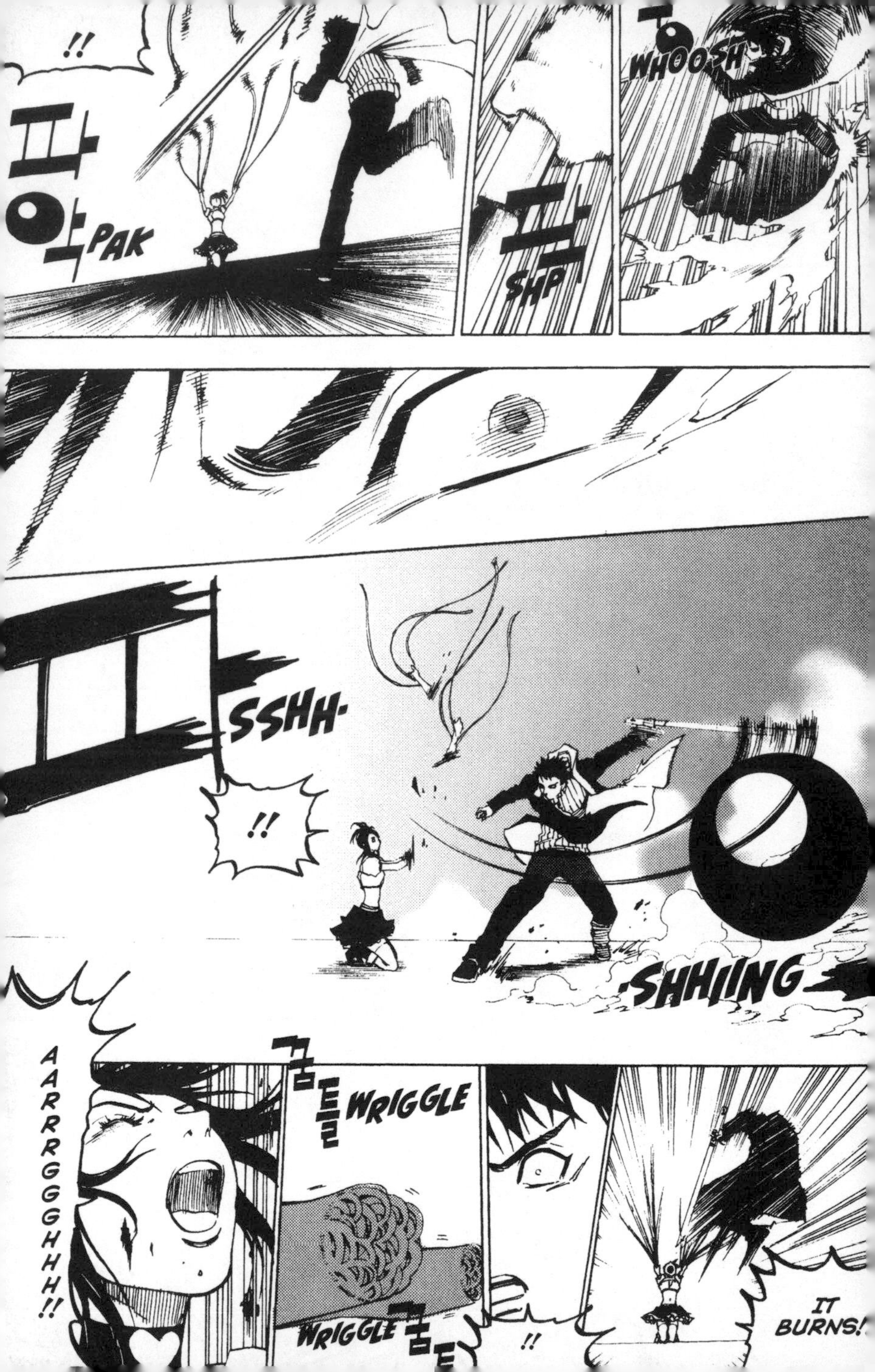
!!
파악 PAK
SHP
WHOOSH
SSHH-
!!
-SHHIING-
AARRRGGGHHH!!
꿈틀 WRIGGLE
WRIGGLE 꿈틀
!!
IT BURNS!

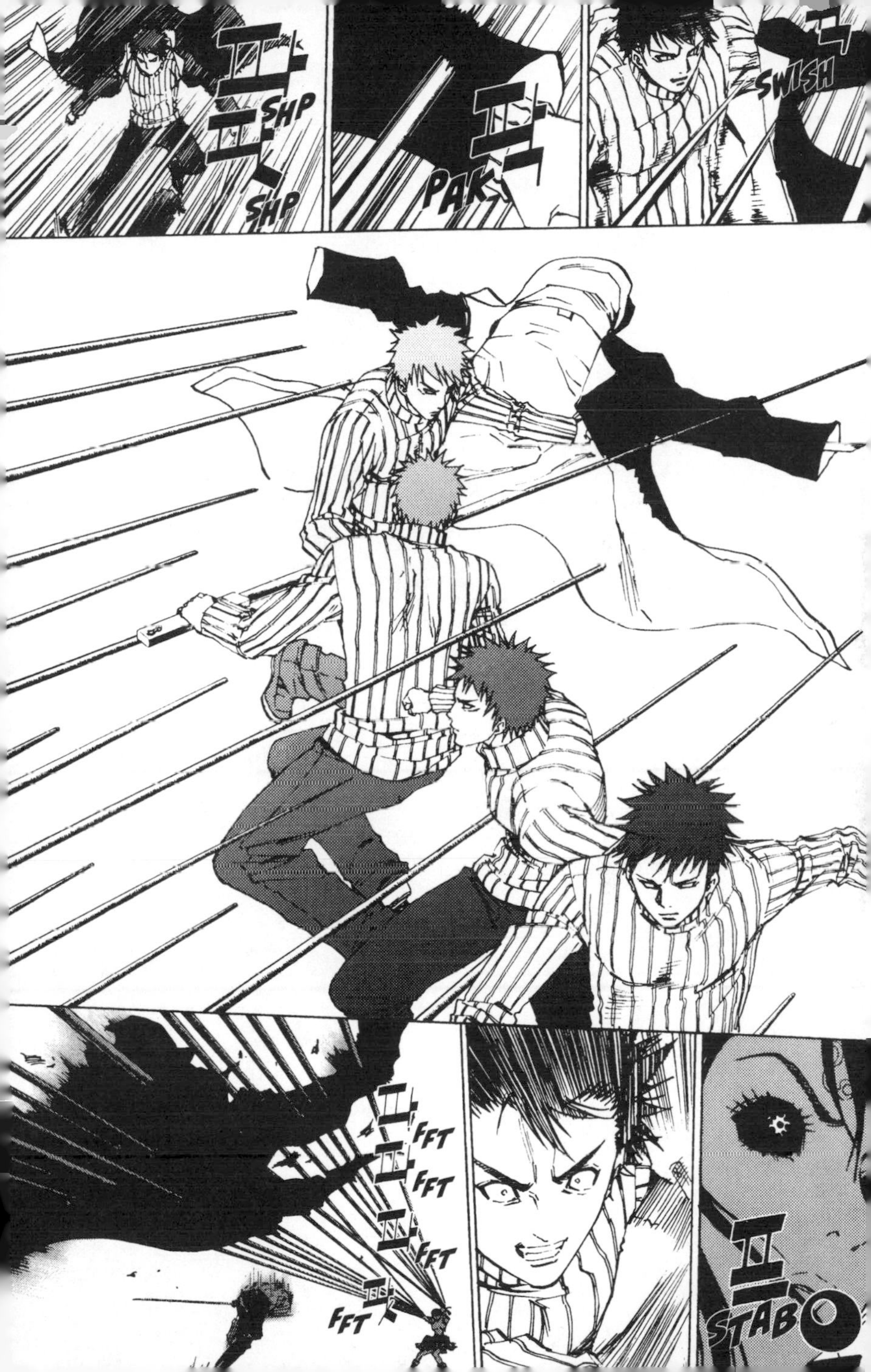
SHP
SHP
PAK
SWISH
FFT
FFT
FFT
FFT
STAB

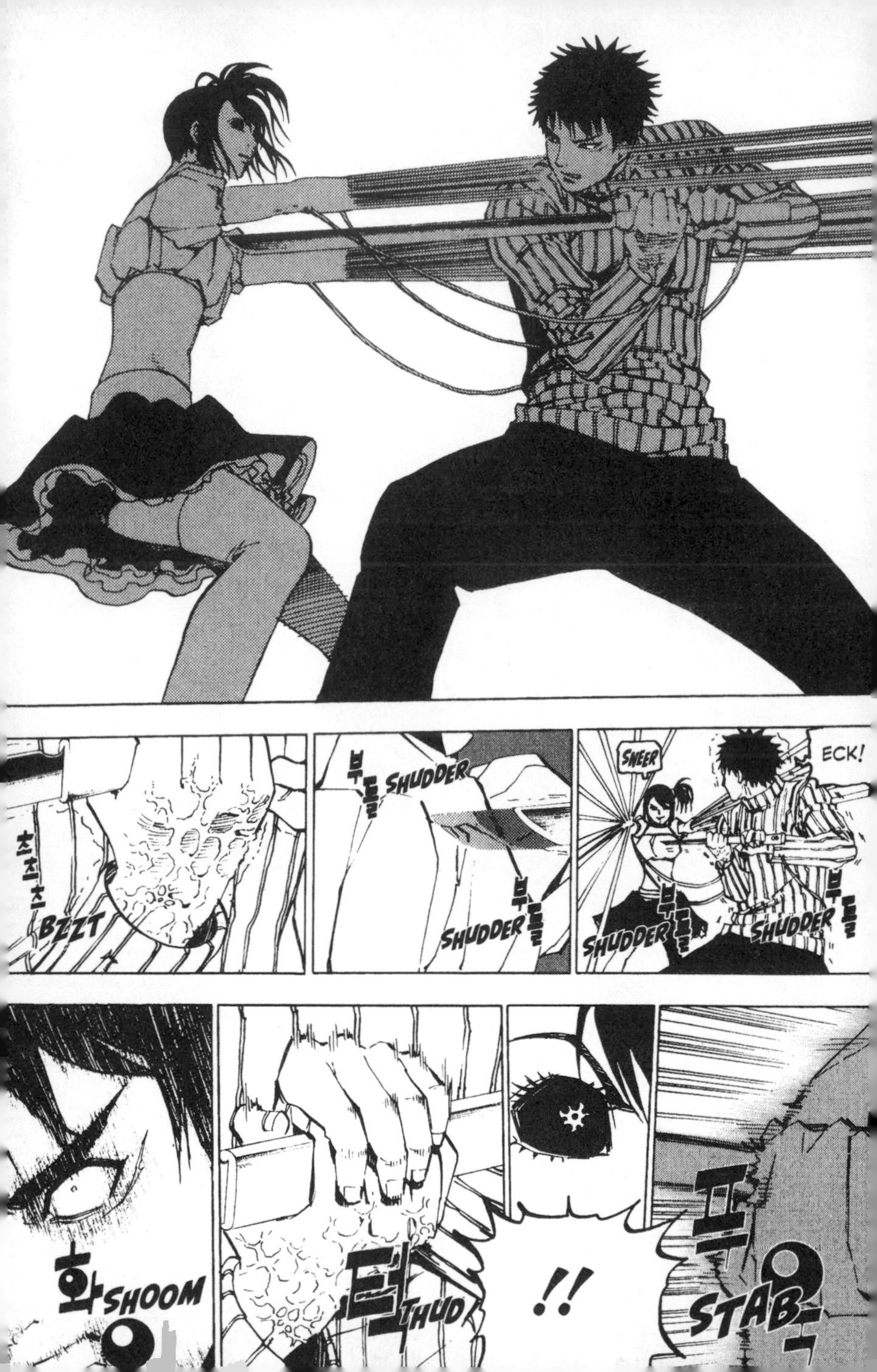
츠츠츠
BZZT
부들
SHUDDER
부들
SHUDDER
SNEER
ECK!
부들
SHUDDER
부들
SHUDDER
화
SHOOM
턱
THUD
!!
푸욱
STAB

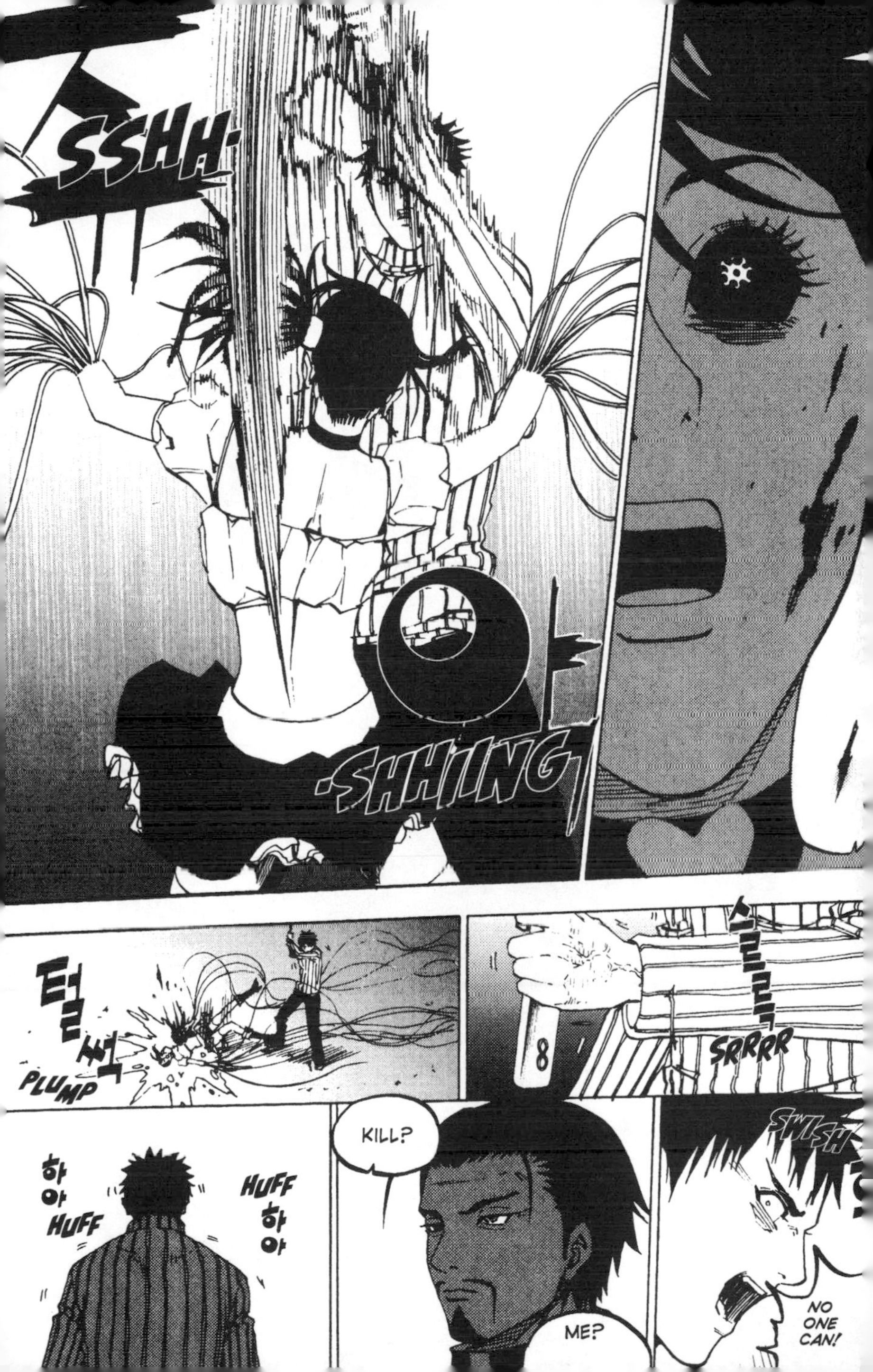
SSHH-
-SHHING
털썩
PLUMP
SRRRR
하아
HUFF
HUFF
하아
KILL?
ME?
SWISH
NO ONE CAN!

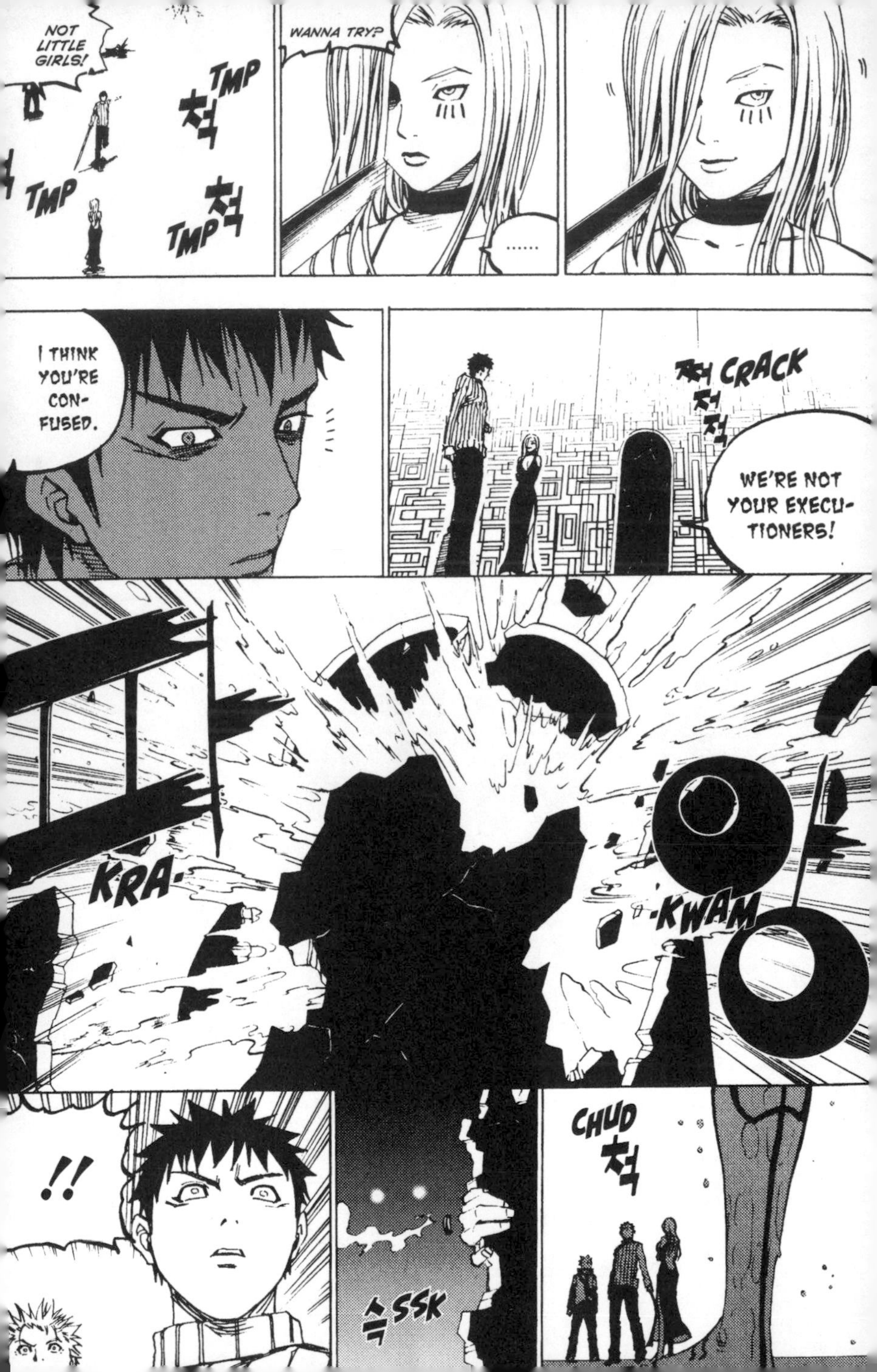
NOT LITTLE GIRLS!
TMP 척
TMP
TMP 척
WANNA TRY?
......
I THINK YOU'RE CON-FUSED.
쩍 CRACK
쩍
쩍
WE'RE NOT YOUR EXECU-TIONERS!
KRA-
-KWAM
!!
슥 SSK
CHUD
척

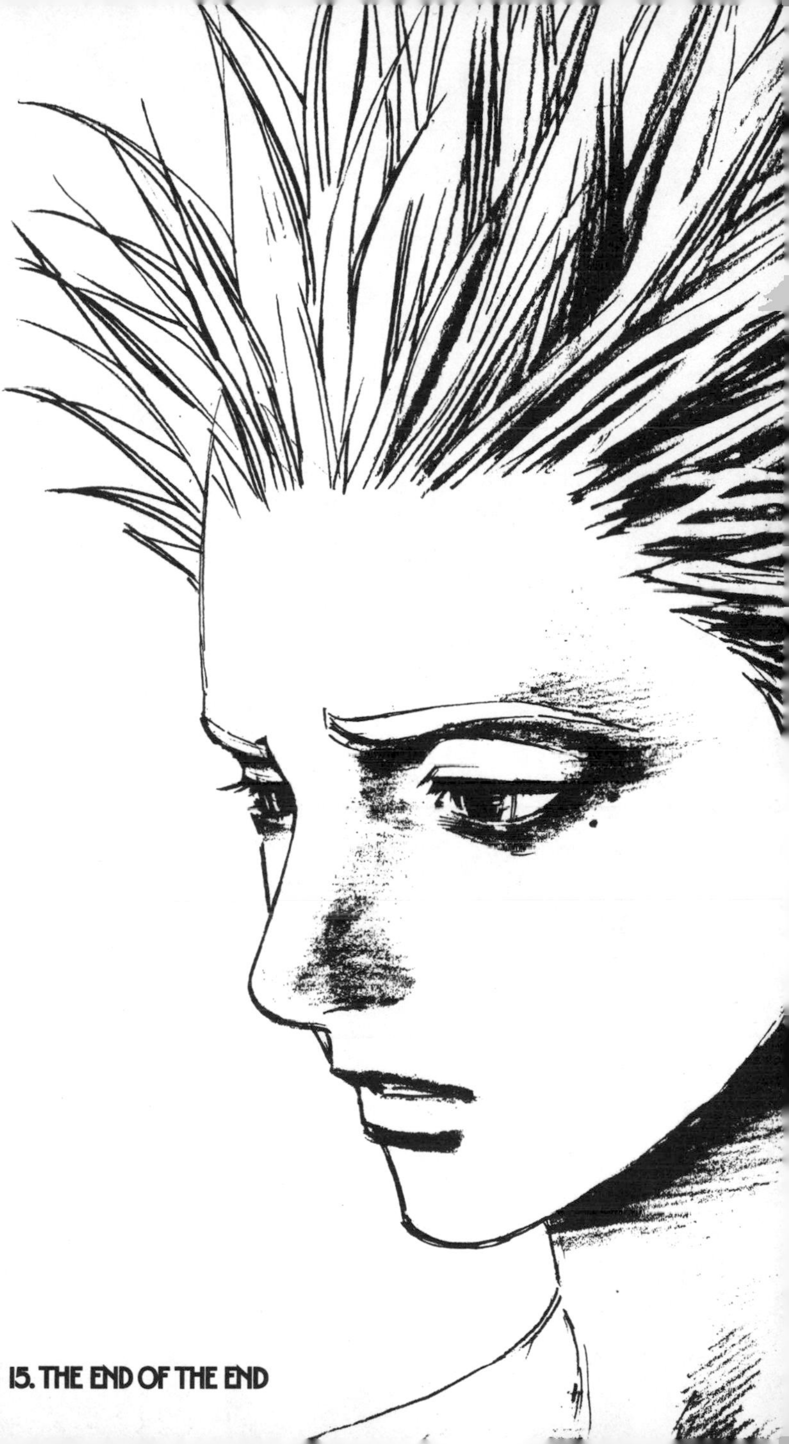

## CAR 15. THE END OF THE END

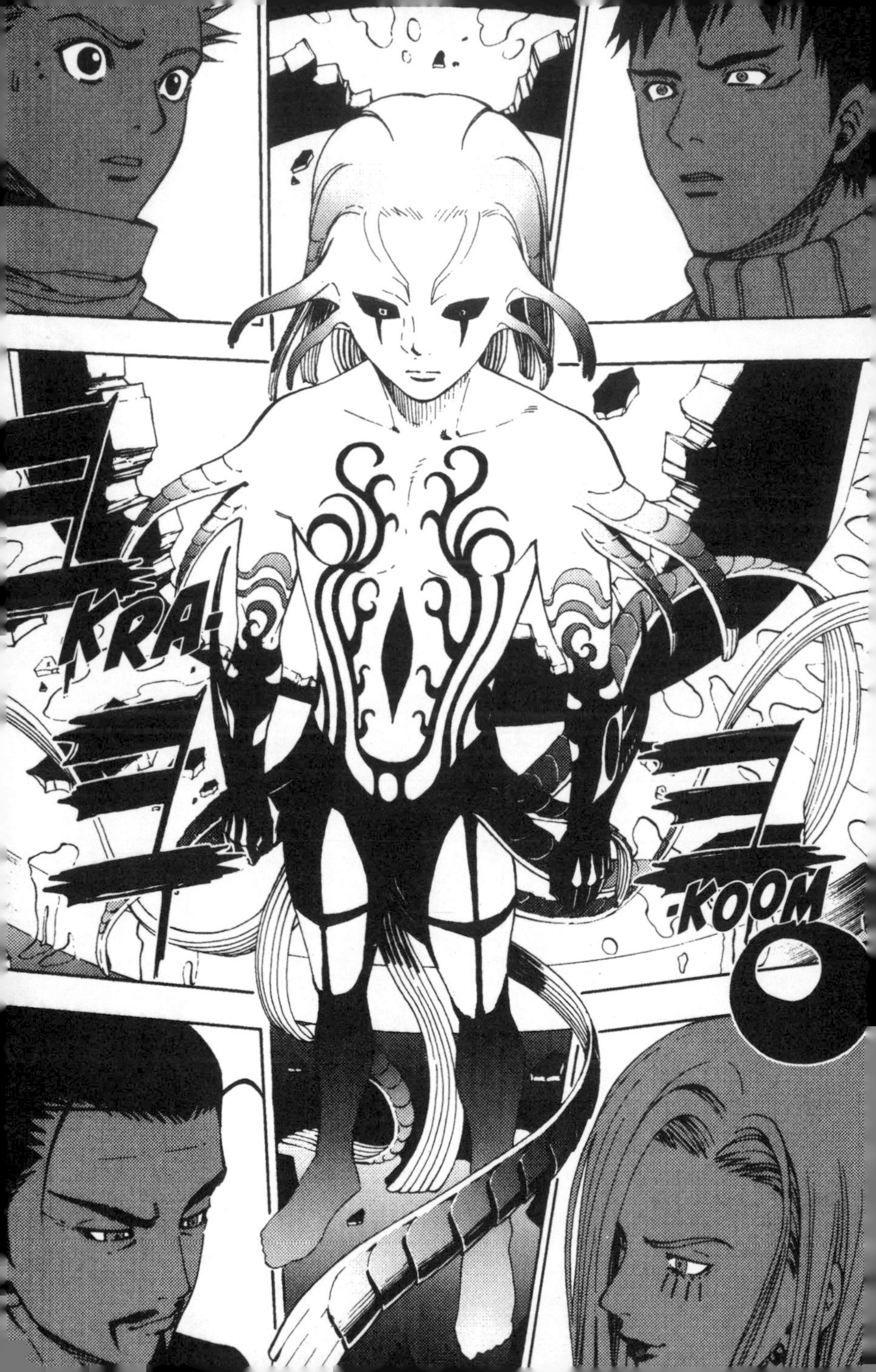
KRA-
-KOOM

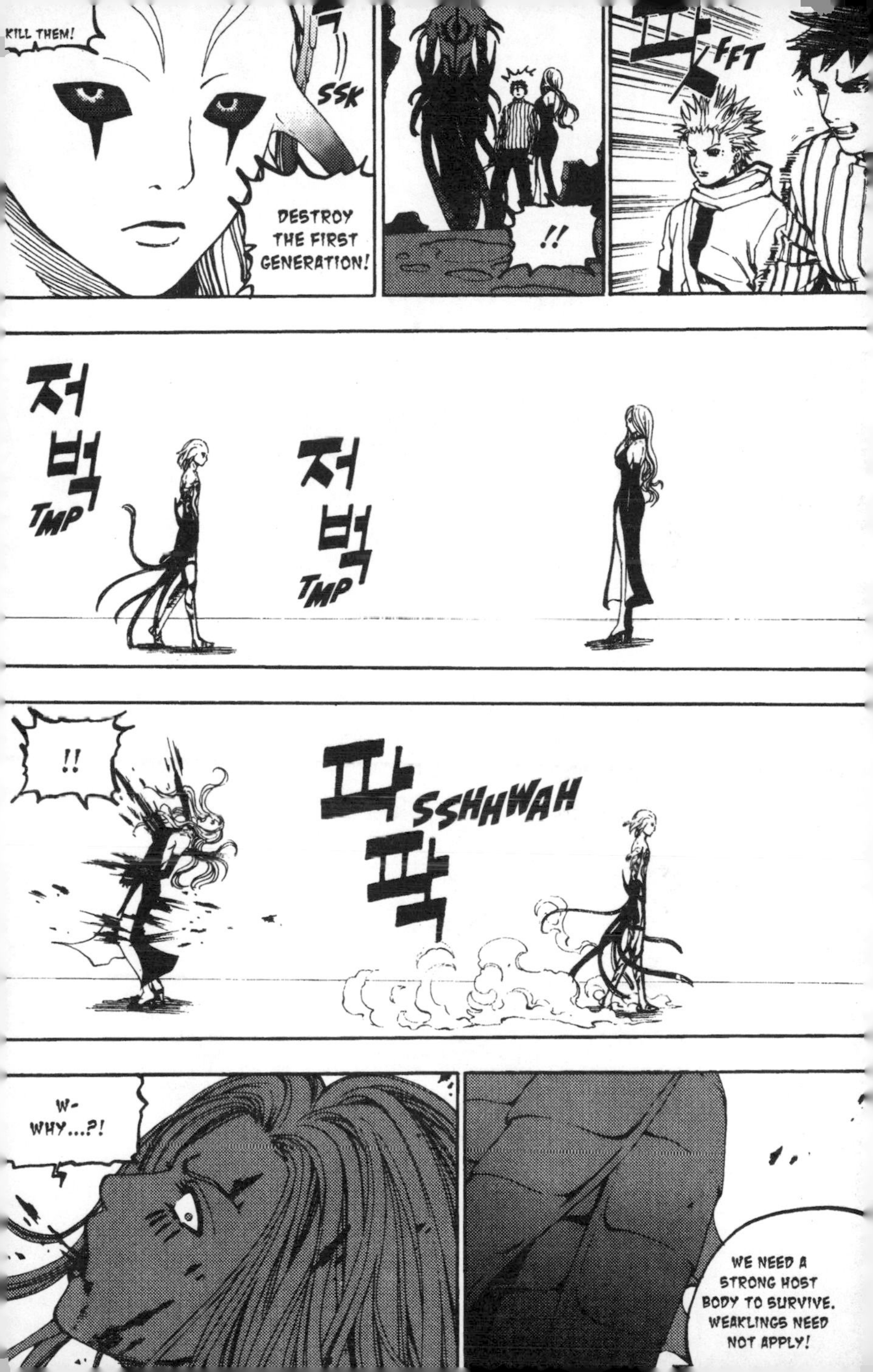
KILL THEM!
SSK
DESTROY THE FIRST GENERATION!
!!
FFT
저벅
TMP
저벅
TMP
!!
파
SSHHWAH
팍
W- WHY...?!
WE NEED A STRONG HOST BODY TO SURVIVE. WEAKLINGS NEED NOT APPLY!

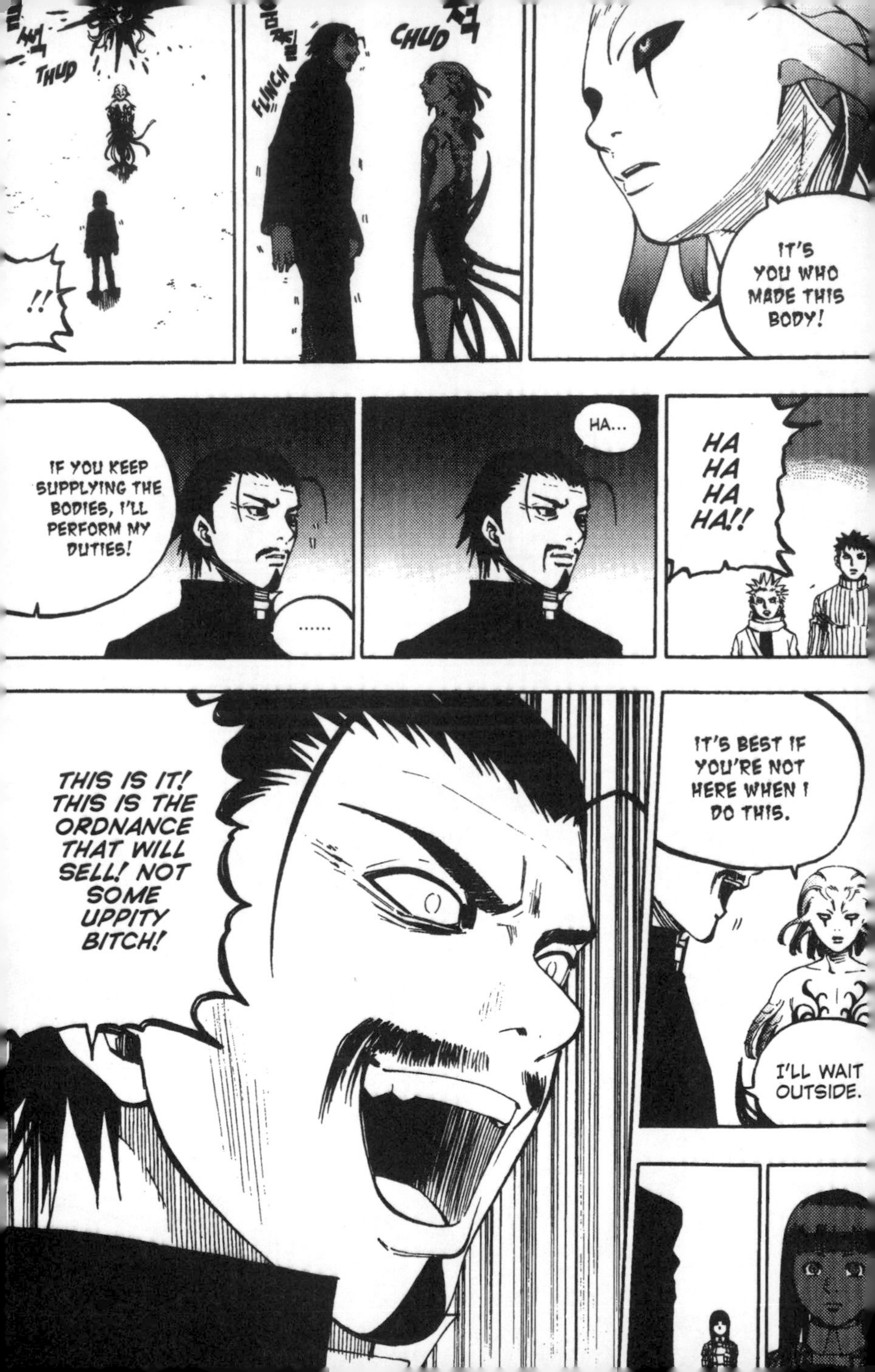
THUD
!!
FLINCH
CHUD
IT'S YOU WHO MADE THIS BODY!
IF YOU KEEP SUPPLYING THE BODIES, I'LL PERFORM MY DUTIES!
......
HA...
HA HA HA HA!!
THIS IS IT! THIS IS THE ORDNANCE THAT WILL SELL! NOT SOME UPPITY BITCH!
IT'S BEST IF YOU'RE NOT HERE WHEN I DO THIS.
I'LL WAIT OUTSIDE.

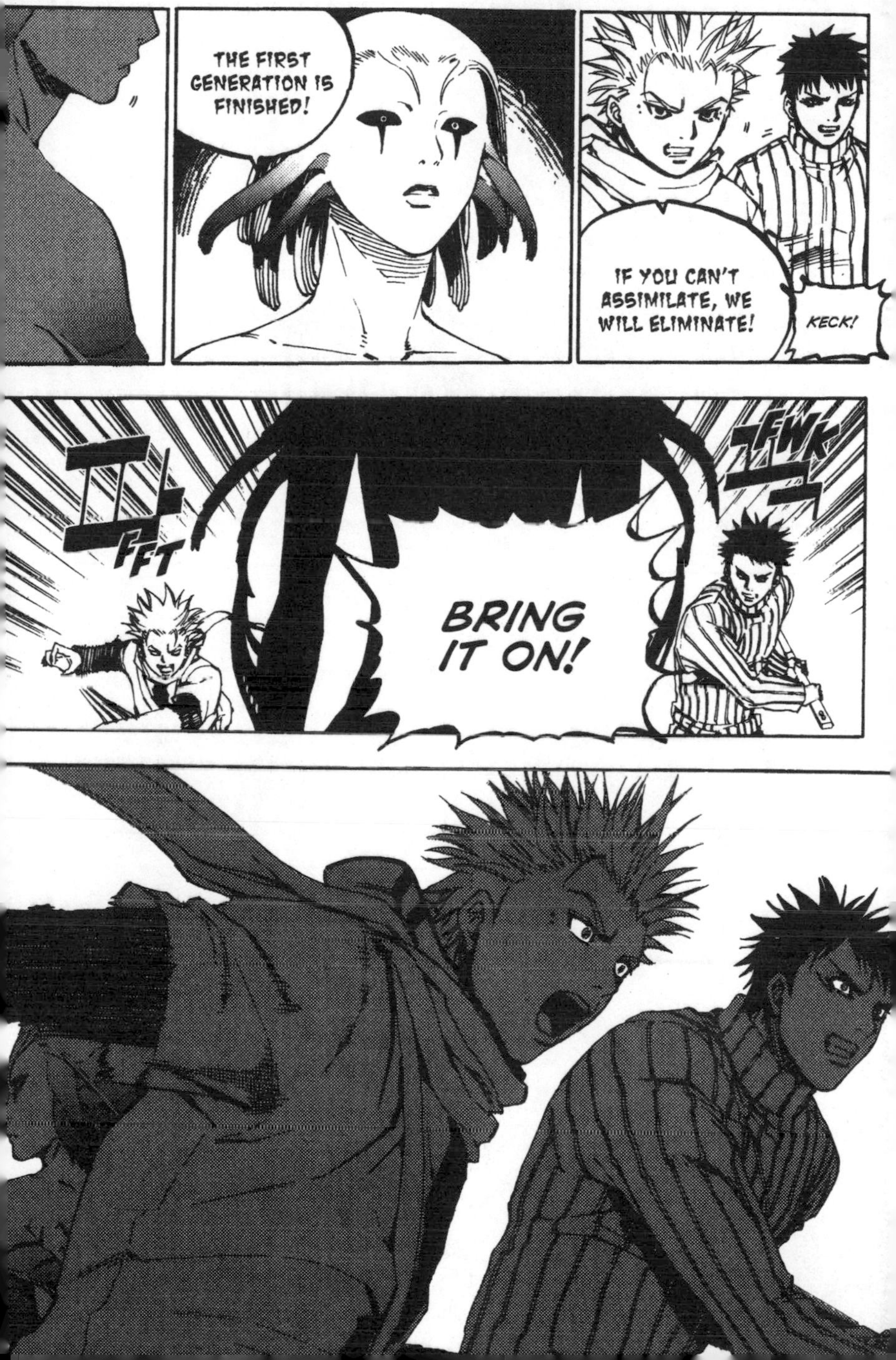
THE FIRST GENERATION IS FINISHED!
IF YOU CAN'T ASSIMILATE, WE WILL ELIMINATE!
KECK!
FFT
FWK
BRING IT ON!

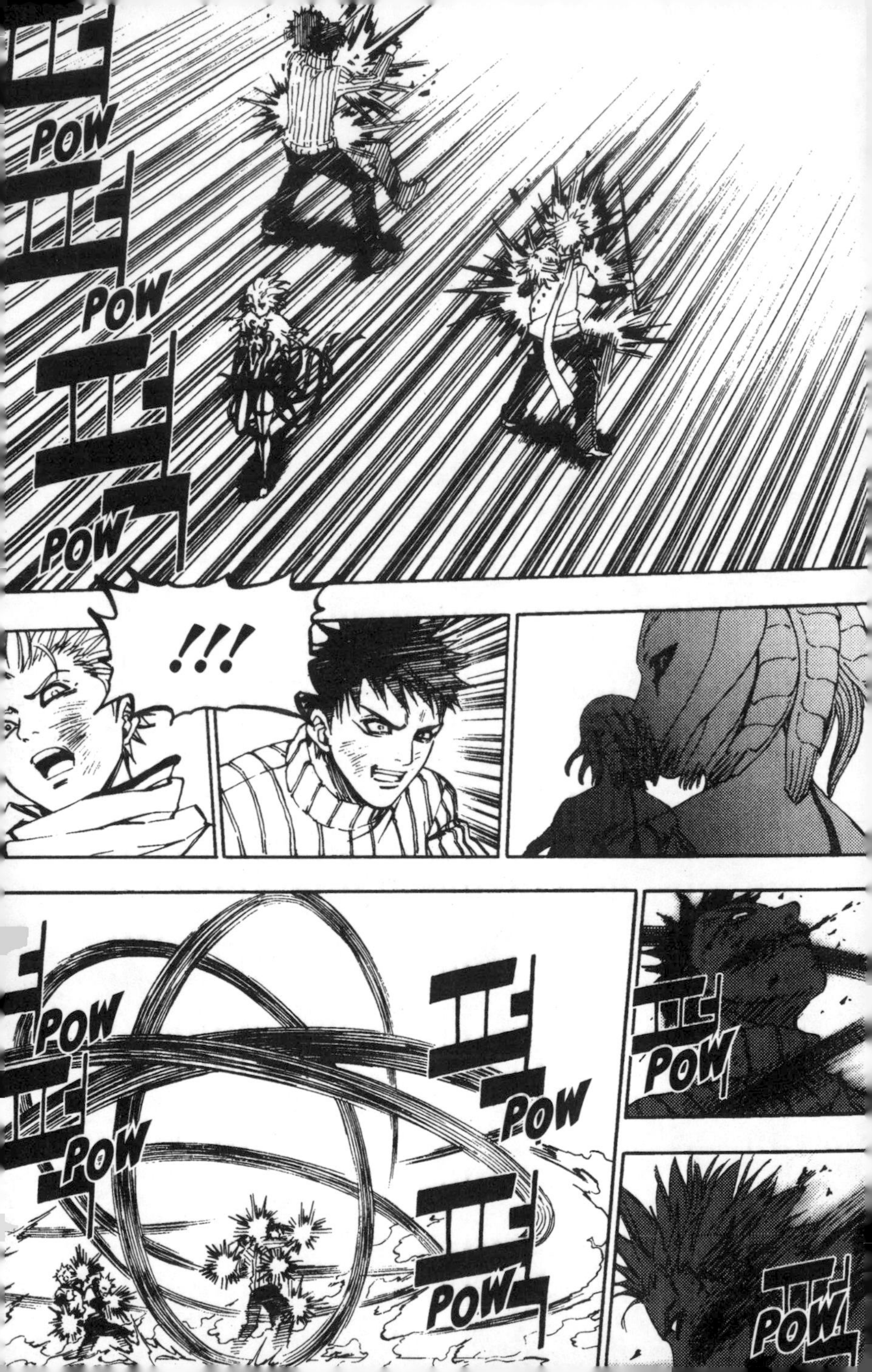
POW
POW
POW
!!!
POW
POW
POW
POW
POW
POW

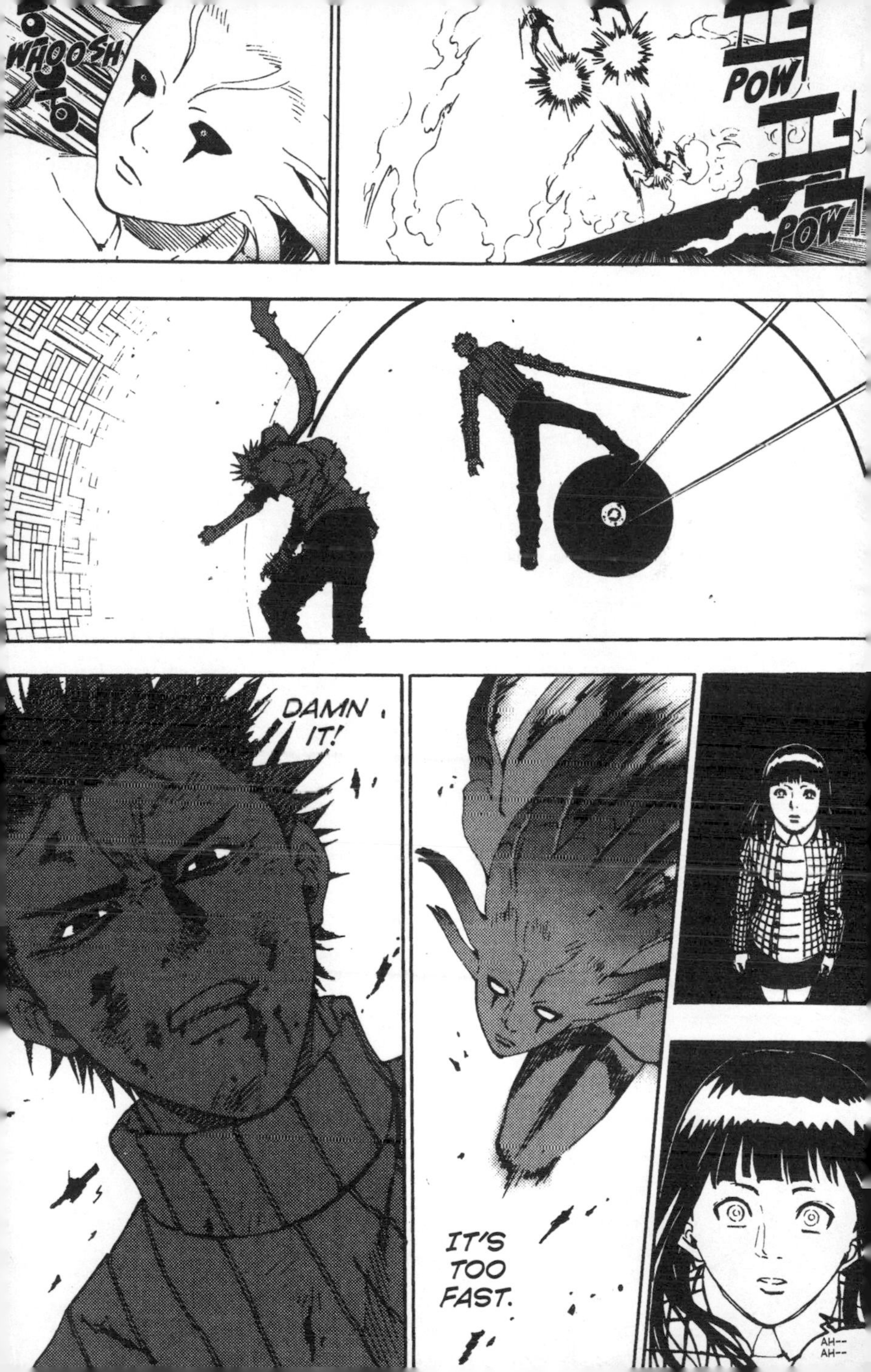
WHOOSH
POW
POW
DAMN IT!
IT'S TOO FAST.
AH-- AH--

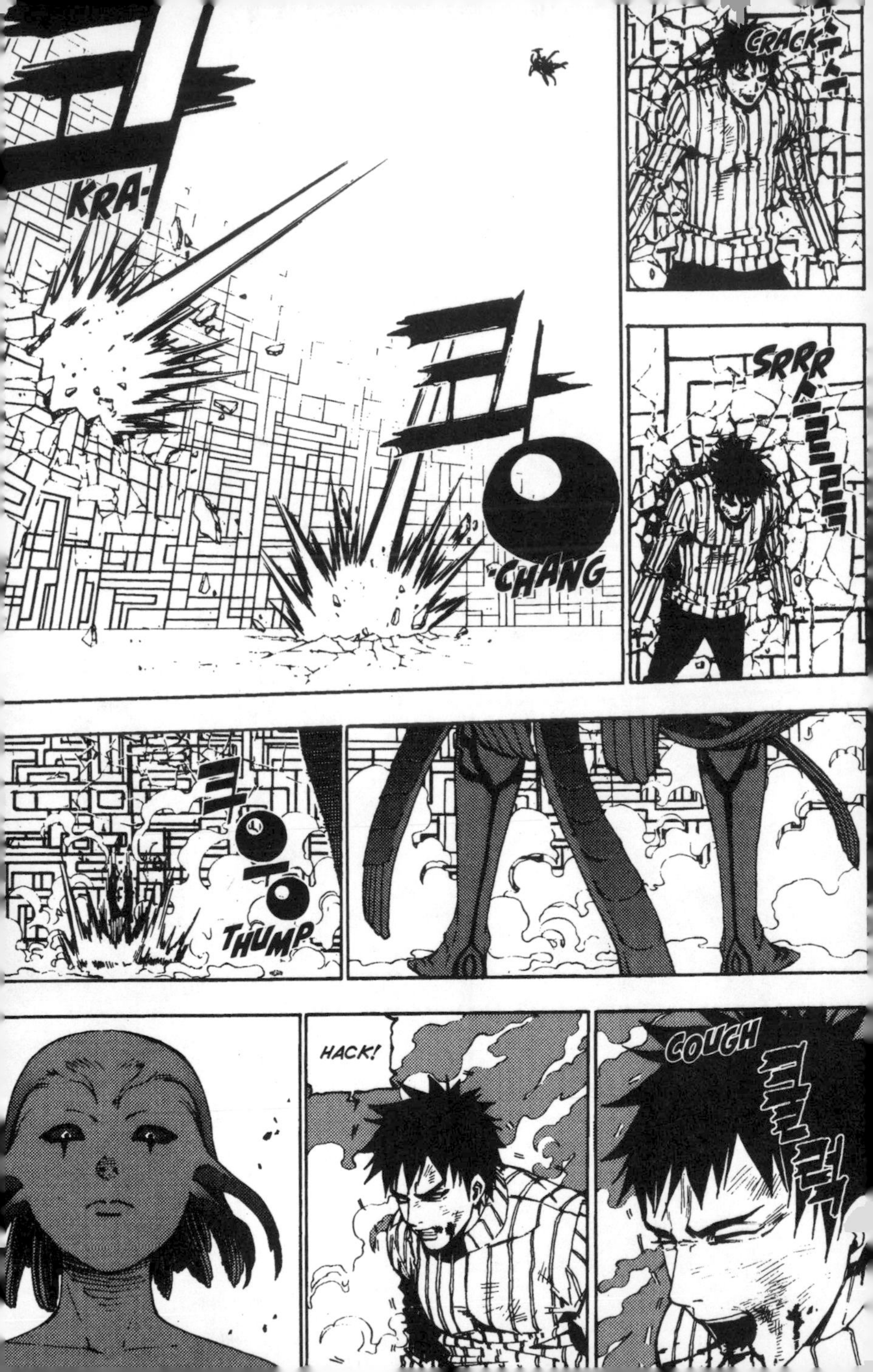
KRA-
-CHANG
CRACK
SRRR
THUMP
HACK!
COUGH

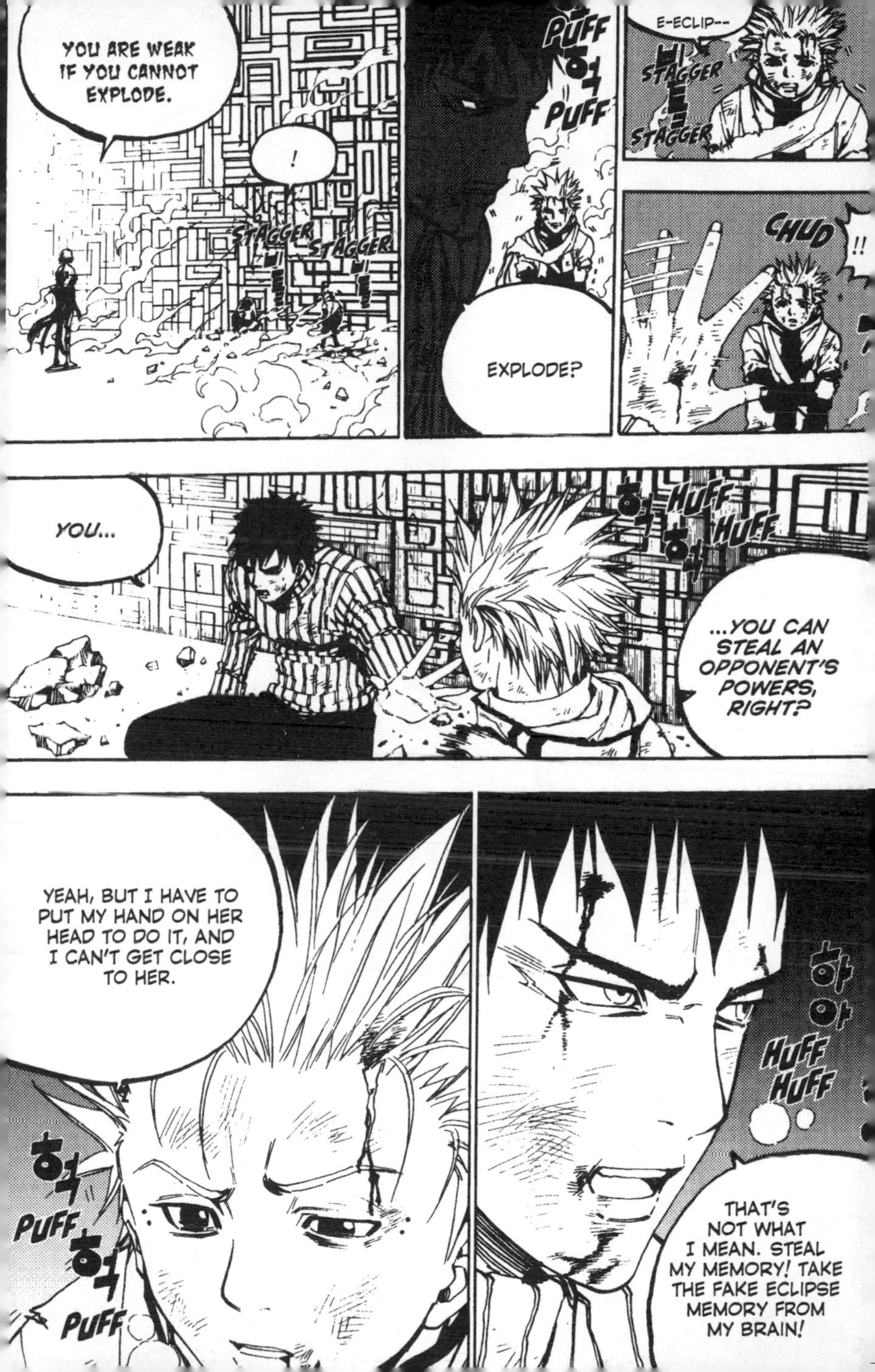
YOU ARE WEAK IF YOU CANNOT EXPLODE.
!
STAGGER
STAGGER
PUFF 헉 PUFF
EXPLODE?
E-ECLIP--
STAGGER
STAGGER
CHUD
!!
YOU...
헉 헉
HUFF HUFF
...YOU CAN STEAL AN OPPONENT'S POWERS, RIGHT?
YEAH, BUT I HAVE TO PUT MY HAND ON HER HEAD TO DO IT, AND I CAN'T GET CLOSE TO HER.
헉 PUFF 헉 PUFF
하아
HUFF HUFF
THAT'S NOT WHAT I MEAN. STEAL MY MEMORY! TAKE THE FAKE ECLIPSE MEMORY FROM MY BRAIN!

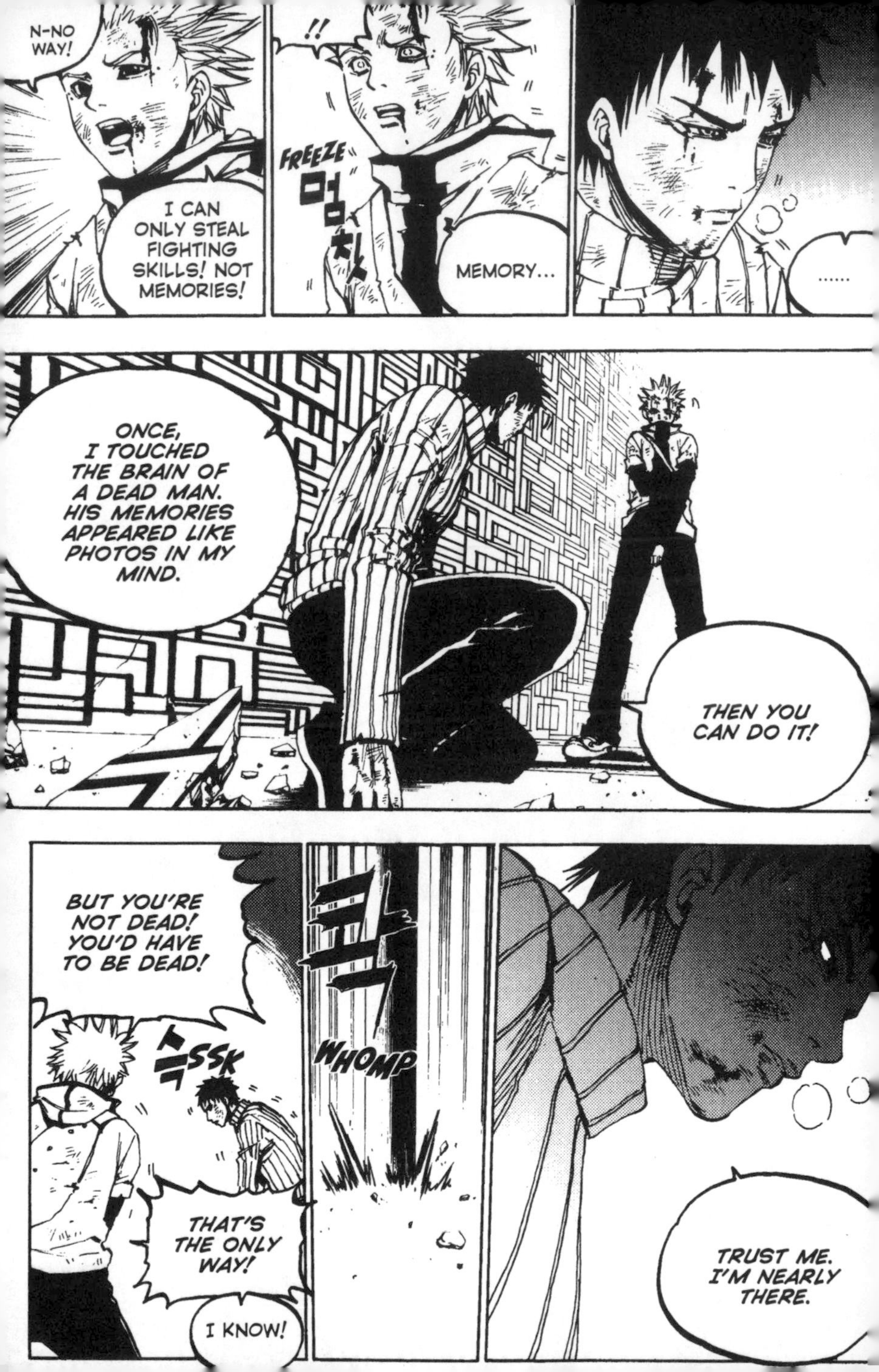
N-NO WAY!
I CAN ONLY STEAL FIGHTING SKILLS! NOT MEMORIES!
!!
FREEZE
멈칫
MEMORY...
......
ONCE, I TOUCHED THE BRAIN OF A DEAD MAN. HIS MEMORIES APPEARED LIKE PHOTOS IN MY MIND.
THEN YOU CAN DO IT!
BUT YOU'RE NOT DEAD! YOU'D HAVE TO BE DEAD!
SSK
THAT'S THE ONLY WAY!
I KNOW!
쿵
WHOMP
TRUST ME. I'M NEARLY THERE.

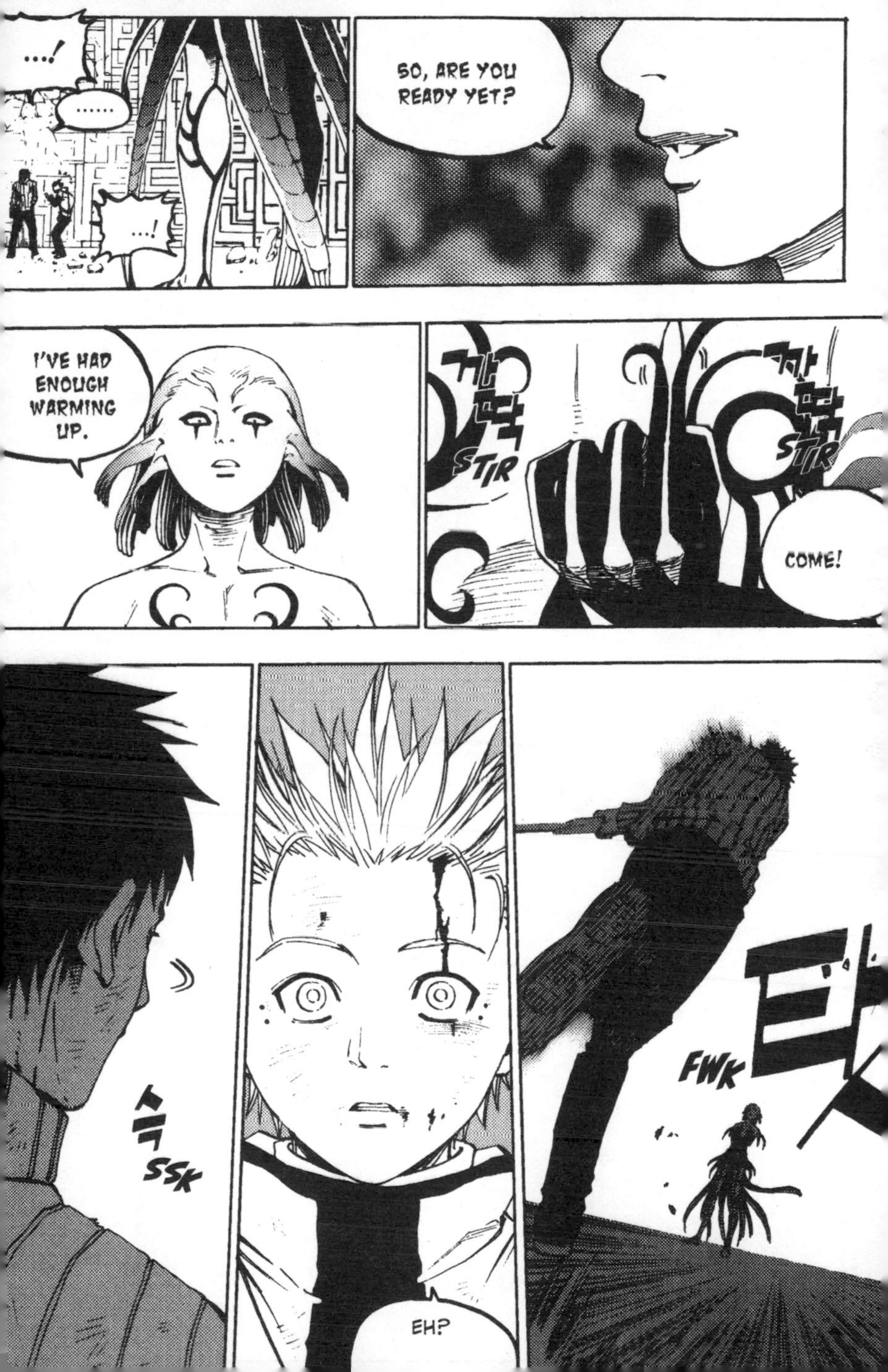

....!
.......
....!
SO, ARE YOU READY YET?
I'VE HAD ENOUGH WARMING UP.
STIR
STIR
COME!
SSK
EH?
FWK

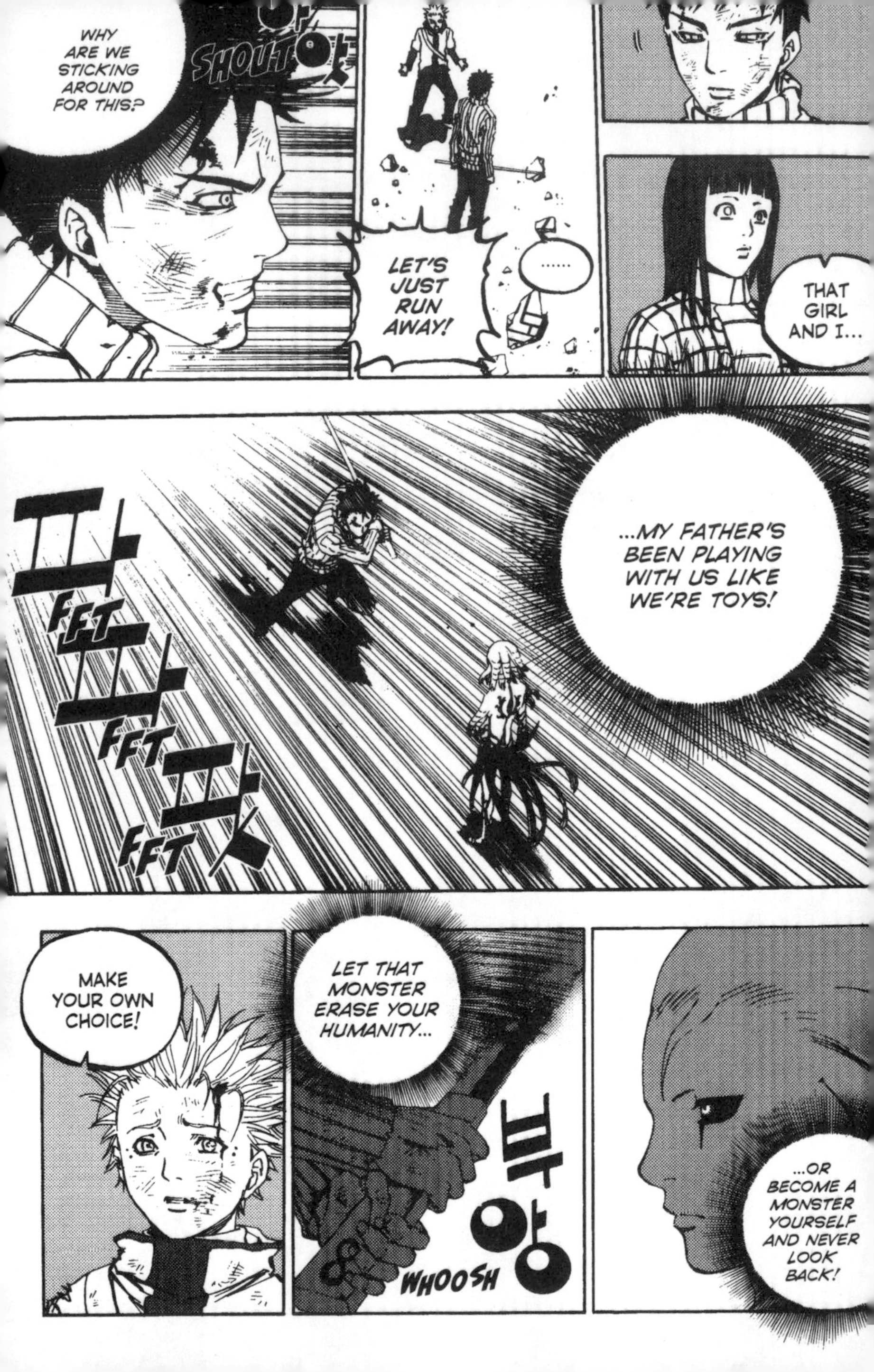
WHY ARE WE STICKING AROUND FOR THIS?
SHOUT
LET'S JUST RUN AWAY!
......
THAT GIRL AND I...
FFT
FFT
FFT
...MY FATHER'S BEEN PLAYING WITH US LIKE WE'RE TOYS!
MAKE YOUR OWN CHOICE!
LET THAT MONSTER ERASE YOUR HUMANITY...
WHOOSH
...OR BECOME A MONSTER YOURSELF AND NEVER LOOK BACK!

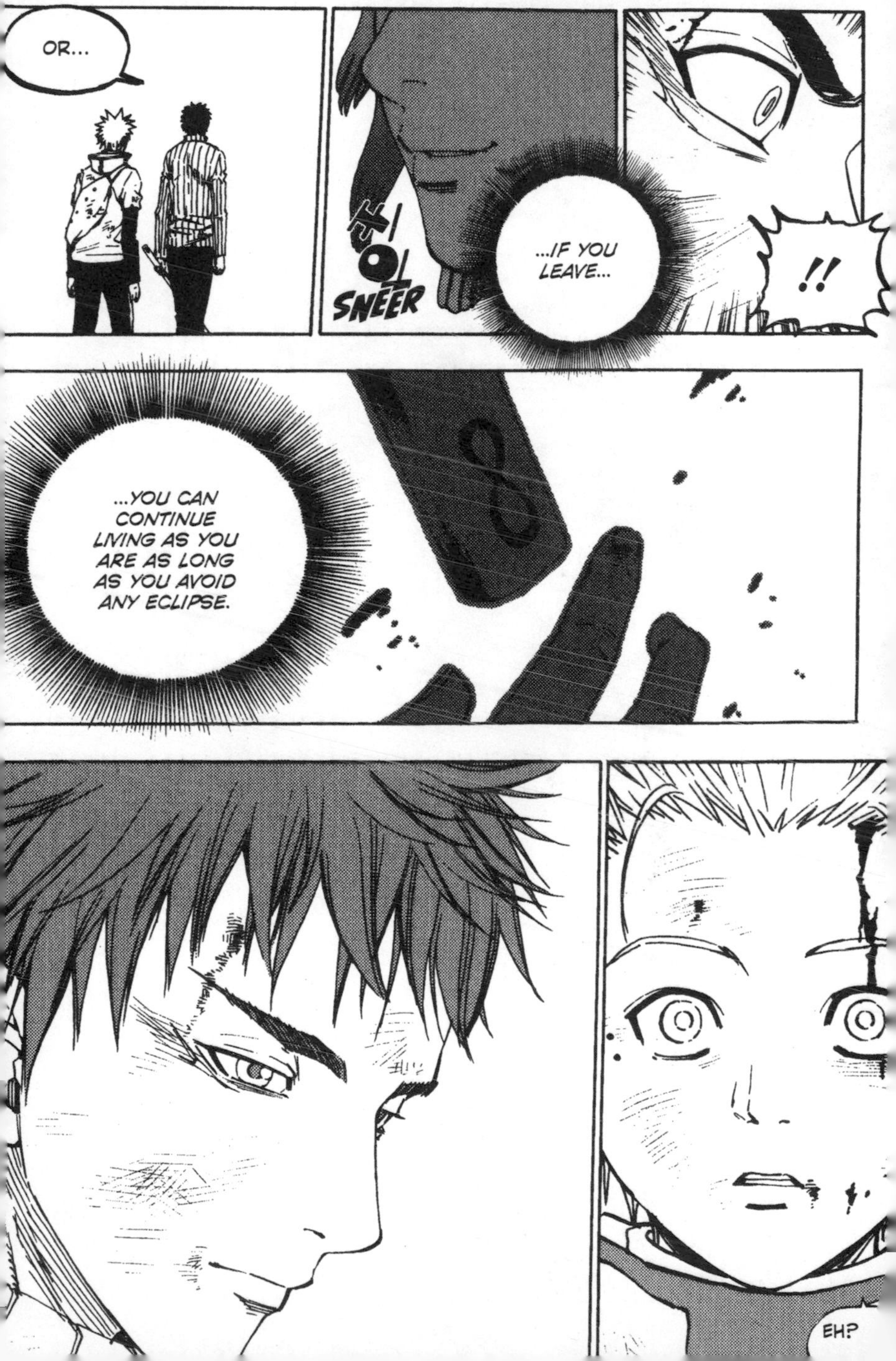
OR...
SNEER
...IF YOU LEAVE...
!!
...YOU CAN CONTINUE LIVING AS YOU ARE AS LONG AS YOU AVOID ANY ECLIPSE.
EH?

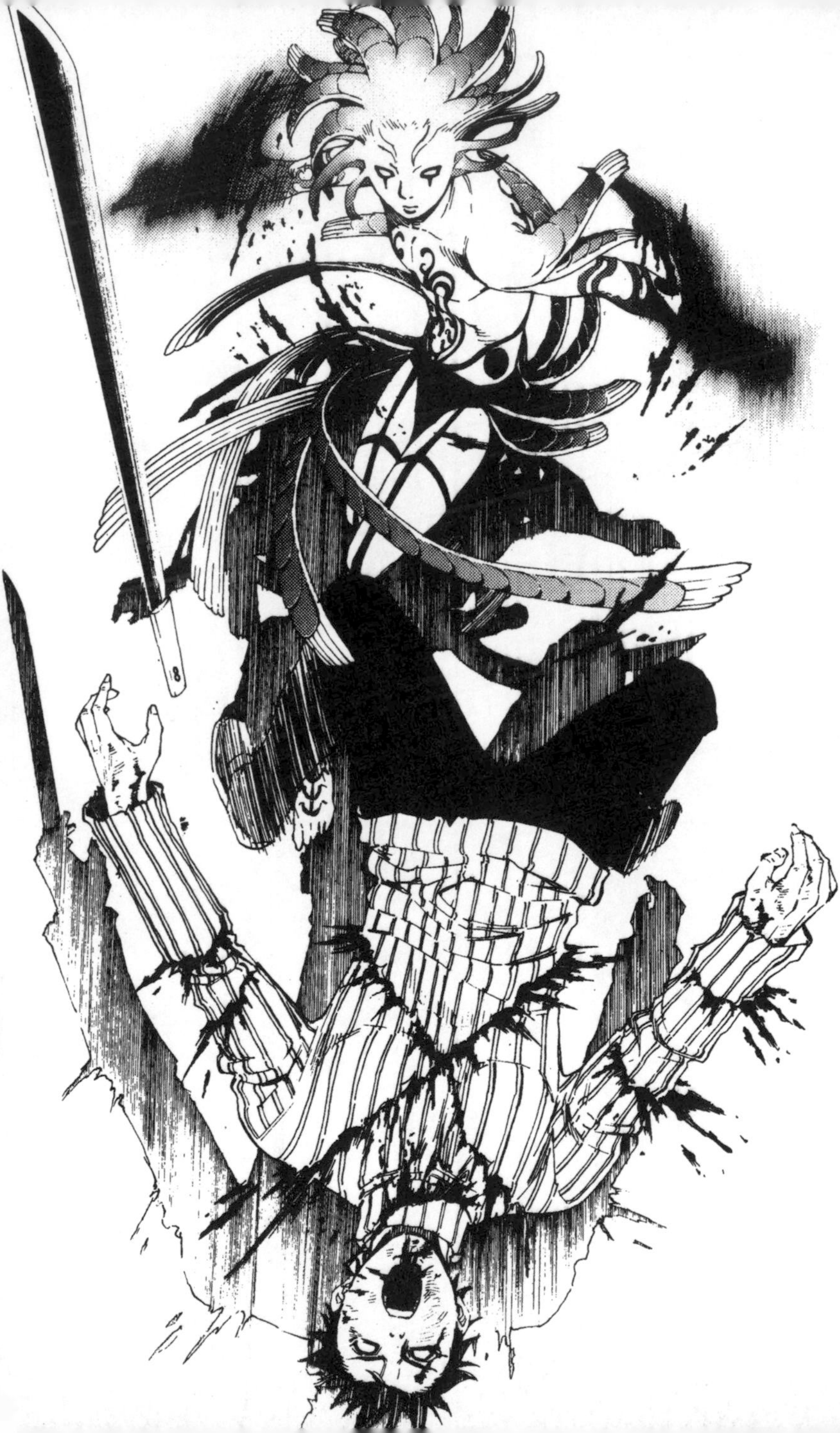

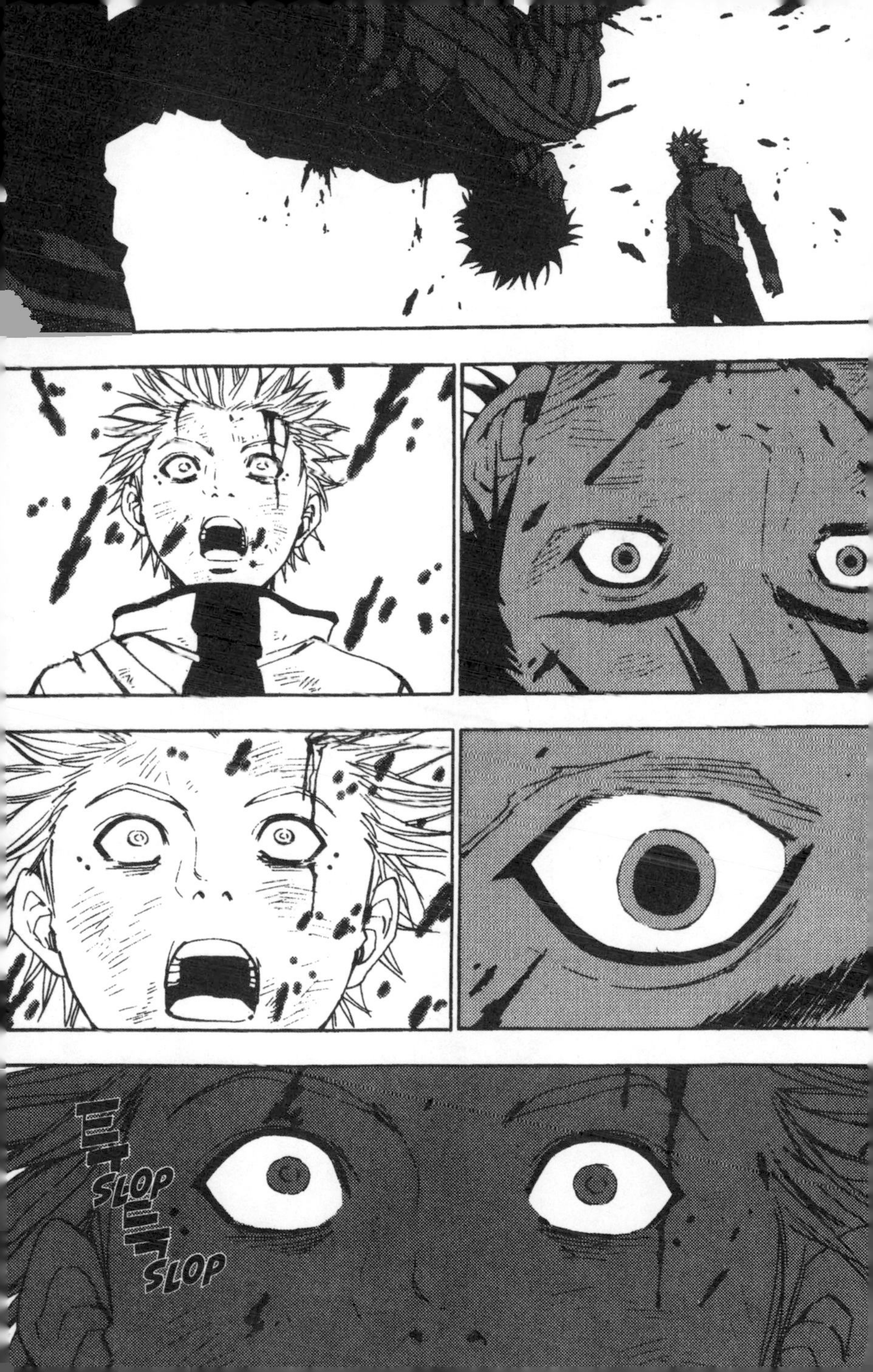
SLOP
SLOP

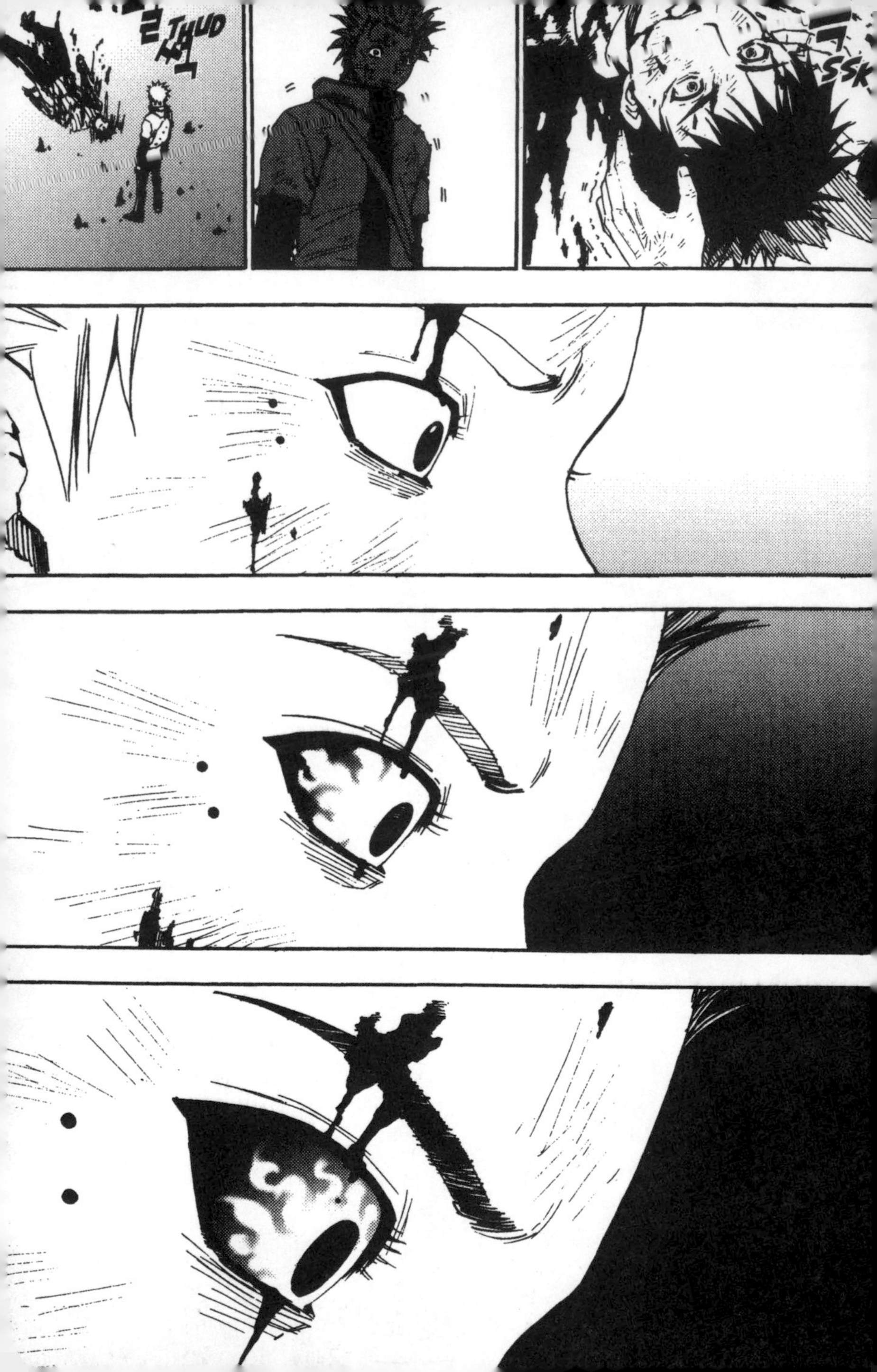
THUD
SSK

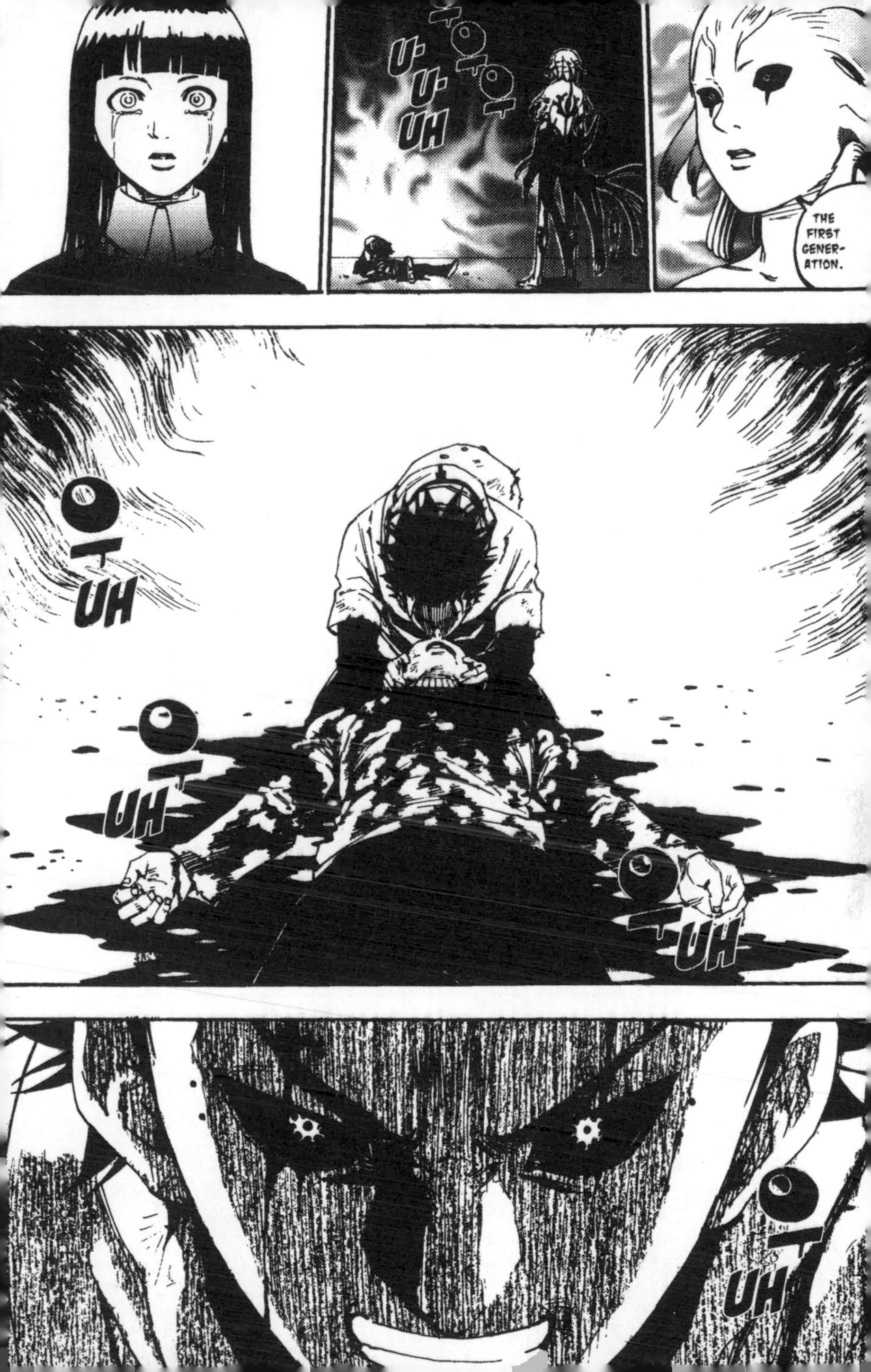
U-U-UH
THE FIRST GENERATION.
UH
UH
UH
UH

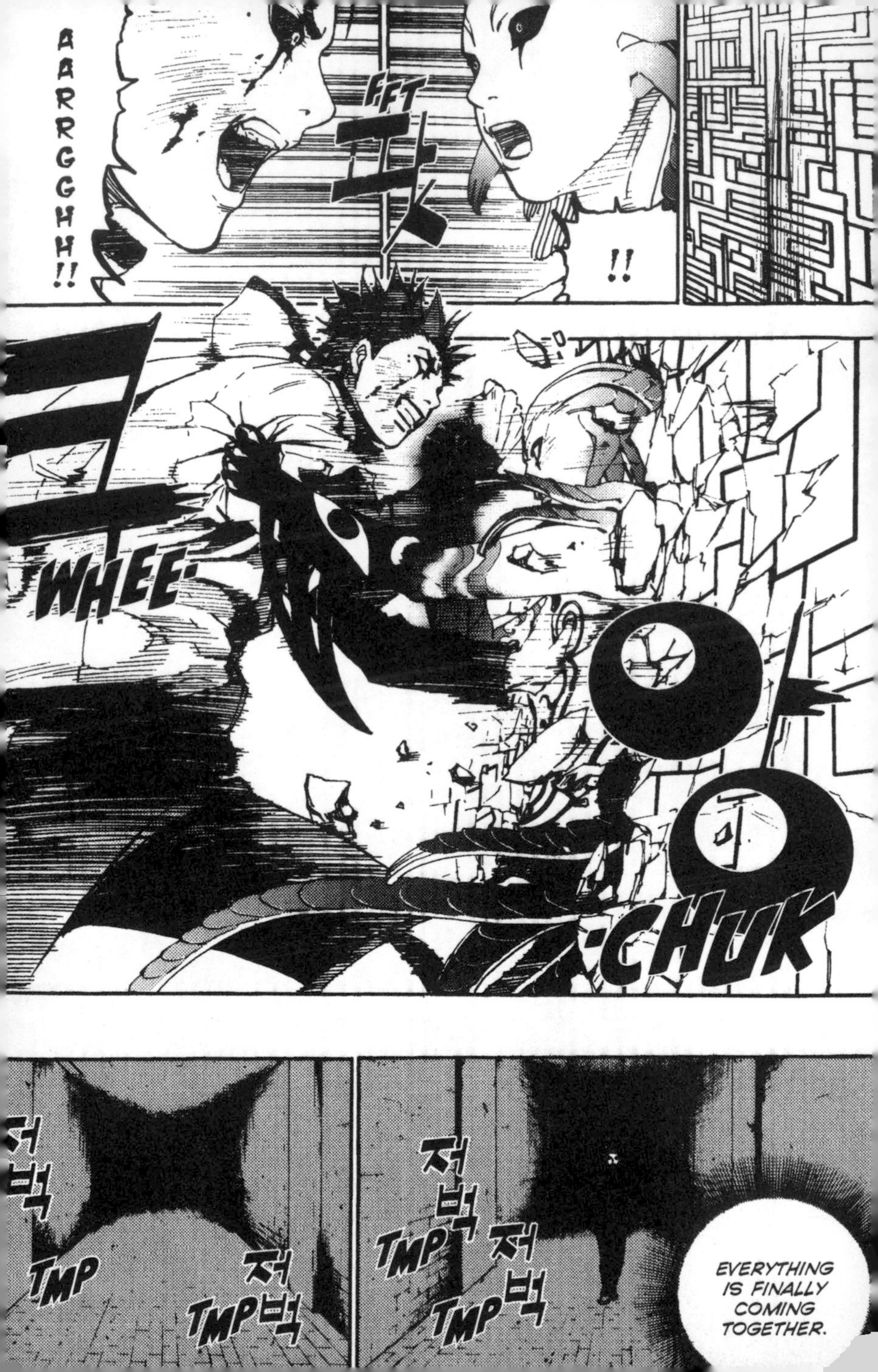
AARRGGHH!!
FFT
!!
WHEE-
-CHUK
TMP
TMP
TMP
TMP
EVERYTHING IS FINALLY COMING TOGETHER.

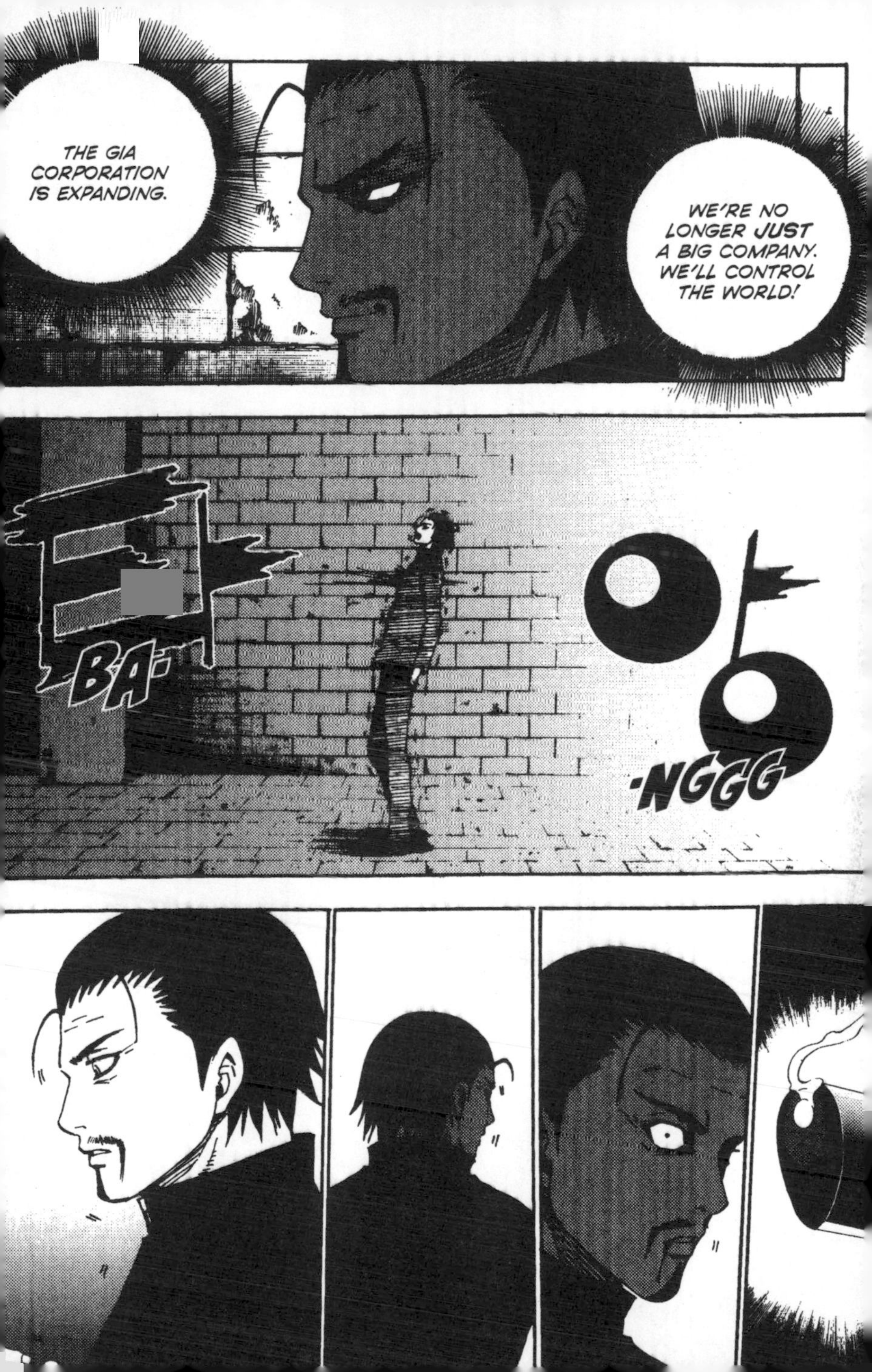
THE GIA CORPORATION IS EXPANDING.
WE'RE NO LONGER JUST A BIG COMPANY. WE'LL CONTROL THE WORLD!
BA-
-NGGG

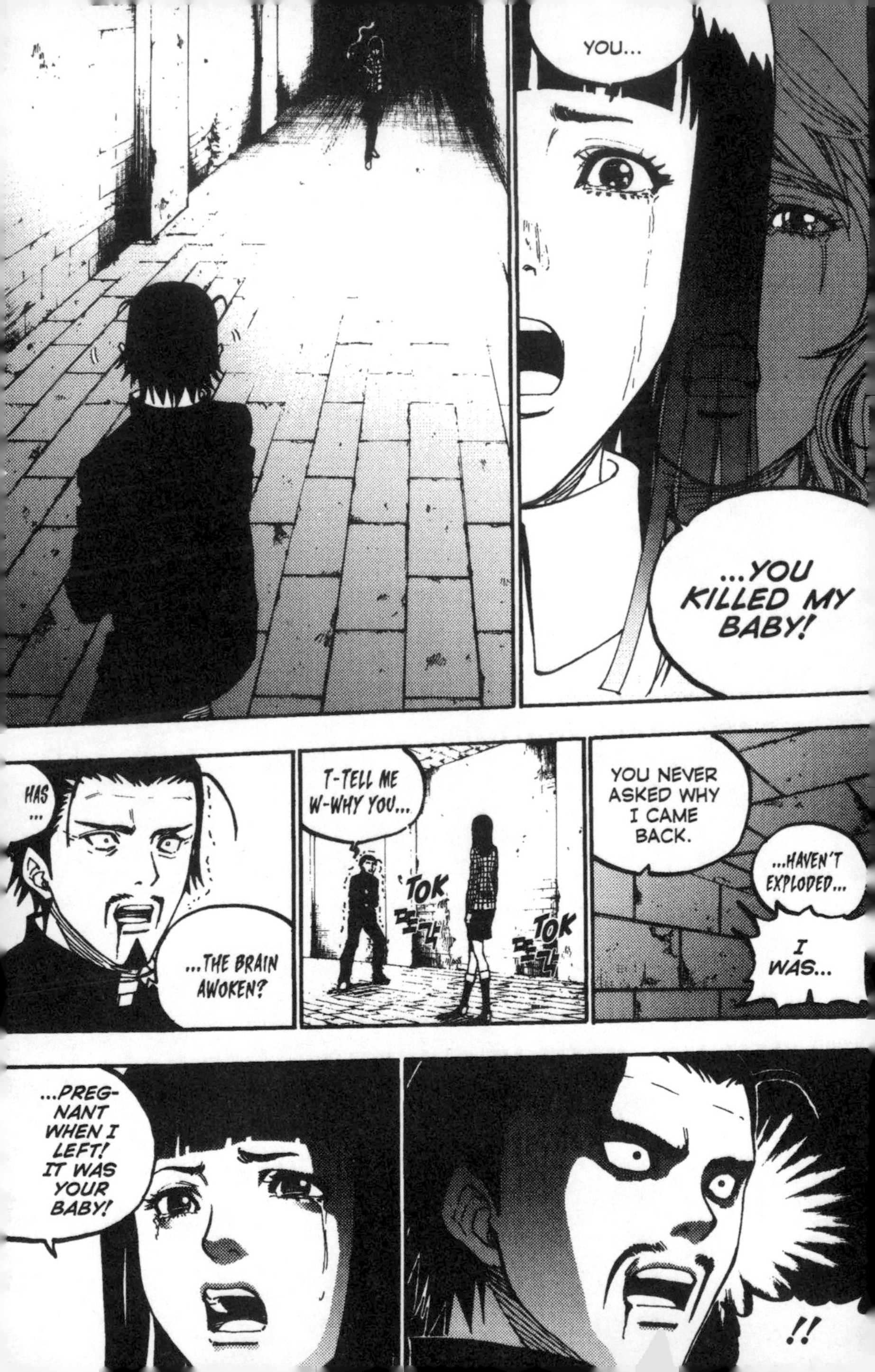
YOU...
...YOU KILLED MY BABY!
HAS ...
...THE BRAIN AWOKEN?
T-TELL ME W-WHY YOU...
TOK
TOK
YOU NEVER ASKED WHY I CAME BACK.
...HAVEN'T EXPLODED...
I WAS...
...PREG-NANT WHEN I LEFT! IT WAS YOUR BABY!
!!

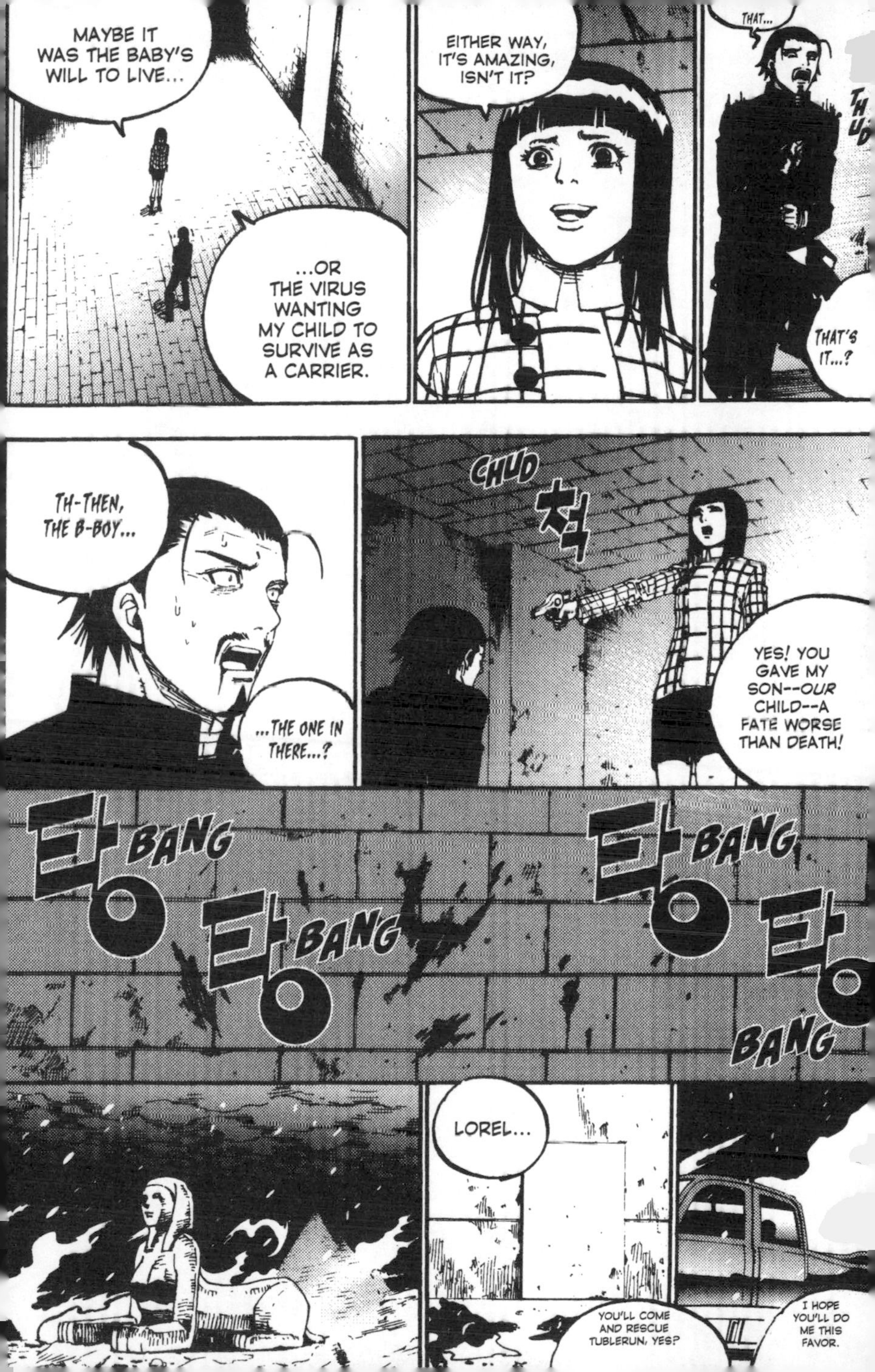
MAYBE IT WAS THE BABY'S WILL TO LIVE...
...OR THE VIRUS WANTING MY CHILD TO SURVIVE AS A CARRIER.
EITHER WAY, IT'S AMAZING, ISN'T IT?
THAT...
THUD
THAT'S IT...?
TH-THEN, THE B-BOY...
...THE ONE IN THERE...?
CHUD
척
YES! YOU GAVE MY SON--*OUR* CHILD--A FATE WORSE THAN DEATH!
탕
BANG
탕
BANG
탕
BANG
탕
BANG
LOREL...
YOU'LL COME AND RESCUE TUBLERUN, YES?
I HOPE YOU'LL DO ME THIS FAVOR.

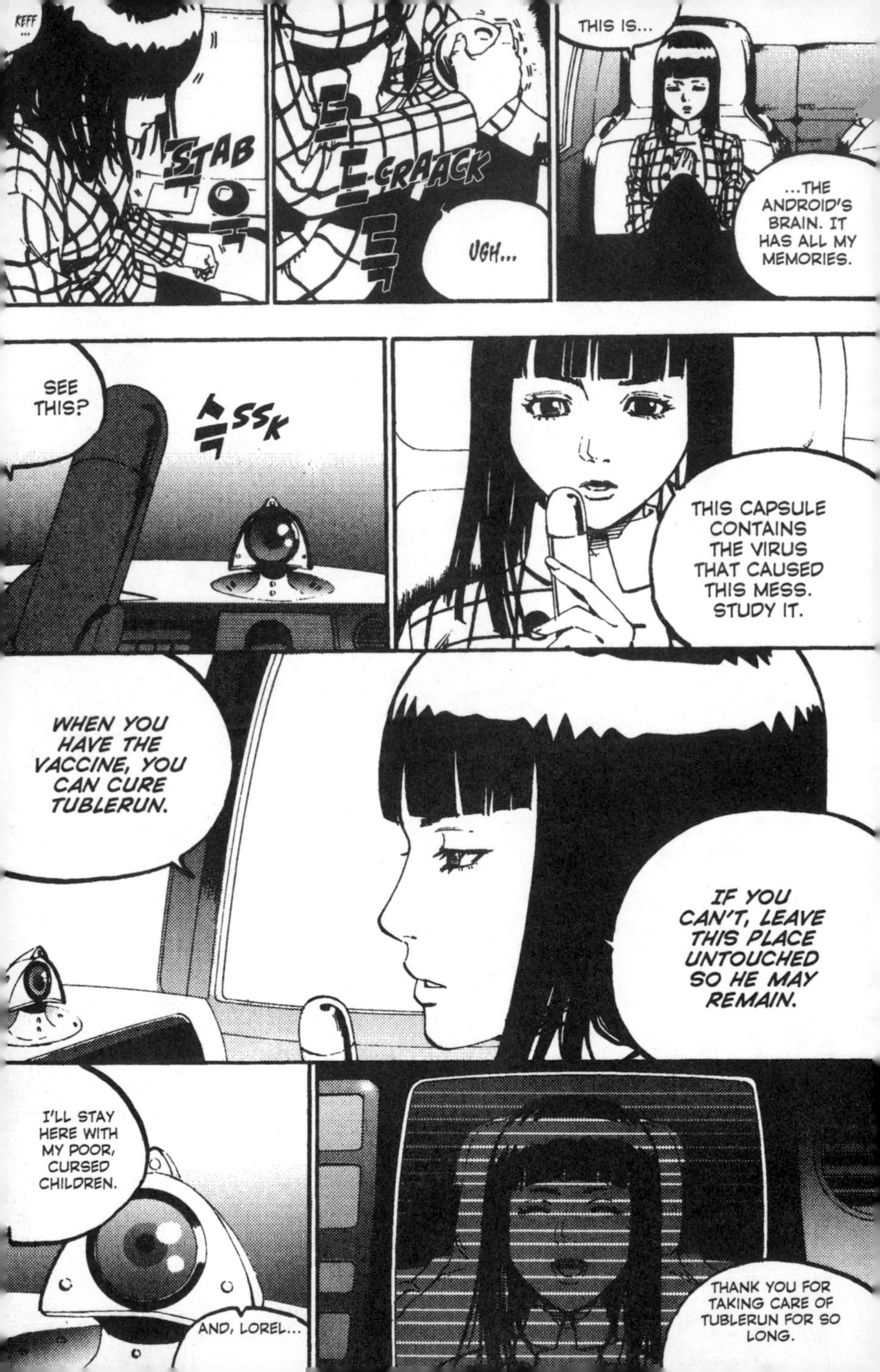
KEFF...
STAB
TH
E-E-CRAACK
UGH...
THIS IS...
...THE ANDROID'S BRAIN. IT HAS ALL MY MEMORIES.
SEE THIS?
SSK
THIS CAPSULE CONTAINS THE VIRUS THAT CAUSED THIS MESS. STUDY IT.
WHEN YOU HAVE THE VACCINE, YOU CAN CURE TUBLERUN.
IF YOU CAN'T, LEAVE THIS PLACE UNTOUCHED SO HE MAY REMAIN.
I'LL STAY HERE WITH MY POOR, CURSED CHILDREN.
AND, LOREL...
THANK YOU FOR TAKING CARE OF TUBLERUN FOR SO LONG.

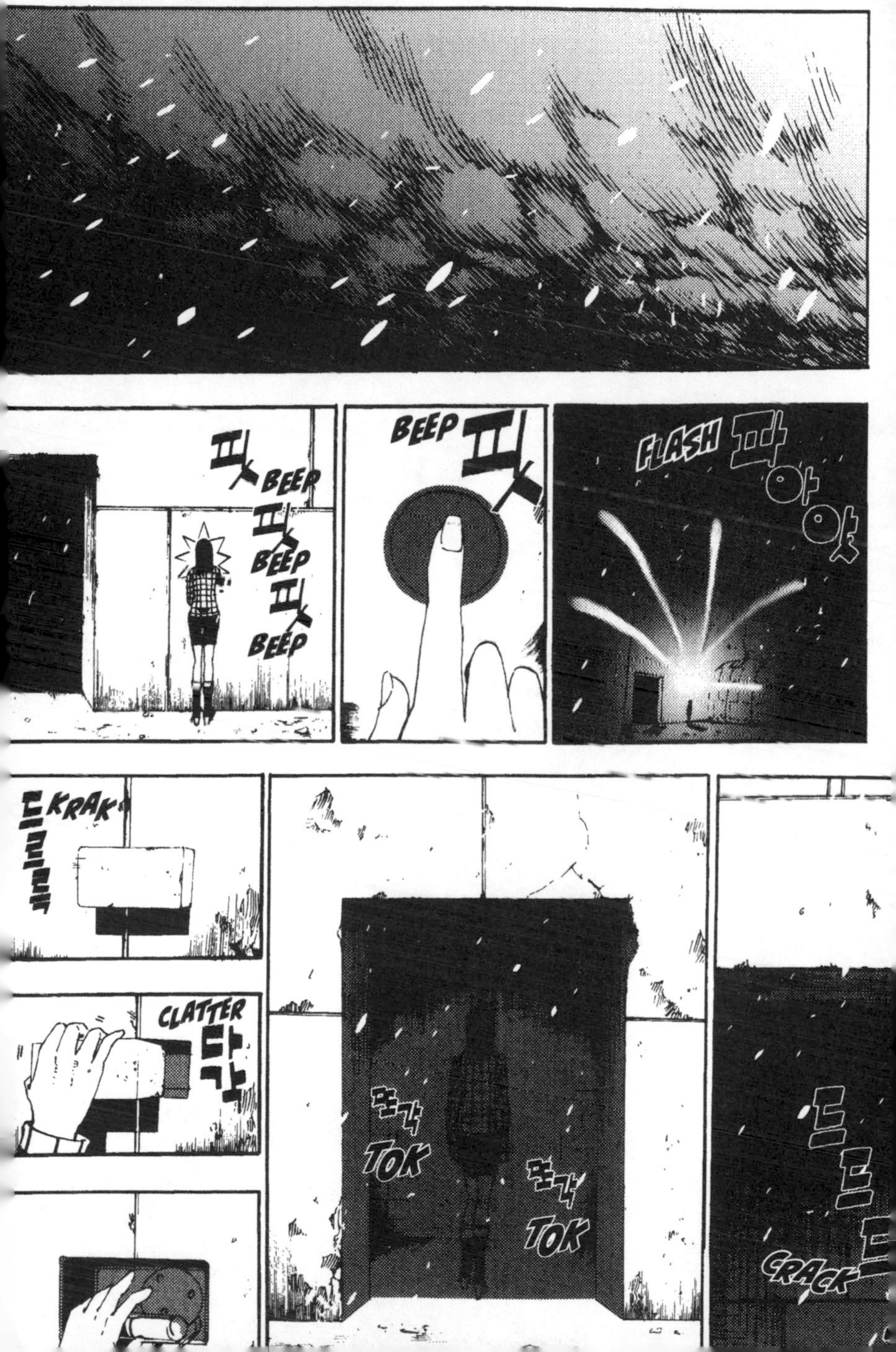
BEEP
BEEP
BEEP
BEEP
FLASH
파아앗
KRAK
CLATTER
또각
TOK
또각
TOK
CRACK

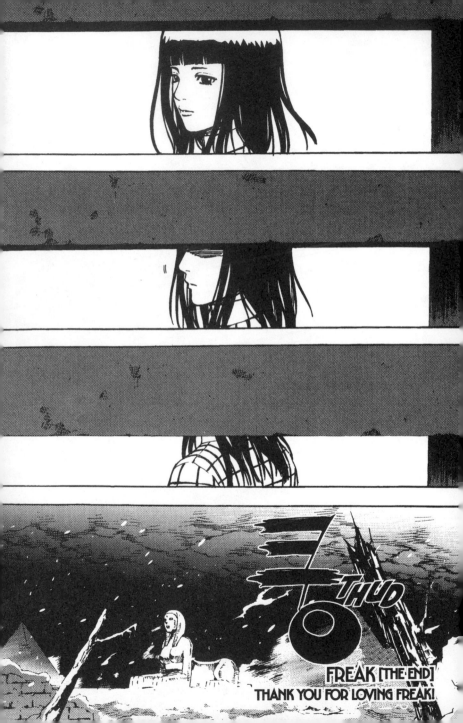

FREAK [THE END]
THANK YOU FOR LOVING FREAK!

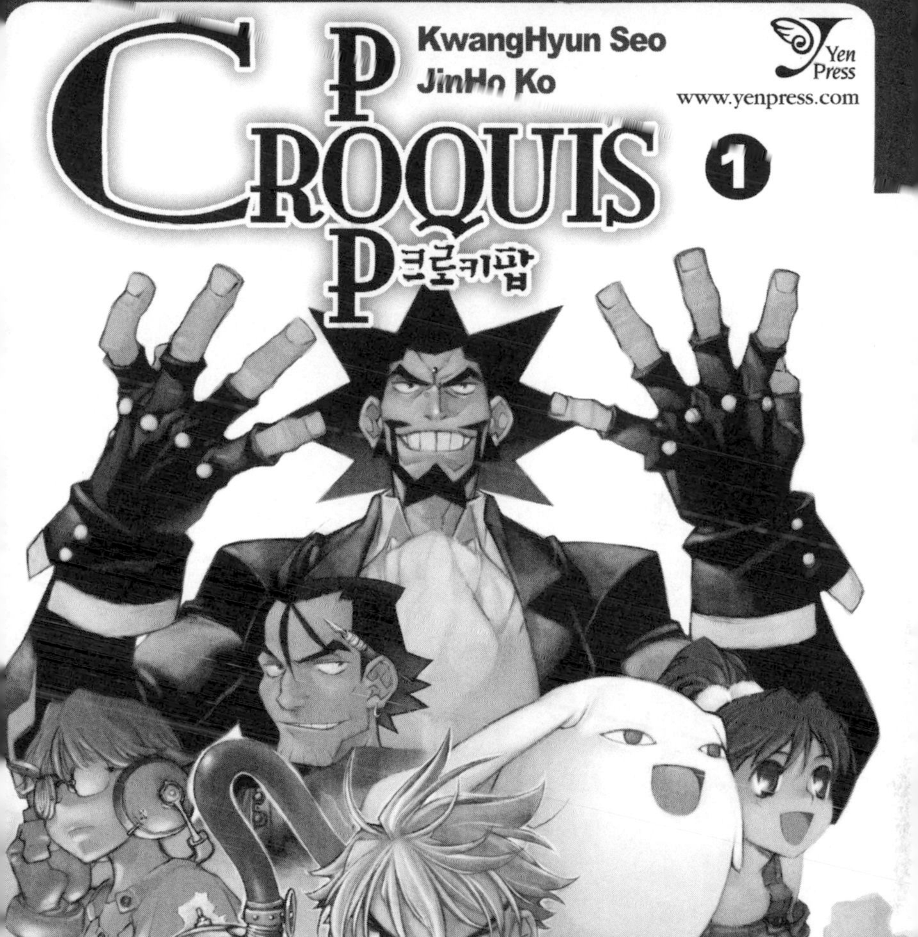

KwangHyun Seo
JinHo Ko

Yen Press
www.yenpress.com

# CROQUIS POP
크로키팝

**1**

## The world you create becomes the world in the book!!

Da-Il has a new job working for a famous comic creator — not that Da-Il has any artistic ability. At least that's what he thinks until he meets Mu-Huk, a ghost whose appearance Da-Il's creativity gives shape. The budding artist soon learns he has the skills of a "Croquer," someone whose talent gives form to ghosts — ghosts it is Mu-Huk's job to dispatch. It's a lot for a young man to absorb, especially when Da-Il learns he'll be the main character in his boss's new comic — CROQUIS POP!

# FREAK

## 1~3

## Legend of the Nonblonds

Story/Yi DongEun

Art/ Yu Chung

THERE IS NOTHING THAT THE NON-
BLONDS CAN'T STEAL FOR A CLIENT.
ONLY THE BEST CAN SURVIVE IN THE
WORLD OF PROFESSIONAL THIEVES.
AND TUBLERUN IS THE BEST OF THE
BEST OF THIEVES. MEANWHILE, CHROMA
IS THE BEST BOUNTY HUNTER OUT
THERE. SO, WHAT HAPPENS WHEN THE
BEST THIEF AND THE BEST BOUNTY
HUNTER CROSS PATHS?

## THE BOUNTY HUNTERS OF THE FUTURE — NOTHING CAN STOP THEM!!

Yen Press

www.yenpress.com

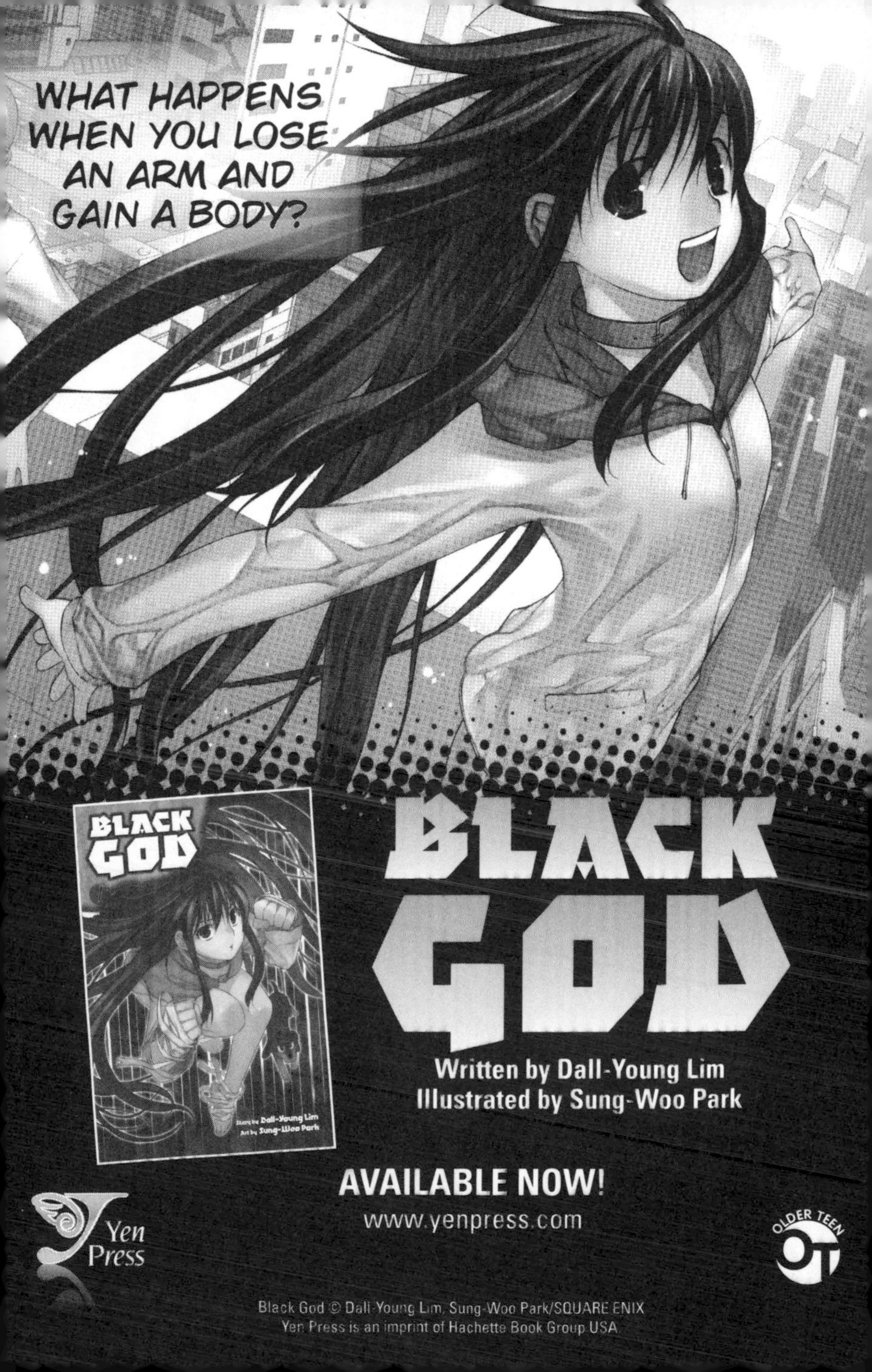
WHAT HAPPENS WHEN YOU LOSE AN ARM AND GAIN A BODY?
BLACK GOD
Story by Dall-Young Lim
Art by Sung-Woo Park
BLACK GOD
Written by Dall-Young Lim
Illustrated by Sung-Woo Park
AVAILABLE NOW!
www.yenpress.com
Yen Press
OLDER TEEN
OT
Black God © Dall-Young Lim, Sung-Woo Park/SQUARE ENIX
Yen Press is an imprint of Hachette Book Group USA

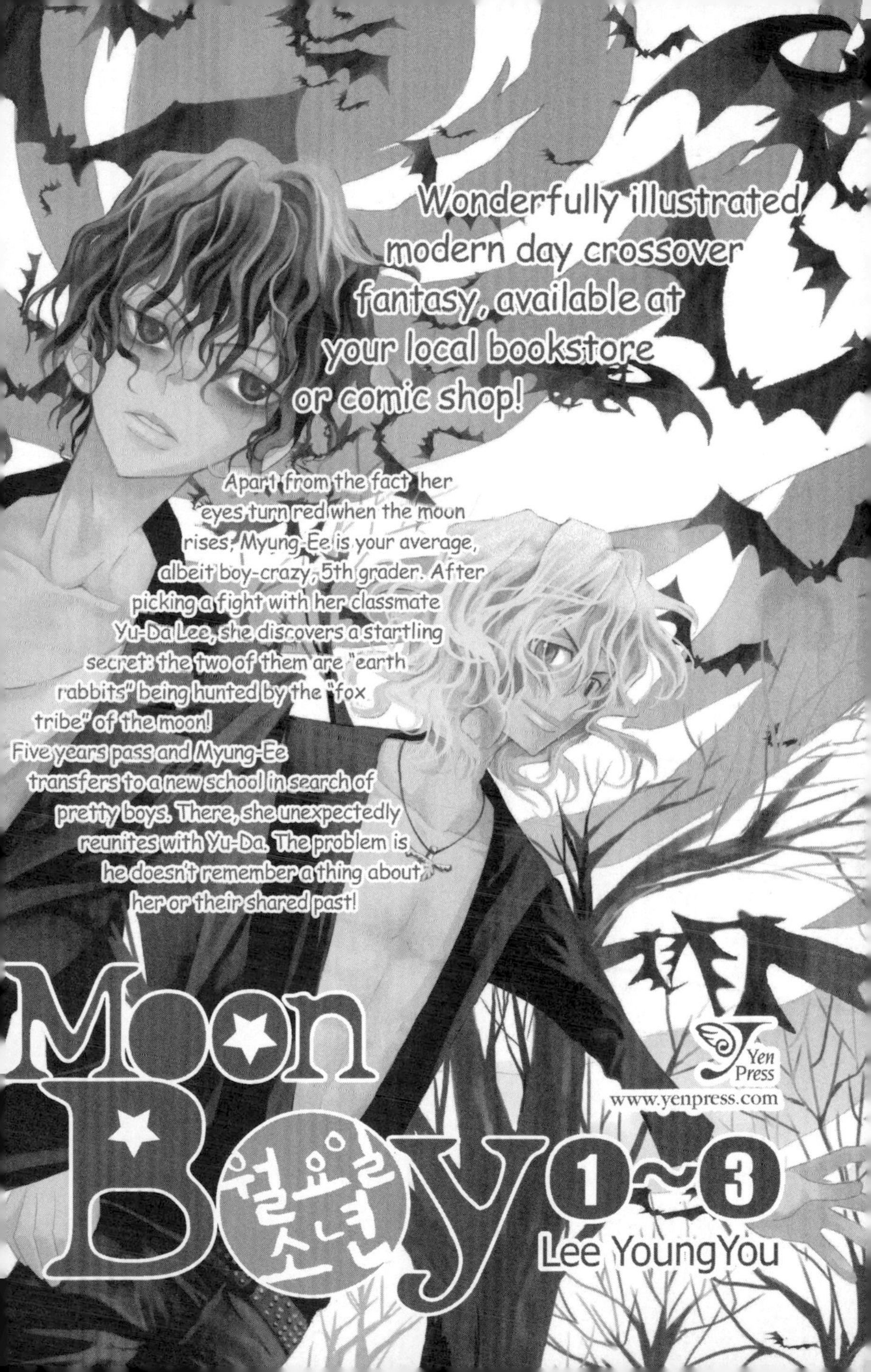
Wonderfully illustrated modern day crossover fantasy, available at your local bookstore or comic shop!
Apart from the fact her eyes turn red when the moon rises, Myung-Ee is your average, albeit boy-crazy, 5th grader. After picking a fight with her classmate Yu-Da Lee, she discovers a startling secret: the two of them are "earth rabbits" being hunted by the "fox tribe" of the moon! Five years pass and Myung-Ee transfers to a new school in search of pretty boys. There, she unexpectedly reunites with Yu-Da. The problem is he doesn't remember a thing about her or their shared past!
Moon Boy
월요일 소년
1~3
Lee YoungYou
Yen Press
www.yenpress.com

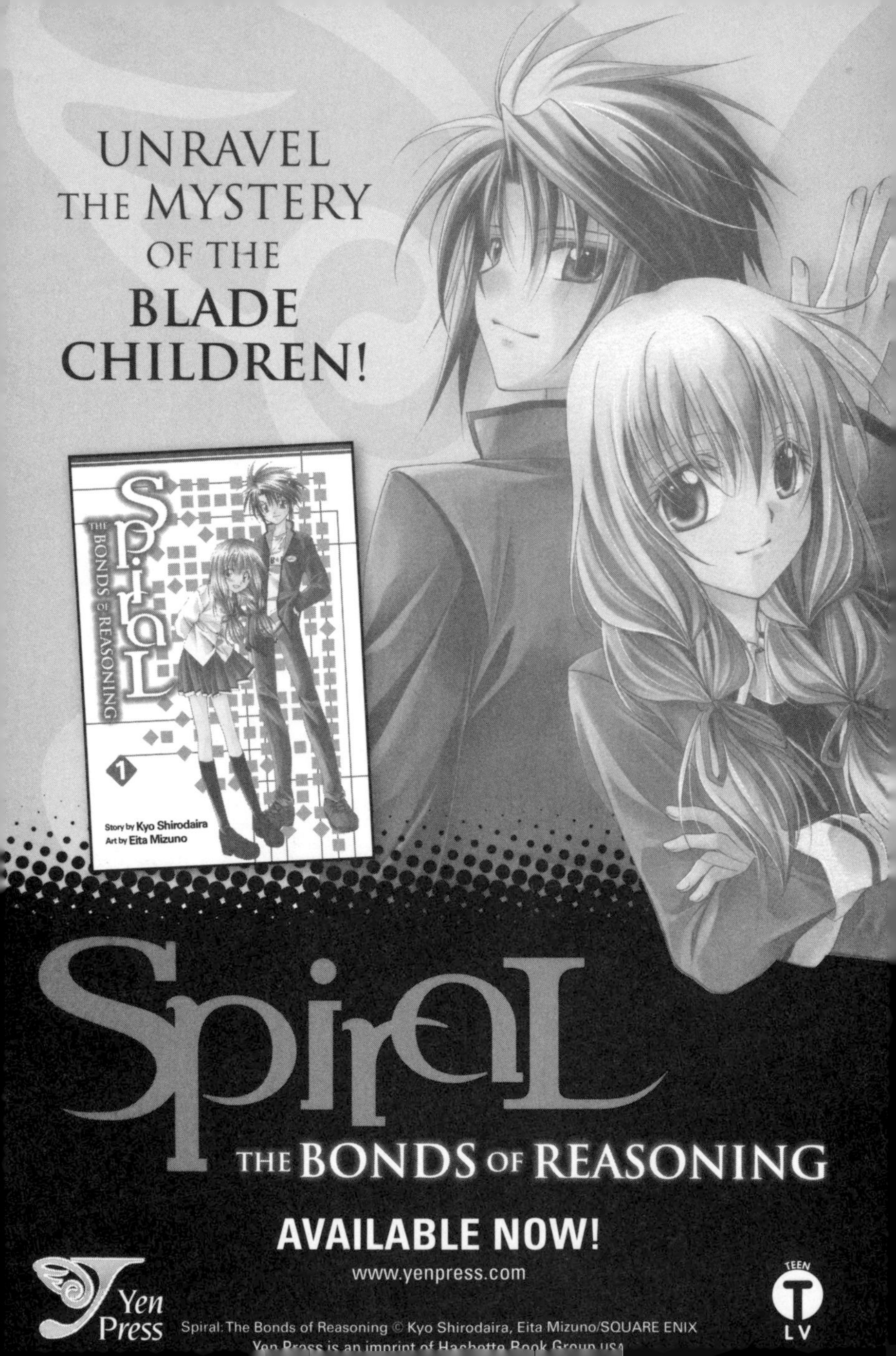
UNRAVEL
THE MYSTERY
OF THE
BLADE
CHILDREN!
Spiral
THE BONDS OF REASONING
1
Story by Kyo Shirodaira
Art by Eita Mizuno
Spiral
THE BONDS OF REASONING
AVAILABLE NOW!
www.yenpress.com
Yen Press
TEEN
T
LV
Spiral: The Bonds of Reasoning © Kyo Shirodaira, Eita Mizuno/SQUARE ENIX
Yen Press is an imprint of Hachette Book Group USA

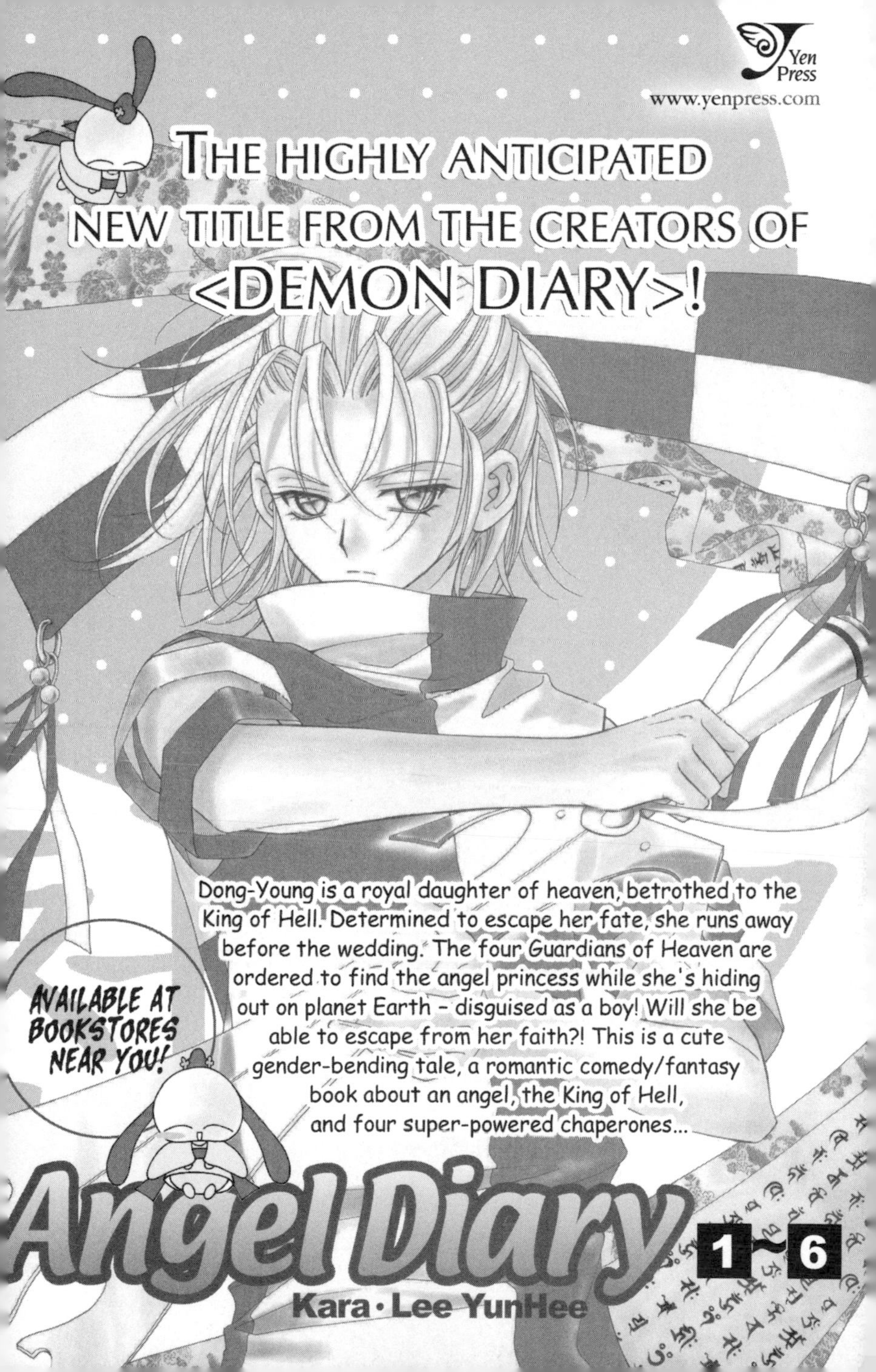
Yen Press
www.yenpress.com
THE HIGHLY ANTICIPATED NEW TITLE FROM THE CREATORS OF <DEMON DIARY>!
Dong-Young is a royal daughter of heaven, betrothed to the King of Hell. Determined to escape her fate, she runs away before the wedding. The four Guardians of Heaven are ordered to find the angel princess while she's hiding out on planet Earth – disguised as a boy! Will she be able to escape from her faith?! This is a cute gender-bending tale, a romantic comedy/fantasy book about an angel, the King of Hell, and four super-powered chaperones...
AVAILABLE AT BOOKSTORES NEAR YOU!
Angel Diary
1~6
Kara · Lee YunHee

Yen Press

# Freak vol. 4

Story by Dong Eun Yi
Art by Chung Yu

Translation: JiEun Park
English Adaptation: Jamie S. Rich
Lettering: Jose Macasocol, Jr.

FREAK Vol. 4 © 2006 Yi Dong Eun · Yu Chung. All rights reserved.
First published in Korea in 2006 by Haksan Publishing Co., Ltd. English
translation rights in U.S.A., Canada, UK, and Republic of Ireland
arranged with Haksan Publishing Co.,Ltd.

English translation © 2008 Hachette Book Group, Inc.

Yen Press
Hachette Book Group
237 Park Avenue, New York, NY 10017

Visit our Web sites at www.HachetteBookGroup.com and
www.YenPress.com.

Yen Press is an imprint of Hachette Book Group, Inc. The Yen Press name
and logo are trademarks of Hachette Book Group, Inc.

First Yen Press Edition: October 2008

ISBN-10: 0-7595-2958-2
ISBN-13: 978-0-7595-2958-8

10 9 8 7 6 5 4 3 2 1

BVG

Printed in the United States of America